Working with Youth Violence

Relevant for experienced and emerging social work and human service practitioners alike, this book explores the uniquely challenging, yet seemingly ubiquitous issue of youth violence. It provides an authentic and accessible discussion of the theories and evidence that inform practice with youth violence alongside the voices of practitioners and the young people they work with.

These voices are drawn from work with the Name.Narrate.Navigate (NNN) program for youth violence. NNN provides a trauma-informed, culturally safe preventive-intervention for young people who use and experience violence, and specialist training for the workers who support them. The program embraces creative methods as a bridge between contemporary evidence on trauma and violence and Aboriginal healing practice. The dual focus of the program is informed and interconnected by action research involving Aboriginal Elders and community members, practitioners, and key service stakeholders, including young people with a lived experience of violence.

This book is ideal for use in professional cross-disciplinary programs, such as criminology, sociology, social work, and psychology, across post-secondary, vocational, and university sectors.

Tamara Blakemore, University of Newcastle, Australia, leads the Name.Narrate.Navigate (NNN) program for youth violence. She is a social work practitioner, researcher, and educator whose work focuses on violence, abuse, and trauma. Her work for the Royal Commission into Institutional Child Sexual Abuse and the Longitudinal Study of Australian Children contributes to high-level social policy.

Chris Krogh, University of Newcastle, Australia, provides human and social service sector expertise to NNN. He has worked across counselling, child protection, and out-of-home care, youth sector development, NSW government policy, and program evaluation. Chris'

PhD investigated effects of practice documentation on those written about, finding, despite attempts to lessen impacts, they often provoke anger and frustration.

Shaun McCarthy, University of Newcastle, Australia, provides expertise on the criminal justice system to NNN. He is the Director of the University of Newcastle Legal Centre (UNLC) and Program Convenor of the Practical Legal Training Program. He provides clinical supervision to law students at the UNLC and teaches in the law school's practice program and bachelor of laws and juris doctor degrees.

Louise Rak, University of Newcastle, Australia, is the program manager of NNN. She has undertaken a PhD in social work exploring young women's use of violence. Louise regularly contributes to policy analysis in areas of homelessness and domestic violence, bringing a wealth of cross-sector experience to her work. She is the Chair of the Board for Nova for Women and Children.

Graeme Stuart, University of Newcastle, Australia, brings almost 40 years' experience in family and community work to his role as facilitator and practitioner working party chair in NNN. Graeme is active in the Alternatives to Violence Project (AVP) and convenes the AVP International research team, is the person behind the *Sustaining Community* blog, and is a proud father.

Working with Youth Violence

The Name.Narrate.Navigate Program

Tamara Blakemore, Louise Rak, Chris Krogh, Shaun McCarthy, and Graeme Stuart

LONDON AND NEW YORK

Designed cover image: Getty No. 688275839

First published 2024
by Routledge
4 Park Square, Milton Park, Abingdon, Oxon OX14 4RN

and by Routledge
605 Third Avenue, New York, NY 10158

Routledge is an imprint of the Taylor & Francis Group, an informa business

British Library Cataloguing-in-Publication Data
A catalogue record for this book is available from the British Library

Library of Congress Cataloging-in-Publication Data
Names: Blakemore, Tamara, author. | Rak, Louise, author. | Krogh, Chris, author. | McCarthy, Shaun (College teacher), author. | Stuart, Graeme, author.
Title: Working with youth violence : the Name Narrate Navigate program / Tamara Blakemore, Louise Rak, Chris Krogh, Shaun McCarthy, and Graeme Stuart.
Description: Abingdon, Oxon ; New York, NY : Routledge, 2024. | Includes bibliographical references and index.
Identifiers: LCCN 2023030883 (print) | LCCN 2023030884 (ebook) | ISBN 9781032012551 (hardback) | ISBN 9781032012490 (paperback) | ISBN 9781003177883 (ebook)
Subjects: LCSH: Youth and violence—Australia. | Juvenile delinquents—Services for—Australia.
Classification: LCC HQ799.2.V56 B53 2024 (print) | LCC HQ799.2.V56 (ebook) | DDC 303.60835—dc23/eng/20230817
LC record available at https://lccn.loc.gov/2023030883
LC ebook record available at https://lccn.loc.gov/2023030884

ISBN: 978-1-032-01255-1 (hbk)
ISBN: 978-1-032-01249-0 (pbk)
ISBN: 978-1-003-17788-3 (ebk)

DOI: 10.4324/9781003177883

Typeset in Sabon
by Apex CoVantage, LLC

Contents

Figures

Tables

Preface

This book explores the complexities of work with young people who use violence. The chapters that follow foreground the voices of practitioners and young people involved with the Name.Narrate.Navigate (NNN) program, supplemented by a critical review of existing literature on the multiple topics examined. NNN is a trauma-informed and culturally safe intervention for youth violence. Developed in 2018 by practitioner-academics in regional Australia, NNN is informed by contemporary understandings of trauma and relational practices consistent with Aboriginal ways of knowing and doing. It aims to strengthen self-awareness, self-regulation, and skills for connection for young people who have experienced and used violence and the workers who support them. In this preface, we discuss the origins of this book and provide background to the development of NNN. We hope this will set the scene for readers and contextualise the following chapters which will highlight findings from analysis of data collected as part of action research associated with NNN and evaluation of the program completed in 2021.

Beginning thoughts, aims, and objectives

When we started thinking about a book about youth violence, it was important to us to foreground practice and the voice of practitioners and the young people we work with. Like Lipsey and Howell (2012), we have long lamented the lack of importance attributed to practitioner voice, recognising that how practitioners perceive, define, and make sense of youth violence is likely to be an important determinant of how they work and, in turn, the effectiveness of that work. A logical place for us to start then, with some vulnerability, was our own practice. We identify ourselves as practitioner-academics; we are social workers, lawyers, and human services and community practitioners who teach and research and have a collective passion for cross-disciplinary and community-engaged social justice.

The work we present in this book was instigated by a conversation with our local Children's Court Magistrate Tracy Sheedy in 2016. Magistrate Sheedy observed what we were familiar with in practice – that young people subject to care and protection proceedings often, over time, also became involved in crime. Magistrate Sheedy also observed that while these young people seemed to have a protracted engagement with the justice system, they were often disengaged from and by education and disaffected with the social services. We all wanted to understand these experiences better and how contextual factors borne of history, religion, culture, social and economic capital, and relationships between people and place have simultaneously shaped the experiences of this cohort as well as our practice with them.

We started with a small pilot study (Blakemore et al., 2018, 2019), exploring practitioner narratives about the young people they worked with, the crimes the young people were involved with, what the practitioners thought contributed to these crimes, and whether these might be the same things that influenced young people's engagement (or disengagement) with supports and education. Semi-structured interviews were conducted with 37 practitioners across sectors of policing, juvenile justice, physical and mental health, child protection and out-of-home care (OOHC), education, and Aboriginal-specific services. Data from these interviews (presented in Chapters 1 and 3) were rich and nuanced, describing observations of the complex contexts in which young people become involved in crime. In fact, a defining feature of practitioner narratives were that they were context heavy. Practitioners spoke about their work with young people who had used crime with a firm gaze cast on location, socioeconomic and sociocultural factors, and relational transactions and interactions that surrounded them and gave them meaning.

At first, we questioned whether our work in regional New South Wales (NSW), Australia, might be of value. We wondered whether there was any real difference between the underpinning ideas and values and theoretical and practice perspectives of our work compared to practitioners in urban settings elsewhere in Australia or overseas. We came to realise, however, that the context of our work was not insignificant. While not unique, our location is characterised by both considerable strengths and challenges, and, in comparison to the rest of Australia, it fares worse in terms of unemployment, youth unemployment, and high school completion rates. High rates of child protection reports, out-of-home care (OOHC) placements, and domestic and family violence (DFV) in the region, particularly around sites of declining heavy industry, further contextualise it as rich in potential but often, in parts, disconnected from education, early intervention, and opportunity. Not unrelatedly, the region is also recognised as an epicentre of historic institutional child sexual abuse (McPhillips, 2018). The intergenerational effects of abuse that occurred across church dioceses here are evident in the socioeconomic realities of some parts of the region. Despite these challenges, both people and place are characterised by steely resilience. The human and social service workforce is relatively stable and staffed by skilled and committed employees with real and often long-term ties to the community.

An unexpected but welcome outcome of the pilot study (Blakemore et al., 2018) was a collective belief amongst those involved that our region, with its characteristic contexts, was, in fact, well-placed to develop community-driven, ground-up solutions to working with youth violence and that there may be broader relevance of our work to other communities and practitioners working with similar challenges. This was the impetus for the NNN program (Blakemore et al., 2021). NNN was designed with and for the community as a preventive intervention for youth violence. Uniquely, the program has a dual focus of working with young people who use and experience violence as well as with the workers who support them. It aims to strengthen self-awareness, self-regulation, and skills for connection to support readiness for deeper work or the migration of identity towards safer outcomes. The program was developed and is continuously improved through community-based participatory (action) research involving a practitioner working party, a steering committee of key sector stakeholders, a cultural reference group led by an acknowledged Aboriginal Elder living locally, and an advisory consortium of young people with a lived experience of violence. Acknowledging that many young people who use violence have also experienced violence and the tragic overrepresentation of Aboriginal and Torres Strait Islander young people (hereafter respectfully referred to as Aboriginal young people) involved with both the child protection and criminal justice system, the program intentionally merges the neuroscience of trauma with ways of working that are consistent with Aboriginal ways of relating, knowing, and doing. It embraces creative and culturally endorsed methods, including Photovoice, to prioritise, centre, and give voice to young people's experiences and to foster storytelling and the co-creation of narratives of youth violence to inform more responsive practice. Since 2018, the program has worked with over 150 young people and close to 1000 practitioners. Evaluation of the program (Rayment-McHugh et al., 2021) identified it as having significant promise in forwarding a trauma-informed and culturally safe way of working with youth violence.

In writing this book, we aim to present a point-in-time description of practice with youth violence that has emerged from research associated with the NNN program. This research has found that practice in this context is complex and that many of the challenges faced by practitioners exist almost symbiotically with the experiences of young people who use and experience violence. Findings from the pilot study (Blakemore et al., 2018) identified practitioner narratives of young people's involvement in crime (including their use of violence) as a means of communication and/or connection – that is, a means of redressing injustice and redistributing power and control and/or finding and forming identity, being seen, and heard. Yet, despite being well-intentioned and invested, common to the narratives we heard from practitioners were signs that the work takes its toll, sometimes articulated as cynicism, detachment, and despondency about the experiences and likely outcomes of young people, sometimes expressed as disconnection from the worlds inhabited by them. For us, as practitioner-academics hearing these narratives, it felt like we were observers to an almost parallel process for workers and their clients, with both wanting to be heard yet lacking an authentic and safe common language.

Tamara Blakemore

References

Blakemore, T., Agllias, K., Howard, A., & McCarthy, S. (2019). The service system challenges of work with juvenile justice involved young people in the Hunter Region, Australia. *Australian Journal of Social Issues*, *54*(3), 341–356. https://doi.org/10.1002/ajs4.69

Blakemore, T., McCarthy, S., Rak, L., McGregor, J., Stuart, G., & Krogh, C. (2021). *Postcards from practice: Learnings from Name.Narrate.Navigate (NNN)*. University of Newcastle. https://nova.newcastle.edu.au/vital/access/manager/Repository/uon:37573

Blakemore, T., Rak, L., Agllias, K., Mallett, X., & McCarthy, S. (2018). Crime and context: Understandings of youth perpetrated interpersonal violence among service providers in regional Australia. *Journal of Applied Youth Studies*, *2*(5), 53–69.

Lipsey, M. W., & Howell, J. C. (2012). A broader view of evidence-based programs reveals more options for state juvenile justice systems. *Criminology & Public Policy*, *11*(3), 515–523. https://doi.org/10.1111/j.1745-9133.2012.00827.x

McPhillips, K. (2018). The royal commission investigates child sexual abuse: Uncovering cultures of sexual violence in the Catholic church. In C. Blyth, E. Colgan, & K. Edwards (Eds.), *Rape culture, gender violence, and religion: Christian perspectives* (pp. 53–71). Palgrave Macmillan. https://doi.org/10.1007/978-3-319-72685-4_4

Rayment-McHugh, S., McKillop, N., Adams, D., & Hull, I. (2021). *Name.Narrate.Navigate: A prevention initiative for youth violence: Evaluation report* [Unpublished report]. Sexual Violence Research and Prevention Unit, University of the Sunshine Coast.

Acknowledgements

The authors recognise the strength, resilience, and knowledge of the Aboriginal and Torres Strait Islander peoples. We acknowledge them as custodians of Australian lands, air, and waters and pay our respects to Elders past, present, and all Aboriginal people on whose land we live, work, and learn. We extend that respect to First Nations peoples across lands this writing may reach.

The findings of this book are based on our work with young people who use and experience violence and the practitioners who support them in our Name.Narrate.Navigate (NNN) program. We have been very fortunate to have many champions for our NNN work. So fortunate that it is difficult to acknowledge everyone here. We are grateful for the funding we have received to run NNN from the University of Newcastle; the Australian Government Department of Social Services and Department of Industry, Sciences, and Resources; the New South Wales Department of Communities and Justice; and Westpac.

Our work would not be possible without the guidance of our steering committee, practitioner working party, and cultural reference groups – we thank them for all their experience, skills, and insight. Most importantly, we acknowledge and thank all the young people involved in this research. They have been generous and giving of their time, stories, and experience.

1 Youth violence, complexity, and context

Louise Rak and Tamara Blakemore

Acknowledgement

This chapter presents data from interviews with practitioners conducted as part of the Juvenile Justice and Education Equity project, a small pilot study preceding the development of NNN. Some of this data was collected by Professor Amanda Howard and Conjoint Associate Professor Nicola Ross, and we acknowledge their contribution.

Youth violence, complexity, and context

This book uses the Name.Narrate.Navigate (NNN) program as a case study to explore social work and human service practice with young people who use and experience violence. In this and the following two chapters we sketch for you, the reader, the complex contexts in and through which NNN has emerged. Here, and throughout the book, we draw on evidence both *for* and *from* practice. We begin by charting contemporary and seminal evidence about youth violence outlining issues of definition and terminology, scope and scale, conceptualisation, and understanding. We complement this literature review with observations and insights from practitioners who work with youth violence. Presented in textboxes throughout, this information was captured (with appropriate ethics approval) through semi-structured interviews conducted in the pilot study which was the impetus to the NNN program (for more information see the Preface) Blakemore et al., 2018, 2019). We hope that, like us, you find stories of and from practice a valuable and accessible way to engage with, think about, and grow a deeper appreciation of the complex realities of young people and their uses of violence.

Youth violence

Whenever violence is discussed, written about, or played out across any medium, how it is viewed, understood, and typified will be influenced

DOI: 10.4324/9781003177883-1

by individual and collective beliefs shaped by historic, sociocultural, and political factors (Staudigl, 2013). It is perhaps both instructive and symptomatic of the lived experience of youth violence that shared understandings are often mired by divergent terms, lack of concise definition, and jurisdictional difference. Confusingly, the term "youth violence" has been used to refer to young peoples' experience of, or exposure to, violence (Atkinson, 2002) as well as young peoples' use of violence (Freeman, 2018). The crossover of the terms here is somewhat appropriate, considering young people use *and* experience violence more often than adults (Finkelhor et al., 2009), with some socioeconomic and gender groups disproportionately affected (Atkinson, 2002; Baidawi, 2020; Rak & Warton, 2023). Robust evidence substantiates that many young people who use violence are also victims of violence (Baidawi, 2020; Blakemore et al., 2021; Rak & Warton, 2023). While this book will focus on young people's use of violence, it is important to acknowledge that the experience and use of violence can be interconnected. Youth violence can refer to the experience and/or exposure to acts including assault; threats; coercion; intimidation; property damage; psychological abuse; neglect; financial abuse; and other forms of controlling or coercive behaviours, including verbal and emotional abuse; *or*, in turn, the use of these behaviours in interpersonal, family, or domestic relationships with peers, partners, parents, siblings, carers, or with or towards others in the wider community (Cox et al., 2016; Moulds et al., 2016).

Young people's use of violence is often categorised according to either the nature of the relationships between the parties involved or the situations and settings in which it occurs. In Australia, this commonly includes differentiations between violence among young people or peer violence (Cox et al., 2016), adolescent relationship violence (Daff et al., 2021), adolescent violence in the home (Moulds et al., 2019), adolescent domestic and family violence (Cox et al., 2016), or adolescent family violence (Voce et al., 2020). The World Health Organization defines youth violence as violence between people aged 10–29 years old who may or may not be known to each other. This violence can occur anywhere and take multiple forms, including threats; bullying; physical, sexual, and emotional abuse; and assault and murder (Russell, 2021). Most prominently discussed in the existing literature is young people's use of violence in the home and towards parents or carers. Conceptualisations of domestic and family violence (DFV) are, as a rule, complex, and this seems to be more so when it is a young person who is using violence (Cox et al., 2016; Moulds et al., 2016). Seminal work by Harbin and Madden (1979) coined the term "battered parent syndrome" to refer to adolescent violence towards parents. Operationalisation of this term lacked measurement specificity, which meant that it had limited utility in better understanding and responding to the phenomenon of youth violence (Edenborough et al., 2008). Subsequent research has tended to focus on family dynamics to understand young people's use of violence towards parents/carers (e.g., Murphy-Edwards & van Heugten, 2015). Generally, adolescent to parent/carer violence occurs amid a more expansive understanding of familial violence and dysfunction, with adolescent to parent/carer violence acting as one component of familial interactions and patterns of behaviour that may also include violence between caregivers, or from one caregiver to another, and violence from one or more caregivers towards children or dependents (Daly & Wade, 2015; Downey, 1997). Consistent with this conceptualisation, familial violence is understood as a dynamic process, produced and reproduced in different patterns that change and repeat over time without a unidirectional or binary cause and effect (Downey, 1997).

The problem with this understanding is that parents, and especially mothers, can be simultaneously blamed and disbelieved for their child's use of violence. Mother-blaming (and shaming) is understood as an artefact of social constructions of mothering, women, and the family. Fear of shame and blame can deter families from seeking police assistance, counselling, and intervention to address youth violence (Edenborough et al., 2008; Moulds et al., 2016). This may be particularly the case when young people use violence towards grandparent caregivers (Fitzpatrick, 2004). McDonald and Martinez (2016) and Khan and Rogers (2015) similarly suggest violence among siblings is underreported, noting it may go undetected as parents and carers overlook this form of aggression and minimise disagreements as rivalry or a normal part of growing up (Coogan, 2011; Khan & Rogers, 2015).

Violence is also widespread in young people's intimate partner and dating relationships and transcends class, culture, and gender (Foshee et al., 2007; Reyes et al., 2015; Simmons et al., 2017; Sinnott & Artz, 2016). Johnson's (1995, 2005, 2010, 2011) extensive work on interpersonal violence posits this can take the form of "intimate terrorism" (behaviours that aim to obtain and maintain control and power over another person) or "situational couple violence" (resulting from (unmanaged) conflict situations). While acknowledging that young people use violence in their intimate partner relationships, Messinger et al. (2014) argue Johnson's typology of violence has limited application for this cohort. In applying Johnson's typology to a female adolescent sample, Messinger et al. (2014) found key differences in adolescent interpersonal violence patterns when compared with those of adults. For example, where violence was present, it was mutual, often contained physical violence, with both parties attempting to exert high levels of control. This is not consistent with Johnson's (2010) findings in relation to adult interpersonal violence, which indicate that mutual high levels of control are less common.

A further defining situational context of youth violence is out-of-home care (OOHC) (Fitzpatrick, 2004). In Australia, OOHC refers to the state-legislated removal and placement of children and young people substantiated to be at risk of significant harm in the family of origin (Australian Institute of Health and Welfare [AIHW], 2019). Children and young people in OOHC in Australia are commonly placed with grandparents or other family members in both formal and informal kinship care arrangements (Fitzpatrick, 2004). Where familial placement is not available, children and young people may be placed into residential or foster care arrangements (Mendes et al., 2014; Mendes & Moslehuddin, 2009). Young people can use and/or experience violence in OOHC placements. Carer burden, generational or cultural difference, pre-existing trauma, and ensuing behavioural challenges, combined with physical and mental ill health and external stressors, can contribute to physical altercations and violence that are either reciprocated or perpetrated from one party towards the other (Fitzpatrick, 2004; Moulds et al., 2016). Historically, care environments across the world have reproduced risk of violence for young people in care, particularly physical, sexual, and psychological forms of abuse and violence (Blakemore et al., 2017). Abuse in care environments (both historically and currently in some circumstances) has been facilitated and contextualised through physical distance and through practices of disconnection from family and culture, depersonalisation, and deprivation of basic needs (Blakemore et al., 2017).

Definitions of youth violence have also sought to differentiate forms of violence accounting for motivation and intent. Gallagher (2004) categorises violence used by young people as being either expressive or instrumental. Expressive violence refers to reactionary violence, borne out of frustration or anger, whereas instrumental violence is described as fit-for-purpose violence used to control the actions of others (Gallagher, 2004). Daly and Wade (2015) similarly categorise young people's use of violence as either reactive or controlling. Howard (2011) suggests young people who use violence towards their parents or carers may employ coercive strategies that are consistent with those of adults who use violence to gain and maintain power and control. By comparison to coercive behaviours used by adults, the motivation or intent of these behaviours for young people is often to coerce the caregiver into giving them something rather than to limit the freedom of the parent (Daly & Wade, 2015; Routt & Anderson, 2014). Strategies used by young people in these contexts can include threats, intimidation, coercion, property destruction, and physical violence (Howard, 2011). Where violence is used with an objective to coerce a parent or carer, threats to siblings can also be viewed as threats, by proxy, to the parent or carer (Cox et al., 2016; Howard & Rottem, 2008; Moulds et al., 2016).

Regardless of relational dynamics, situation, or motivation, violence used by young people rarely occurs in isolation from other forms of violence (Rak & Warton, 2023). Practitioners we spoke to describe young people they work with as using violence towards their parents (notably mothers), siblings, and other family members as well as care providers, often alongside acts of property damage.

Box 1.1 What practitioners tell us . . .

> "At the moment . . . we're getting a lot of DV stuff. I think DV stuff on the whole is quite a common offence for young people to come in . . . most young people, if not the majority, come to us with AVOs in place, various family members or neighbours or whatever". (Practitioner 20)

> "They assault our staff, or they might damage the property or steal our cars. . . . They're in an escalation because of the behavioural issues that they have and why they're with us and the trauma that comes from that. A lot of the time it's them not being able to self-regulate and reacting. Unfortunately, that leads to criminalisation of them, really". (Practitioner 13)

Prevalence

Consistent with the observations of practitioners we spoke to, evidence suggests that youth violence is a complex issue of significant scope and scale. In Australia, there is no comprehensive national data source on young people who use and experience violence; rather, our understanding of the prevalence of these often-overlapping experiences is drawn from administrative datasets of different states and territories and national survey data. These data sources can provide some insight into the prevalence of young people's use and experience of violence in Australia, but because of issues related to reporting and recording this data, they are likely to underestimate the true extent of young people's involvement with violence (AIHW, 2021).

Understanding how many young people experience and/or use violence is complicated by definition differences and a reliance on either self-reports or official records related to criminal charges. All these factors are likely to produce an underestimate of the experience and/or use of violence by young people. Definitional differences will mean that some, but not all, experiences will be captured. Where data is captured, definitional differences make combining or comparing reported rates of crime difficult. Not all violence that occurs is reported. The interpersonal dynamics that perpetuate risk for violence, in many contexts, can also contribute to it continuing and operate as powerful disincentives to disclose its occurrence. It is also important to note that most research and reported crime statistics related to youth violence use heteronormative pronouns, taking a biological approach to understanding and defining gender (Reuter & Whitton, 2018; Sylaska & Walters, 2014).

What is well-established is that young people are frequently exposed to violence. In the United States (US), it has been estimated that three in five young people, or up to 46 million young people per year, are exposed to violence (Finkelhor et al., 2009). According to the Australian Bureau of Statistics' (ABS, 2021) 16,345 young people aged under 18 years were recorded as victims of sexual assault, kidnapping/abduction, robbery, homicide, murder, manslaughter, attempted murder, or armed robbery in 2021. Sexual assault accounted for most of these cases. There were also around 28,800 other assault offences (which included grievous bodily harm, torture, and use of a weapon perpetrated against young people aged 15–24) in the six jurisdictions for which data were available – New South Wales (NSW), Western Australia (WA), South Australia (SA), Tasmania (TAS), the Australian Capital Territory (ACT), and the Northern Territory (NT) (ABS, 2021).

When it comes to estimating how common it is for young people to use violence, limitations of definition consistency and reporting fidelity become even more pronounced. Rather than relying on a report of harm to child welfare agencies, what we know about the prevalence of young people's use of violence is primarily drawn from crime statistics. Consistent with the experience of violence, there are often powerful disincentives to disclose victimisation at the hands of a young person, particularly in familial contexts (Fitz-Gibbon et al., 2018). Howard (2015) notes, "Most families do not report their child to the police due to embarrassment, guilt, a sense of needing to manage their own children, and/or a fear of judgment about their own parental capacities" (Howard, 2015, p. b3). As a result, actual prevalence rates of youth-perpetrated violence, particularly in familial contexts, are unclear (Moulds et al., 2016).

In Australia, over time, there has been a general decrease in the size of the population of justice-involved young people (ABS, 2021). However, there is some evidence to suggest that more young people are being charged with violent crimes, at a younger age (Papalia et al., 2015). In NSW, where our work is located, "acts to cause injury" were the most common criminal offence young people were charged with during 2017–2018 (ABS, 2019). The NSW Bureau of Crime Statistics and Research (NSW BOCSAR) has similarly noted significant increases in the rates at which young people are charged with DFV offences, citing growth from

154.5 per 100,000 people in 2008 to 195.7 per 100,000 in 2017 (Freeman, 2018). Based on current police reporting of DFV matters, approximately 10% of NSW police proceedings are against offenders under the age of 18 (Freeman, 2018). Further, more than half of young people charged also had at least one charge related to DFV offences in the two years prior (Freeman, 2018). During this same time, DFV offence rates for adult offenders stabilised, indicating that rather than an artefact of a general increase in DFV in the community, the rates reflected a rise in youth-specific offending and reoffending (Freeman, 2018).

In NSW, when young people are charged with DFV-related offences, most are found to have used violence against their parents or carers (44%), followed by other family members (particularly grandparents) (20%), partners and siblings (15%), or OOHC workers (6%) (Freeman, 2018). In 2019–20, the number of young people aged 10–17 charged with any criminal offence was around 47,000, a rate of 1,914 offenders per 100,000, the lowest rate since the time series began in 2008–09 (3,187 per 100,000) (ABS, 2021). In 2017–18, 40 young people aged 15–24 were charged with homicide, representing a rate of 1.3 young per 100,000 young people (AIHW, 2021). This rate is lower than for people aged 25–34 (2.0 per 100,000) and 35–44 (1.7 per 100,000) but higher than all other age groups. The majority (80%) of young people charged with homicide were male (AIHW, 2021). There is some suggestion that location differences exist in rates of violent offending, reoffending, or sentencing, particularly for DFV-related offences. This phenomenon is described by Grover (2017, p. 13) as "postcode justice" or "justice by geography". In Australia, Grech and Burgess (2011) report that of the 20 local government areas with the highest per capita rates of DFV in 2010, 19 were in regional or remote locations. These findings may, in part, be attributable to reoffending rates, suggesting that young people from regional areas are more likely to reoffend than those from metropolitan areas (Shirley, 2017).

Data from longitudinal studies of youth development in both Australia and overseas identify an early and stable trajectory of antisocial behaviour, including tendencies towards using violence (Dishion & Patterson, 2015). These studies indicate that there are those who will "naturally desist" and those who will continue with certain behaviours. This stable trajectory typically includes less than 15% of youth, and even within this group, violence is not a universal behaviour. Indeed, most youth do not engage in antisocial or more extreme violent behaviours (e.g., Moffitt et al., 2011). The work of McGee et al. (2021) outlines a trajectory for some young people known as "persistent offenders," who continue to commit offences long after their peers have ceased and who make up a small number of the population committing approximately half of all youth offences.

Terminology

You will have noticed by now that, in this book, we predominantly use the person-first phrasing "(young) people who have experienced violence" and "(young) people who have used violence". While not ignoring important critical discussions about person-first language not being universally endorsed by people experiencing the issue (Meadows & Daníelsdóttir, 2016), this person-first terminology acknowledges context and that labelling through other terms can entrench stigma, especially for young people. Person-first language also recognises the significant unresolved debate that exists around the appropriateness of the terms victim/survivor and perpetrator/offender (Williamson & Serna, 2018). Contrasting viewpoints are each informed by and manifest historical, cultural, gender, and economic symbolism (Bourke, 2012).

Advocates for the term "victim" argue that not all victims survive (Bourke, 2012, 2015) and that the term "survivor" has a significant cultural relevance that prefaces the experience and perception of the white middle class (Spencer, 2016). Like the reclamation of names and labels that have negative connotations for marginalised groups, "victim" is also a label that some suggest needs to be reclaimed (Lacerda, 2015). Hill (2019) believes that the use of "victim" justifiably places responsibility on the perpetrator, while proponents of the term "survivor" argue that it is a braver, more action-oriented and less passive descriptor of an individual who has experienced violence (Lamb, 1999). Maintaining a binary approach to the use of "victim" and "survivor" ignores the reality that identity and perceptions of self are fluid and dynamic. It precludes contemplating a space and place for those people who do not identify with either label (Williamson & Serna, 2018) and the reality of dual identities or shifting identities over time. In Australia, the terms "perpetrator" and "offender" are commonly used interchangeably, especially outside the context of legal proceedings (Phillips et al., 2015), wherein it is more common to find the terms "offender" and "alleged offender" used as they relate to criminal offences and associated charges (Australian Institute of Family Studies [AIFS], 2012).

Understandings

No one factor or causal pathway has been associated with youth violence, but, rather, multiple influences have been implicated, theorised as part of complex and dynamic combinations over time and across situations and settings (Bushman et al., 2016). Explored in detail in the following chapters: potential drivers of youth violence have been located in the challenges young people experience in recognising and regulating emotions, accurately appraising situations, and taking the perspective of others in enacting agency and choice. These individual challenges are variously understood to arise as artefacts of complex and interacting processes of acculturation, socialisation and learning, marginalisation, and oppression. In the following sections, we briefly describe how the use of violence has been understood for young men and young women and across culture before exploring identified risk factors for youth violence.

Young male violence

Most understandings of youth violence concentrate on male violence (Farrington, 2003; Jolliffe et al., 2019). The disproportionate use of violence by men towards women has been explained by various theories as a learned and reinforced behaviour. Social learning theories suggest that violence, and particularly DFV, is a pattern of learned behaviour, observed through dyadic relationships in the family (e.g., parent to child or male parent/caregiver to female parent/caregiver) and repeated in future relationships. From this perspective, children, in particular, sons, learn the aggressive behaviours of their male parents/caregivers through the process of behavioural modelling (Bandura & Walters, 1977). Male violence has also been linked to socially constructed hegemonic masculinity and resulting power imbalances reproduced within and between genders, classes, ethnicities, and institutional settings and enacted through behaviours and actions at micro and macro levels (Crawshaw et al., 2010).

As Rak and Warton (2023) note, the role of hegemonic masculinity in understanding the use of violence emerges as hegemonic masculinity itself becomes (or is perceived to become) destabilised through intersectionality from other power sources such as wealth, age, class, gender, race, and religion (Connell & Messerschmidt, 2005), which go on to re-influence relations, in almost an action/consequence stimulus response (Jefferson, 2002). Hegemonic masculinity and violence, in this sense, must be considered within the context of positionality, hierarchy, and intersectionality and treated as a gender ideology, influencing relationships between men and women as well as relationships between men and other men across a variety of settings. Warton's (2020) work with young Australian males on remand for their use of violence and other offences situates youth violence by its relationship with identity and identity formation. Warton's (2020) findings suggest that the intersection of the use of violence and social identity was a key theme for young men who used violence. As with the work of Staff and Kreager (2008), Warton's (2020) work highlights the role of violence, acceptance, identity, and status for many young men, particularly those from backgrounds of less access and advantage and those who consider themselves as marginalised.

Young female violence

While violence tends to be thought of as a gendered experience, with men predominantly using violence against women, the proportions of males versus females using and experiencing violence is different for young people in Australia. According to Freeman (2018), one-third of all young people proceeded against by police for domestic and family violence (DFV) in NSW were female, and males were victims in one in three cases. There is a common perception, including among practitioners, that young female violence is increasing with almost a third of the practitioners we spoke to reporting they believed there had been an increase in young female violence (Blakemore et al., 2018).

Box 1.2 What practitioners tell us . . .

> "We're getting more girls, and the girls that we're getting are more violent and have more mental health issues. There's definitely an escalation in the number of girls and the level of violence that they perpetrate, probably . . . over the last 10 years there's been quite an escalation". (Practitioner 30)
>
> "We've found that girls are becoming more violent in their assaults. It's almost like girls have to prove themselves, or they're just . . . they're becoming more violent than the boys". (Practitioner 27)

Distinct conceptualisations of young women's or other genders' violence is largely missing from the existing evidence base (Craig & Trulson, 2019), though Carrington (2013) has long argued feminist theorists could play an important role in theorising young women's use of violence. Feminist theorists argue that intimate partner violence stems from male oppression against women, situated within the context of an enduring patriarchal system. Within this context and understanding, men are the main causes of violence and women are the main victims of violence, with men continuing violence against women to maintain power and control (Miller & Mullins, 2017). Carrington (2006, 2014) argues traditional feminist theories do not do enough to explain or seek to understand why women use violence. Feminist criminologists recognise the role of intersectionality in young women's engagement in crime but don't go as far as to draw clear links between this intersectional understanding and the impacts of the patriarchy on this process, as per traditional feminist theory (Miller & Mullins, 2009, 2017). Carrington (2014) suggests this gap is exacerbated by the inherent challenges many feminist theorists have in recognising that women may have agency to use violence as opposed to being victims of violence only.

Young women's use of violence presents policy and practice with challenging issues interconnected with the ways in which youth violence and young women themselves have been understood (Bock & James, 2005; Segal, 2015). As discussed in Blakemore et al. (2021), young women who use violence have, in the past, been routinely positioned as victims, of either biology (with violence stemming from illness or inability) or oppression (where violence stems from their own experience of violence) (Boxall et al., 2020; Chesney-Lind & Eliason, 2006). A contrasting historic discourse is that of the "bad girl" (Brown, 2011). This girl is portrayed as equal parts dangerous, conniving, and violent and as a risk to wider society because of her promiscuous and troubling ways and her insatiable desire to have a voice and a role outside the traditional confines of her gender (Brown, 2011; Chesney-Lind & Irwin, 2008). More recent understandings of young women, their places in society, and their experiences and uses of violence have centred on the (somewhat incongruous) intersection of the "girlhood in crisis" and "girl power" discourses. This situates young women as simultaneously having the world as their oyster (Scharff, 2016) while having to navigate an unrelenting patriarchal system still informed by traditional notions of femininity (Pomerantz et al., 2013; Scharff, 2016). This creates a neoliberal ideal of a girl as one who chases girl power, assuaging girlhood in crisis as a state of being that lacks the resilience and grit to acquire girl power status (Scharff, 2016). Critiques of these discourses question how young women from differing socioeconomic and sociocultural contexts might effectively subscribe to girl power, noting it requires access to and control over social, cultural, and economic resources and capital (Harris et al., 2005) and, where they sit outside these contexts, how they access girl power without having their actions perceived as wilful, disobedient, and potentially deviant (Reay, 2005; Segal, 2015; Walkerdine et al., 2001).

Youth violence and culture

In Australia, Aboriginal and Torres Strait Islander young people (hereafter respectfully referred to as Aboriginal young people) are more vulnerable to poorer justice-related outcomes, including younger age of initial police charges and greater likelihood of convictions for violent offences compared to their non-Aboriginal peers (Baidawi, 2020). Aboriginal young people are 18 times more likely to be incarcerated than their non-Aboriginal peers (AIHW, 2018) and make up 59% of incarcerated youth in Australia, despite comprising only 5% of the overall youth population (Anthony & Blagg, 2021). Over-representation of Aboriginal young people at every level of the justice system is similar across other colonised countries such as Canada, Aotearoa/New Zealand (NZ), and the US (Anthony & Blagg, 2021). Through our practice, we recognise that violence in any Aboriginal communities is not cultural and will not be understood without the recognition and acknowledgement of contextual factors that contribute to the ongoing impacts of colonisation (Rak et al., 2022). These impacts include the exclusion of Aboriginal voices in making meaning of violence, the past and ongoing removal of Aboriginal children from their kin and community, and the implicit and explicit silencing of Aboriginal cultures (Cunneen & Tauri, 2019b). The pervasive impact of structural violence on Aboriginal people has been described by Menzies (2019) as being a collective trauma, one that may manifest across and between generations of people, emerging as expressions of violence, towards others and the self, reproducing violence as an experience and activity (Atkinson, 2002). Ignoring the intersectionality between experiences of violence, discrimination, and marginalisation whitewashes their relationships to violence and, in the process, risks pathologising Aboriginal peoples and communities as "other" (Cunneen & Tauri, 2019a).

Risk factors for youth violence

A major focus of efforts to understand youth violence has been on identifying factors that increase risk for young people experiencing or using violence. By definition, risk factors are characteristics or experiences whose presence is significantly associated with an increased likelihood that adverse outcomes will occur at some later stage (Nash & Bowen, 1999). Importantly, while risk factors precede the associated outcome, they may not necessarily be directly causal. Risk factors are merely markers of high susceptibility or increased likelihood and do not equate to causal factors (Finkelhor & Baron, 1986). Risk factors for youth violence have been identified through descriptive and diagnostic understandings of the personalities, family backgrounds, and demographic characteristics of young people who have experienced and used violence and the sociocultural and economic circumstances that shape their experiences. Individual, family, and social (structural) factors can constitute both risk and/or protective factors for youth violence. Practitioners we spoke to identified individual risk factors they considered likely contributors to the use of violence as including a complex and connected mix of antisocial attitudes and beliefs, a lack of communication and self-regulation skills, and diagnosed and undiagnosed mental health issues, learning disabilities, and/or developmental delay.

Box 1.3 What practitioners tell us . . .

> "It's complicated to know where the antisocial behaviour starts. I think some kids – most of the kids that we get involved with have some kind of learning disability. It's really hard to know where their learning disability comes from because if they've got a dysfunctional family background and the kids are often anxious or distressed and are put in no-win situations through punitive parenting, they often don't learn the skills of learning, so going to school to learn is difficult for them. They become frustrated, I think, at school, frustrated with their parents' expectations or their parents' dysfunction. They can't cope. They rebel and they become angry, resentful, and they become antisocial habitually". (Practitioner 1)

Young people with intellectual disability or below average intelligence quotient (IQ) have also been shown to have higher levels of engagement with the criminal justice system in Australia (Frize et al., 2008; Haysom et al., 2014; Indig et al., 2011), and adolescents of Aboriginal origin who are engaged in the criminal justice system have an even higher incidence of intellectual disability and below average IQ than non-Aboriginal young people (Frize et al., 2008; Haysom et al., 2014; Indig et al., 2011). These observations are likely linked to education disengaging from the young people and potentially to the impacts of trauma (Rak & Warton, 2023). Data retrieved from the 2002 National Aboriginal and Torres Strait Islander Social Survey found that participation in high school education significantly lowered the likelihood of engagement in the criminal justice system (Ferrante, 2013; Reeve & Bradford, 2014), with Ferrante (2013) noting that the protective effect was greatest for those who reached senior high school. Yet, as noted in our pilot study (Blakemore et al., 2019) and observed by Indig et al. (2011), engagement in school for young people who use violence seems to be a fraught experience, with young people who use and experience violence being less likely to be regularly attending school when compared to their counterparts who did not use violence (Rak & Warton, 2023).

Box 1.4 What practitioners tell us . . .

Practitioners observed young people they worked with "had a problem with authority".

> "They don't seem to trust authority figures or even . . . just adults in general. I'm not really sure where that's stemmed from, whether it's like a history of trauma or whether it's because they've been caught and now they resent authority". (Practitioner 10)

Practitioners linked this to (possibly intergenerational) experiences of disadvantage and trauma.

> "Kids who have experienced a lot of family violence end up distrusting authority figures. They see authority figures as disappointing, unreliable, duplicitous, self-serving, and disinterested in them. Their behaviour and their antisocial behaviour evolves out of that general mistrust and expectation that people are . . . are unreliable". (Practitioner 1)

Practitioner observations are consistent with evidence of other individual risk factors for the use of violence including gender; age; ability and cognition (Howard & Rottem, 2008; Routt & Anderson, 2011); prior experiences of violence abuse and trauma (Moulds et al., 2016); peer group influences (Cox et al., 2016; Howard & Rottem, 2008); and prior offending (Freeman, 2018). Young people's use of violence often coincides and coexists with the commission of other types of crime (Freeman, 2018; Moulds et al., 2016). Young people who have been charged with criminal offences are more likely to have had a domestic or interpersonal-related charge within a two-year timeframe, and the use of crime often coexists with the use of violence in the adolescent cohort (Freeman, 2018).

Familial risk factors for youth violence can include parental youth, poor mental health (Moulds et al., 2016; Simmons et al., 2017), parental absence, family dynamics and functioning, domestic and family violence (Bobic, 2004; Cox et al., 2016; Simmons et al., 2017), parenting practices (Morris, 2009; Walsh & Krienert, 2009), and intergenerational experiences of violence abuse and trauma (Atkinson, 2002). The family and social circumstances of young people are not only the site and settings of violence but are also correlates of involvement with the criminal justice system. Young people who use violence have frequently experienced or been exposed to DFV and other forms of violence, abuse, and neglect in childhood (Bollinger et al., 2017; Moulds et al., 2016). Several specific precursors to crime are believed to have a greater effect on young females compared with young males – namely, parental relationship instability, financial insecurity, and childhood abuse and associated trauma (Bollinger et al., 2017; Ford & Hawke, 2012; Thompson & McGrath, 2012). Young women who use violence are likely to have experienced inconsistent discipline from a caregiver and have a broken or dysfunctional relationship with their female caregiver (Thompson & McGrath, 2012). Young women who use violence are also more likely to have had periods of homelessness or are at greater risk of homelessness compared with young males (Rak, 2022; Thompson & McGrath, 2012).

Family and individual factors are likely to intersect and may be dynamic or static; for example, family of origin is considered static, while drug and alcohol mis/use is considered dynamic (Douglas & Skeem, 2005; Van der Put et al., 2012). However, they intersect in situations such as communal drug mis/use within a family setting (Baglivio et al., 2018). Practitioners described how the family context can be a gateway to involvement in crime, including the use of violence. In this way, however, crime was also a means of connection. Practitioners detailed familial and peer transfer of behaviour and experience and a sense of acculturation to pro-criminal ideas and actions that engendered a sense of connection and belonging.

Box 1.5 What practitioners tell us . . .

> "Yeah pro-criminal attitudes and beliefs are then just prevalent. . . . It's a known behaviour. Often siblings are committing crimes together. So there's that connection". (Practitioner 20)

> "We've had like parents actually take their child to a place that has been set up to have a fight, and they've been present while this has happened. . . . It actually happens, multiple times that has happened, and if you asked them about it, they would say I'd rather she/he got it out of the way . . . I know what's happened, I'm here, I can control it". (Practitioner 4)

These quotes give an insight into how practitioners perceived some families as modelling and supporting behaviours outside the law and outside normative developmental behaviour, including familial transfer of drugs and alcohol, engagement in antisocial behaviour, and aiding and abetting interpersonal violence in the community (Blakemore et al., 2018). Crime in this context was described alternately as a bonding experience and as an inevitability of intergenerational disadvantage and disengagement with systems and structures. While current theory and literature attests to the importance and benefits of belonging for the health and wellbeing of young people, it often assumes a wholesome type of belonging that is consistent with prosocial values and socially acceptable relationships. When belonging is discussed in relation to juvenile crime, it tends to examine the degree of association between peers and the transmission of antisocial values, norms, and behaviours that are reinforced though intrinsic and tangible rewards (Seddig, 2013; Silverman & Caldwell, 2008).

Social-structural risk factors for youth violence can include placement in OOHC; intergenerational experiences of violence; abuse and neglect; disadvantage (Simmons et al., 2017; Walsh & Krienert, 2009); and collective colonialist experiences of violence, abuse, and trauma (Atkinson, 2002). Children in OOHC are noted to be at significant risk of involvement with the criminal justice system (Borzycki, 2005; Mendes, 2009), with this risk associated with the use of violence, substance use, relationship breakdowns, financial instability or hardship, and significant learning or intellectual disabilities (Mendes et al., 2014; Mendes & Moslehuddin, 2009). Young women in OOHC are more likely to be charged with violence-related offences that their non-care leaver counterparts may not be charged with – for example, property damage (Bollinger et al., 2017; McFarlane, 2011). For young women, an experience of OOHC and/or protracted engagement with the child protection system are identified risk factors for juvenile recidivism (Bollinger et al., 2017; McFarlane, 2011). This may be because young women who are involved with both the child protection and juvenile justice systems may be more likely to be early parents and to also have their children removed due to child protection concerns (Mendes et al., 2014). Young Aboriginal women who have an experience of care tend to have poorer outcomes and a greater association with the criminal system compared with their Aboriginal peers without experience of care. These young women are up to five times more likely to be incarcerated than their non-Indigenous, non-OOHC counterparts (McFarlane, 2011), commonly having become involved in property-related crime and theft with cousins and siblings.

Theoretically, risk factor approaches to understanding youth violence map to an ecological systems model of understanding human development. Brofenbrenner's ecosystems framework (1979) articulates five nested interacting systems or ecologies, including the microsystem, mesosystem, exosystem, macrosystem, and chronosystem. These interacting systems are theorised as the situations and settings through which young people find and form relationships with family and friends and in and through which they navigate relationships with institutions, including school, community, and culture and the wider sociopolitical structures that govern experience across each system. From an ecosystems perspective, the young person's environment is a complex and interwoven set of systems that shift and change, operating simultaneously at different levels (Bronfenbrenner, 1979, 1994; Johns et al., 2017). Bronfenbrenner's (1995) concept of "proximal processes" underpins ecological ideas and theories of how the cycle of youth crime may occur. As children and young people age and develop, their interactions with others become deeper, more complex, and reciprocal in nature (Bronfenbrenner, 1995; Johns et al., 2017). Through their natural development, children and young people use these interactions to make meaning of their immediate surroundings and their role within them (Bronfenbrenner, 1995). Proximal process – that is, the deeply relational interaction between the individual and temporal and spatial contexts as well as where and how these interactions are situated in wider systemic processes – contribute to identity formation as well as an understanding of power and control (Bronfenbrenner, 1995; Johns et al., 2017). Discussed in the following chapters, understandings of risk and criminogenic risk factors have been highly influential in shaping both justice- and practice-based responses to youth violence.

Conclusion

This chapter has outlined the complex set of factors that combine to form and contextualise youth violence. Youth violence frequently takes place within individual, familial, and community settings and is often associated with disadvantage and disconnection. The next chapter discusses how the justice system responds to and interacts with youth violence. The legal processes relevant to youth use and experiences of violence are analysed and discussed through a literature review. A vital part of this discussion is a comparison between the reflections and feedback from young people who have a lived experience of violence and the findings presented in the literature review.

References

Anthony, T., & Blagg, H. (2021). Hyperincarceration and indigeneity. In *Oxford research encyclopedias: Criminology and criminal justice*. Oxford University Press. https://doi.org/10.1093/acrefore/9780190264079.013.656

Atkinson, J. (2002). *Trauma trails, recreating song lines*. Spinifex Press.

Australian Bureau of Statistics. (2019). *Youth offenders, 2017–18*. www.abs.gov.au/ausstats/abs@.nsf/Lookup/by%20Subject/4519.0~2017-18~Main%20Features~Youth%20Offenders~4

Australian Bureau of Statistics. (2021). *Recorded crime – victims*. www.abs.gov.au/statistics/people/crime-and-justice/recorded-crime-victims/latest-release

Australian Institute of Family Studies. (2012). *Reporting on sexual assault*. https://aifs.gov.au/publications/reporting-sexual-assault/what-sexual-assault

Australian Institute of Health and Welfare (AIHW). (2018). *Aboriginal and Torres Strait Islander adolescent and youth health and wellbeing 2018*. Canberra: AIHW. www.aihw.gov.au/reports/indigenous-australians/atsi-adolescent-youth-health-wellbeing-2018/contents/summary

Australian Institute of Health and Welfare (AIHW). (2019). *Child protection in Australia*. www.aihw.gov.au/reports/child-protection/child-protection-australia-2017-18/formats

Australian Institute of Health and Welfare (AIHW). (2021). *Crime and violence*. www.aihw.gov.au/reports/children-youth/crime

Baglivio, M. T., Wolff, K. T., Howell, J. C., Jackowski, K., & Greenwald, M. A. (2018). The search for the holy grail: Criminogenic needs matching, intervention dosage, and subsequent recidivism among serious juvenile offenders in residential placement. *Journal of Criminal Justice*, *55*, 46–57. https://doi.org/10.1016/j.jcrimjus.2018.02.001

Baidawi, S. (2020). Crossover children: Examining initial criminal justice system contact among child protection-involved youth. *Australian Social Work*, *73*(3), 280–295. https://doi.org/10.1080/0312407X.2019.1686765

Bandura, A., & Walters, R. H. (1977). *Social learning theory* (Vol. 1). Prentice-Hall.

Blakemore, T., Agllias, K., Howard, A., & McCarthy, S. (2019). The service system challenges of work with juvenile justice involved young people in the Hunter Region, Australia. *Australian Journal of Social Issues*, *54*(3), 341–356. https://doi.org/10.1002/ajs4.69

Blakemore, T., Herbert, J. L., Arney, F., & Parkinson, S. (2017). The impacts of institutional child sexual abuse: A rapid review of the evidence. *Child Abuse & Neglect*, *74*, 35–48. https://doi.org/10.1016/j.chiabu.2017.08.006

Blakemore, T., Rak, L., Agllias, K., Mallett, X., & McCarthy, S. (2018). Crime and context: Understandings of youth perpetrated interpersonal violence among service providers in regional Australia. *Journal of Applied Youth Studies*, *2*(5), 53–69.

Blakemore, T., Randall, E., Rak, L., & Cocuzzoli, F. (2021). Deep listening and relationality: Cross-cultural reflections on practice with young women who use violence. *Australian Social Work*, *75*(3), 304–316. https://doi.org/10.1080/0312407X.2021.1914697

Bobic, N. (2004). *Adolescent violence towards parents*. Australian Domestic & Family Violence Clearinghouse.

Bock, G., & James, S. (Eds.). (2005). *Beyond equality and difference: Citizenship, feminist politics and female subjectivity*. Routledge. https://doi.org/10.4324/9780203982266

Bollinger, J., Scott-Smith, S., & Mendes, P. (2017). How complex developmental trauma, residential out-of-home care and contact with the justice system intersect. *Children Australia*, *42*(2), 108–112. https://doi.org/10.1017/cha.2017.9

Borzycki, M. (2005). *Interventions for prisoners returning to the community: A report prepared by the Australian Institute of criminology for the community safety and justice branch of the Australian government attorney-general's department*. Australian Government. https://doi.org/10.1037/e669922010-001

Bourke, J. (2012). Sexual violence, bodily pain, and trauma: A history. *Theory, Culture & Society*, *29*(3), 25–51. https://doi.org/10.1177/0263276412439406

Bourke, J. (2015). *Rape: A history from 1860 to the present*. Virago.

Boxall, H., Morgan, A., & Brown, R. (2020). The prevalence of domestic violence among women during the COVID-19 pandemic. *Australasian Policing*, *12*(3), 38–46. https://doi.org/10.52922/sb04718

Bronfenbrenner, U. (1979). *The ecology of human development*. Harvard University Press.

Bronfenbrenner, U. (1994). Ecological models of human development. *Readings on the Development of Children*, *2*(1), 37–43.

Bronfenbrenner, U. (1995). Developmental ecology through space and time: A future perspective. In P. Moen, G. H. Elder Jr & K. Lüscher (Eds.), *Examining lives in context: Perspectives on the ecology of human development* (pp. 619–647). American Psychological Association. https://doi.org/10.1037/10176-018

Brown, J. (2011). "Brown girl in the ring": Poly Styrene, Annabella Lwin, and the politics of anger. *Journal of Popular Music Studies*, *23*(4), 455–478. https://doi.org/10.1111/j.1533-1598.2011.01306.x

Bushman, B. J., Newman, K., Calvert, S. L., Downey, G., Dredze, M., Gottfredson, M., Jablonski, N., Masten, A. S., Morrill, C., Neill, D. B., Romer, D., & Webster, D. W. (2016). Youth violence: What we know and what we need to know. *American Psychologist*, *71*(1), 17–39. https://doi.org/10.1037/a0039687

Carrington, K. (2006). Does feminism spoil girls? Explanations for official rises in female delinquency. *Australian & New Zealand Journal of Criminology*, *39*(1), 34–53. https://doi.org/10.1375/acri.39.1.34

Carrington, K. (2013). Girls, crime and violence: Toward a feminist theory of female violence. *International Journal for Crime, Justice and Social Democracy*, *2*(2), 63–79. https://doi.org/10.5204/ijcjsd.v2i2.101

Carrington, K. (2014). *Feminism and global justice*. Routledge. https://doi.org/10.4324/9781315748368

Chesney-Lind, M., & Eliason, M. (2006). From invisible to incorrigible: The demonization of marginalized women and girls. *Crime, Media, Culture*, *2*(1), 29–47. https://doi.org/10.1177/1741659006061709

Chesney-Lind, M., & Irwin, K. (2008). Girls' violence: Beyond dangerous masculinity. *Sociology Compass*, *2*(3), 837–855. https://doi.org/10.1111/j.1751-9020.2008.00120.x

Connell, R. W., & Messerschmidt, J. W. (2005). Hegemonic masculinity: Rethinking the concept. *Gender & Society*, *19*(6), 829–859. https://doi.org/10.1177/0891243205278639

Coogan, D. (2011). Child-to-parent violence: Challenging perspectives on family violence. *Child Care in Practice*, *17*(4), 347–358. https://doi.org/10.1080/13575279.2011.596815

Cox, E., Leung, R., Baksheev, G., Day, A., Toumbourou, J. W., Miller, P., Kremer, P., & Walker, A. (2016). Violence prevention and intervention programmes for adolescents in Australia: A systematic review. *Australian Psychologist*, *51*(3), 206–222. https://doi.org/10.1111/ap.12168

Craig, J. M., & Trulson, C. R. (2019). Continuity of the delinquent career behind bars: Predictors of violent misconduct among female delinquents. *Aggression and Violent Behavior*, *49*, Article 101301. https://doi.org/10.1016/j.avb.2019.06.002

Crawshaw, P., Scott-Samuel, A., & Stanistreet, D. (2010). Masculinities, hegemony, and structural violence. *Criminal Justice Matters, 81*(1), 2–4. https://doi.org/10.1080/09627251.2010.505383

Cunneen, C., & Tauri, J. M. (2019a). Indigenous peoples, criminology, and criminal justice. *Annual Review of Criminology, 2*, 359–381. https://doi.org/10.1146/annurev-criminol-011518-024630

Cunneen, C., & Tauri, J. M. (2019b). Violence and Indigenous communities. In W. S. DeKeseredy, C. M. Rennison, & A. K. Hall-Sanchez (Eds.), *The Routledge international handbook of violence studies* (pp. 350–361). Routledge. https://doi.org/10.4324/9781315270265-33

Daff, E. S., McEwan, T. E., & Luebbers, S. (2021). Australian adolescents' experiences of aggression and abuse by intimate partners. *Journal of Interpersonal Violence, 36*(9–10), NP5586–NP5609. https://doi.org/10.1177/0886260518801936

Daly, K., & Wade, D. (2015). Gender and adolescent-to-parent violence: A systematic analysis of typical and atypical cases. In *Working with adolescent violence and abuse towards parents* (pp. 162–182). Routledge. https://doi.org/10.4324/9781315750781-19

Dishion, T. J., & Patterson, G. R. (2015). The development and ecology of antisocial behavior in children and adolescents. In *Developmental psychopathology: Volume 3: Risk, disorder, and adaptation* (pp. 503–541). https://doi.org/10.1002/9780470939406.ch13

Douglas, K. S., & Skeem, J. L. (2005). Violence risk assessment: Getting specific about being dynamic. *Psychology, Public Policy, and Law, 11*(3), 347–383. https://doi.org/10.1037/1076-8971.11.3.347

Downey, L. (1997). Adolescent violence: A systemic and feminist perspective. *Australian and New Zealand Journal of Family Therapy, 18*(2), 70–79. https://doi.org/10.1002/j.1467-8438.1997.tb00272.x

Edenborough, M., Jackson, D., Mannix, J., & Wilkes, L. M. (2008). Living in the red zone: The experience of child-to-mother violence. *Child & Family Social Work, 13*(4), 464–473. https://doi.org/10.1111/j.1365-2206.2008.00576.x

Farrington, D. P. (2003). Key results from the first forty years of the Cambridge study in delinquent development. In T. P. Thornberry & M. D. Krohn (Eds.), *Taking stock of delinquency: An overview of findings from contemporary longitudinal studies* (pp. 137–183). Kluwer/Plenum. https://doi.org/10.1007/0-306-47945-1_5

Ferrante, A. M. (2013). Assessing the influence of "standard" and "culturally specific" risk factors on the prevalence and frequency of offending: The case of Indigenous Australians. *Race and Justice, 3*(1), 58–82. https://doi.org/10.1177/2153368712462410

Finkelhor, D., & Baron, L. (1986). Risk factors for child sexual abuse. *Journal of Interpersonal Violence, 1*(1), 43–71.

Finkelhor, D., Turner, H., Ormrod, R., & Hamby, S. L. (2009). Violence, abuse, and crime exposure in a national sample of children and youth. *Pediatrics, 124*(5), 1411–1423. https://doi.org/10.1542/peds.2009-0467

Fitz-Gibbon, K., Elliott, K., & Maher, J. (2018). *Investigating adolescent family violence in Victoria: Understanding experiences and practitioner perspectives.* Monash Gender and Family Violence Research Program, Faculty of Arts, Monash University.

Fitzpatrick, M. (2004). *Grandparents raising grandchildren*. Council on the Ageing.

Ford, J. D., & Hawke, J. (2012). Trauma affect regulation psychoeducation group attendance is associated with reduced disciplinary incidents and sanctions in juvenile detention facilities. *Journal of Aggression, Maltreatment, and Trauma*, *21*, 365–384. https://doi.org/10.1080/10926771.2012.673538

Foshee, V. A., Bauman, K. E., Linder, F., Rice, J., & Wilcher, R. (2007). Typologies of adolescent dating violence: Identifying typologies of adolescent dating violence perpetration. *Journal of Interpersonal Violence*, *22*(5), 498–519. https://doi.org/10.1177/0886260506298829

Freeman, K. (2018). *Domestic and family violence by juvenile offenders: Offender, victim and incident characteristics*. NSW Bureau of Crime Statistics and Research.

Frize, M., Kenny, D., & Lennings, C. (2008). The relationship between intellectual disability, Indigenous status and risk of reoffending in juvenile offenders on community orders. *Journal of Intellectual Disability Research*, *52*, 510–519. https://doi.org/10.1111/j.1365-2788.2008.01058.x

Gallagher, E. (2004). Parents victimised by their children. *Australian and New Zealand Journal of Family Therapy*, *25*(1), 1–12. https://doi.org/10.1002/j.1467-8438.2004.tb00573.x

Grech, K., & Burgess, M. (2011). *Trends and patterns in domestic violence assaults: 2001 to 2010*. NSW Bureau of Crime Statistics and Research.

Grover, C. (2017). *Youth justice in Victoria*. www.parliament.vic.gov.au/publications/research-papers/download/36-research-papers/13806-youth-justice-in-victoria

Harbin, H. T., & Madden, D. J. (1979). Battered parents: A new syndrome. *American Journal of Psychiatry*, *136*(10), 1288–1291. https://doi.org/10.1176/ajp.136.10.1288

Harris, A., Gonick, M., & Aapola, S. (2005). *Young femininity: Girlhood, power and social change*. Palgrave Macmillan.

Haysom, L., Indig, D., Moore, E., & Gaskin, C. (2014). Intellectual disability in young people in custody in New South Wales, Australia – prevalence and markers. *Journal of Intellectual Disability Research*, *58*, 1004–1014. https://doi.org/10.1111/jir.12109

Hill, J. (2019). *See what you made me do: Power, control and domestic abuse*. Black Inc.

Howard, J. (2011). *Adolescent violence in the home: The missing link in family violence prevention and response* (Stakeholder Paper No. 11). Australian Domestic & Family Violence Clearinghouse.

Howard, J. (2015). Adolescent violence in the home: How is it different to adult family violence? *Journal of the Home Economics Institute of Australia*, *22*(3), 32.

Howard, J., & Rottem, N. (2008). *It all starts at home: Male adolescent violence to mothers: A research report*. Inner South Community Health Services Inc and Child Abuse Research Australia, Monash University.

Indig, D., Vecchiato, C., Haysom, L., Beilby, R., Carter, J., Champion, U., Gaskin, C., Heller, E., Kumar, S., Mamone, N., Muir, P., van den Dolder, P., & Whitton, G. (2011). *2009 NSW young people in custody health survey: Full report*. NSW Health. www.justicehealth.nsw.gov.au/publications/ypicks-full.pdf

Jefferson, T. (2002). Subordinating hegemonic masculinity. *Theoretical Criminology*, *6*(1), 63–88. https://doi.org/10.1177/136248060200600103

Johns, D. F., Williams, K., & Haines, K. (2017). Ecological youth justice: Understanding the social ecology of young people's prolific offending. *Youth Justice*, *17*(1), 3–21. https://doi.org/10.1177/1473225416665611

Johnson, M. P. (1995). Patriarchal terrorism and common couple violence: Two forms of violence against women. *Journal of Marriage and the Family*, *57*(2), 283–294. https://doi.org/10.2307/353683

Johnson, M. P. (2005). Domestic violence: It's not about gender – or is it? *Journal of Marriage and Family*, *67*(5), 1126–1130. https://doi.org/10.1111/j.1741-3737.2005.00204.x

Johnson, M. P. (2010). *A typology of domestic violence: Intimate terrorism, violent resistance, and situational couple violence*. Northeastern University Press.

Johnson, M. P. (2011). Gender and types of intimate partner violence: A response to an anti-feminist literature review. *Aggression and Violent Behavior*, *16*(4), 289–296. https://doi.org/10.1016/j.avb.2011.04.006

Jolliffe, D., Farrington, D. P., Brunton-Smith, I., Loeber, R., Ahonen, L., & Palacios, A. P. (2019). Depression, anxiety and delinquency: Results from the Pittsburgh youth study. *Journal of Criminal Justice*, *62*, 42–49. https://doi.org/10.1016/j.jcrimjus.2018.08.004

Khan, R., & Rogers, P. (2015). The normalization of sibling violence: Does gender and personal experience of violence influence perceptions of physical assault against siblings? *Journal of Interpersonal Violence*, *30*(3), 437–458. https://doi.org/10.1177/0886260514535095

Lacerda, T. (2015). "Victim": What is hidden behind this word? *International Journal of Transitional Justice*, *10*(1), 179–188. https://doi.org/10.1093/ijtj/ijv028

Lamb, S. (Ed.). (1999). *New versions of victims: Feminists struggle with the concept*. New York University Press. https://doi.org/10.18574/nyu/9780814752913.001.0001

McDonald, C., & Martinez, K. (2016). Parental and others' responses to physical sibling violence: A descriptive analysis of victims' retrospective accounts. *Journal of Family Violence*, *31*(3), 401–410. https://doi.org/10.1007/s10896-015-9766-y

McFarlane, K. (2011). From care to custody: Young women in out-of-home care in the criminal justice system. *Current Issues in Criminal Justice*, *22*(3), 345–353. https://doi.org/10.1080/10345329.2010.12035890

McGee, T. R., Whitten, T., Williams, C., Jolliffe, D., & Farrington, D. P. (2021). Classification of patterns of offending in developmental and life-course criminology, with special reference to persistence. *Aggression and Violent Behavior*, *59*, 101460.

Meadows, A., & Daníelsdóttir, S. (2016). What's in a word? On weight stigma and terminology. *Frontiers in Psychology*, *7*, 1527. https://doi.org/10.3389/fpsyg.2016.01527

Mendes, P. (2009). Young people transitioning from state out of home care: Jumping hoops to access employment. *Family Matters*, (83), 32–38.

Mendes, P., & Moslehuddin, B. (2009). Transitioning from state care to state prison: A critical analysis of the relationship between leaving out of home care and involvement in the criminal justice system. *Social Alternatives*, *28*(3), 51–56.

Mendes, P., Snow, P., & Baidawi, S. (2014). The views of service providers on the challenges facing young people also involved in the youth justice system transitioning from out-of-home care. *Journal of Policy Practice*, *13*(4), 239–257. https://doi.org/10.1080/15588742.2014.929074

Menzies, K. (2019). Understanding the Australian Aboriginal experience of collective, historical and intergenerational trauma. *International Social Work*, *62*(6), 1522–1534. https://doi.org/10.1177/0020872819870585

Messinger, A. M., Fry, D. A., Rickert, V. I., Catallozzi, M., & Davidson, L. L. (2014). Extending Johnson's intimate partner violence typology: Lessons from an adolescent sample. *Violence Against Women*, *20*(8), 948–971. https://doi.org/10.1177/1077801214546907

Miller, J., & Mullins, C. W. (2009). Feminist theories of girls' delinquency. In *The delinquent girl* (pp. 30–49). Temple University Press.

Miller, J., & Mullins, C. W. (2017). The status of feminist theories in criminology. In *Taking stock* (pp. 217–249). Routledge. https://doi.org/10.4324/9781315130620-9

Moffitt, T. E., Arseneault, L., Belsky, D., Dickson, N., Hancox, R. J., Harrington, H., Houts, R., Poulton, R., Roberts, B. W., Ross, S., Sears, M. R., Thomson, W. M., & Caspi, A. (2011). A gradient of childhood self-control predicts health, wealth, and public safety. *Proceedings of the National Academy of Sciences*, *108*(7), 2693–2698. www.pnas.org/doi/full/10.1073/pnas.1010076108

Morris, A. (2009). Gendered dynamics of abuse and violence in families: Considering the abusive household gender regime. *Child Abuse Review*, *18*(6), 414–427. https://doi.org/10.1002/car.1098

Moulds, L., Day, A., Mayshak, R., Mildred, H., & Miller, P. (2019). Adolescent violence towards parents – prevalence and characteristics using Australian police data. *Australian & New Zealand Journal of Criminology*, *52*(2), 231–249. https://doi.org/10.1177/0004865818781206

Moulds, L., Day, A., Mildred, H., Miller, P., & Casey, S. (2016). Adolescent violence towards parents – the known and unknowns. *Australian and New Zealand Journal of Family Therapy*, *37*(4), 547–557. https://doi.org/10.1002/anzf.1189

Murphy-Edwards, L., & van Heugten, K. (2015). Domestic property violence: A distinct and damaging form of parent abuse. *Journal of Interpersonal Violence*, *33*(4), 617–636. https://doi.org/10.1177/0886260515613341

Nash, J. K., & Bowen, G. L. (1999). Perceived crime and informal social control in the neighborhood as a context for adolescent behavior: A risk and resilience perspective. *Social Work Research*, *23*(3), 171–186. https://doi.org/10.1093/swr/23.3.171

Papalia, N., Thomas, S. D., Ching, H., & Daffern, M. (2015). Changes in the prevalence and nature of violent crime by youth in Victoria, Australia. *Psychiatry, Psychology, and Law*, *22*(2), 213–223. https://doi.org/10.1080/13218719.2014.937476

Phillips, J., Dunkley, A., Muller, D., & Lorimer, C. (2015). *Domestic violence: Issues and policy challenges* (Research Paper Series 2015–16). Parliamentary Library.

Pomerantz, S., Raby, R., & Stefanik, A. (2013). Girls run the world? Caught between sexism and post-feminism in school. *Gender & Society*, *27*(2), 185–207. https://doi.org/10.1177/0891243212473199

Rak, L. (2022). Making the invisible, visible: Seeking the voices of justice involved young women in homelessness discourse. *Parity*, *35*(1), 42–43.

Rak, L., Cocuzzoli, F., & Randall, E. (2022). No filter needed: Interweaving deep listening with visual methods in practice with young justice-involved Aboriginal women. In *FRSA Conference E-Journal* (5th ed.). https://aifs.gov.au/resources/news-and-events/peer-reviewed-papers-frsa-2022-national-conference

Rak, L., & Warton, T. (2023). His, hers and theirs: Comparative narratives from young people who use violence. *Safer Communities*, *22*(1), 42–55. https://doi.org/10.1108/SC-08-2022-0033

Reay, D. (2005). "Spice girls," "nice girls," "girlies" and "tomboys": Gender discourses, girls' cultures and femininities in the primary classroom. In *Feminist critique of education* (pp. 63–77). Routledge.

Reeve, R., & Bradford, W. (2014). Aboriginal disadvantage in major cities of New South Wales: Evidence for holistic policy approaches. *Australian Economic Review*, *47*(2), 199–217. https://doi.org/10.1111/1467-8462.12061

Reuter, T. R., & Whitton, S. W. (2018). Adolescent dating violence among lesbian, gay, bisexual, transgender, and questioning youth. In D. A. Wolfe & J. R. Temple (Eds.), *Adolescent dating violence* (pp. 215–231). Academic Press. https://doi.org/10.1016/B978-0-12-811797-2.00009-8

Reyes, H. L. M., Foshee, V. A., Fortson, B. L., Valle, L. A., Breiding, M. J., & Merrick, M. T. (2015). Longitudinal mediators of relations between family violence and adolescent dating aggression perpetration. *Journal of Marriage and Family*, *77*(4), 1016–1030. https://doi.org/10.1111/jomf.12200

Routt, G., & Anderson, L. (2011). Adolescent violence towards parents. *Journal of Aggression, Maltreatment & Trauma*, *20*(1), 1–19. https://doi.org/10.1080/10926771.2011.537595

Routt, G., & Anderson, L. (2014). *Adolescent violence in the home: Restorative approaches to building healthy, respectful family relationships*. Routledge. https://doi.org/10.4324/9780203517994

Russell, K. (2021). *What works to prevent youth violence: A summary of the evidence*. Scottish Violence Reduction Unit.

Scharff, C. (2016). *Repudiating feminism: Young women in a neoliberal world*. Routledge. https://doi.org/10.4324/9781315605517

Seddig, D. (2013). Peer group association, the acceptance of norms and violent behaviour: A longitudinal analysis of reciprocal effects. *European Journal of Criminology*, *11*, 319–339. https://doi.org/10.1177/1477370813496704

Segal, L. (2015). *Why feminism? Gender, psychology, politics*. John Wiley & Sons.

Shirley, K. (2017). The cautious approach: Police cautions and the impact on youth reoffending. *Crime Statistics Agency*, *9*, 1–23.

Silverman, J. R., & Caldwell, R. M. (2008). Peer relationships and violence among female juvenile offenders: An exploration of differences among four racial/ethnic populations. *Criminal Justice and Behavior*, *35*(3), 333–343. https://doi.org/10.1177/0093854807311114

Simmons, M., McEwan, T. E., Purcell, R., & Ogloff, J. R. (2017). Sixty years of child-to-parent abuse research: What we know and where to go. *Aggression and Violent Behavior*, *38*, 31–52. https://doi.org/10.1016/j.avb.2017.11.001

Sinnott, T., & Artz, S. (2016). What's in a name? The negative implications of gender neutrality in the intimate partner violence prevention and intervention literature. *Gender Issues*, *33*(3), 271–284. https://doi.org/10.1007/s12147-016-9166-5

Spencer, B. (2016). The impact of class and sexuality-based stereotyping on rape blame. *Sexualization, Media, & Society*, *2*(2). https://doi.org/10.1177/2374623816643282

Staff, J., & Kreager, D. A. (2008). Too cool for school? Violence, peer status and high school dropout. *Social Forces*, *87*(1), 445–471. https://doi.org/10.1353/sof.0.0068

Staudigl, M. (2013). Towards a relational phenomenology of violence. *Human Studies*, *36*(1), 43–66. https://doi.org/10.1007/s10746-013-9269-x

Sylaska, K. M., & Walters, A. S. (2014). Testing the extent of the gender trap: College students' perceptions of and reactions to intimate partner violence. *Sex Roles*, *70*(3–4), 134–145. https://doi.org/10.1007/s11199-014-0344-1

Thompson, A. P., & McGrath, A. (2012). Subgroup differences and implications for contemporary risk-need assessment with juvenile offenders. *Law and Human Behavior*, *36*(4), 345–355. https://doi.org/10.1037/h0093930

Van der Put, C. E., Stams, G. J. J., Hoeve, M., Deković, M., Spanjaard, H. J. M., van der Laan, P. H., & Barnoski, R. P. (2012). Changes in the relative importance of dynamic risk factors for recidivism during adolescence. *International Journal of Offender Therapy and Comparative Criminology*, *56*(2), 296–316. https://doi.org/10.1177/0306624X11398462

Voce, I., Boxall, H., Morgan, A., & Coughlan, M. (2020). *Responding to adolescent family violence: Findings from an impact evaluation* (Trends and Issues in Crime and Criminal Justice No. 601). Australian Institute of Criminology.

Walkerdine, V., Lucey, H., & Melody, J. (2001). *Growing up girl: Psychosocial explorations of gender and class*. Palgrave Macmillan. https://doi.org/10.5040/9781350392793

Walsh, J. A., & Krienert, J. L. (2009). A decade of child-initiated family violence: Comparative analysis of child – parent violence and parricide examining offender, victim, and event characteristics in a national sample of reported incidents, 1995–2005. *Journal of Interpersonal Violence*, *24*(9), 1450–1477. https://doi.org/10.1177/0886260508323661

Warton, T. J. (2020). *The development of a criminal identity amongst adolescent males* [Doctoral dissertation]. Monash University.

Williamson, J., & Serna, K. (2018). Reconsidering forced labels: Outcomes of sexual assault survivors versus victims (and those who choose neither). *Violence Against Women*, *24*(6), 668–683. https://doi.org/10.1177/1077801217711268

2 Justice responses to youth violence

Shaun McCarthy, Tamara Blakemore, and Louise Rak

Acknowledgement

This chapter presents data from interviews with NNN graduates. Some of this data was collected by Dr Joel McGregor, and we acknowledge his contribution. We also acknowledge Stephanie Simm's literature review used in these interviews and this chapter.

Justice responses to youth violence

This chapter examines justice responses to youth violence, focusing largely on the legal process in Australia and in New South Wales (NSW), the location of our NNN work. Where relevant, we provide a brief discussion of general differences and points of interest as they relate to other jurisdictions. The chapter describes findings from the literature on young people's experience of legal process and introduces readers to "Ray" and "Jazz" (not their real names) – two young people with a lived experience of the justice system. In this chapter, Ray and Jazz provide unique and raw insights into the evidence about young people's justice involvement, often recounting their own experiences and perspectives on the legal process described. Presented in textboxes throughout, this information was captured (with appropriate ethics approval) through a shared reading and reflection on the literature reviewed.

Terms and conditions

How we conceptualise and understand youth violence (as discussed in Chapter 1) shapes policy and practice-based responses. In its simplest way, this is evidenced in the terms used to refer to young people subject to justice intervention. In our work, we use the term "justice-involved youth" to represent the legal situation of the young people we work with. The terms "young offenders," "juvenile offenders", or "juvenile delinquents" are often used interchangeably to refer to this cohort. Each

DOI: 10.4324/9781003177883-2

of these terms are influenced by, and representative of, varying historic, sociocultural, and political ideas about the actions and agency of young people. For example, "offending" indicates a person's behaviour is outside the law, whereas "delinquency" refers to behaviour outside legal and *moral* requirements of the prevailing social order (Wilson, 2013). The term "young offender" is commonly used in Australia, whereas "delinquent" is more commonly used in the United States (US) and in parts of Asia.

Terms used to refer to justice-involved young people also reflect wider debates about what constitutes an appropriate response to youth offending. Referencing the work of Cunneen and Goldson (2015), Sheehan et al. (2023) suggest these debates broadly align to either a "justice" or "welfare" model of youth justice (p. 299). The authors suggest these models are underpinned by different philosophical approaches. A justice approach, influenced by behaviourist worldviews, emphasises that behaviour is modified by reinforcing boundaries through predictable and consistent consequences (Cunneen & Goldson, 2015). A welfare approach, by contrast, is influenced by evidence of intersectional experiences of justice-involved young people and focuses on addressing welfare-related drivers of crime to reduce recidivism (Baidawi & Sheehan, 2019).

Justice responses to youth violence in Australia are typically shared between the Children's Court (responsible for adjudicating and sentencing) and Youth Justice Systems (who supervise orders imposed by the Courts in either the community or detention centres). Noting differences across jurisdictions, we refer to the Children's Court as a collective noun describing the judicial settings where matters relating to crimes alleged to have been committed by children and young people are adjudicated. In Australia, Children's Courts and Youth Justice Systems are bound in their responses by jurisdiction-based laws. Australian states and territories have distinct and separate laws specifically dealing with youth offending. Most commonly referenced in this chapter is the *Children (Criminal Proceedings) Act* 1987. which provides a legislative regime for young people who have committed crimes in NSW. Different legislation and policy across jurisdictions infer different policing practices and types of legal orders relating to young people across Australia (Australian Institute of Health and Welfare [AIHW], 2022). Common law jurisdictions, including the United Kingdom (UK), Aoetearoa/New Zealand (NZ), and some states in the United States (US), have analogous approaches and processes for justice-involved youth.

Age of criminal responsibility

The age of criminal responsibility refers to the applicable age range to which relevant criminal laws apply, with the lower limit representing the minimum age at which a person can be charged with a criminal offence. Almost all countries have a minimum age of criminal responsibility (MACR), notable exceptions being Panama, Brunei, and Saudi Arabia (Hazel, 2008). The United Nations Committee on the Rights of the Child (UNCRC) (UNCRC, 2019) advocates for an internationally accepted MACR of 14 years. In Australia, the MACR is 10 years, though TAS and the ACT regions made commitments to raise it 14 years (Drabsch, 2022; Jaensch, 2022). This responds to widespread advocacy for raising the MACR in Australia to least 14 years, commensurate with the recommendations of the UNCRC (2019) and Amnesty International (2018). Cunneen (2020) notes that at 10 years, the MACR in Australia is out of step with contemporary practice in other countries. Comparing the youth justice systems of 90 countries, Hazel (2008) found that MACR ranged from 6 years (North Carolina, US) to 18 years (Luxemburg). The most common MACR was 14 years, which was reported for 25% of the countries studied (Hazel, 2008).

Doli incapax

In legal practice, the age of criminal responsibility can operate in conjunction with the common law doctrine of *doli incapax*, a legal principle acknowledging the inherent vulnerabilities and capacities of young people charged with a criminal offence. In some jurisdictions, it operates to shield young people between the ages of 10 and 13 from criminal liability unless the prosecution can prove beyond reasonable doubt that the young person knew at the time of the offence that it was seriously wrong to engage in the conduct (as opposed to just misbehaving) (Fitz-Gibbon & O'Brien, 2019). *Doli incapax* is often raised as a reason why we *don't* need to increase the MACR; however, it is a rebuttable common law presumption (as opposed to a criminal legal defence) and may be displaced if the court is satisfied that the defendant knew the alleged conduct committed was seriously wrong. *Doli incapax* applies in all states and territories in Australia with the High Court deciding the case of *RP v The Queen* [2016] HCA 53, clearly setting out the law on *doli incapax*. However, *doli incapax* was abolished in England and Wales in 1998 and varies in its use throughout international jurisdictions.

Status offending

In considering the age of criminal responsibility, it is also worth briefly exploring the concept of status offending. Freiburger and Burke (2011) note that in the US, the juvenile court was designed with the goal of protecting children and young people, with an emphasis placed on treatment rather than punishment and protecting young people from their own bad behaviours. This paternalist philosophy, the authors suggest, has justified the inclusion of non-criminal offences considered deviant when exercised by young people (Freiburger & Burke, 2011). These offences are referred to as status offences, meaning that they are only criminal offences by virtue of the juvenile status (age) of the offender (Holden & Kapler, 1995). Peck et al. (2014) identify common status offences as truancy, curfew violation, and running away from home. Over time, there has been considerable controversy around status offences, not least because of their differential impact on young women compared to young men and young people from racial and ethnic minorities compared to those from the dominant white culture. The *U.S. Juvenile Justice and Delinquency Prevention Act* (JJDP Act) of 1974 and its subsequent reauthorisations (especially in 1992) have attempted to ensure greater equality in the handling of matters before the U.S. juvenile courts for all young people (Peck et al., 2014). However, evidence suggests that young women continue to be disproportionately brought before juvenile courts for moral rather than criminal offences (Chesney-Lind & Sheldon, 2004) and judged more harshly, often based on concerns for their moral wellbeing rather than their criminality (Abrams & Curran, 2000). Similar concerns have been raised in relation to the experiences of young people from minority groups and across racial profiles (Bishop et al., 2010).

Legal process

Across jurisdictions, the justice involvement of young people tends to involve similar legal processes. This includes being charged by police, going to court, and deliberations towards legal outcomes. These outcomes commonly include youth justice conferencing, community-based orders (which may include supervision), or detention. Figure 2.1 presents an illustrative overview of the legal process involved in the vast majority of cases that come before the Children's Court (NSW). Of note, it does not reflect the process applied if a young person is charged with a serious children's indictable offence.

Introducing Ray and Jazz

Much has been written about how young people experience this legal process, highlighting challenges and opportunities for greater responsivity to young people's needs. The following sections provide an overview of aspects of the legal process and what the literature says about how young people experience them. Textboxes provide commentary from Ray and Jazz, two young people we initially met through their participation in NNN. Later, they would go on to work in the program, contributing their knowledge and skills to its continuous improvement and delivery. With their consent, we introduce them here and share their stories, describing their lived experience of the justice system.

Box 2.1 Introducing Ray . . .

Ray is an Aboriginal young man. When we met Ray, he had been involved with youth justice services for most of his adolescence. He described an early exposure to the criminal justice system via the interactions of his family members.

> "When I was 8, mum got locked up. I went to school till year 7, and when I was in year 7, mum got out of jail, and then like "monkey see monkey do". Mum went and done drugs – I went and done drugs. My older brother went and got on drugs. – I went and got on drugs. It was the only connection me and my brother and my mum ever had for years. Then like, I got locked up". (Ray)

Box 2.2 Introducing Jazz . . .

Jazz is a young woman living independently, working, studying, and raising a young family. When we first met Jazz, she had 106 criminal charges in the year prior. She was involved with youth justice services for most of her adolescence. Jazz was last consistently engaged in education when she was in primary school (at age 12). Since then, her housing had been insecure. Her parents struggled with issues related to substance abuse and poor mental health, and older siblings, with their own experience of the criminal justice system, were sometime supports for her. Reflecting on her experiences, at one time Jazz remarked that kids like her were "stuck in the system".

Getting charged by the police

Police in Australia routinely investigate matters where it has been alleged that a young person has committed a criminal offence. A young person is required to be cautioned by police that they do not have to take part in any police interview where they are a suspect and that anything that is said during the interview may be subsequently used in court as evidence. A support person must be present when a young person suspected of committing a criminal offence is interviewed by police. By law, children and young people have the right to obtain legal advice before giving a statement to police. Young people's right to legal advice remains constant throughout all stages of the criminal legal process and is funded by the government.

As illustrated in Figure 2.1, following an investigation, police can decide not to proceed with legal action and/or issue a caution or warning.

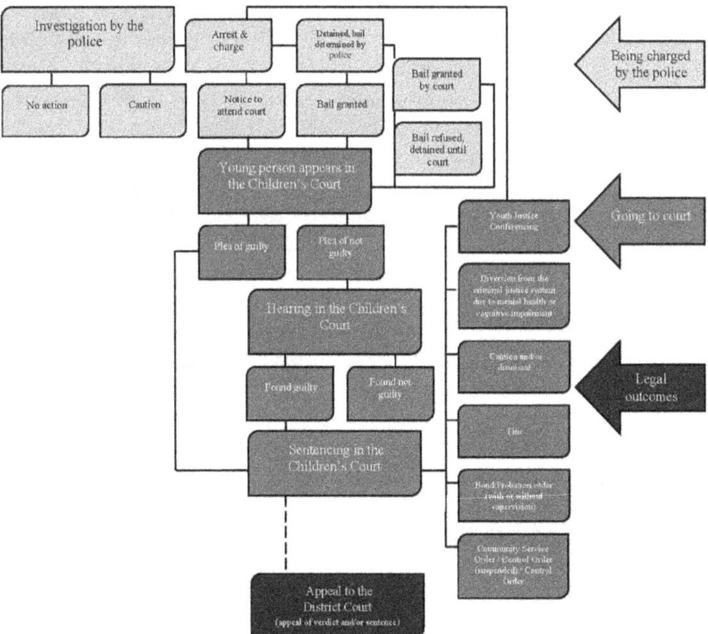

Figure 2.1 Overview of legal process for justice-involved young people in NSW

Source: Adapted from information published by the NSW Office of the Director of Public Prosecutions (2021)

Should police decide to proceed against a young person, they can issue a court attendance notice requiring them to attend court, or they may arrest the young person and charge them with allegedly committing a criminal offence and then determine whether bail should be granted. If bail is refused, young people can then seek bail through the Children's Court. The AIHW (2023) notes that young people are proceeded against by police for allegedly committing a criminal offence more often when compared to those against adults. Data from the Australian Bureau of Statistics (ABS) (2023) crime statistics note that in 2020–21 police proceeded against young people aged 10–17 years at a rate of 178 per 10,000 and against adults at a rate of 161 per 10,000 people.

Encounters with police are typically the first point of entry to the criminal justice system. How young people experience these encounters is likely to "spill over" and influence how they perceive the entire legal process (Baker et al., 2014). Young people's perceptions of police may have direct and long-lasting effects through what has been termed "legal cynicism" (Pollock & Menard, 2015). Research consistently finds that justice-involved young people report policing practices as unjust and unfair. Alder et al. (1992) interviewed 382 young people and found that 70% reported being yelled at or sworn at by police. A decade later the Youth Justice Coalition (2002) found that 42% of those interviewed reported that they were not fairly treated by police. Age, gender, and ethnicity all influence young people's perceptions of police. Young men express more negative perceptions of police compared to young women (Brick et al., 2009). Findings suggesting that Aboriginal and ethnic minority youth report more negative experiences, and perceptions of police have been reported across several countries, including Australia (e.g., Sivasubramaniam & Goodman-Delahunty, 2008), the US (e.g., Zhang et al., 2020), Canada (e.g., Samuels-Wortley, 2021), and Nordic countries (e.g., Haller et al., 2020). Young people's perceptions of police may also be shaped by "legal socialisation" – an orientation to law and legal authorities that develops across childhood and adolescence and is shaped by familiarity, including direct and vicarious experiences of peers, family, and the community (Fagan & Tyler, 2005). Research also suggests negative perceptions of police might be underpinned by a lack of understanding of police practices. Bevan (2016) described young people in the UK as having a patchy understanding of their legal rights when dealing with the police. While in Australia, the Youth Justice Coalition (2002) reported that young people are often unaware of their right to silence during police questioning, with one study participant saying, "I later found out I could say 'no comment' " (p. vii).

Box 2.3 Feedback from Ray and Jazz . . .

Ray and Jazz demonstrated a sophisticated understanding of police practices shaped by witnessing interactions between family and police. Jazz recounted that only days before she was first arrested (at age 14), her mother, stepfather, and brother had all been arrested. From this, she was aware that police couldn't talk to her until she had a support person there.

Ray, like Jazz, said that his parents had "*been in and out of the system*" and had "*told him what to say*". Despite this, Ray said when he was first picked up by the police, he didn't have a clear understanding of what would happen to him. He recalls:

> "I didn't even know about cautions. The cops said, like, you aren't going to juvie, you can go home, you're on bail. I was, like, sweet, and then I'm just, like, yeah, mum, what's that mean?".

Going to court

In Australia, the Children's Courts adjudicate and sentence most criminal cases (with the exception of serious children's indictable offences) where the defendant is under 18 years of age at the time of the alleged offence. While the Children's Court operates within an adversarial system, measures are taken to reduce the formality of legal process and to ensure that young people understand the nature and implications of legal proceedings. For example, legal practitioners remain seated throughout the hearing of evidence and when making submissions to the judicial officer. A police prosecutor represents the state bringing the prosecution and presents the evidence on behalf of police regarding the criminal charge. Should a young person plead guilty to the alleged offence, the defence lawyer will make a plea in mitigation to the judicial officer regarding the proposed penalty for the commission of the offence. Should a young person plead not guilty, the criminal defence lawyer can test the prosecution evidence, including cross-examining police and lay witnesses, and make submissions regarding the defence of their client.

Following the hearing of evidence, the judicial officer will determine whether the criminal charges have been proved beyond reasonable doubt and make a finding as to whether the young person is guilty or not guilty of the criminal offence. If the young person is found guilty, the case proceeds to a sentencing hearing (see Figure 2.1). The Children's Court is guided by the principle that young people should be detained only as a matter of last resort and for the shortest possible period (AIHW, 2022), and all efforts are made to divert young people away from the justice system. The main ways this happens are through an order under the *Young Offenders Act* 1997 (NSW) for youth justice conferencing, cautions or warnings, or diversion to the health system for young people with mental health concerns or cognitive impairments, pursuant to the *Mental Health and Cognitive Impairment Forensic Provisions Act* 2020 (NSW). Young people may also have their matters transferred to the Youth Koori Court, where the court's process may give, among other things, services to the young person which will hopefully lead to a finding that they have good prospects of rehabilitation, inferring a positive impact on eventual sentencing. Alternatively, if the matter proceeds through the court and the charge is proven, the court may impose various orders with or without recording a criminal conviction (AIHW, 2022).

Despite its child-centric ethos, young people report being perplexed by the "alien nature of the court system" (Legal and Constitutional References Committee, 2004, p. 156). Young people in Scotland (Deuchar & Sapouna, 2016) and NZ (Lount et al., 2018) have reported unease and confusion about their court appearances, citing that they didn't know what to expect and found it difficult to know what was going on. These findings echo early work by O'Connor (1991) who found that young people can misunderstand and misconstrue what happens in court and can perceive it as a place they are brought to be dealt with rather than a place of inquiry into the allegation (O'Connor, 1991). Young people in this study explained that their feelings of confusion and frustration were often exacerbated by court processes that hindered their ability to actively participate in the proceedings (O'Connor, 1991). When asked to describe their subjective experiences in court, young people recounted sitting and standing on command and being talked at and talked about by their lawyer, the prosecutor, or the judge but rarely involved in any meaningful dialogue about their case (O'Connor, 1991). Research since consistently finds that young people struggle to have a "voice" in court (Appell, 2007; Natapoff, 2005). Cox (2013) notes young people are frustrated by experiences of "voicelessness," remarking, "We can't even speak in the courtroom" (p. 141). Greene et al. (2010) found that when young people experience the court as confusing and unprofessional, they are more likely to view the entire justice system as less legitimate. Baker et al. (2014) added that having a voice, feeling you can "have your say" or have your questions answered, is also a key determinant of whether young people perceive the court as fair and legitimate.

Box 2.4 Feedback from Ray . . .

Agreeance and a weary acceptance of the findings discussed in the previous section were apparent in Ray's demeanour and attitude about the court as he shrugged dismissively, reporting that he felt he couldn't speak in court:

> Half the time we think that we can't even talk to the judge. Like, we sit there, we shut up, until, like, the only time we'll ever talk to them is when he asks us, "Do you understand that?" We don't even talk. We sit there and shake our head, like, yeah.

Lawyers

Access to lawyers and legal services is fundamental to ensuring that young people's rights are upheld and that they are supported throughout the justice process. In Australia, young people can access free public legal services via Legal Aid, the Aboriginal Legal Service, community legal centres, and private criminal lawyers funded by Legal Aid. The role of the lawyer in the Children's Court is to explain the case against the young person, give advice, and represent the young person in court. Lawyers describe their most critical work as occurring pre-court when they examine elements of the criminal charge, explain the relevant aspects of law to the young person, and provide advice towards a plea (Naffine & Wundersitz, 1991). Standard practice in this regard is described as hearing the young person's perspective on events and checking with the prosecution to elicit police allegations (such as documented in a "Facts Sheet"). If accounts conflict and the young person disputes allegations made, the lawyer may seek to negotiate with the prosecution to establish a common view of the events acceptable to, and in the best interests of, the young person (Naffine & Wundersitz, 1991).

Cashmore and Bussey (1994) note that young people often hold different expectations of what the lawyer's role is in representing them than might be held by the lawyer themselves. Interviews with young people find they can come to court believing their lawyer will represent their point of view or explain contexts surrounding alleged crimes and are confused and disappointed when their lawyer instead concentrates on matters of law (Cashmore & Bussey, 1994; Pennington & Farrell, 2019). Similar sentiments were reported by Peterson-Badali et al. (2007): "[my lawyer] was supposed to do what I wanted, but he didn't listen to me.

He just did what he wanted" (p. 392). Cashmore and Bussey (1994) found that lawyers interviewed in these same contexts felt they had done a good job in representing the young person and their best interests. The idea that young people may have limited understanding of the legal process and the role of lawyers is important to their equitable access in securing legal representation.

In a study of young people's experience of the *Young Offenders Act* 1997 (NSW), Turner (2002) found that 76% of young people interviewed did not understand the importance of obtaining legal advice, with one interviewee commenting that they did not have a solicitor present during their interview with police because they "didn't know how solicitors work" (p. vii). Similar findings have been reported in Canada, where Peterson-Badali et al. (1999) found 76% of young people interviewed did not phone a lawyer before being questioned by police because they didn't know they could have access to a lawyer. A lack of understanding about legal rights can be associated with mistrust of lawyers (Pierce & Brodsky, 2002). Beliefs about lawyers can be influenced by the media (Asimow, 1999) and through "legal socialisation" – a process inclusive of the young person's own experiences and those of peers, family, and fellow community members (Brunson, 2007).

The quality of communication between lawyers and young clients can be critical to establishing or rebalancing a sense of legal legitimacy. Research finds, however, that justice-involved young people find the way lawyers communicate unfamiliar and hard to understand (Alder et al., 1992) and that they often feel unheard by their lawyers (Chui & Cheng, 2015). Lawyers can contribute to young people's feelings of angst in the legal process by simply "not listening" (Tillack et al., 2018, p. 6). Wigzell et al. (2015) emphasise ineffective communication is a primary cause for young people's reported dissatisfaction with lawyers and that "[a good advocate] should just listen" (p. 32). Hughes (2006) found that simple acts of listening, keeping in touch, and spending time with the client were considered by young people as constituting good lawyering and were the primary determinants of satisfaction with the lawyer.

Box 2.5 Feedback from Ray and Jazz . . .

When reflecting on his experience with lawyers, Ray lamented, "You just have your good lawyers and bad ones I guess". Ray reported positive interactions with his lawyers coincided with being listened to: "Yeah. Yeah, they'd sit, ask me, some of them would even make time to, like, go out of their way, ask me how I'm going and that. What I get up to in my spare time".

Whereas negative interactions coincided with not being listened to and feeling invalidated when his opinions or concerns were dismissed:

> "I wouldn't talk to (some of) my lawyers . . . I'd talk to my last one but that's, like, cause I had a good relationship with him. The other ones would just, you know, take the piss [i.e., be dismissive of Ray's opinions and point of view]".

While Jazz saw herself as legally self-reliant, she was able to draw parallels to her own experience when reflecting on these findings. She indicated that even though she had gained some useful tips from lawyers over time:

> "I just learnt it as I went along. The lawyer told me when I first got arrested, just said 'don't do an interview'. And then ever since then, the lawyer's said every time on the phone 'don't do an interview, don't do an interview'. . . . You do an interview, you're a snitch". (Jazz)

This advice, and perhaps the way in which it was communicated, clearly resonated with Jazz and seemed to lend legitimacy to the lawyer's role in her mind.

Judicial officers

Judicial officers preside over Children's Court matters. Young people's perceptions and experiences of judges and magistrates may be linked to perceptions of "procedural justice," or how fair they believe the processes of the court to be. Blader and Tyler (2003) explain that judgements about procedural fairness are based on how fairly people feel they have been treated and how fair they believe decision-making processes to be. Procedural justice is important because it fosters the legitimacy of the legal process and its outcomes. When young people perceive legal process as unfair or feel they have been treated unfairly (including not being listened to or given a say in proceedings), they are less likely to comply with court orders (Piquero et al., 2004). Conversely, early work by Tyler et al. (1989) found that when people feel they have been treated fairly they were more willing to accept court outcomes, even if they were not in their favour.

Research has found that young people's views about the magistrate or judge hearing their case significantly influence their beliefs about the legitimacy of the legal system (Burdziej et al., 2019; Sprott & Greene,

2010). Cox (2009) suggests that important to understanding this finding is the connection between perceived fairness and the notion of respect. Cox (2009) notes that some young people in her study emphasised their respect for the fair decisions made by a judge in their case, particularly if they felt the judge had taken time to understand them and their circumstances. When asked what made a good judge, young people stressed the idea of "giving someone a go," even if this involved second, or third, chances: "a good trait in a judge would be one who is willing to give the person a chance . . . to make themselves into something" (Cox, 2009, p. 5).

Box 2.6 Feedback from Jazz . . .

The idea of "good judge" really resonated with Jazz. She recalled her interactions with a senior judge who she felt was fair, had given her many chances, and who expressed an understanding of her circumstances. Jazz clearly articulated her knowledge of court systems, knowing when in the week to present to police to gain appearance in front of this judge for the best or most minimal sentencing.

> "She's like so good. She's the best judge ever, like ever. I used to hand myself in on the Sunday just so I could go before her . . . they said to me, we used to see you like two to three times a week and you weren't even from our area . . . it's only Tuesdays and Fridays that you can. Like, if you get locked up in [X town] on a Tuesday you go to [Y town] court, if you get locked up on a Monday, Wednesday, and Friday, you go to [Z town] court . . . so I'd always try to get her because she'd always give me bail. I even ran out of her courthouse, and she still gave me bail". (Jazz)

Legal outcomes

The welfare-oriented approach of Australian sentencing policies for justice-involved youth (Green et al., 2020) prioritises the diversion of young people away from the criminal justice system. The rationale for this approach centres around increasing opportunities to support a young person's development by addressing factors potentially affecting criminogenic risk. Supporting this, legislative frameworks across Australian jurisdictions have formalised diversionary measures for young people found guilty of a criminal offence. The use of diversionary measures is predicated on the young person admitting they have committed the criminal offence with which they have been charged.

Diversionary measures can involve coordination of services attended by police, youth justice agencies, and the broader human and social service systems and can be implemented either prior to and without the need to proceed to court or as an outcome of the court proceedings. NSW legislation identifies a hierarchy of measures that can be issued regarding young people, including warnings, police cautions, and youth justice conferencing (discussed later) (Bargen et al., 2005). Elsewhere in Australia, counselling and infringement notices are frequently used options (AIHW, 2020). Cleland (2016) reported that in NZ, diversion from formal justice processes (involving the courts) is undertaken by over 80% of young people who are charged with a criminal offence. The success of diversionary measures has been well-documented (e.g., Atkinson, 2018; Cunningham, 2007; Lulham et al., 2009), with positive outcomes identified for safer communities, cost efficiencies, and reduced recidivism (White & Gooda, 2017). Yet, despite positive sentiments, reports identify that diversionary measures can be underused or not used systematically, particularly for Aboriginal young people (Office of the Auditor General Western Australia, 2017).

For matters proceeding to court, orders can include a dismissal and/or caution, a good behaviour bond with or without supervision, a fine, a referral to a youth justice conference, conditional or unconditional probation, a community service (supervision) order, or a (control) order that confines the young person to a period of detention (see Figure 2.1). Incorporated into legislation regarding the sentencing of young people across all Australian jurisdictions are principles that affirm that young people should only be detained as a last resort and for the shortest possible period (AIHW, 2022).

Sentencing

In a sentencing hearing, the young person is called to the court and the prosecutor outlines the facts of the case and details of prior criminal offences with the defence counsel in response making a plea of mitigation (Travers, 2007). Thereafter the judicial officer delivers their sentence (Travers, 2007). When a sentence is handed down, the court matter is finalised (though matters may also be finalised through transfer to another court or when a matter is withdrawn by the prosecution). Data sourced from NSW Bureau of Crime Statistics and Research (BOSCAR) (2023) revealed that from July 2021 to June 2022, 5,295 matters were finalised in the Children's Court (NSW). Almost 80% of defendants in these matters were found guilty of at least one charge. Table 2.1 describes the distribution of penalties issued to these young people.

Table 2.1 Principal penalty issued for defendants found guilty in the Children's Court (NSW)

Principal penalty	*Number*	*Percent*
Control order (full time custody in a youth detention centre)	237	5.8%
Community service order/control order (suspended)	1277	30.9%
Bond/probation order (with or without supervision).	804	19.5%
Fine	166	4.0%
Other*	1643	39.8%
Total	4127	100.0%

Source: Data sourced from the NSW Bureau of Crime and Research Statistics. Other* penalties include no conviction recorded or action taken, dismissal with or without caution, a caution issued, or the matter dismissed after youth justice conferencing (BOSCAR, 2023)

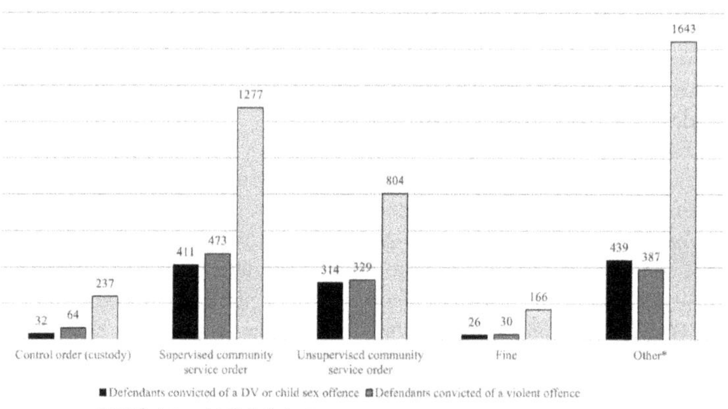

Figure 2.2 Finalised matters in the Children's Court (NSW) July 2021–June 2022

Source: Data sourced from the NSW Bureau of Crime Statistics and Research

Control orders were the least often issued, representing less than 6% of all penalties, and were noted to have decreased by 17.4% over the past five years (BOSCAR, 2023). The average (mean) duration of custodial sentences imposed was a period of 4.6 months. The average length of time from arrest to finalisation of matters in the Children's Court (NSW) is 160 days, and the average length of time from when young people first presented at court until their matter is finalised is 99 days. The Australian Government Productivity Commission (2022) reported that young people (or their representatives) attend court on average 6.2 times before a matter is finalised. This includes attendances that are adjourned or rescheduled. Attendance is highest in the NT (10.2) and lowest in VIC (4.2).

In Figure 2.2, the distribution of penalties issued for all defendants with finalised matters in the Children's Court (2021–22) is shown in the lightest shading, finalised matters relating to violence offences are shown in the next darkest shading, and finalised matters relating to domestic violence (DV) and child sex-related offences are shown in the darkest shading. Data reported illustrates that almost 90% of guilty findings for violent offences relate to DV offences, 50% of these being property damage. Diversionary measures and supervised community service orders were the most common penalties issued for this cohort.

As noted in Chapter 1, in Australia, so-called "postcode" effects have long been observed in the sentencing of young people, with those from rural and remote areas at increased likelihood of receiving harsher and more often custodial sentences (Fernandez et al., 2013, 2014). Indeed, one criminal defence solicitor interviewed by Fernandez et al. (2014) commented that "sentencing generally works pretty well in the specialist Sydney Children's Court. In country courts, where they may not have a specialist children's magistrate . . . sentences by comparison are a lot harsher" (p. 21). These observations are substantiated by data from the AIHW (2022), noting that young people from remote areas are six times more likely to be under either community or custodial-based supervision compared to peers in major cities, while young people from very remote areas were nine times more likely. Aboriginal young people were reported to be 16 times more likely than non-Aboriginal peers to receive supervision orders (AIHW, 2022).

White and Cunneen (2006) note intersections of age, disability, location, ethnicity, gender, and disadvantage contextualise the complex process of legal decision-making *about* young people charged with a criminal offence, yet these same intersections also contextualise the often-protracted experience of going to court and how young perceive the justice system. This is relevant to evidence that guilty pleas and plea bargaining are extremely common for young defendants in the justice system (Grisso et al., 2003; Viljoen et al., 2005). Cabell and Marsh (2020) suggest legal, developmental, and social factors all influence young people's decisions on whether to plead guilty or enter into a negotiated plea. Like adults, young people are found to be more likely to plead guilty or enter into plea negotiations if they believe the evidence against them is strong (Viljoen et al., 2005), but, more than adults, their decisions are motivated by a desire to end the legal process (Zottoli & Daftary-Kapur, 2019). Feld (2013) suggests this reflects young people's developmentally (and possibly contextually) appropriate focus on more immediate rather than long-term consequences.

Box 2.7 Feedback from Ray and Jazz . . .

Both Ray and Jazz discussed their experiences of sentencing and specifically their decision-making about whether to enter a guilty plea to a criminal offence.

> "So, they [plead guilty] to get a lighter sentence. 25% off. 'Cause half the time, they didn't do it. Or half the time it's just stupid, and their mums and dads tell them if you don't plead guilty, you're gonna fucking wish you did when you get home. Like, I've sat there and plead guilty a few times, for something that I, like, half the time, it was not even me doing it". (Ray)

> "I reckon about half the time I plead guilty to stuff I didn't do just to get reduced time in case they found me guilty anyway". (Jazz)

Youth justice conferencing

Youth justice conferencing (YJC) is a common diversionary approach reducing the likelihood of criminal convictions for justice-involved youth (Trimboli, 2000). In NSW, young people may be referred to conferencing for certain criminal offences, including summary offences or less serious matters. For a referral to be made, the young person must admit to the offence and generally agree that the matter is to be dealt with by way of a conference. Trimboli (2000) provides an illustrative overview of the key elements of YJC, noting it begins with the conference convenor outlining the role of participants in the process and facilitating introductions centred around the participants' relationship to the person who experienced harm. Notionally, this invites the young person who has caused harm to identify their acts at the commencement of the process. Trimboli (2000) notes the convenor outlines the conference agenda, stressing conditions of confidentiality, mutual respect, participation, collaboration, and voluntary participation before inviting reciprocal reflections on the experience and impact of the offence. This is an opportunity for the person who has caused harm to express remorse prior to the development of an outcome plan to achieve reparation. The plan developed is to be mutually agreeable with the parties and able to be completed within a set period.

Based on both frameworks of dispute resolution and restorative justice, YJC endeavours to promote accountability and facilitate some form of resolution, including the reintegration of the young person who has caused harm back into their family and community (Zappavigna &

Martin, 2017). YJC has been lauded for its relative successes compared to formal legal responses with favourable outcomes reported in relation to victim satisfaction and fairness (Trimboli, 2000; Zappavigna & Martin, 2017). A closer review of the literature indicates that young peoples' positive receptions of YJC are, perhaps, underscored by their ability to actively participate in the process and influence the decisions made (Trimboli, 2000). Wagland et al. (2013) reported that a thematic consistency in young people's motivations for attending a YJC was the opportunity to speak with the person harmed and describe in their own words what happened. Yet Webber (2012) cautions perceptions of greater procedural fairness associated with YJC may be specific to conferences that occur either early in the young person's engagement with the criminal justice system or quickly after an arrest is made. Similar findings were reported by Moore (2011), who found that the length of time it takes for court-referred conferences to reach finalisation appears to impact on perceived satisfaction with the process.

Box 2.8 Feedback from Ray . . .

Ray was nonplussed about his experience of YJC. His reflections giving a different insight into the lived experience of accepting responsibility for your actions:

> "I got locked up for a reason, like, you know? So, I'm not gonna sit there and apologise for it and talk my way through it. It's just, like, fuck off, leave me be. You go your way, I'll go my way. Stay in your lane, I'll stay in mine". (Ray)

He further elaborated on the inherent power imbalance that can occur in YJCs and how efforts made in the child's best interest might not necessarily align with the child's or young person's wants or needs:

> "I've had them try and, like, get me back into school and that, like, with juvenile justice. I've sat there, and I've been around, like, a table of adults and me being the only kid, and I was, like, 14. And then, yeah, it was, like, fucking weird". (Ray)

Smith and Weatherburn (2012) claim offence-related data suggests that YJCs are no more effective than more formal sanctions of the Children's Court in reducing reoffending. Hayes (2017) emphasise this may be particularly so for Aboriginal young people; however, Allard et al. (2010) highlight Aboriginal young people in NSW, SA, and WA are less likely to be issued with diversionary sanctions either by police or the courts. Murphy et al. (2010) suggest low rates of diversion away from the courts may contribute to the over-representation of Aboriginal young people in the justice system. More nuanced conceptualisations suggest that experience in and of the criminal justice system is the most powerful predictor of recidivism and that all attempts at early diversion, including greater use of cautions, should be encouraged. Vignaendra and Fitzgerald (2006) report 42% of young people cautioned in NSW reoffend within five years, compared to 58% of those diverted to a conference. Similarly, Cunningham (2007) found 39% of young people before the courts in the NT reoffend within 12 months, compared to 21% of those diverted to a conference and 19% of those persons who received a warning. Relevant to the use of early diversion strategies are complex considerations of the intersection between the type of criminal offence, appropriateness to YJC, and likelihood of reoffending. Bun et al. (2020) argue consequences of being arrested and found guilty of a criminal offence are more far-reaching for the young person than imposition of sanctions by the court, particularly as they relate to stigma, shame, and self-perception. Craig et al. (2020) explain experiences of prior adjudication; experience of formal court sanctions, especially incarceration; length of incarceration; and experiences during incarceration are likely the most relevant explanations of repeat offending.

Supervision orders

In Australia and around the world, a major feature of youth justice systems is the supervision of young people on legal orders by the state and territory agencies responsible for youth justice. Young people may be supervised either in their communities or in secure detention facilities. The AIHW (2023) reports that across Australia, in 2021–22, a total of 8,932 young people aged 10 and over were subject to supervision orders. The majority (82%) were supervised in the community with significantly less (18%) supervised in custody. Young men represented the majority of supervisees in the community (80%) and in custody (90%). Nearly all (96%) were aged over 14 years; however, WA and the ACT had the largest proportion (7.5%) of younger cohorts (10–13) followed by the NT (5.3%). Younger cohorts may have greater numbers of Aboriginal young people, with data confirming that on average both male and female Aboriginal young people under supervision are younger, with more than a third first supervised before they were aged 10, compared to 14% of their non-Aboriginal peers. Young people from remote and very remote communities (largely representative of Aboriginal people) were eight times more likely than their peers in major cities to be under supervision, either in the community or detention. Two-thirds of young people under supervision in 2021–22 had been supervised in the previous year, with this being more common for those on community supervision orders (71%) compared to detention (59%). When all time spent under supervision during 2021–22 is considered (including multiple periods and periods that were not yet completed), young people who were supervised during the year spent an average of 185 days (about six months) under supervision. Rates of youth justice supervision vary among the states and territories, reflecting, in part, the differences in legislation, policies, and practices between each state and territory. In 2021–22, the rate of young people aged 10–17 under supervision on an average day ranged from 5.8 per 10,000 in VIC to 46 per 10,000 in the NT.

The experience of young people under supervision has been more commonly explored from the perspective of those in detention rather than community-based supervision. The Office for the Advocate for Children and Young People (NSW) (2019) highlights that justice responses are inherently biased towards assumed motivations, experiences, and needs of men. Implications of this for young women span placement in mixed-gender facilities, having access only to programs developed for males, and being served meals dense in carbohydrates, often leading to weight gain (Advocate for Children and Young People, 2019). Young women interviewed for this report drew attention to time imposts on workers necessitated by bail conditions requiring secured housing prior to release: "caseworkers spend a lot of time consumed with trying to find accommodation for people on Section 28" (Advocate for Children and Young People, 2019, p. 32). In its harshest reality, some young women described having to "stay in custody because they were unable to meet the accommodation requirement of their bail conditions" (Advocate for Children and Young People, 2019, p. 7).

Box 2.9 Feedback from Jazz . . .

Jazz agreed with sentiments about food in detention, acknowledging weight gain and its impact on self-esteem and general wellbeing. Jazz also recounted positives about her experience in detention that were challenging to hear:

> "My best Christmas ever was in [x detention centre], we got, like, a crop top bra and undies and body wash and deodorant and stuff. It was the best ever". (Jazz)

Reflections on issues regarding housing were raw and immediate for Jazz. The experience of insecure housing having extended prior to and post her justice-involvement.

> "Like the biggest issue in my life at the moment is housing, so what I feel like doing is chucking my hands up in the air and not worrying about, but I have to . . . but . . . sometimes doing something is positive, sometimes not doing something is positive too". (Jazz)

Conclusion

This chapter described justice responses to youth violence, outlining legal processes that justice-involved young people are likely to encounter. It presented a brief review of evidence relating to young people's experience of these processes and the actors involved. Ray and Jazz provided insights into the lived experiences of both, highlighting with raw effect the uneasy parallels between dynamics of the justice system and those intertwined with perpetuating experiences of adversity and trauma. How practice has responded to youth violence will be explored in the next chapter, with the following picking up the threads of trauma visible across the work so far to examine its place in work with youth violence.

References

Abrams, L. S., & Curran, L. (2000). Wayward girls and virtuous women: Social workers and female juvenile delinquency in the progressive era. *Affilia*, *15*(1), 49–64. https://doi.org/10.1177/08861090001500104

Advocate for Children and Young People (NSW). (2019). *What children and young people in juvenile justice centres have to say*. Office for the Advocate of Children and Young People.

Alder, C., O'Connor, I., Warner, K., & White, R. (1992). *Perceptions of the treatment of juveniles in the legal system*. National Youth Affairs Research Scheme.

Allard, T., Stewart, A., Chrzanowski, A., Ogilvie, J., Birks, D., & Little, S. (2010). *Police diversion of young offenders and Indigenous over-representation* (Trends & Issues in Crime and Criminal Justice No. 390). Australian Institute of Criminology.

Amnesty International. (2018). *The sky is the limit: Keeping young children out of prison by raising the age of criminal responsibility*. www.amnesty.org.au/wp-content/uploads/2018/09/The-Sky-is-the-Limit-FINAL-1.pdf

Appell, A. R. (2007). Representing children representing what: Critical reflections on lawyering for children. *Columbia Human Rights Law Review*, *39*, 573.

Asimow, M. (1999). Bad lawyers in the movies. *Nova Law Review*, *24*, 533. https://doi.org/10.2139/ssrn.159295

Atkinson, B. (2018). *Report on youth justice*. Youth Justice Taskforce, Department of Child Safety, Youth and Women.

Australian Bureau of Statistics. (2023). *Recorded crime – offenders, 2021–22*. www.abs.gov.au/statistics/people/crime-and-justice/recorded-crime-offenders/latestrelease#key-statistics

Australian Government Productivity Commission. (2022, January 28). *Report on government services 2022–7 courts*. www.pc.gov.au/ongoing/report-on-government-services/2022/justice/courts

Australian Institute of Health and Welfare. (2020). *Young people under youth justice supervision and in child protection 2018–19*. https://doi.org/10.25816/ech1-dg08

Australian Institute of Health and Welfare. (2022). *Youth justice in Australia 2020–21*. https:///doi.org/10.25816/53k2-5w18

Australian Institute of Health and Welfare. (2023). *Youth justice in Australia 2021–22* (Catalogue Number JUV 140). www.aihw.gov.au/getmedia/3fe01ba6-3917-41fc-a908-39290f9f4b55/aihw-juv-140.pdf.aspx?inline=true

Baidawi, S., & Sheehan, R. (2019). *"Cross-over kids": Effective responses to children and young people in the youth justice and statutory child protection systems: Report to the criminology research advisory council*. Australian Institute of Criminology. https://doi.org/10.4324/9780429291517

Baker, T., Pelfrey, W. V. Jr., Bedard, L. E., Dhungana, K., Gertz, M., & Golden, K. (2014). Female inmates' procedural justice perceptions of the police and courts: Is there a spill-over of police effects? *Criminal Justice and Behavior*, *41*(2), 144–162. https://doi.org/10.1177/0093854813497479

Bargen, J., Clancey, G., & Chan, J. (2005). Development of the young offenders act. In J. B. L. Chan (Ed.), *Reshaping juvenile justice* (pp. 17–24). Institute of Criminology Series no. 22. The Institute of Criminology.

Bevan, M. (2016). *Investigating young people's awareness and understanding of the criminal justice system: An exploratory study*. https://howardleague.org/wp-content/uploads/2016/06/Investigating-young-people%E2%80%99s-awareness-and-understanding-of-the-criminal-justice-system.pdf

Bishop, D. M., Leiber, M., & Johnson, J. (2010). Contexts of decision making in the juvenile justice system: An organizational approach to understanding minority overrepresentation. *Youth Violence and Juvenile Justice*, *8*(3), 213–233. https://doi.org/10.1177/1541204009361177

Blader, S. L., & Tyler, T. R. (2003). A four-component model of procedural justice: Defining the meaning of a "fair" process. *Personality and Social Psychology Bulletin*, *29*(6), 747–758. https://doi.org/10.1177/0146167203029006007

Brick, B. T., Taylor, T. J., & Esbensen, F. A. (2009). Juvenile attitudes towards the police: The importance of subcultural involvement and community ties. *Journal of Criminal Justice*, *37*, 488–495. https://doi.org/10.1016/j.jcrimjus.2009.07.009

Brunson, R. K. (2007). "Police don't like black people": African-American young men's accumulated police experiences. *Criminology & Public Policy*, *6*(1), 71–101. https://doi.org/10.1111/j.1745-9133.2007.00423.x

Bun, M. J., Kelaher, R., Sarafidis, V., & Weatherburn, D. (2020). Crime, deterrence and punishment revisited. *Empirical Economics*, *59*, 2303–2333. https://doi.org/10.1007/s00181-019-01758-6

Burdziej, S., Guzik, K., & Pilitowski, B. (2019). Fairness at trial: The impact of procedural justice and other experiential factors on criminal defendants' perceptions of court legitimacy in Poland. *Law & Social Inquiry*, *44*(2), 359–390.

Cabell, J. J., & Marsh, S. C. (2020). Swing and a miss: Reflections on the "voluntariness" of pleas in juvenile court. *Children and Youth Services Review*, *117*, Article 105300. https://doi.org/10.1016/j.childyouth.2020.105300

Cashmore, J., & Bussey, K. (1994). Perceptions of children and lawyers in care and protection proceedings. *International Journal of Law, Policy and the Family*, *8*(3), 319–336. https://doi.org/10.1093/lawfam/8.3.319

Chesney-Lind, M., & Sheldon, R. G. (2004). *Girls, delinquency and juvenile justice* (3rd ed.). Wadsworth/Thomson Learning.

Children (Criminal Proceedings) Act 1987 No. 55 (NSW). https://legislation.nsw.gov.au/view/html/inforce/current/act-1987-055

Chui, W. H., & Cheng, K. K. Y. (2015). Young people's perception of lawyers in Hong Kong: A comparison between offenders, youth-at-risk and students. *International Journal of Law, Crime and Justice*, *43*(4), 481–495. https://doi.org/10.1016/j.ijlcj.2014.12.001

Cleland, A. (2016). Portrait of the accused as a young man: New Zealand's harsh treatment of young people who commit serious crimes. *The Round Table*, *105*(4), 377–387. https://doi.org/10.1080/00358533.2016.1205360

Cox, A. (2009). Rooting respect: Young people's perspectives on respect, responsibility and government in the criminal courts. *Childhoods Today*, *3*(1), 1–21.

Cox, A. (2013). New visions of social control? Young people's perceptions of community penalties. *Journal of Youth Studies*, *16*(1), 135–150. https://doi.org/10.1080/13676261.2012.697136

Craig, J. M., Trulson, C. R., DeLisi, M., & Caudill, J. W. (2020). Toward an understanding of the impact of adverse childhood experiences on the recidivism of serious juvenile offenders. *American Journal of Criminal Justice*, *45*, 1024–1039. https://doi.org/10.1007/s12103-020-09524-6

Cunneen, C. (2020). *Arguments for raising the age of criminal responsibility*. Jumbunna Institute for Indigenous Education and Research, UTS.

Cunneen, C., & Goldson, B. (2015). Restorative justice? A critical analysis. In *Youth, crime and justice* (2nd ed., pp. 137–156). SAGE Publications.

Cunningham, T. (2007). *Pre-court diversion in the Northern Territory: Impact on juvenile reoffending* (Trends & Issues in Crime & Criminal Justice No. 339). Australian Institute of Criminology.

Deuchar, R., & Sapouna, M. (2016). "It's harder to go to court yourself because you don't really know what to expect": Reducing the negative effects of court exposure on young people – findings from an evaluation in Scotland. *Youth Justice*, *16*(2), 130–146. https://doi.org/10.1177/1473225415606815

Drabsch, T. (2022, March 1). *Age of criminal responsibility*. Parliament of New South Wales. www.parliament.nsw.gov.au/researchpapers/Pages/ageofcriminalresponsibility.aspx

Fagan, J., & Tyler, T. R. (2005). Legal socialization of children and adolescents. *Social Justice Research*, *18*, 217–241. https://doi.org/10.1007/s11211-005-6823-3

Feld, B. C. (2013). The youth discount: Old enough to do the crime, too young to do the time. *Ohio State Journal of Criminal Law*, *11*, 107–148.

Fernandez, E., Bolitho, J., Hansen, P., & Hudson, M. (2013). The children's court in New South Wales. In R. Sheehan & A. Borowski (Eds.), *Australia's children's courts today and tomorrow* (Vol. 7, pp. 27–44). Children's well-being: Indicators and research. Springer International Publishing. https://doi.org/10.1007/978-94-007-5928-2_3

Fernandez, E., Bolitho, J., Hansen, P., Hudson, M., & Kendall, S. (2014). *A study of the Children's Court of New South* Wales. https://ssrn.com/abstract=3439191

Fitz-Gibbon, K., & O'Brien, W. (2019). A child's capacity to commit crime: Examining the operation of doli incapax in Victoria (Australia). *International Journal for Crime, Justice and Social Democracy*, *8*(1), 18–33. https://doi.org/10.5204/ijcjsd.v8i1.1047

Freiburger, T. L., & Burke, A. S. (2011). Status offenders in the juvenile court: The effects of gender, race, and ethnicity on the adjudication decision. *Youth Violence and Juvenile Justice*, *9*(4), 352–365. https://doi.org/10.1177/1541204011399933

Green, R., Gray, R. M., Bryant, J., Rance, J., & MacLean, S. (2020). Police decision-making with young offenders: Examining barriers to the use of diversion options. *Australian & New Zealand Journal of Criminology*, *53*(1), 137–154. https://doi.org/10.1177/0004865819879736

Greene, C., Sprott, J. B., Madon, N. S., & Jung, M. (2010). Punishing processes in youth court: Procedural justice, court atmosphere and youths' views of the legitimacy of the justice system. *Canadian Journal of Criminology and Criminal Justice*, *52*(5), 527–544. https://doi.org/10.3138/cjccj.52.5.527

Grisso, T., Steinberg, L., Woolard, J., Cauffman, E., Scott, E., Graham, S., Lexcen, F., Reppucci, N. D., & Schwartz, R. (2003). Juveniles' competence to stand trial: A comparison of adolescents' and adults' capacities as trial defendants. *Law and Human Behavior*, *27*(4), 333–363. https://doi.org/10.1023/A:1024065015717

Haller, M. B., Solhjell, R., Saarikkomäki, E., Kolind, T., Hunt, G., & Wästerfors, D. (2020). Minor harassments: Ethnic minority youth in the Nordic countries and their perceptions of the police. *Criminology & Criminal Justice*, *20*(1), 3–20. https://doi.org/10.1177/1748895818800744

Hayes, H. (2017). Emotion and language in restorative youth Justice. In A. Deckert & R. Sarre (Eds.), *The Palgrave handbook of Australian and New Zealand criminology, crime and justice* (pp. 407–419). Palgrave Macmillan. https://doi.org/10.1007/978-3-319-55747-2_27

Hazel, N. (2008). *Cross-national comparison of youth justice*. https://usir.salford.ac.uk/id/eprint/50528/

Holden, G. A., & Kapler, R. A. (1995). Deinstitutionalizing status offenders: A record of progress. *Juvenile Justice*, 2, 3. https://doi.org/10.1037/e381542004-001

Hughes, T. (2006). A paradigm of youth client satisfaction: Heightening professional responsibility for children's advocates. *Columbia Journal of Law and Social Problems*, *40*, 551.

Jaensch, R. (2022, June 8). *Raising the minimum age of detention*. Premier of Tasmania. www.premier.tas.gov.au/site_resources_2015/additional_releases/raising_the_minimum_age_of_detention

Juvenile Justice and Delinquency Prevention Act 1974 (US). https://ojjdp.ojp.gov/about/legislation

Legal and Constitutional References Committee. (2004). *Inquiry into legal aid and access to justice* (Ch. 8). Parliament of Australia.

Lount, S. A., Hand, L., Purdy, S. C., & France, A. (2018). Tough talk: Youth offenders' perceptions of communicating in the Youth Justice system in New Zealand. *Australian & New Zealand Journal of Criminology*, *51*(4), 593–618. https://doi.org/10.1177/0004865817740404

Lulham, R., Weatherburn, D., & Bartels, L. (2009). The recidivism of offenders given suspended sentences: A comparison with full-time imprisonment. *Crime and Justice Bulletin*, (136). https://www.bocsar.nsw.gov.au/Publications/CJB/cjb136.pdf

Moore, E. (2011). *Youth Justice conferences versus children's court: A comparison of time to finalisation* (Crime and Justice Statistics Bureau Brief, Issue Paper No. 174). NSW Bureau of Crime Statistics and Research.

Murphy, P., McGinness, A., & McDermott, T. (2010). *Review of effective practice in juvenile justice Report for the Minister for Juvenile Justice*. Noetic Solutions.

Naffine, N., & Wundersitz, J. (1991). Lawyers in the children's court: An Australian perspective. *Crime & Delinquency*, *37*(3), 374–392. https://doi.org/10.1177/0011128791037003005

Natapoff, A. (2005). *Speechless: The silencing of criminal defendants* (Loyola-LA Legal Studies Paper No. 2005–12). https://doi.org/10.2139/ssrn.709363

O'Connor, I. (1991). *Can the children's court prevent further offending?* [Unpublished manuscript]. Department of Social Work, University of Queensland.

Office of the Auditor General Western Australia. (2017). *Diverting young people away from court*. https://audit.wa.gov.au/reports-and-publications/reports/diverting-young-people-away-court/auditor-generals-overview/

Office of the Director of Public Prosecutions. (2021, June 30). *Charges involving a young person*. www.odpp.nsw.gov.au/prosecution-guidance/charges-involving-young-person

Peck, J. H., Leiber, M. J., & Brubaker, S. J. (2014). Gender, race, and juvenile court outcomes: An examination of status offenders. *Youth Violence and Juvenile Justice*, *12*(3), 250–267. https://doi.org/10.1177/1541204013489713

Pennington, L., & Farrell, A. (2019). Role of voice in the legal process. *Criminology*, *57*(2), 343–368. https://doi.org/10.1111/1745-9125.12205

Peterson-Badali, M., Abramovitch, R., Koegl, C. J., & Ruck, M. D. (1999). Young people's experience of the Canadian youth justice system: Interacting with police and legal counsel. *Behavioral Sciences & the Law*, *17*(4), 455–465. https://doi.org/10.1002/(SICI)1099-0798(199910/12)17:4<455::AID-BSL358>3.0.CO;2-R

Peterson-Badali, M., Care, S., & Broeking, J. (2007). Young people's perceptions and experiences of the lawyer – client relationship. *Canadian Journal of Criminology and Criminal Justice*, *49*(3), 375–401. https://doi.org/10.3138/cjccj.49.3.375

Pierce, C. S., & Brodsky, S. L. (2002). Trust and understanding in the attorney – juvenile relationship. *Behavioral Sciences & the Law*, *20*(1–2), 89–107. https://doi.org/10.1002/bsl.478

Piquero, A. R., Gomez-Smith, Z., & Langton, L. (2004). Discerning unfairness where others may not: Low self-control and unfair sanction perceptions. *Criminology*, *42*(3), 699–734. https://doi.org/10.1111/j.1745-9125.2004.tb00534.x

Pollock, W., & Menard, S. (2015). Perceptions of unfairness in police questioning and arrest incidents: Race, gender, age, and actual guilt. *Journal of Ethnicity in Criminal Justice*, *13*(3), 237–253. https://doi.org/10.1080/15377938.2015.1015197

RP v The Queen (2016). *HCA 53*.

Samuels-Wortley, K. (2021). To serve and protect whom? Using composite counter-storytelling to explore Black and Indigenous youth experiences and perceptions of the police in Canada. *Crime & Delinquency*, *67*(8), 1137–1164. https://doi.org/10.1177/0011128721989077

Sheehan, R., Baidawi, S., & Chipp, L. (2023). Children and young people in court. In *Australian courts: Controversies, challenges and change* (pp. 297–320). Springer International Publishing. https://doi.org/10.1007/978-3-031-19063-6_13

Sivasubramaniam, D., & Goodman-Delahunty, J. (2008). Ethnicity and trust: Perceptions of police bias. *International Journal of Police Science & Management*, *10*(4), 388–401. https://doi.org/10.1350/ijps.2008.10.4.094

Smith, N., & Weatherburn, D. (2012). *Youth justice conferences versus children's court: A comparison of re-offending* (Crime and Justice Bulletin No. 160). NSW Bureau of Crime Statistics and Research.

Sprott, J. B., & Greene, C. (2010). Trust and confidence in the courts: Does the quality of treatment young offenders receive affect their views of the courts? *Crime & Delinquency*, *56*(2), 269–289. https://doi.org/10.1177/0011128707308176

Tillack, K., Raineri, T., Cahill, A., & McDowall, J. J. (2018). *Youth justice report: Consultation with young people in out-of-home care about their experiences with police, courts, and detention*. Create Foundation. https://create.org.au/wp-content/uploads/2021/07/CREATEs-Youth-Justice-Report-Young-Persons-Version-2018.pdf

Travers, M. (2007). Sentencing in the children's court: An ethnographic perspective. *Youth Justice*, *7*(1), 21–35. https://doi.org/10.1177/1473225406074817

Trimboli, L. (2000). *An evaluation of the NSW youth justice conferencing scheme*. NSW Bureau of Crime Statistics and Research. www.bocsar.nsw.gov.au/Publications/Legislative/l12.pdf

Turner, S. (2002). *Young people's experiences of the young offenders act*. Youth Justice Coalition, Law and Justice Foundation of New South Wales.

Tyler, T. R., Caspi, J. D., & Fisher, B. (1989). Maintaining allegiance toward political authorities. *American Journal of Political Science*, *33*, 629–625. https://doi.org/10.2307/2111066

United Nations Committee on the Rights of the Child. (2019). *General comment No 24 (2019) on children's rights in the child justice system, UN Doc CRC/C/GC/24 (18 September 2019)*. https://undocs.org/en/CRC/C/GC/24

Vignaendra, S., & Fitzgerald, J. (2006). *Reoffending among young people cautioned by police or who participated in a youth justice conference* (Crime and Justice Bulletin No. 103). NSW Bureau of Crime Statistics and Research.

Viljoen, J. L., Klaver, J., & Roesch, R. (2005). Legal decisions of preadolescent and adolescent defendants: Predictors of confessions, pleas, communication with attorneys, and appeals. *Law and Human Behavior*, *29*, 253–277.

Wagland, P., Blanch, B., & Moore, E. (2013). *Participant satisfaction with youth justice conferencing* (Crime and Justice Bulletin No. 170). NSW Bureau of Crime Statistics and Research.

Webber, A. (2012). *Youth justice conferences versus children's court: A comparison of cost-effectiveness* (Crime and Justice Bulletin No. 164). NSW Bureau of Crime Statistics and Research.

White, M., & Gooda, M. (2017). *Report of the royal commission and board of inquiry into the protection and detention of children in the Northern Territory* (p. 9). Northern Territory Government.

White, R., & Cunneen, C. (2006). Social class, youth crime and juvenile justice. In B. Goldson & J. Muncie (Eds.), *Youth crime and justice* (pp. 17–29). SAGE Publications.

Wigzell, A., Kirby, A., & Jacobson, J. (2015). *The youth proceedings advocacy review: Final report*. Bar Standards Board. https://eprints.bbk.ac.uk/id/eprint/13577/

Wilson, P. (2013). Delinquency. In *The Handbook of child and adolescent psychotherapy* (pp. 311–327). Routledge.

Youth Justice Coalition. (2002). *Young people's experiences of the Young Offenders Act*. Marrickville Legal Centre.

Zappavigna, M., & Martin, J. R. (2017). *Discourse and diversionary justice: An analysis of youth justice conferencing*. Springer International Publishing.

Zhang, G., Nakamoto, J., & Cerna, R. (2020). Racial and ethnic disparities in youth perceptions of police in the community and school: Considering the effects of multilevel factors. *Policing: An International Journal*, *43*(5), 831–844. https://doi.org/10.1108/PIJPSM-05-2020-0075

Zottoli, T. M., & Daftary-Kapur, T. (2019). Guilty pleas of youths and adults: Differences in legal knowledge and decision making. *Law and Human Behavior*, *43*(2), 166–179. https://doi.org/10.1037/lhb0000314

3 Practice responses to youth violence

Tamara Blakemore, Louise Rak, and Chris Krogh

Acknowledgement

This chapter presents data from interviews with practitioners conducted as part of the Juvenile Justice and Education Equity project, a pilot study preceding the development of NNN. Some of this data was collected by Professor Amanda Howard and Conjoint Associate Professor Nicola Ross, and we acknowledge their contribution.

Practice responses to youth violence

This chapter explores practice responses to youth violence. It considers how evidence for practice with youth violence has pondered questions of, what is to be done?, what works?, and what doesn't work? and poses the question, what are we missing? The voice of practitioners bookends the chapter, situating review of the evidence for practice in the realities of frontline practitioners. Presented in textboxes throughout, this information was captured (with appropriate ethics approval) through semi-structured interviews conducted in the pilot study impetus to the NNN program (for more information see the Preface; Blakemore et al., 2018, 2019).

Lessons from history

The history of practice responses to "what is to be done" for youth violence have seemingly flip-flopped between juxtaposed positions of punitive deterrence and rehabilitation. These positions mirror shifting sociopolitical ideals influenced by human rights advocacy and evolving awareness of human development and the impact of adversity and stress on brains, bodies, and behaviour. They also reflect changing ways in which we have thought about and understood the use of violence. The modern era of practice in this field got off to a rough start when criminologist Robert Martinson (1974) published a review on prison

DOI: 10.4324/9781003177883-3

rehabilitation reporting that preliminary analyses found no effect of criminal justice interventions. The metric of success (or failure) for these interventions was recidivism, measured by re-arrest and/or reconviction. While he did note that this might be because interventions weren't good enough or weren't delivered in the right way (p. 49), Martinson's (1974) summary was so pessimistic that the review came to be nicknamed "Nothing Works!" These findings seemed to take on a life of their own, as Hollin (1999, p. 361) observed the "Nothing Works!" doctrine was transformed from a theoretical argument to a socially constructed reality, "resulting in the elimination of intervention and treatment programs for justice-involved cohorts in the United States (US)".

While rehabilitation seemed largely doomed, several commentators, most notably fellow criminologists Paul Gendreau and Robert Ross (1987), produced demonstrably successful examples of intervention with justice-cohorts establishing that "Something Works!" (Prescott, 2013, p. 70). Just what that something was, for whom, and in what ways were more difficult to identify. What has (somewhat) helped in this endeavour is the use of meta-analytic techniques (whereby summary statistics for multiple, individual studies form data points for statistical analysis of aggregated data) (Izzo & Ross, 1990). Meta-analytic studies of justice-related data have explored both clinical (personal wellbeing) and criminogenic (recidivism) outcomes and, with a somewhat rigid emphasis on recidivism, have progressed the field to an understanding of "What Works!" (McGuire, 1995). The challenge for practice with youth violence, then, is to translate findings of "What Works!" into intervention and program delivery.

Across the US, the UK, and Australia, this has commonly involved adopting an "at risk" approach to thinking about young people's involvement with crime (including violence) and their risk of reoffending (Sampson & Themelis, 2009). As described in Chapter 1, theoretically, this approach maps to an ecological framework understanding of youth crime – identifying multiple and intersecting risk and protective factors across community, family, school, peer, and individual domains (Bronfenbrenner, 1979; Cox et al., 2016). Risk and protective factors are understood to be dynamic, emerging or becoming more salient at different points across developmental trajectories, with their cumulative experience being more crucial than exposure to any one factor (Cox et al., 2016). By implication, the aims and objectives of practice informed by this approach are to target and minimise known risk factors for the use of violence (and recidivism) and enhance those factors known to moderate, mediate, or decrease its likelihood (Coie et al., 1993). Highly influential in this regard has been the application of principles of risk, need, and responsibility to shaping effective youth justice interventions (Andrews & Bonta, 2010).

The risk-need-responsivity (RNR) model suggests the risk principle dictates intervention should be appropriately matched to assessed risk of reoffending. Young people assessed to be at high risk should receive intensive, high-dose interventions (Andrews & Bonta, 2010). The authors identify what they term the "Big 4" risk factors: 1) antisocial attitudes and antisocial associates; 2) antisocial personality and behaviours; 3) impulsivity and aggressive energy, egocentrism, and thrill-seeking; 4) poor problem-solving and poor self-regulation (Andrews & Bonta, 2010). Assessment of risk counts many risk factors young people experience, noting risk factors change their meaning with use (Kemshall & Wilkinson, 2015) and are often context-specific (Pitts, 2003). As Sampson and Themelis (2009) emphasise, "While the presence of risk factors may be a necessary condition for offending, they are not sufficient to explain the actual committing of offences" (p. 124).

The need principle relates to things that need to change to reduce the risk of reoffending. Examples include changing criminal interests, attitudes, and beliefs; changing faulty cognitive schemas; and upskilling in self-regulation, problem-solving, and coping skills. Of interest to us is the conceptualisation of needs as driven by evidence for, not from, practice. Barnao and Ward (2015, p. 81) write, "The need principle *stipulates* interventions *should address empirically based* dynamic risk factors or criminogenic needs" (emphasis our own). Similarly, Prescott (2013, p. 74) states, "Effective treatment programs look at what *research* has identified as meaningful treatment goals" (again, emphasis here is our own). Herein lies a tension relating to practitioner observations that if the work is not seen as meaningful to young people, how do we hope to support their change? (Blakemore et al., 2018, 2019).

The third principle of the RNR model (Andrews et al., 1990) may go some way to addressing these concerns. The responsivity principle is described by Barnao and Ward (2015) as the "how" of intervention, noting effective practice should be responsive to young people's preferences, abilities, circumstances, and culture. While responsivity will not reduce the likelihood of reoffending on its own, it can strengthen engagement with goals for intervention (Prescott, 2013). The RNR model (Andrews et al., 1990) has best been described as an "umbrella framework" specifying the basic conditions that diverse interventions for youth violence need to meet to be effective (Polaschek, 2012).

Interventions for youth violence

Interventions for youth violence have included boot camps and relationship education, anger management and life skills, peer mentoring and sports, parent training and family therapy, cognitive therapies, and deterrence (Farrell & Flannery, 2006). Interventions focus on criminogenic needs that contextualise or constitute risk for violence. They differ in delivery and focus and in the theories held about what is likely to support and sustain change. Some interventions aim to address multiple risk factors for violence, while others are focused on shifting cognitive and behavioural responses (World Health Organisation [WHO], 2015). Interventions are delivered by trained psychologists, social workers, case managers, and youth workers and sometimes by trained community members on an individual or group basis and may sometimes involve family members or carers. It is useful to distinguish interventions as practice approaches (detailing focus, method, and informing theories of change) from programs (strategies to implement a practice approach). The following sections provide a brief description of common intervention approaches informed by cognitive behavioural theory, the strengths perspective, and the social development model.

Cognitive-behavioural interventions

Interventions informed by cognitive-behavioural theory focus on changing cognitive schemas to support more adaptive behavioural response to emotionally charged situations. Cognitive-behavioural interventions are delivered one-on-one to individuals and inform group-based programs and family-focused interventions. There is good empirical support for their effectiveness in reducing aggression and improving wellbeing and reducing recidivism in adult cohorts (e.g., Allen et al., 2001; Milkman & Wanberg, 2007; Shingler, 2004). A systematic review of outcomes for justice-involved young people similarly finds that cognitive-behavioural therapy (CBT) can reduce reoffending by 25% (Lipsey et al., 2007). Though other results are more modest (Garrido & Morales, 2007). Some commentators caution an over-reliance on cognitive interventions, suggesting they should be considered in conjunction with interventions that allow for a deeper understanding of other drivers of violence (Gilbert & Daffern, 2010).

Anger management

Novaco's (1975) model of anger management is a cognitive-behavioural intervention that describes how cognitive appraisals, emotional arousal, and angry responses are interdependent to support participants to both understand and better manage their experiences. The model is widely used, including with justice-cohorts. However, McGuire (2008) notes that despite indications of effectiveness in non-justice cohorts, implementing anger management programs in justice settings has not been uniformly successful, with some findings suggesting marginal success.

Howell (2003) reporting on Australian research in prison settings suggest that anger management can be useful but not as a "blanket approach", with latter work further emphasising the importance of participants' readiness for change in determining program outcomes (Howells & Day, 2003). Polaschek and Reynolds (2004) remind us that uncontrolled anger may contribute to some violence, but this is not a universal experience.

Aggression replacement therapy

Aggression replacement therapy (ART) is a multimodal cognitive-behavioural intervention for aggression (Goldstein & Glick, 2001). ART aims to reduce antisocial and aggressive behaviour through activities that support strengthening social skills, moral reasoning, and anger management (Glick & Gibbs, 2010). It is informed by Bandura's (1973) social learning theory, Novaco's (1975) anger control research, and Kohlberg's (1973) theory of moral reasoning. ART is an intensive thrice weekly group work program (Goldstein et al., 1998), widely implemented since the 1990s with adaptations delivered to justice-involved young people (Holmqvist et al., 2009). ART is suggested as particularly useful for justice-involved young people impacted by trauma (Kowalski, 2019). Evaluations report positive effects on recidivism but do not distinguish for violent recidivism (McGuire, 2008), with more recent meta-analyses (Brännström et al., 2016) suggesting there is insufficient evidence to claim that it is an effective intervention for reducing offending in young people.

Dialectical behaviour therapy

Dialectical behaviour therapy (DBT) is a cognitive-behavioural intervention developed to strengthen emotional and behavioural regulation through enhancing skills for mindfulness, distress tolerance, emotional recognition and regulation, and interpersonal effectiveness (Linehan, 1993). DBT embraces the notion of the "dialectic" and encourages participants to replace dichotomous (or black-and-white) thinking with perspective-taking. It emphasises self-awareness and skills for self-soothing and distraction. DBT has been found to be an effective intervention for anger and aggressive behaviour (Frazier & Vela, 2014) and has been implemented with both adult and youth justice-involved cohorts (Cunningham, 2004; Follette, 2006; Witkiewitz et al., 2005). The relevance of DBT to young people who use violence relates to its focus on criminogenic needs of self-regulation, self-control (Sapouna et al., 2011), emotional regulation (Chitsabesan et al., 2006; Vitacco et al., 2010), and cognitive and behavioural flexibility (Fazel et al., 2008). Differing from other interventions, DBT is characterised by a relational approach where practitioners use skills of reciprocal communication to validate experiences of trauma as contexts for behaviour, without invalidating its consequences (Linehan, 1993). Frank, irreverent communication and problem-solving are used to name and address issues as they arise in the group rather than excluding participants for disruptive behaviour (Linehan, 1993; Quinn & Shera, 2009).

Multisystemic therapy

Multisystemic therapy (MST) is a family-focused intervention informed by family and cognitive-behavioural therapies (Welsh et al., 2014). MST targets factors associated with the development of antisocial and violent behaviour, including family relationships, parenting and parent wellbeing, poor social support, negative peer associations, and chronic stress (Henggeler et al., 1992; Sood & Berkowitz, 2016). MST supports parents to gain or strengthen skills for managing challenging behaviour and helps young people to develop skills to manage and problem-solve around issues that arise with peers, in school, or in the community (Henggeler et al., 1992). MST is delivered in the home or community settings by trained practitioners, with treatment lasting on average four months (Henggeler et al., 1992). Evaluation of MST under robust conditions has provided strong support for its effectiveness in reducing the likelihood of recidivism and reducing the use of violence (Borduin et al., 1990, 1995; Curtis et al., 2004; Fain et al., 2014). A narrative review of outcomes (University of Colorado, 2014) reports participation in MST was associated with a 50% reduction in arrests and convictions, including for violent crime. Longitudinal studies (Schaeffer & Borduin, 2005; Wagner et al., 2014) suggest positive effects are long-lasting and observed more than 20 years later. Despite these findings, other studies (Cunningham, 2002; Henggeler et al., 1992; Sundell et al., 2008) report MST offers no significant benefit over other interventions. Littell et al. (2005) note these findings prevent a firm conclusion from being drawn on superiority of MST over alternative interventions but do not diminish the positive outcomes observed in other studies.

Strengths-based interventions

Strengths-based interventions encourage identifying and fostering the personal strengths, skills, and resources people need to create a personally meaningful, satisfying, and safe life (Ward & Gannon, 2006). Strengths-based approaches were developed in response to deficit-focused ways of working with vulnerable populations. Saleebey (1996, p. 297) explains, "The appreciations and understandings of the strengths perspective are an attempt to correct this destructive emphasis on what is wrong, what is missing, and what is abnormal". Tyler et al. (2020) note strengths-based approaches are relatively recent in work with justice-involved cohorts. While many strengths-based interventions are emerging in the justice literature, functional family therapy (FFT) and the Good Lives Model (GLM) are the most notable.

Functional family therapy

Functional family therapy is described as a strengths-based, short-term, structured family intervention (Alexander et al., 2013). FFT aims to reduce recidivism by strengthening relationships and effective communication among family members. It involves modelling and reinforcing communication strategies to minimise conflict and linking with supports to ensure gains are sustained (Alexander & Parsons, 1973; Sood & Berkowitz, 2016). FFT can be delivered in home or community settings and involves families working with a practitioner over three to four months (Alexander et al., 2013). FFT has been widely used for over 40 years (Sexton & Turner, 2010). It has been demonstrated to be associated with decreased recidivism for justice-involved young people, including those who have used violence (Aos et al., 2001; Greenwood, 2006; University of Colorado, 2014). There is some suggestion positive effects are long-lasting with lower rates of recidivism reported into adulthood (Gordon et al., 1988). Sexton and Turner (2010) note that critical to these outcomes is a practitioner's strict adherence to the treatment model.

The Good Lives Model

The Good Lives Model is a strengths-based approach to rehabilitation for justice-involved cohorts (Marshall et al., 2017). Best understood as an overarching framework, the GLM encourages building strengths and resources to achieve "a good life" in socially acceptable ways (Ward & Maruna, 2007). Tyler et al. (2020) explain the GLM embraces the idea that all behaviour is motivated by "human goods". Barnao and Ward (2015) describe these as activities, experiences, or situations that bring happiness and fulfillment. People seek human goods through their own capacities and skills or the resources and capital available to them (Tyler et al., 2020). Absence of these goods or difficulty obtaining them can lead to psychological distress and potentially harmful behaviour (Ward & Maruna, 2007). The GLM understands offending (including the use of violence) as an attempt to secure human goods in the context of internal and external obstacles (including impulsivity, compromised social skills and supports, dysfunction, and disadvantage) (Barnao & Ward, 2015). Objectives of the GLM include increasing personal agency and developing or strengthening an internal locus of control (Wainwright & Nee, 2014).

Social development interventions

Social development interventions are informed by the social development model (Catalano & Hawkins, 1996). Building on ecological theory (Bronfenbrenner, 1979), the social development model suggests pro- and anti-social behaviours are learned from socialisation that occurs in the family, school, and community (Catalano & Hawkins, 1996). It argues that young people are socialised through developmental processes involving opportunities for connecting and interaction with others, the intensity of this involvement or interaction, the skills developed and used in these interactions, and the reinforcement they receive from these interactions (Herrenkohl et al., 2001). Social development interventions for youth violence target protective factors by improving competency and social skills (Mercy et al., 2002).

Life skills interventions

Life skills interventions with young people who have used violence focus on strengthening self-awareness, self-regulation, and skills for connection, targeting criminogenic needs related to a lack of social skills and poor conflict management. Life skills interventions can be self-administered (Ralph & Sanders, 2004) or implemented with groups (Paterson et al., 2002; Stallman & Ralph, 2007; Toumbourou & Gregg, 2002). These interventions typically use cognitive-behavioural methods and can incorporate experiential learning (Fagan & Catalano, 2013). Life skills interventions have been delivered to universal, selected, and indicated cohorts with good effect. Evidence for the effectiveness of life skills interventions draws on data from implementations of these interventions in schools. Both meta-analyses (Wilson & Lipsey, 2007) and systematic reviews (Hahn et al., 2007; Mytton et al., 2006) report reductions in aggressive and violent behaviour after participation in life skills interventions.

Mentoring interventions

Mentoring describes a relational experience involving a more experienced person sharing knowledge, skills, information, and perspective to aid the prosocial development of a young person (Tolan et al., 2008).

Mentoring interventions assume that social learning situated in the relationship between the mentor and mentee will enhance handling of day-to-day problems and model alternative ways to deal with conflict (WHO, 2015). Mentoring interventions are appealing and have a long history with the Big Brothers and Big Sisters program dating back to 1904 (De Wit et al., 2007). While meta-analyses and systematic reviews suggest modest positive effects on aggression, no studies have assessed the effectiveness of mentoring for severe violence (WHO, 2015).

Relationship education interventions

Relationship education interventions aim to strengthen young people's understanding of and skills to form and maintain positive, equal, respectful, and safe relationships and to develop positive strategies for resolving conflict without violence (Pfitzner et al., 2022; WHO, 2015). These interventions span public health strategies from social marketing campaigns through to programs delivered to small groups of young people (Carmody, 2015). Relationship education programs are commonly a universal intervention mainly delivered in schools by teachers or community members. Universities are also a significant site for education relationship programs as well as broader safer relationship initiatives (McCall et al., 2023). Programs aiming to prevent relationship violence represent a range of theoretical perspectives, including social learning and feminist empowerment (Weisz & Black, 2009) and, over time, have reflected a range of discourses from women's risk avoidance to developing skills for bystander interventions and ethically negotiating sexual situations (Carmody, 2015). No research was identified reporting experiences of young people who use violence in these programs, though Weisz and Black (2009) report that practitioners acknowledge that the young people attending these programs may have experienced violence or acted violently prior to participating. Meta-analyses of program evaluations for 36 relationship education interventions found that objectives rarely matched measured outcomes (Benham-Clarke et al., 2022). This means it is difficult to know whether they effect changes in knowledge, attitudes and beliefs, skills, and behaviour.

What works

The majority of what we know about the effectiveness of interventions for youth violence comes from the US (Bellis et al., 2012). Evidence is commonly drawn from systematic reviews and meta-analyses that synthesise findings across multiple evaluations of different interventions (Matjasko et al., 2012). An influential example is Lipsey's (2007) meta-analysis of interventions for justice-involved young people in the

US. Findings from this study assessed interventions as demonstrating either above-average effects, average effects, or below-average effects in reducing recidivism. Interventions associated with above-average effects included CBT, group counselling, vocational training, mentoring, and some forms of treatment for young people exhibiting sexually harmful behaviour or experiencing substance abuse issues. Average effects were associated with family-focused interventions, individual counselling, life skills interventions, MST, and educational interventions. Below-average effects were reported for recreational and restorative interventions as well as intensive supervision. In considering what contributed to the effectiveness (or lack thereof) of these interventions, Lipsey (2007) notes the importance of the type of intervention, the fidelity of implementation, and the assessed risk level of the participants.

Efficacy versus effectiveness

We are increasingly encouraged to consider not only what intervention works but also how and why it works (McNeil & Weaver, 2010). Sapouna et al. (2011) explain this is known as the "efficacy" versus "effectiveness" debate (p. 97). Efficacy is the "extent to which an intervention works under ideal circumstances" and effectiveness is "whether an intervention works when provided under usual circumstances" (Kim, 2013, p. 227). What we learn from "gold standard" evaluations, employing randomised control trials (RCTs), is the efficacy of an intervention rather than its effectiveness (Glasgow et al., 2006). Andrews and Bonta (2006, p. 329) estimate the real-life implementation of effective interventions results in reductions of recidivism "a little more than 50%" of that reported in (controlled) evaluation conditions. This is because implementation involves dynamic interactions between policy, practice, and participants, each capable of effecting unintended consequences on the work (Sampson, 2010). Realist evaluation addresses this by moving from the question of, *what works?*, to, *what works, for whom, in what circumstances, and how?* (Pawson et al., 1997). Merging the two approaches, realist RCTs have been trialled in the broader youth violence field and found to be "philosophically coherent, practically feasible and able to produce nuanced findings" (Warren et al., 2022, p. 82). While we wait for this field of evidence production to grow, what then should we make of our existing evidence base? Hough (2010) suggests evidence we have from RCTs is valuable in demonstrating what *can* work but that we should also be thinking about the elements and mechanisms that support interventions that work best. Pooley (2020) suggests we consider what the essential core components of interventions are that make them effective. She discerns that when interventions are found to be effective, core components of those interventions are associated with reductions in the use of violence (or re-arrest) and conversely when interventions are found to be ineffective, the absence of core components are associated with increases in the use of violence (or re-arrest) (Pooley, 2020).

Core components of effective interventions

Lipsey's (2009) meta-analysis of 548 studies with justice-involved young people aged 12–21 identified five core components of effective interventions: (1) the primary service, (2) supplementary services, (3) treatment amount, (4) treatment quality, and (5) youth risk level. These findings seem to have withstood the test of time, with contemporary evidence strengthening our understanding of the importance of each core component. Herein, we understand "treatment" and "service" to be synonymous with "intervention" and adopt this terminology in the following brief description of each core component.

Primary intervention

Lipsey's (2009) study found the most effective interventions were those underpinned by therapeutic principles – those aligned to the (criminogenic) needs of participants and which supported positive change (O'Connor & Waddell, 2015). Key amongst these were skill-building interventions that used cognitive- behavioural techniques to develop skills for prosocial engagement. These interventions were associated with a 26% reduction in recidivism (Lipsey, 2009). Skill-building interventions can be multimodal or multifaceted, can focus on one area of need or many, and can be delivered to individuals or groups. Evidence suggests skill-based interventions are particularly well-suited to group delivery. Lipsey (2009) found that group-based skill-building interventions were associated with a 22% reduction in recidivism. Those who support group-based work argue that it offers a relatively safe way for young people to build skills for being in a group, which is an important skill in society, intensified by peer group dynamics throughout adolescence (Harvey, 1997; Linehan, 1993). Studies of intervention with young people who used violence in the home have found group work to be effective in providing a safe space for sharing and creative problem-solving (Correll et al., 2017; Messiah & Johnson, 2017; Moulds et al., 2019). Skill-building interventions are suggested to impact recidivism through responsivity to criminogenic needs and through their capacity to enhance self-agency and self-efficacy (McIvor et al., 2009).

Supplementary interventions

Supplementary interventions (where participants are simultaneous supported by other services) are critical to the effectiveness of interventions because they provide a way to address a broader range of criminogenic needs than are usually within scope for any one service or intervention. Supplementary interventions can also support through-care options to maintain positive outcomes achieved by an intervention (Lipsey, 2009). This may be especially relevant when working with participants where there are diverse, complex, and/or conflicting needs (Correll et al., 2017). Of course, the prospect of supplementary interventions often involves cross-agency work, which can introduce or compound complex dynamics between participants and "the system". Prior, concomitant, and cumulative experiences of systemic disadvantage and denial of care will shape expectations (and sometimes outcomes) of service engagement. How supplementary services are experienced by participants is, therefore, also an important determinant of the effectiveness of intervention for youth violence.

Intervention amount

Intervention amount, also referred to as "dosage", a core component of effective interventions, refers to how often and for how long an intervention is delivered (Pooley, 2020). Dosage is found to be particularly important to the effectiveness of interventions underpinned by what Lipsey (2009) refers to as a "therapeutic philosophy" (Adler et al., 2016; Lipsey, 2009). Dosage, however, can have the opposite effect on supervision-focused interventions because an increased frequency of contact can mean an increased likelihood of detecting involvement in crime (Bouchard & Wong, 2018).

Intervention quality

Intervention quality, sometimes equated to implementation fidelity (O'Connor & Waddell, 2015), refers to how well an intervention is implemented. This involves skilful and relational practice. Positive and collaborative relationships between practitioners and young people are critical to effectiveness of interventions for youth violence (Dowden & Andrews, 2004; Gendreau et al., 1996; Trotter, 2006, 2013). Demonstration of shared states of emotion or experience, flexibility, and compassion on behalf of the practitioner may stimulate mutual respect and a collaborative working alliance. This, in turn, can increase the likelihood that young people will engage with (and complete) interventions; see them as fair, reasonable, and useful; and ultimately achieve positive change (Cramer et al., 2019; Prior & Mason, 2010). In this way, positive, open, and nonjudgemental relationships between practitioners and young people may be associated with reduced recidivism (Adler et al., 2016; Prior & Mason, 2010; Sampson & Themelis, 2009).

Youth risk level

Youth risk level relates to the finding that interventions work best when they are delivered to high-risk participants. This finding references the "risk principle" (Andrews et al., 1990), which suggests that effective interventions will have a greater impact on higher-risk cohorts because they have more room for improvement than lower-risk cohorts.

What doesn't work

Having explored what works, it is just as important to know what doesn't work and, in fact, whether some interventions might make matters worse. Evidence exists that many interventions make, at best, no difference and can be associated with increased recidivism. Lipsey (2007) reports these include punishment regimes, "Scared Straight" programs, boot camps, restrictive out-of-home care (OOHC) or residential placements, psychiatric hospitalisation, and long-term confinement in large custodial facilities. Interventions least effective are those based on deterrence and/or discipline (O'Connor & Waddell, 2015).

Deterrence-based interventions

Lipsey (2009) explains deterrence-based interventions attempt to motivate desistence through scare tactics designed to confront the young person with the possible consequences of their actions. Petrosino et al. (2005) report several studies have examined effectiveness of deterrence-based interventions, with none finding a positive impact on recidivism and a number reporting that these interventions led to an increase in violence and crime. Perhaps the most infamous example of this is the "Scared Straight" program in the US, which involved providing first-hand observations of prison life and interaction with adult inmates. Petrosino et al. (2013) note participating in this intervention increased the odds of a young person engaging in crime by between 60% and 96%. Despite this, Petrosino et al. (2013) observe "Scared Straight"–type programs continued to be delivered across many countries.

Discipline-based interventions

Lipsey (2009) describes discipline-based interventions as being informed by an ethos that enforces structure, hardship, and punishment, which can motivate prosocial behaviour. Most common amongst these types of interventions are military-style "boot camps" (Wilson et al., 2005). A systematic review of the effectiveness of boot camps notes they are no more effective at reducing recidivism than probation or incarceration (Wilson et al., 2005). The group-based implementation of these programs is suggested by some to effect "group contagion," whereby deviant peer association undermines any beneficial effect of the intervention or, worse, contributes to actual harm (Dishion & Piehler, 2009; Welsh & Rocque, 2014). However, other interventions of this same style show more promising effects (Jolliffe et al., 2013), possibly due to a more structured and supervised format that also incorporates rehabilitative aspects (Cécile & Born, 2009).

Practice considerations

Mason and Prior (2008) observe that studies of effective interventions provide a paucity of insights into practice skills and techniques to implement interventions effectively. Where evidence does exist, it is primarily concentrated on the relational quality of practice and how this motivates the positive *engagement* of young people towards desistence (Adler et al., 2016).

Box 3.1 What practitioners tell us . . .

Practitioners report that systemic processes often set up conditions wherein engagement is brief, transactional, and impersonal.

> "I remember seeing a young person who was sent by [agency] and there they were told if they turned up for 5 minutes, that would look better in a court than if they didn't turn up at all. So, they turned up for 5 minutes; I encouraged them to come back. They turned up for [another] 5 minutes and wanted to leave again". (Practitioner 10)

Practitioners also recognise that systemic practice can contribute to difficulties with engagement and a lack of motivation for change.

> "The biggest challenge just is getting the young person onside, because all the time, they just think that – you're someone else talking down to them. They get that a lot, and it's just hard to get them to be invested in their own rehabilitation. I think

that's the biggest challenge. You can throw service after service after service at them . . . if they're not really interested or motivated – and I think that's the hardest thing. I think that's – I still don't know how to unlock that". (Practitioner 2)

These reflections highlight how engagement can be contextualised and reinforced by systemic processes and practice and potentially by the young person's "readiness to change" (Day & Howells, 2008). Also described as "treatment readiness," this refers to the ability of young people to engage with and benefit from an intervention and the likelihood of intervention completion (Kemshall & Wilkinson, 2015). Readiness to change is influenced by both individual and situational factors that can, in and of themselves, influence the likelihood of engagement with and completion of interventions. Referred to as the "completion effect," starting but not completing interventions can be associated with recidivism (Hatcher & Palmer, 2008; Hatcher et al., 2012).

Box 3.2 What practitioners tell us . . .

Practitioners relate frustration at some young people's readiness for change.

> "Unless the kid is there and wanting help and wanting – at times it can be wasted effort. That sounds really negative doesn't it, but just at times you think [argh]". (Practitioner 24)

Practitioners also observe, however, that readiness to change can develop over time.

> "Often that just shows that the young person doesn't really have an insight into what their behaviour is leading to and the motivation to change isn't there. Like to be able to perform any sort of intervention and put these things in place, they have to be at least contemplating some sort of change in their world. But the majority of the clients that we get are pretty contemplative. But whether that's an age thing or just a maturity thing [is unclear]". (Practitioner 20)

Consistent with these observations, other studies suggest readiness to change can develop during interventions as the working alliance between the young person and practitioner strengthens (Day & Howells, 2008). These findings caution pre-emptive assumptions about likely outcomes and further encourage relational practice. Considering existing practice response to youth violence also gives us pause to consider whether something is missing. This is not to disregard efforts, achievements, and success of practitioners and young people. Rather, it reflects a palpable sense of inertia in the work that seems to be sustained by parallel "insider–outsider" experiences. Practitioners are commonly positioned as an outsider to the young people they work with because of their role, knowledge of "the system", and differential access to and control over resources, including power.

Box 3.3 What practitioners tell us . . .

Practitioner positionality can mean we see the motivations and experiences of young people in stark contrast to our own experience of the world.

> "[Eighteen] and they haven't even bothered to try and get a licence or any of the things that I wanted when I was that age. That was my goal . . . I want to get a licence; I want to get a car. No, they don't even think about it". (Practitioner 23)

The uneasiness of an outsider perspective can also contribute to a feeling of ineffectiveness in practice.

> "If you can just get through to them, to reducing recidivism. But how do you get through to them? How do you relate to them? Often you're – for me, I'm from a different culture with my clients. I'm a different gender. How do you [get through?]" (Practitioner 2)

In these circumstances, parallel insider–outsider experiences can influence how each party understands and works with the other and can easily contribute to young people's behaviours being pathologised, labelled, and othered.

What are we missing?

When we consider many existing practice responses to youth violence, it seems to us that something is missing. This is not to disregard efforts, achievements, and success of practitioners and young people. Rather, it reflects a palpable sense of inertia in the work that seems to be sustained by parallel "insider–outsider" experiences. Practitioners are commonly positioned as an outsider to the young people they work with because of their role, knowledge of "the system", and differential access to and control over resources, including power. A key observation for us in our work is that many interventions for youth violence do not fit with, understand, nor respond to young people's gender, culture, and trauma. These service gaps and neglected needs can contribute to an increased risk of recidivism. The following sections describe the need for gender-, culture-, trauma-, and power-responsive interventions.

Gender-responsive interventions

While the proportion of young women in the youth justice population has grown, there has been no corresponding progress in developing, implementing, and evaluating gender-responsive interventions (Leve et al., 2015). Chesney-Lind et al. (2008) argue this effectively silences young women's presence, needs, and potency in the justice system. This has been attributed to "young men being more noticeable and noticed than young women" (Alder, 1995, p. 3) and young women's crimes being deemed less of a risk to public safety and property than young men's. The (criminogenic) needs of young women who use violence are often intertwined with and compounded by complex and intergenerational experiences of trauma as well as gendered and structural disadvantage and discrimination. These experiences are associated with fractured relationship systems and schemas that mean that family-focused interventions can be inappropriate or even unsafe (Schaffner, 2006).

Culturally responsive interventions

Richards et al. (2011) stress the need for Aboriginal community involvement in the design, delivery, and dissemination of information about interventions aimed at addressing Aboriginal young people's justice involvement. Programs designed with and for Aboriginal young people are more effective at reducing recidivism and are preferred because of their capacity to empower and strengthen Aboriginal communities (Borowski, 2010; McGuinness et al., 2017). Richards et al. (2011) explain interventions need to be holistic and build on existing strengths in Aboriginal communities to address justice involvement in collaborative ways. Incorporating culturally appropriate activities, engaging practitioners from the same cultural background, using preferred languages, and embedding traditions and norms are also important for intervention effectiveness (Fazal, 2014). Positive relationships centred in shared place, language, histories, and beliefs are central to this work (Fazal, 2014; Lopes et al., 2013). Stringfellow et al. (2022) emphasise a relational approach is important because it supports addressing young people's involvement in crime in a way that is contextualised by lived experience. This echoes sentiments of Edwards-Groves and Murray (2008), who argue there is a need for culturally responsive work that views young people not through a deficit lens but rather listens to and validates their lived experience, acknowledging and affirming their connection to culture as a valuable part of their identity.

Trauma-responsive interventions

The experience of adversity and developmental trauma among justice-involved young people seems to be at once commonly acknowledged yet ignored in practice responses to youth violence. Despite evidence that many justice-involved young people have trauma histories (Malvaso et al., 2022), that trauma is an established risk factor for the use of violence (Kerig & Becker, 2010), and that prior trauma can be compounded by experiences in the justice system (Ferrito et al., 2017), there is a paucity of trauma-informed interventions for youth violence (Gueta et al., 2022). In practice, and substantiated by the literature, it seems this may be a consequence of the deeply polarised positions taken regarding those who have experienced violence and those have used violence, despite the empirical overlap between the two (Jennings et al., 2012; Sindicich et al., 2014). Trauma-responsive interventions often incorporate aspects of CBT, which is found to be effective in reducing violence and recidivism in youth justice cohorts (Aos & Drake, 2013). Further, trauma-responsive interventions actively target (criminogenic) needs, including impulsivity, emotional dysregulation, and poor self-awareness (Wolff et al., 2015). With emerging evidence of their effectiveness for use with justice-involved cohorts (Zettler, 2021), there is significant impetus for furthering trauma-responsive interventions for youth violence.

Power-responsive interventions

Dynamics of power and control are central to understandings of domestic, family, and intimate partner violence. Tools such as the Duluth model's "Power and Control Wheel" (Duluth Model, 2021) are often used in violence prevention and intervention (Gilman & Walker, 2020). These interventions focus exclusively on the use of violence against women, consistent with evidence that most violence is used by men, often in domestic, family, and intimate partner relationships, against women. Very little has been written about interventions that attend to dynamics of power and control in young people's use of violence outside these contexts. Likewise, despite justice-involved young people's daily experience of systemic and structural power, little has been written about whether or how interventions with young people who use violence articulate practitioner power in this work. This would address what Jenkins (2009, p. 14) calls the "politics of intervention," recognising that work with violence occurs within dominant social power structures and that practitioners largely represent these social dynamics, including working within powerful institutions and carrying significant social privileges. Jenkins (2009) argues, "We have a responsibility to be vigilant for and to critique violent practices whether they are enacted by our clients, statutory and community institutions or (especially) by ourselves" (p. 10). Echoing lessons from critical youth theory, which describes much youth work as involving "pastoral power" (Hodgson, 2018) and/or disciplinary power (Gray & Smith, 2021; Lohmeyer & McGregor, 2022; McCallum, 2009; McGregor, 2017) to insinuate individualised self-responsiblisation of young people, practice in this area requires greater (and more transparent) reflexivity and efforts to balance power.

Conclusion

This chapter has described practice responses to youth violence. It has considered the aims and objectives of practice with youth violence and how understandings of risk, need, responsivity, desistence, and change have shaped practice responses over time. Practitioner feedback provided an insight into the real-life experience of these constructs. The chapter presented a brief overview of different intervention approaches for youth violence, exploring what works, what doesn't work, and what's missing from our current practice. The chapter has contextualised the development of a new way of working with youth violence that will be explored in the following chapter.

References

Adler, J. R., Edwards, S., Scally, M., Gill, D., Puniskis, M. J., Gekoski, A., & Horvath, M. A. (2016). *What works in managing young people who offend? A summary of the international evidence*. www.gov.uk/government/publications/what-works-in-managing-young-people-who-offend

Alder, C. (1995). *Delinquency prevention with young women*. Paper presented at the Delinquency Prevention Conference, Terrigal, New South Wales, Australia.

Alexander, J. F., & Parsons, B. V. (1973). Short-term behavioral intervention with delinquent families: Impact on family process and recidivism. *Journal of Abnormal Psychology*, *81*, 219–225. https://doi.org/10.1037/h0034537

Alexander, J. F., Waldron, H. B., Robbins, M. S., & Neeb, A. A. (2013). *Functional family therapy for adolescent behavior problems*. American Psychological Association. https://doi.org/10.1037/14139-000

Allen, L. C., MacKenzie, D. L., & Hickman, L. J. (2001). The effectiveness of cognitive behavioral treatment for adult offenders: A methodological, quality-based review. *International Journal of Offender Therapy and Comparative Criminology*, *45*(4), 498–514. https://doi.org/10.1177/0306624X01454009

Andrews, D. A., & Bonta, J. (2006). *The psychology of criminal conduct* (4th ed.). Matthew Bender.

Andrews, D. A., & Bonta, J. (2010). *The psychology of criminal conduct* (5th ed.). Routledge.

Andrews, D. A., Bonta, J., & Hoge, R. D. (1990). Classification for effective rehabilitation: Rediscovering psychology. *Criminal Justice and Behavior*, *17*(1), 19–52. https://doi.org/10.1177/0093854890017001004

Aos, S., & Drake, E. (2013). *Prison, police and programs: Evidence-based options that reduce crime and save money*. Washington State Institute for Public Policy.

Aos, S., Phipps, P., Barnoski, R., & Lieb, R. (2001). *The comparative costs and benefits of programs to reduce crime* (Version 4.0). Washington State Institute of Public Policy.

Bandura, A. (1973). *Aggression: A social learning analysis*. Prentice-Hall. https://doi.org/10.2307/1227918

Barnao, M., & Ward, T. (2015). Sailing uncharted seas without a compass: A review of interventions in forensic mental health. *Aggression and Violent Behavior*, *22*, 77–86. https://doi.org/10.1016/j.avb.2015.04.009

Bellis, M. A., Hughes, K., Perkins, C., & Bennett, A. (2012). *Protecting people, promoting health: A public health approach to violence prevention for England*. North West Public Health Observatory at the Centre for Public Health. www.gov.uk/government/publications/apublic-health-approach-to-violence-prevention-in-england

Benham-Clarke, S., Roberts, G., Janssens, A., & Newlove-Delgado, T. (2022). Healthy relationship education programmes for young people: Systematic review of outcomes. *Pastoral Care in Education*. https://doi.org/10.1080/02643944.2022.2054024

Blakemore, T., Agllias, K., Howard, A., & McCarthy, S. (2019). The service system challenges of work with juvenile justice involved young people in the Hunter Region, Australia. *Australian Journal of Social Issues*, *54*(3), 341–356. https://doi.org/10.1002/ajs4.69

Blakemore, T., Rak, L., Agllias, K., Mallett, X., & McCarthy, S. (2018). Crime and context: Understandings of youth perpetrated interpersonal violence among service providers in regional Australia. *Journal of Applied Youth Studies*, *2*(5), 53–69.

Borduin, C. M., Henggeler, S. W., Blaske, D. M., & Stein, R. J. (1990). Multisystemic treatment of adolescent sexual offenders. *International Journal of Offender Therapy and Comparative Criminology*, *34*(2), 105–113. https://doi.org/10.1177/0306624X9003400204

Borduin, C. M., Mann, B. J., Cone, L. T., Henggeler, S. W., Fucci, B. R., Blaske, D. M., & Williams, R. A. (1995). Multisystemic treatment of serious juvenile offenders: Long-term prevention of criminality and violence. *Journal of Consulting and Clinical Psychology*, *63*(4), 569–578. https://doi.org/10.1037/0022-006X.63.4.569

Borowski, A. (2010). Indigenous participation in sentencing young offenders: Findings from an evaluation of the Children's Koori Court of Victoria. *Australian and New Zealand Journal of Criminology*, *43*(3), 465–484. https://doi.org/10.1375/acri.43.3.465

Bouchard, J., & Wong, J. S. (2018). Examining the effects of intensive supervision and aftercare programs for at-risk youth: A systematic review and meta-analysis. *International Journal of Offender Therapy and Comparative Criminology*, 62(6), 1509–1534. https://doi.org/10.1177/0306624X17690449

Brännström, L., Kaunitz, C., Andershed, A. K., South, S., & Smedslund, G. (2016). Aggression replacement training (ART) for reducing antisocial behavior in adolescents and adults: A systematic review. *Aggression and Violent Behavior*, *27*, 30–41. https://doi.org/10.1016/j.avb.2016.02.006

Bronfenbrenner, U. (1979). *The ecology of human development: Experiments by nature and design*. Harvard University Press.

Carmody, M. (2015). *Sex, ethics, and young people*. Palgrave Macmillan. https://doi.org/10.1057/9781137405975

Catalano, R. F., & Hawkins, J. D. (1996). The social development model: A theory of antisocial behaviour. In J. D. Hawkins (Ed.), *Delinquency and crime: Current theories* (pp. 149–198). Cambridge University Press.

Cécile, M., & Born, M. (2009). Intervention in juvenile delinquency: Danger of iatrogenic effects? *Children and Youth Services Review*, *31*, 1217–1221. https://doi.org/10.1016/j.childyouth.2009.05.015

Chesney-Lind, M., Morash, M., & Stevens, T. (2008). Girls troubles, girls' delinquency, and gender responsive programming: A review. *Australian and New Zealand Journal of Criminology*, *41*(1), 162–189. https://doi.org/10.1375/acri.41.1.162

Chitsabesan, P., Kroll, L., Bailey, S. U. E., Kenning, C., Sneider, S., MacDonald, W., & Theodosiou, L. (2006). Mental health needs of young offenders in custody and in the community. *British Journal of Psychiatry*, *188*(6), 534–540. https://doi.org/10.1192/bjp.bp.105.010116

Coie, J. D., Watt, N. F., West, S. G., Hawkins, J. D., Asarnow, J. R., Markman, H. J., Ramey, S. L., Shure, M. B., & Long, B. (1993). The science of prevention: A conceptual framework and some directions for a national research program. *American Psychologist*, *48*(10), 1013–1022. https://doi.org/10.1037/0003-066X.48.10.1013

Correll, J. R., Walker, S. C., & Edwards, T. C. (2017). Parent perceptions of participating in a program for adolescents who are violent at home. *Journal of Family Violence*, 32(2), 243–255. https://doi.org/10.1007/s10896-016-9847-6

Cox, E., Leung, R., Baksheev, G., Day, A., Toumbourou, J. W., Miller, P., Kremer, P., & Walker, A. (2016). Violence prevention review. *Australian Psychologist*, *51*, 206–222. https://doi.org/10.1111/ap.12168

Cramer, L., Esthappan, S., Lynch, M., & Goff, M. (2019). *Considerations for justice-involved youth programming: Lessons learned and recommendations from the Arches, AIM, and NYC Justice Corps Evaluations*. Urban Institute. www.urban.org/research/publication/considerations-justice-involved-youth-programming

Cunningham, A. (2002). Lessons learned from a randomized study of multisystemic therapy in Canada. *One Step Forward*, 1–31.

Cunningham, R. (2004). Structured living environments in Canadian federal institutions for women. In *Forum on corrections research* (Vol. 16, No. 1, pp. 9–10).

Curtis, N. M., Ronan, K. R., & Borduin, C. R. (2004). Multisystemic treatment: A metaanalysis of outcome studies. *Journal of Family Psychology*, *18*, 411–419. https://doi.org/10.1037/0893-3200.18.3.411

Day, A., & Howells, K. (2008). Assessing treatment readiness in violent offenders. *Journal of Interpersonal Violence*, *24*, 618–635.

De Wit, D. J., Lipman, E., Manzano-Munguia, M., Bisanz, J., Graham, K., Offord, D. R., O'Neill, E., Pepler, D., & Shaver, K. (2007). Feasibility of a randomized controlled trial for evaluating the effectiveness of the big brothers big sisters community match program at the national level. *Children and Youth Services Review*, *29*(3), 383–404. https://doi.org/10.1016/j.childyouth.2006.09.003

Dishion, T. J., & Piehler, T. F. (2009). Deviant by design: Peer contagion in development, interventions, and schools. In K. H. Rubin, W. M. Bukowski, & B. Laursen (Eds.), *Handbook of peer interactions, relationships, and groups* (pp. 589–602). The Guilford Press.

Dowden, C., & Andrews, D. A. (2004). The importance of staff practice in delivering effective correctional treatment: A meta-analytic review of the literature. *International Journal of Offender Therapy and Comparative Criminology*, *48*(2), 203–214. https://doi.org/10.1177/0306624X03257765

Duluth Model. (2021, April 24). *Wheels: Domestic Abuse Intervention Programs*. www.theduluthmodel.org/wheels/

Edwards-Groves, C. with Murray, C. (2008). Enabling voice: Perceptions of schooling from rural Aboriginal youth at risk of entering the juvenile justice system. *The Australian Journal of Indigenous Education*, *37*(1), 165–177. https://doi.org/10.1017/S1326011100016203

Fagan, A. A., & Catalano, R. F. (2013). What works in youth violence prevention: A review of the literature. *Research on Social Work Practice*, *23*(2), 141–156. https://doi.org/10.1177/1049731512465899

Fain, T., Greathouse, S. M., Turner, S. F., & Weinberg, H. D. (2014). Effectiveness of multisystemic therapy for minority youth: Outcomes over 8 years in Los Angeles County. *Journal of Juvenile Justice*, *3*(2), 24.

Farrell, A. D., & Flannery, D. J. (2006). Youth violence prevention: Are we there yet? *Aggression and Violent Behavior*, *11*(2), 138–150. https://doi.org/10.1016/j.avb.2005.07.008

Fazal, S. M. (2014). *Safely home: Reducing youth incarceration and achieving positive youth outcomes for high and complex need youth through effective community-based programs*. Youth Advocate Programs Policy & Advocacy Centre. https://chronicleofsocialchange.org/publication/safely-home-reducing-youth-incarceration/7344

Fazel, S., Doll, H., & Långström, N. (2008). Mental disorders among adolescents in juvenile detention and correctional facilities: A systematic review and metaregression analysis of 25 surveys. *Journal of the American Academy of Child & Adolescent Psychiatry*, *47*(9), 1010–1019. https://doi.org/10.1097/CHI.0b013e31817eecf3

Ferrito, M., Needs, A., & Adshead, G. (2017). Unveiling the shadows of meaning: Meaning-making for perpetrators of homicide. *Aggression and Violent Behavior*, *34*, 263–272. https://doi.org/10.1016/j.avb.2016.11.009

Follette, V. M., & Ruzek, J. I. (2006). *Cognitive-behavioral therapies for trauma* (2nd ed.). Guilford Press.

Frazier, S. N., & Vela, J. (2014). Dialectical behavior therapy for the treatment of anger and aggressive behavior: A review. *Aggression and Violent Behavior*, *19*(2), 156–163. https://doi.org/10.1016/j.avb.2014.02.001

Garrido, V., & Morales, L. A. (2007). Serious (violent or chronic) juvenile offenders: A systematic review of treatment effectiveness in secure corrections. *Campbell Systematic Reviews*, *3*(1), 1–46. https://doi.org/10.1002/CL2.34

Gendreau, P., Little, T., & Goggin, C. (1996). A meta-analysis of the predictors of adult offender recidivism: What works. *Criminology*, *34*(4), 575–608. https://doi.org/10.1111/j.1745-9125.1996.tb01220.x

Gendreau, P., & Ross, R. R. (1987). Revivification of rehabilitation: Evidence from the 1980s. *Justice Quarterly*, *4*(3), 349–407. https://doi.org/10.1080/07418828700089411

Gilbert, F., & Daffern, M. (2010). Integrating contemporary aggression theory with violent offender treatment: How thoroughly do interventions target violent behavior? *Aggression and Violent Behavior*, *15*, 167–180. https://doi.org/10.1016/j.avb.2009.11.003

Gilman, A. B., & Walker, S. C. (2020). Evaluating the effects of an adolescent family violence intervention program on recidivism among court-involved youth. *Journal of Family Violence*, *35*(2), 95–106. https://doi.org/10.1007/s10896-019-00070-2

Glasgow, R. E., Klesges, L. M., Dzewaltowski, D. A., Estabrooks, P. A., & Vogt, T. M. (2006). Evaluating the overall impact of health promotion programs: Using the RE-AIM framework for decision making and to consider complex issues. *Health Education Research*, *21*(5), 688–694. https://doi.org/10.1093/her/cyl081

Glick, B., & Gibbs, J. C. (2010). *Aggression replacement training: A comprehensive intervention for aggressive youth*. Research Press.

Goldstein, A. P., & Glick, B. (2001). Aggression replacement training: Application and evaluation management. In G. A. Bernfeld, D. P. Farrington, & A. W. Leschied (Eds.), *Offender rehabilitation in practice: Implementing and evaluating effective programs* (pp. 121–148). John Wiley & Sons.

Goldstein, A. P., Glick, B., & Gibbs, J. C. (1998). *Aggression replacement training: A comprehensive intervention for aggressive youth* (Rev. Ed.). Research Press.

Gordon, D. A., Arbuthnot, J., Gustafson, K. E., & McGreen, P. (1988). Home-based behavioral-systems family therapy with disadvantaged juvenile delinquents. *American Journal of Family Therapy*, *16*(3), 243–255. https://doi.org/10.1080/01926188808250729

Gray, P., & Smith, R. (2021). Shifting sands: The reconfiguration of neoliberal youth penality. *Theoretical Criminology*, *25*(2), 304–324. https://doi.org/10.1177/1362480619872262

Greenwood, P. W. (2006). *Changing lives: Delinquency prevention as crime-control policy*. University of Chicago Press. https://doi.org/10.7208/chicago/9780226307237.001.0001

Gueta, K., Chen, G., & Ronel, N. (2022). Trauma-oriented recovery framework with offenders: A necessary missing link in offenders' rehabilitation. *Aggression and Violent Behavior*, *63*, Article 101678. https://doi.org/10.1016/j.avb.2021.101678

Hahn, R., Fuqua-Whitley, D., Wethington, H., Lowy, J., Crosby, A., Fullilove, M., Johnson, R., Liberman, A., Moscicki, E., Price, L., Snyder, S., Tuma, F., Cory, S., Stone, G., Mukhopadhaya, K., Chattopadhyay, S., Dahlberg, L., & Task Force on Community Preventive Services. (2007). Effectiveness of universal school-based programs to prevent violent and aggressive behavior: A systematic review. *American Journal of Preventive Medicine*, *33*(2), S114–S129. https://doi.org/10.1016/j.amepre.2007.04.012

Harvey, A. R. (1997). Group work with African-American youth in the criminal justice system: A culturally competent model. In G. L. Grief & R. H. Ephross (Eds.), *Group work with populations at risk* (pp. 160–174). Oxford University Press.

Hatcher, R., McGuire, J., Bilby, C., Palmer, E., & Hollin, C. (2012). Methodological considerations in the evaluation of offender interventions: The problem of attrition. *International Journal of Offender Therapy and Comparative Criminology*, *56*, 447–464. https://doi.org/10.1177/0306624X11403271

Hatcher, R., & Palmer, E. (2008). Aggression replacement training with adult male offenders within community settings: A reconviction analysis. *The Journal of Forensic Psychiatry & Psychology*, *19*, 517–532. https://doi.org/10.1080/14789940801936407

Henggeler, S. W., Melton, G. B., & Smith, L. A. (1992). Family preservation using multisystemic therapy: An effective alternative to incarcerating serious juvenile offenders. *Journal of Consulting and Clinical Psychology*, *60*(6), 953–961. https://doi.org/10.1037/0022-006X.60.6.953

Herrenkohl, T. I., Huang, B., Kosterman, R., Hawkins, J. D., Catalano, R. F., & Smith, B. H. (2001). A comparison of social development processes leading to violent behavior in late adolescence for childhood initiators and adolescent initiators of violence. *Journal of Research in Crime and Delinquency*, *38*, 45–63. https://doi.org/10.1177/0022427801038001003

Hodgson, D. (2018). Disciplining the conduct of young people in compulsory education policy and practice. *Discourse: Studies in the Cultural Politics of Education*, *39*(1), 1–14. https://doi.org/10.1080/01596306.2016.1160031

Hollin, C. R. (1999). Treatment programs for offenders: Meta-analysis, "what works," and beyond. *International Journal of Law and Psychiatry*, *22*(3–4), 361–372. https://doi.org/10.1016/S0160-2527(99)00015-1

Holmqvist, R., Hill, T., & Lang, A. (2009). Effects of aggression replacement training in young offender institutions. *International Journal of Offender*

Therapy and Comparative Criminology, *53*(1), 74–92. https://doi.org/10.1177/0306624X07310452

Hough, M. (2010). Gold standard or fool's gold: The pursuit of certainty in experimental criminology. *Criminology Criminal Justice*, *10*(1), 11–22. https://doi.org/10.1177/1748895809352597

Howell, J. C. (2003). *Preventing and reducing juvenile delinquency: A comprehensive framework*. SAGE Publications.

Howells, K., & Day, A. (2003). Readiness for anger management: Clinical and theoretical issues. *Clinical Psychology Review*, *23*(2), 319–337. https://doi.org/10.1016/S0272-7358(02)00228-3

Izzo, R. L., & Ross, R. R. (1990). Meta-analysis of rehabilitation programs for juvenile delinquents: A brief report. *Criminal Justice and Behavior*, *17*, 134–142. https://doi.org/10.1177/0093854890017001008

Jenkins, A. (2009). *Becoming ethical: A parallel, political journey with men who have abused*. Russell House Publishing.

Jennings, W. G., Piquero, A. R., & Reingle, J. M. (2012). On the overlap between victimization and offending: A review of the literature. *Aggression and Violent Behavior*, *17*(1), 16–26. https://doi.org/10.1016/j.avb.2011.09.003

Jolliffe, D., Farrington, D. P., & Howard, P. (2013). How long did it last? A 10-year reconviction follow-up study of high intensity training for young offenders. *Journal of Experimental Criminology*, *9*, 515–531.

Kemshall, H., & Wilkinson, B. (2015). *What works in work with violent offenders: An overview*. https://dora.dmu.ac.uk/bitstream/handle/2086/12145/Kemshall_et_al_What_Works_in_Work_Overview_2015.pdf

Kerig, P. K., & Becker, S. P. (2010). From internalizing to externalizing: Theoretical models of the processes linking PTSD to juvenile delinquency. In S. J. Egan (Ed.), *Posttraumatic stress disorder (PTSD): Causes, symptoms and treatment* (pp. 33–78). Nova Science Publishers.

Kim, S. Y. (2013). Efficacy versus effectiveness. *Korean Journal of Family Medicine*, *34*(4), 227. https://doi.org/10.4082/kjfm.2013.34.4.227

Kohlberg, L. (1973). Stages and aging in moral development – some speculations. *The Gerontologist*, *13*(4), 497–502. https://doi.org/10.1093/geront/13.4.497

Kowalski, M. A. (2019). Adverse childhood experiences and justice-involved youth: The effect of trauma and programming on different recidivistic outcomes. *Youth Violence and Juvenile Justice*, *17*(4), 354–384. https://doi.org/10.1177/15412040188098

Leve, L. D., Chamberlain, P., & Kim, H. K. (2015). Risks, outcomes, and evidence-based interventions for girls in the US juvenile justice system. *Clinical Child and Family Psychology Review*, *18*, 252–279. https://doi.org/10.1007/s10567-015-0186-6

Linehan, M. M. (1993). *Skills training manual for treating borderline personality disorder*. Guilford Press.

Lipsey, M. W. (2007). *A standardized program evaluation protocol for programs serving juvenile probationers*. Vanderbilt University.

Lipsey, M. W. (2009). The primary factors that characterize effective interventions with juvenile offenders: A meta-analytic overview. *Victims and Offenders*, *4*(2), 124–147. https://doi.org/10.1080/15564880802612573

Lipsey, M. W., Landenberger, N. A., & Wilson, S. J. (2007). Effects of cognitive-behavioral programs for criminal offenders. *Campbell Systematic Reviews*, *3*(1), 1–27. https://doi.org/10.1002/CL2.42

Littell, J. H., Popa, M., & Forsythe, B. (2005). Multisystemic therapy for social, emotional, and behavioral problems in youth aged 10–17. *Campbell Systematic Reviews*, *1*(1), 1–63. https://doi.org/10.4073/csr.2005.1

Lohmeyer, B. A., & McGregor, J. R. (2022). A critical examination of Australian youth case management: Compounding governing spaces and infantilising self-management. *Journal of Youth Studies*, *25*(4), 530–546. https://doi.org/10.1080/13676261.2021.1910222

Lopes, J., Flouris, A., & Lindeman, M. A. (2013). Youth development programs in Central Australian Aboriginal communities: A review of the literature. *Youth Studies Australia*, *32*(1), 55–62.

Malvaso, C. G., Cale, J., Whitten, T., Day, A., Singh, S., Hackett, L., Delfabbro, P. H., & Ross, S. (2022). Associations between adverse childhood experiences and trauma among young people who offend: A systematic literature review. *Trauma, Violence, & Abuse*, *23*(5), 1677–1694. https://doi.org/10.1177/15248380211013132

Marshall, W. L., Marshall, L. E., & Olver, M. E. (2017). An evaluation of strength-based approaches to the treatment of sex offenders: A review. *Journal of Criminal Psychology*, *7*(3), 221–228. https://doi.org/10.1108/JCP-04-2017-0021

Martinson, R. (1974). What works? Questions and answers about prison reform. *The Public Interest*, *35*, 22–54.

Mason, P., & Prior, D. (2008). *Keeping young people engaged: Source document*. Youth Justice Board.

Matjasko, J. L., Vivolo-Kantor, A. M., Massetti, G. M., Holland, K. M., Holt, M. K., & Cruz, J. D. (2012). A systematic meta-review of evaluations of youth violence prevention programs: Common and divergent findings from 25 years of meta-analyses and systematic reviews. *Aggression and Violent Behavior*, *17*(6), 540–552. https://doi.org/10.1016/j.avb.2012.06.006

McCall, D., Luu, X., Krogh, C., Phelan, L., Dempsey, A., Acosta, C., Marshall, F., Svejkar, D., Pruscino, C., & Beres, M. A. (2023). A comparative account of institutional approaches to addressing campus-based sexual violence in Australia and Aotearoa New Zealand. *Violence Against Women*, 1–28. Online first. https://journals.sagepub.com/doi/abs/10.1177/10778012231183654

McCallum, D. (2009). Punishing welfare: Genealogies of child abuse. *Griffith Law Review*, *18*(1), 114–128.

McGregor, J. R. (2017). Case management and post-release young people. *Journal of Applied Youth Studies*, *2*(2), 47–60.

McGuinness, A., Tuohy, M., & Rowney, R. (2017). *Youth justice: Effective practice guide*. Noetic Group. https://noeticgroup.com/youth-justice-effective-practice-guide/

McGuire, J. (Ed.). (1995). *What works: Reducing reoffending*. John Wiley & Sons.

McGuire, J. (2008). A review of effective interventions for reducing aggression and violence. *Philosophical Transactions: Biological Sciences*, *363*(1503), 2577–2597. https://doi.org/10.1098/rstb.2008.0035

McIvor, G., Trotter, C., & Sheehan, R. (2009). Women, resettlement and desistance. *Probation Journal*, *56*(4), 347–361. https://doi.org/10.1177/0264550509346515

McNeil, F., & Weaver, B. (2010). *Changing lives: Desistance research and offender management*. www.sccjr.ac.uk/pubs/Changing-Lives-Desistance-Research-and-Offender-Management/255

Mercy, J., Butchart, A., Farringdon, D. P., & Cerda, M. (2002). Youth violence. In E. Krug, L. L. Dalberg, J. A. Mercy, A. B. Zwi, & R. Lozano (Eds.), *World report on violence and health* (pp. 25–56). World Health Organization.

Messiah, A. P., & Johnson, E. J. (2017). Social work intervention in adolescent-to-parent abuse. *Journal of Human Behavior in the Social Environment*, *27*(3), 187–197. https://doi.org/10.1080/10911359.2016.1270868

Milkman, H., & Wanberg, K. (2007). *Cognitive-behavioral treatment: A review and discussion for corrections professionals*. National Institute of Corrections.

Moulds, L. G., Malvaso, C., Hackett, L., & Francis, L. (2019). The kind program for adolescent family and dating violence. *Australian and New Zealand Journal of Family Therapy*. https://doi.org/10.1002/anzf.1364

Mytton, J. A., DiGuiseppi, C., Gough, D., Taylor, R. S., & Logan, S. (2006). School-based secondary prevention programmes for preventing violence. *Cochrane Database of Systematic Reviews*, *3*. https://doi.org/10.1002/14651858.CD004606.pub2

Novaco, R. W. (1975). *Anger control: The development and evaluation of an experimental treatment*. Lexington.

O'Connor, R. M., & Waddell, S. (2015). *What works to prevent gang involvement, youth violence and crime: A Rapid Review of Interventions Delivered in the UK and Abroad*. Early Intervention Foundation.

Paterson, R., Luntz, H., Perlesz, A., & Cotton, S. (2002). Adolescent violence towards parents: Maintaining family connections when the going gets tough. *Australian & New Zealand Journal of Family Therapy*, *23*(2), 90–100. https://doi.org/10.1002/j.1467-8438.2002.tb00493

Pawson, R., Tilley, N., & Tilley, N. (1997). *Realistic evaluation*. SAGE Publications.

Petrosino, A., Turpin-Petrosino, C., & Buehler, J. (2005). "Scared straight" and other juvenile awareness programmes for preventing juvenile delinquency. *Campbell Collaboration Systematic Review*, *1*(1). https://doi.org/10.4073/csr.2004.2

Petrosino, A., Turpin-Petrosino, C., Hollis-Peel, M. E., & Lavenberg, J. G. (2013). Scared straight and other juvenile awareness programs for preventing juvenile delinquency: A systematic review. *Campbell Systematic Reviews*, *9*(1), 1–55. https://doi.org/10.4073/csr.2013.5

Pfitzner, N., Ollis, D., Stewart, R., Allen, K. A., Fitz-Gibbon, K., & Flynn, A. (2022). *Respectful relationships education in Australian: National stocktake and gap analysis of respectful relationships education material and resources final report*. Monash Gender and Family Violence Prevention Centre.

Pitts, J. (2003). *The new politics of youth crime*. Palgrave Macmillan.

Polaschek, D. L. (2012). An appraisal of the risk – need – responsivity (RNR) model of offender rehabilitation and its application in correctional treatment.

Legal and Criminological Psychology, *17*(1), 1–17. https://doi.org/10.1111/j.2044-8333.2011.02038.x
Polaschek, D. L., & Reynolds, N. (2004). Assessment and treatment: Violent offenders. In C. R. Hollin (Ed.), *The essential handbook of offender assessment and treatment* (pp. 201–218). John Wiley & Sons.
Pooley, K. (2020). *What are the characteristics of effective youth offender programs?* (Trends and Issues in Crime and Criminal Justice No. 604). Australian Institute of Criminology. https://doi.org/10.52922/ti04701
Prescott, D. S. (2013). Principles and programs for young offenders. *Resource Material Series*, *91*, 69–79.
Prior, D., & Mason, P. (2010). A different kind of evidence? Looking for "what works" in engaging young offenders. *Youth Justice*, *10*(3), 211–226. https://doi.org/10.1177/1473225410381688
Quinn, A., & Shera, W. (2009). Evidence-based practice in group work with incarcerated youth. *International Journal of Law and Psychiatry*, *32*(5), 288–293. https://doi.org/10.1016/j.ijlp.2009.06.002
Ralph, A., & Sanders, M. R. (2004). *The "Teen Triple P" positive parenting program: A preliminary evaluation* (Trends and Issues in Crime and Criminal Justice No. 282). Australian Institute of Criminology.
Richards, K., Rosevear, L., & Gilbert, R. (2011). *Promising interventions for reducing Indigenous juvenile offending*. Indigenous Justice Clearinghouse, Australian Institute of Criminology.
Saleebey, D. (1996). The strengths perspective in social work practice: Extensions and cautions. *Social Work*, *41*(3), 296–305.
Sampson, A., & Themelis, S. (2009). Working in the community with young people who offend. *Journal of Youth Studies*, *12*(2), 121–137. https://doi.org/10.1080/13676260802558854
Sampson, R. J. (2010). Gold standard myths: Observations on the experimental turn in quantitative criminology. *Journal of Quantitative Criminology*, *26*(4), 489–500. https://doi.org/10.1007/s10940-010-9117-3
Sapouna, M., Bisset, C., & Conlong, A.-M. (2011). *What works to reduce reoffending: A summary of the evidence – Justice analytical services – Scottish government*. https://digital.nls.uk/pubs/scotgov/2015/9781785443336.pdf
Schaeffer, C. M., & Borduin, C. M. (2005). Long-term follow-up to a randomized clinical trial of multisystemic therapy with serious and violent juvenile offenders. *Journal of Consulting and Clinical Psychology*, *73*, 445–453. https://doi.org/10.1037/0022-006X.73.3.445
Schaffner, L. (2006). *Girls in trouble with the law*. Rutgers University Press.
Sexton, T., & Turner, C. W. (2010). The effectiveness of functional family therapy for youth with behavioral problems in a community practice setting. *Journal of Family Psychology*, *24*(3), 339–348. https://doi.org/10.1037/a0019406
Shingler, J. (2004). A process of cross-fertilization: What sex offender treatment can learn from dialectical behaviour therapy. *Journal of Sexual Aggression*, *10*(2), 171–180. https://doi.org/10.1080/13552600412331289050
Sindicich, N., Mills, K. L., Barrett, E. L., Indig, D., Sunjic, S., Sannibale, C., Rosenfeld, J., & Najavits, L. M. (2014). Offenders as victims: Post-traumatic stress disorder and substance use disorder among male prisoners. *The Journal*

of Forensic Psychiatry & Psychology, *25*(1), 44–60. https://doi.org/10.1080/14789949.2013.877516

Sood, A. B., & Berkowitz, S. J. (2016). Prevention of youth violence: A public health approach. *Child and Adolescent Psychiatric Clinics*, *25*(2), 243–256. https://doi.org/10.1016/j.chc.2015.11.004

Stallman, H. M., & Ralph, A. (2007). Reducing risk factors for adolescent behavioral and emotional problems: A pilot randomised controlled trial of a self-administered parenting intervention. *Australian E-Journal for the Advancement of Mental Health*, 6(2), 125–137. https://doi.org/10.5172/jamh.6.2.125

Stringfellow, R., Tauri, J., & Richards, K. (2022). *Prevention and early intervention programs for Indigenous young people in Australia and Aotearoa New Zealand*. Indigenous Justice Clearinghouse, Australian Institute of Criminology.

Sundell, K., Hansson, K., Löfholm, C. A., Olsson, T., Gustle, L. H., & Kadesjö, C. (2008). The transportability of multisystemic therapy to Sweden: Short-term results from a randomized trial of conduct-disordered youths. *Journal of Family Psychology*, *22*(4), 550–560. https://doi.org/10.1037/a0012790

Tolan, P., Henry, D., Schoeny, M., & Bass, A. (2008). Mentoring interventions to affect juvenile delinquency and associated problems. *Campbell Systematic Reviews*, *4*(1), 1–112. https://doi.org/10.4073/csr.2008.16

Toumbourou, J. W., & Gregg, M. E. (2002). Impact of an empowerment-based parent education program on the reduction of youth suicide risk factors. *Journal of Adolescent Health*, *31*(3), 277–285. https://doi.org/10.1016/S1054-139X(02)00384-1

Trotter, C. (2006). *Working with involuntary clients: A guide to practice* (2nd ed.). SAGE Publications.

Trotter, C. (2013). Reducing recidivism through probation supervision: What we know and don't know from four decades of research. *Federal Probation*, *77*(2), 43–46.

Tyler, N., Heffernan, R., & Fortune, C. A. (2020). Reorienting locus of control in individuals who have offended through strengths-based interventions: Personal agency and the good lives model. *Frontiers in Psychology*, *11*, Article 553240. https://doi.org/10.3389/fpsyg.2020.553240

University of Colorado. (2014, December 15). *Providing a registry of experimentally proven programs*. Blueprints for Healthy Youth Development. www.blueprintsprograms.org

Vitacco, M. J., Neumann, C. S., & Caldwell, M. F. (2010). Predicting antisocial behavior in high-risk male adolescents: Contributions of psychopathy and instrumental violence. *Criminal Justice and Behavior*, *37*(8), 833–846. https://doi.org/10.1177/0093854810371358

Wagner, D. V., Borduin, C. M., Sawyer, A. M., & Dopp, A. R. (2014). Long-term prevention of criminality in siblings of serious and violent juvenile offenders: A 25-year follow-up to a randomized clinical trial of multisystemic therapy. *Journal of Consulting and Clinical Psychology*, *82*(3), 492–499. https://doi.org/10.1037/a0035624

Wainwright, L., & Nee, C. (2014). The good lives model – new directions for preventative practice with children? *Psychology, Crime & Law*, *20*(2), 166–182. https://doi.org/10.1080/1068316X.2013.770851

Ward, T., & Gannon, T. A. (2006). Rehabilitation, etiology, and self-regulation: The comprehensive good lives model of treatment for sexual offenders. *Aggression and Violent Behavior*, *11*(1), 77–94. https://doi.org/10.1016/j.avb.2005.06.001

Ward, T., & Maruna, S. (Eds.). (2007). *Rehabilitation: Key ideas in criminology*. https://doi.org/10.4324/9780203962176

Warren, E. A., Melendez-Torres, G. J., & Bonell, C. (2022). Are realist randomised controlled trials possible? A reflection on the INCLUSIVE evaluation of a whole-school, bullying-prevention intervention. *Trials*, *23*(1), 82–92. https://doi.org/10.1186/s13063-021-05976-1

Weisz, A. N., & Black, B. M. (2009). *Programs to reduce teen dating violence and sexual assault: Perspectives on what works*. Columbia University Press.

Welsh, B. C., Braga, A. A., & Sullivan, C. J. (2014). Serious youth violence and innovative prevention: On the emerging link between public health and criminology. *Justice Quarterly*, *31*(3), 500–523. https://doi.org/10.1080/07418825.2012.690441

Welsh, B. C., & Rocque, M. (2014). When crime prevention harms: A review of systematic reviews. *Journal of Experimental Criminology*, *10*, 245–266. https://doi.org/10.1007/s11292-014-9199-2

Wilson, D. B., MacKenzie, D. L., & Mitchell, F. N. (2005). Effects of correctional boot camps on offending. *Campbell Collaboration Systematic Review*, *1*(1). https://doi.org/10.4073/csr.2005.6

Wilson, S. J., & Lipsey, M. W. (2007). School-based interventions for aggressive and disruptive behavior: Update of a meta-analysis. *American Journal of Preventive Medicine*, *33*(2), S130–S143. https://doi.org/10.1016/j.amepre.2007.04.011

Witkiewitz, K., Marlatt, G. A., & Walker, D. (2005). Mindfulness-based relapse prevention for alcohol and substance use disorders. *Journal of Cognitive Psychotherapy*, *19*(3), 211–228. https://doi.org/10.1891/JCOP.2005.19.3.211

Wolff, N., Huening, J., Shi, J., Frueh, B. C., Hoover, D. R., & McHugo, G. (2015). Implementation and effectiveness of integrated trauma and addiction treatment for incarcerated men. *Journal of Anxiety Disorders*, *30*, 66–80. https://doi.org/10.1016/j.janxdis.2014.10.009

World Health Organization. (2015). *Preventing youth violence: An overview of the evidence*. World Health Organization.

Zettler, H. R. (2021). Much to do about trauma: A systematic review of existing trauma-informed treatments on youth violence and recidivism. *Youth Violence and Juvenile Justice*, *19*(1), 113–134. https://doi.org/10.1177/1541204020939645

4 The Name.Narrate. Navigate (NNN) program

Louise Rak, Tamara Blakemore, Graeme Stuart, Chris Krogh, and Shaun McCarthy

The Name.Narrate.Navigate program

This book uses the Name.Narrate.Navigate (NNN) program as a case study to explore social work and human service practice with young people who use and experience violence. This chapter describes the program, sketching its development, core components, and theory, and outlines its embedded action research strategy. It starts by describing the program and the community-based participatory research frame integral to its design and continuous improvement and ends with an outline of data collection and analysis methods and evaluation findings.

Program description

The Name.Narrate.Navigate (NNN) program has evolved as a community-engaged response to an unmet need for trauma-informed and culturally safe interventions for young people who use and experience violence and for accessible specialist training for workers who support them. NNN has a dual focus on working with young people and practitioners, towards mutual goals of self-awareness, self-regulation, and skills for connection. The program encompasses:

- **NNN for Young People:** a group work program for young people aged 12–18 who have used and experienced violence.
- **NNN Practice Pathways:** a professional education and training program for practitioners who work with youth violence.
- **Now.See.Hear:** a project focused on the development of trauma-informed and culturally safe resources and tools for working with youth violence.
- **Ongoing research and evaluation:** involving young people, social service sector stakeholders and practitioners, Aboriginal Elders, and community members.

DOI: 10.4324/9781003177883-4

This book is focused on the NNN program for young people. Hereafter where we refer to NNN or 'the program', we are (except where noted) referring to our work with young people who use and experience violence. We refer to NNN as a (new) way of working with youth violence that is trauma-informed and recognises the value of reflexive and relational practice, grounded in an ethic of care, shared power, and reciprocity, consistent with Aboriginal ways of knowing and doing. It recognises the prevalence of trauma in the lives of justice-involved young people (Dierkhising et al., 2013) and the over-representation of Aboriginal young people in criminal justice populations (Baidawi, 2020),

NNN respects the intrinsic fit between what is needed to heal from trauma and Aboriginal knowledges and ways of doing that prioritise relationship, connection, and story. The program emphasises cultural safety, recognising it acknowledges power imbalances exist between workers and Aboriginal and Torres Strait Islander young people (Browne & Fiske, 2001). The program embraces cultural safety as a way of ensuring the effects of colonisation are understood when we are working with young people's use and experience of violence. A culturally safe lens helps centre our understanding of young people's violence in the narratives of young people while unpacking social constructions of identity, culture, and Othering. Cultural safety also encompasses how we, as professionals, use reflexive awareness of both our own cultures and the cultures of others, how these assumptions are shaped, and how this and assumptions contribute to our practice (Watts, 2019).

Development

With appropriate ethics approval from the Australian Institute of Aboriginal and Torres Strait Islander Studies (AIATSIS), the University of Newcastle (UON), and New South Wales (NSW) Departments of Education and Justice, NNN was developed and is continuously improved through an iterative, reflexive process of community-based participatory research (CBPR). Minkler and Wallerstein (2003) describe CBPR as a continuum of social justice–informed research approaches, ranging from action research through to participatory action research (PAR), with increasing degrees of active and engaged participation across the continuum. Wallerstein et al. (2017) note CBPR is empowering, participatory, and cooperative, engaging researchers and community members in a collaborative process of problem definition and research design that involves co-learning that contributes to capacity building and systems development.

A CBPR approach positions NNN as accountable to and contextualised by a series of interconnecting relationships with a stakeholder consortium including young people with a lived experience of violence, a cultural reference group of Aboriginal Elders and community members, a working party of practitioners who support justice-involved young people, and a steering committee of key sector stakeholders. Developing NNN commenced with a synthesis of existing evidence for and from practice (including the aforementioned Juvenile Justice and Education Equity pilot project), informing increasingly focused consultation with the stakeholder consortium, who were (and continue to be) key contributors to the design and continuous improvement of NNN. They provide practice and lived experience perspectives, ensure local relevance, challenge assumptions, and test content and activities that become part of the program. Their input is captured through regular, facilitated meetings where written and oral data is collected and thematically analysed to inform intersecting feedback loops between separate parties. This process (see Figure 4.1) has assisted collaborative development of a theoretical and conceptual framework for NNN, grounded in understandings and knowledge from multiple perspectives.

Figure 4.1 Practitioner working party members reviewing program activities

Design

NNN is a preventive intervention that addresses known risks while reinforcing and encouraging protective factors related to the self, family, and community. Cox et al. (2016, p. 207) explain preventive interventions can be delivered to everyone in the community through universal programs, to those identified at increased risk through targeted programs, and to those already displaying behaviours through indicated programs. By this metric, NNN is best described as an indicated program, working with young people who have used violence but also applicable to targeted delivery to young people identified as at risk of using violence.

NNN understands youth violence as a contextualised and multi-determined experience. Important to this is recognising how violence is situated in a broader sense including an understanding of the presence and role of violence in community life, noting young people's use of violence rarely occurs in isolation of other violence and offending (Bromfield et al., 2007). It also involves attention to possible gendered differences in motivations for violence. Work by Warton (2020) and Staff and Kreager (2008) suggests disenfranchised young men from areas of less advantage may connect with peers and antisocial behaviours, including violence, for belonging and acceptance. This is like the work of Blakemore et al. (2018) that indicates young people's use of violence may intersect with identity while also having links to community, place, relationality, gender, and trauma. When considering how female use of violence is conceptualised, it is important to factor in the evolution and historical perspectives of how and why young women use violence (Blakemore et al., 2021). Historically and in public discourse, women's use of violence has been associated with narratives of lack and deficit, where women have been viewed as not being feminine or not meeting society's ideal or where their violence is only due to perceived victimisation (Boxall et al., 2020; Chesney-Lind & Eliason, 2006). Common to these understandings is the compelling role of trauma in the lives and experiences of young women in their use of violence (Swan et al., 2008).

When thinking about the design of NNN, we reflected on what we saw in our own practice, what we were told by practitioners in our pilot study (see Blakemore et al., 2018, 2019), and what emerged from consultations with the NNN stakeholder consortium. As a starting point, we understood that many young people who use and experience violence often find themselves subject to many referrals to different supports but often seem to lack real engagement with these service offers. We started to think about what authentic engagement would look like for a service provider and what it would require of justice-involved young people. We contemplated the often taken-for-granted indicators of engagement in most service contexts – things like behavioural norms of punctuality and being articulate, self-aware, well-regulated, and willing and able to engage in the back and forth of polite conversation in a client–worker context. We pondered whether and how the impact(s) of trauma might interact with any reliable display of these indicators of engagement and wondered whether it was just a case of services needing to do things differently. While this temptingly simple solution might have some validity, we also recognised that the skills young people use to successfully engage with services transfer across situations and settings over the course of their lives. We wondered then whether there was an imperative for situating a preventive intervention that bridged the gap to positive engagement in specialist recidivist-focused interventions by addressing what we identified as "readiness" skills. We were clear that we did not see NNN as replacing ongoing casework or specialist programs; but, instead, we saw it as a way of working that would support young people to a point of readiness by strengthening their skills for self-awareness, self-regulation, and connection.

Theory of change

The theory of change associated with a program or intervention maps a picture of a desired change, why and how that change may occur, and the contexts which situate change (Davis et al., 2015). Working from a trauma-informed and culturally sensitive ethos, the theory of change underpinning NNN recognises that young people need skills to recognise, regulate, and communicate emotions and needs; empathy to respond to others and themselves; an understanding of power, control, and shame; and an opportunity to explore what positive choice might look like in their lives. NNN suggests new knowledge, skills, and behaviours and greater confidence as well as coping and connection that can improve life circumstances, wellbeing, and safety. The aim of the NNN program is to enhance these factors to drive and sustain change towards better, safer outcomes. The theory of change for NNN is presented in Figure 4.2.

Informing evidence base

NNN is informed by a broad body of evidence-based learning and practice approaches, including Kolb's (2015) experiential learning model, universal design learning (UDL) (Rose & Meyer, 2006), dialectical behaviour therapy (DBT) (Linehan, 2015), and Photovoice (Fitzgibbon & Stengel, 2018; Fitzgibbon & Healy, 2019; Wang, 1999). NNN embeds experiential learning throughout program activities and conversations, both guided and organic. Experiential learning (Kolb, 2015)

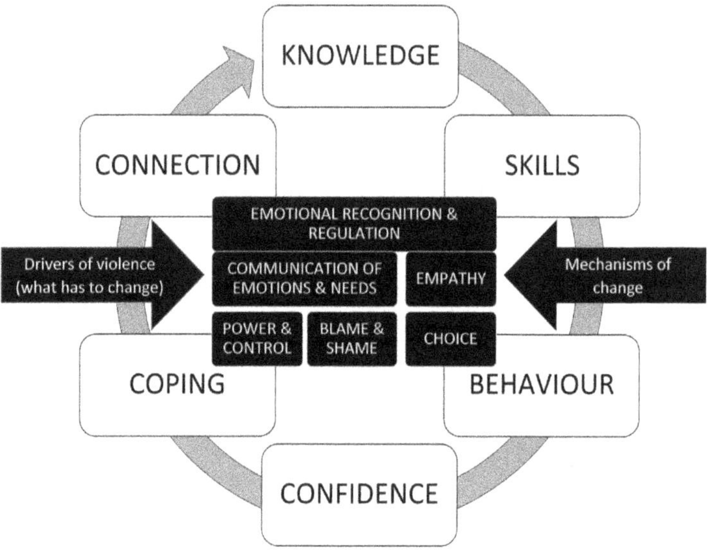

Figure 4.2 NNN theory of change

privileges lived experience and the understanding of concepts, ideas, and new knowledges through active engagement with learning "triggers". NNN presents different and engaging stimuli for learning, actively engages with these learning objects or examples, and reflects on ideas, knowledge, and experience. Experiential learning models are appropriate for young people and people with lower literacy levels as it prefaces practical application over literacy (George et al., 2015).

NNN minimises a reliance on dominant literacies by focusing instead on expression and exploration as a way of knowing and being known. It foregrounds the importance of story, visual representation, and creative methods to explore concepts, experiences, meaning, and impact. The program is informed in design, facilitation, and evaluation by concepts of universal design learning (UDL) (Rose, 2000), which centres on principles of engaging learners through many pathways, having many modes of representation of information, and including multiple ways learners can express themselves through their learning. UDL rejects positivist and individualist understandings of educational breakdown, suggesting that rigid learning environments are the issue and not the individual (Karger & Currie-Rubin, 2013). UDL has been used with justice-involved young people and identified as a promising way to change the way they learn and engage with education (Karger & Currie-Rubin, 2013).

Likewise identified for its potential value in use with justice-involved cohorts is dialectical behaviour therapy (DBT) (Edwards et al., 2022; Fox et al., 2020; Shelton et al., 2011). DBT is a cognitive-behavioural intervention that strengthens skills for communication, self-regulation, and relationships (Linehan, 2015; Mazza et al., 2016). DBT has been found effective in work with people experiencing a wide range of mental health conditions and across inpatient and community settings (Bradley & Follingstad, 2003; Iverson et al., 2009; Nelson-Gray et al., 2006; Shelton et al., 2009). Most informative to the design and delivery of NNN has been components of the DBT skills training program and the concepts and techniques of reciprocal communication and mindfulness. As discussed in following sections of this chapter, these techniques have been helpful in engaging young people in ways that draw attention to and strengthen reflective dialogue about self-awareness and self-regulation.

Also helpful in eliciting narratives and stimulating dialogue is the use of creative methods including photo elicitation (Harper, 2002) and Photovoice (Wang & Burris, 1997). As both a method of intervention and a tool of research, Photovoice involves a combination of photography and focus group discussions to gain rich, multidimensional understandings of social phenomena (Fitzgibbon & Healy, 2019). Photovoice and relatedly therapeutic photography (Loewenthal, 2013) have been used effectively with justice-involved young people to safely share their experiences and stories, increasing self-awareness and skills for self-reflection (Fitzgibbon & Stengel, 2018; Halkola, 2013). Photovoice is noted to be a culturally safe way of working with Aboriginal communities (Adams et al., 2012; Brooks & Poudrier, 2014; Moffitt & Vollman, 2004) because of its synergies with storytelling and how in method and application it attempts to redistribute and equalise power relations between and among participants and practitioners (Creighton et al., 2018). Our commitment to Photovoice is sustained by its trauma-informed and culturally safe ethos and its transformative potential for those involved (Budig et al., 2018).

The NNN program for young people

The following sections outline the who, what, where, how, and why of the NNN program for young people, detailing program specifics, program practice principles, and core components of the program.

Program specifics

The NNN program for young people was designed for young people aged 12–18 years who have experienced violence *and* are identified as having used or being at risk of using violence in their relationships with others. NNN was initially piloted with 112 young people during 2019–2021. These young people were referred by case managers in justice (n=47) and school personnel education (n=65). Roughly equal numbers of participants in this pilot phase identified with either the male or female gender and almost 40% identified as Aboriginal. The program was evaluated in 2021 (Rayment-McHugh et al., 2021) and has continued to be delivered in schools and with justice-involved young people in both community and incarcerated settings.

When we present information about the NNN program to service providers and academic partners, we are often asked about the age range of young people involved. Three key factors have underpinned our decisions thus far to work with young people aged 12–18 years. These include considerations of developmental stage and identity formation, the interaction between this and increasing independence of movement and engagement with potentially antisocial associations or activities, and the likelihood of increasingly engaged responses by the justice system to these activities. The work of Rak and Warton (2023) identifies that early to mid-adolescence, regardless of gender, is an important period in which young people form and develop key relationships with peers and their community which have the potential to contribute to personal and criminal identity formation. This intersects with justice system responses to young people, including the application of the legal provisions *doli incapax* and the assessment of age of criminal responsibility (Sheehan & Baidawi, 2022).

The aim and intent of the NNN program for young people is to increase self-awareness, self-regulation, and skills for connection through psychoeducation and skill development. It is typically delivered as eight weekly sessions (see Table 4.1), facilitated in a safe venue situated in the attendees' community.

The first and last sessions are focused on orientation and review. In these sessions, young people meet with practitioners either individually or with their caseworker or support person. After orientation, participants

Table 4.1 Program structure: Focus of weekly sessions

Program structure	*Session*	*Focus*
		Orientation
	1	Emotions
	2	Voice
	3	Empathy
	4	Power and Control
	5	Shame
	6	Choice
		Review

Table 4.2 Program structure: Weekly session content

Session structure	*Order*	*Focus*
	1	Check in
	2	Brief mindfulness activity
	3	Photo review and theming
	4	New skill content
	5	Photovoice excursion
	6	Postcards to practice
	7	Session feedback
	8	Check out

attend small group sessions lasting from 90 minutes to 2 hours. Groups tend to consist of four to six young people and two practitioners. Group sessions are focused on emotional recognition, invalidation, empathy, power and control, shame, and choice. These factors are thought of as criminogenic needs or drivers of violence. Each group session has a consistent structure (see Table 4.2).

Consistent structure in the delivery of the program helps young people know what to expect week to week. Each session starts and ends with a checking in and out process. This assists practitioners and young people to safely signal how they are feeling week to week. A Post-it note with individual initials is placed next to one of several feeling options. The second activity is always a brief mindfulness activity (discussed further in Chapter 11). These activities change each week and are completed as a group. After this the group reviews photos from the previous week and theme accordingly. New skill content is then delivered and discussed as a group. A Photovoice excursion into the community follows before a shared meal or snack. Then participants complete a "Postcard to Practice" activity (discussed further in Chapter 7) and a session evaluation. After each session, practitioners complete a reflection form, noting changes they've observed or reflections on their own practice for follow-up. At the end of the group program, practitioners try to send young people personalised postcards reflecting on what they've learned, valued, and appreciated from working with them.

Practice principles

As NNN practitioners, we use a deeply relational approach, validating trauma while recognising consequences of violence, supporting mindful engagement, and emphasising power *with* young people while supporting new skills and knowledge for improved safety and wellbeing. Five practice principles summarise "how" we work in NNN and are discussed here.

Reciprocal communication

A distinguishing feature of NNN is its commitment to reciprocal communication (Turney, 2012). Most often associated with DBT, reciprocal communication asks practitioners to deeply listen to the people they are working alongside and to be contemplative and vulnerable in sharing aspects of their own stories (Cargo & Mercer, 2008; Ledwith & Springett, 2010; Linehan, 2015). Reciprocal communication involves responsiveness, self-disclosure, warm engagement, and genuineness (Linehan, 2015). It requires practitioners to make themselves vulnerable to the young people we work with and express this vulnerability in ways that can be heard and understood by them. Reciprocity is in the service of the young people we work with, not for the benefit of the practitioner. Sometimes when we talk to practitioners about our use of reciprocal communication it raises questions about boundaries and personal safety in the work. We suggest that our skills in self-awareness, self-regulation, and trauma-informed and culturally safe connection underpin the relational way that we work in NNN. These skills involve appreciating difference and deeply hearing the experience of the other. Reciprocal communication skills aid balancing power between parties and in establishing conditions for open dialogue and exchange.

In DBT, it is often noted that reciprocal communication is usefully balanced with irreverent communication, which focuses on curiosity, frankness, and humour in engaging as a co-learner in the process (Linehan, 2015). In practice, NNN practitioners use both reciprocal and frank irreverent communication, with an emphasis on the former to elicit reflective discussion about ideas, concepts, and experiences. Steeped in ideas of critical reflexivity, reciprocal communication demands practitioners acknowledge how their own histories, trauma, and past interweave with (Linehan, 2015) and influence their practice (Ledwith & Springett, 2010). Reciprocal communication requires practitioners to be contemplative and self-disclose to induce deeper learning and connection (Linehan, 2015; Pederson, 2015; Sarnat, 2019). Practitioners are not seen as the experts, rather as (optimally) authentic, curious people in the encounter (Linehan, 2015; Pederson, 2015). In NNN, practitioners share their experiences in relation to the skills and concepts being discussed, including feelings that resonate with them. An extended discussion of reciprocal communication is discussed in Chapter 7.

Mindful engagement

NNN embraces mindfulness as a means of building skills for self-regulation in the context of the often-chaotic life circumstances of young people who experience and use violence. Some of us might be familiar with the terms "mindfulness" or "mindful meditation". Definitions of these concepts and what they look like in practice can vary, but consistent with DBT and Linehan (2015), we understand mindfulness to involve focusing your attention on what's happening in the moment without judgement. Mindfulness helps develop self-regulation and self-awareness and reduce symptoms of anxiety and depression. Linehan (2015) pointed to specific evidence of mindfulness helping with emotional regulation (Williams, 2008); distractive, ruminative thoughts and behaviours (Jain et al., 2007); positive emotion (Davidson, 2003); decreased depression and anxiety (Gross et al., 2009; Kabat-Zinn et al., 1992); decreased anger and emotional irritability; confusion and cognitive disorganisation (Speca et al., 2000); and decreased psychological distress and increased wellbeing (Pradhan et al., 2007). A growing body of literature points to the value of mindfulness for justice-involved young people (Evans-Chase, 2015; Himelstein et al., 2012; Owen-Smith et al., 2021; Winters & Beerbower, 2017). In NNN, three different forms of mindful engagement are practiced throughout the program: (1) *participatory mindfulness*: activities that require, or invite, total concentration and involvement; (2) *observatory mindfulness*: activities focused on being aware of and noticing with curiosity things either inside or outside of us, and (3) *descriptive mindfulness*: activities focused on giving voice to what we see and what it means to us while recognising different perspectives and points of view. NNN sessions generally commence with a mindfulness activity. Other aspects of the program, including photo elicitation and Photovoice work, also involve mindfulness. Consistent with the work of Linehan (2015) and Kabat-Zinn (2015), there is a focus across all these activities in staying out of judgement. We focus on practicing noticing, building awareness, but being aware without falling into "black-and-white" thinking and making judgements.

Validation of trauma

Underpinning the principle of validation is a non-judgemental attitude and a genuine desire to better understand, with more sensitivity, the experiences of the young people we work with. An extended discussion of reciprocal communication and (in)validation is discussed in Chapter 7. Consistent with Linehan (2015), validation in our work means acknowledging the experience and perspectives of the young people we work with and acknowledging their perceptions as being true (or at least understandable). In NNN the essence of validation is that often our responses are understandable in the contexts of life circumstance or situation. It does not necessarily mean agreeing with the young people we are working with, and it does not mean that perceptions cannot be questioned. Further, validating trauma does not mean invalidating the consequences of the choices and actions made. This can be a tricky skill to master in practice. Validation can improve our relationships by showing we are listening, reduce negative reactivity, defuse anger, and reduce feeling the need to justify actions (Linehan, 2015). Validation of trauma can help build knowledge that can motivate skill-building and self-awareness for participants in managing distress. Consistent with Linehan (2015), four key practices assist in validating young people's experiences and emotions: (1) demonstrate that you are paying attention by noticing the context of behaviour; (2) without judgement, reflect both feeling and content back to the young person; (3) be attuned to and curious about the needs that might underpin behaviour; and (4) communicate that you are open to trying to understand the contexts that give rise to behaviours, even if you don't agree with them.

Shared power

A central tenet of the NNN "way of working" is that as practitioners we need to be critically aware of our own positionality and power. We recognise that we bring to our practice with young people inherent power by virtue of our role but also our size, age, gender, race, education, and privilege. Being aware of our positionality and power is crucial if our work is to be trauma-informed and culturally safe. The NNN way of working upholds the value of taking a *power with* rather than *power over* approach to our work with young people. We recognise that as practitioners we are often charged with responsibilities that invite us to exercise *power over* the people we work with. This may be in the form of enacting sanctions or consequences but can also include implications of our actions or inactions in advocating for those we work with. There is also the subtle (or not so subtle) invitation in our work to exercise power via our "expert" status in determining what the people we work with need and problem-solving to meet these needs or resolve crises. By contrast, *power with* is shared power that grows out of collaboration and relationships. It is built on respect, mutual support, shared power, solidarity, influence, empowerment, and collaborative decision-making. A *power with* approach can build bridges within groups or across differences (Stuart, 2019) and acknowledges differences in power and attempts to equalise these wherever possible (see Chapter 9 for a more detailed discussion of power).

Skills for connection

Reflecting the theory of change underpinning NNN, there is a focus on building new knowledge, skills, behaviour, confidence, connection, and coping for participants. In NNN this includes emotional recognition and regulation; communicating emotions and needs; improving empathy for others and the self; understanding power, control, and shame; and articulating and exercising positive choice. Encouraged by practitioners, skills for connection develop throughout NNN, both incidentally and by design, through activities, group conversations, shared meals, co-creation, and shared experiences.

Core program components

Core program components are embedded in the consistent structure of each program session. These are discussed next and expanded on in subsequent chapters as noted.

Check-in and check-out

Each group work session starts and finishes with participants and practitioners sharing a check-in and check-out process, using visual and tactile methods. Participants can choose to keep their check-in/check-out anonymous or show their check-in. Participants know that practitioners will check in with them if they select one of the final two options ("I'm having a rough time and need a check-in" or "I'm really struggling") but will do so in a way that's safe and non-identifying. As with all NNN activities, the check-in/check-out board is inclusive of all learning styles and not reliant on written language cues.

Participatory mindfulness

The program includes a key focus on building skills for mindfulness but includes an intentional time in all group sessions where participants engage in participatory mindfulness activities. These involve the young people in activity that requires concentration and sustained focus (see Figure 4.3). As we discuss further in Chapter 11, the participatory mindfulness activities are designed to either raise or drop the heart rate of group members and are deliberately placed within the program to assist uptake of learning and reflection.

Content for experiential learning, knowledge, and skill development

The program generally includes three short activities per group session which engage participants in experiential learning for knowledge development and skill-building. Drawing on Kolb's (2015) model of

Figure 4.3 Participatory mindfulness activity

experiential learning, new knowledge and skill development triggers reflection, contemplation of difference, and new ideas. Experiential learning is used in our session on empathy where participants are asked to reflect on found objects, using them as prompts to guide thinking and understanding themselves and other people in their lives. This activity is explored more in Chapter 8.

Photovoice

Photovoice (Fitzgibbon, 2022; Sutton-Brown, 2014; Wang, 1999) is an important part of the group work sessions in NNN providing valuable insights and data to enhance our understanding of youth violence. Group work sessions (with the exception of the last week) include a photo-making excursion where young people and practitioners take a walking tour of the local area to create photos around themes explored in the session (e.g., take photos of what shame looks like) (see Figure 4.4). The following session starts with inspecting, theming, and adding narratives to the photos taken the session before. This activity

Figure 4.4 Photovoice excursion

engages young people in descriptive and observational mindfulness and models focus and nonjudgemental and curious exploration of a product they've made. Narratives of violence and its key component drivers are elicited through exploration and discussion of the photos created. Photovoice is discussed in more detail in Chapter 6.

Postcards to practice

As a way of modelling reciprocal communication, each session provides young people with the opportunity to contribute a Postcard to Practice – telling practitioners something related to the session's focus they wish adults knew (e.g., "I wish you knew how it feels when . . ."). The Postcard to Practice exercise provides an opportunity for young people to be heard and contribute to discussions on violence, community, identity, and relationships and provides facilitators with new and different insights into the same. The Postcard to Practice process is discussed in detail in Chapter 7.

Session rating scale

Each of the six group sessions ends with the young people completing a paper-based brief session-rating tool, based on an original approach by Miller and Duncan (2000). The young people rate the sessions against four criteria: (1) whether they felt listened to by the practitioners during the session, (2) whether the session covered things that were important to them, (3) whether they liked what they did during the session, and (4) whether they liked the session overall and would want to do more of the same next session. This activity is consistent with principles of universal learning and, as with any NNN activity that requires a level of literacy, young people are supported to complete their session rating scales, either by practitioners or other participants.

Data collection and analysis

The CBPR model informing NNN situates participants, practitioners, and the stakeholder consortium in a triangulated process of action and reflection. When young people are referred to the NNN program, they are advised that there is an attached program of research and that this research aims to better understand young people's experience and use of violence and how we can better respond as practitioners. Young people are invited to contribute to this research by offering de-identified data that arises as part of their participation in NNN for use by the NNN research team. Young people can participate in the program without contributing their data to research.

Data collection

In NNN, data is collected at three timepoints: pre-program, in-program, and post-program. Data is collected from both young people who participate in the program and practitioners who facilitate group sessions. Pre-program or referral information for young people who participate in NNN includes qualitative demographic data, information on current living circumstances, psychosocial wellbeing, educational engagement, and criminogenic risk factors important in determining safety in NNN. Pre- and post-program data explores participant's self-awareness, skills for communication and connection, and contextual precipitants to their referral to NNN. In the pilot phase, this data was collected through qualitative psychosocial assessment and quantitative survey of communication strengths and soft spots (Egan, 2010). An important finding from the evaluation (discussed next) is that these assessment tools were only partially fit for purpose for assessing the young people's circumstances and needs and have limited value for our ongoing understanding of the program's effectiveness and value.

As a result, new data collection methods have since been adopted. These include a mixed methods assessment of individual quality of life using the Schedule for the Evaluation of Individual Quality of Life-Direct Weighting (SEIQoL-DW) tool (Chenhall et al., 2010). This open-ended, conversationally driven measure has been used effectively with justice-involved Aboriginal youth in QLD (Chenhall et al., 2010). The measure yields qualitative data about important things in the young person's life and a quantitative score of reported quality of life. Complementing this is a new tool (in development by the NNN project team) which uses photographic images and conversational prompts to explore capacities for emotional recognition, empathy, prosocial reasoning, and sharing of important experiences that young people believe shape their lives.

In-program (de-identified) data is gathered from participants in the form of qualitative Photovoice narratives and associated photo work, anonymous Postcards to Practice, and quantitative session rating scales. Practitioners facilitating NNN groups contribute data by completing structured reflection form that seeks immediate observations about the experience of delivering each aspect of the program. These observations contribute to the cycles of action research that inform continuous improvement of the program. Practitioners then have a reflective conversation with another member of the NNN team that is focused both on gathering lessons from the implementation as well as ensuring accountable practice and providing an opportunity to address any issues for the practitioner or the young people in the program. In some instances, practitioner reflections have been elicited through the process of Social Yarning (Bessarab & Ng'andu, 2010). Social Yarning is an Aboriginal practice that encourages people to build belonging through the sharing of information. As described in Blakemore et al. (2021), this practice of Yarning about our work in NNN has been organically guided by the chair of the cultural reference group with practitioners meeting with one another to share stories and experience. Practitioner reflections have been a critical source of data for identifying key themes arising from group sessions to date.

Data analysis

Data analysis occurs after each group rollout, with outcomes of analysis then shared with the stakeholder consortium in consultations to inform further development of the program and disseminate findings to appropriate audiences. Data analysis varies depending on the different types of data collected over the course of the program. Quantitative data from session rating scales and the SEIQoL-DW (and formerly the survey of communication strengths and soft spots) are analysed using descriptive and inferential statistics in the SPSS software package. Qualitative information from young people (including psychosocial assessment information, narratives from Photovoice and photo elicitation activities, and Postcards to Practice) are analysed using qualitative thematic analysis (Guest et al., 2011). After initial themes are identified, the visual and other qualitative data collected through work with the young people is coded using axial coding tools to detect additional sub-themes, clarify interpretations, and recognise and categorise descriptive quotes from participants.

Qualitative data from practitioners (including data drawn from Yarning and autoethnographic reflections on practice) have also been analysed using qualitative thematic analysis (Guest et al., 2011). The use of autoethnography as a method for our work reflects a desire to investigate the intersecting experiences of violence, relationships, and connections with society for ourselves as practitioners (Chang, 2008). Through use of reflexive practices and self-exploration, practitioners investigate concepts of culture, connection, belonging, representation, and recognition within the context of working with young people who have used and experienced violence (Bochner & Ellis, 2016; Ellis & Bochner, 2000; Sweet, 2020). An emphasis on culture is important when discussing autoethnography and is reflective of its origins in anthropology (Ellis & Bochner, 2000). Proponents of autoethnography argue that culture is a phenomenon that is inherently about connection, an understanding of which is best accessed via self-exploration, providing that the practitioner/researcher is open to self-exploration in the first instance (Chang, 2008). A core aspect of autoethnographic research is positioning the self in the work (Bochner & Ellis, 2016; Ellis & Bochner, 2000). Our shared experience of autoethnography in NNN has highlighted that it can be challenging to negotiate factors such as violence, relationships, culture, and the self in research, particularly when considering experiences of intersectionality (Johnson & LeMaster, 2020).

Evaluation

In 2021, researchers from the University of the Sunshine Coast's Sexual Violence Research and Prevention Unit completed an evaluation of the pilot rollout of NNN. A realist evaluation framework was implemented, exploring what worked, for whom, in what circumstances, in what respects, and how (Pawson & Tilley, 1997). The evaluation used a mixed methodology involving pre-existing data from the pilot implementation of NNN, including pre- and post-program assessments, session rating scales, and postcards to practice, and newly collected data from focus group and individual interviews with justice-sector stakeholders and young people who had participated in the program. Thematic analysis methods were used to review the available data with validity checking undertaken by an independent researcher (Rayment-McHugh et al., 2021). The evaluation presented a pragmatic review of program achievements and key lessons to date, focusing on how the program worked and what preliminary short-term outcomes could be identified (Rayment-McHugh et al., 2021). Implementation and process considerations (i.e., key change mechanisms and the contextual conditions relevant to success) were a focus of the evaluation to inform improvement and at-scale delivery of the program (Rayment-McHugh et al., 2021).

Evaluation limitations

Robustness of the evaluation was hampered by the volume of data available and, in some instances, its relevance for drawing conclusions about program effects. These limitations may have been due to the length of time between engagement in the program and evaluation follow-up, literacy concerns, and moving away. Despite these limitations, a series of indicative findings were made across nine program areas with recommendations for future program delivery.

Evaluation findings

The evaluation findings were communicated using Johnson et al.'s (2015) realist evaluation-informed EMMIE framework. The EMMIE acronym represents five domains: effects, mechanisms, moderators, implementation, and economic value (Johnson et al., 2015). As the evaluation did not seek a cost-benefit analysis of the program, the economic value dimension of the framework was not used. Key findings from the evaluation (Rayment-McHugh et al., 2021) are summarised in Table 4.3.

Table 4.3 Evaluation key findings

Effects: *What is the overall impact of the program?*
1. NNN shows promise in promoting positive change among participants.
2. NNN also contributes positive benefits for industry stakeholders.
Mechanisms: *What is it about the program that produces these effects?*
3. The program creates safe spaces for young people to explore issues of violence.
4. Creative methods and "deep listening" contributed to positive engagement, reflection, and learning.
Moderators: *What internal or external factors impact program outcomes?*
5. Participant vulnerability and personal challenges moderated success.
6. Professional stakeholder input was essential.
7. The pilot faced additional challenges associated with the COVID-19 pandemic.
Implementation: *What factors are important for program implementation?*
8. Recruiting the "right team" was key to effective implementation.
9. A need for post-program support was identified.

These findings are expanded on throughout the book as they relate to program content and the findings emerging from practitioner reflection.

Ethics

As noted, appropriate ethics approval was gained for all aspects of NNN development, design, implementation, and evaluation from AIATSIS, UON, and the NSW Departments of Education and Justice. Particular attention was paid to the ethical issues surrounding informed consent for young people referred to NNN. In accepting referrals for justice-involved young people to the program, it was important for us to consider whether their participation in the program could detrimentally impact on any ongoing legal processes. For this reason, referrals were only accepted for young people who had already pled or been found guilty of violence-related matters. This applied only to referrals for young people from the justice sector and did not apply to young people referred from education settings.

A further ethical issue related to informed consent which assumed maturity and capacity to consent of young people referred to the program. In all respects, ethical considerations were aligned with The National Statement on Ethical Conduct in Human Research (2018). Referring caseworkers discussed the NNN program and its associated research project with young people prior to any contact with the NNN team. In these discussions, they used a collaboratively designed information statement written in age-appropriate, plain English. Young people referred to the program were expressly assured that their participation was entirely voluntary and that if they chose not to participate, they would not be disadvantaged in any way. This was particularly important for justice-involved young people in case their decision not to participate were to be used against them in ongoing legal matters. Young people were assured that they could participate in the NNN program but not contribute to the research or, if they chose to contribute to the research, that they could withdraw their consent up until the final session of the program. The information statement about the program and its associated research detailed what information was collected and that all data was de-identified.

Referring caseworkers were tasked with assessing the capacity of young people to understand what the program involved and their ability to consent to participate. Where a young person was aged 16 years or younger, parent/guardian consent was also sought for their participation, with caseworkers providing information on the program and its associated research. Because of relationship breakdown or safety concerns, some young people were not able to obtain parental consent. In these instances, caseworkers determined whether the young person was mature enough and competent to provide informed consent on their own. This was particularly relevant for young people living independently, sometimes as young parents themselves. In these instances, caseworkers co-signed consent forms to note that they had assessed maturity and competency to consent.

Participant and researcher safety

In the design and delivery of NNN, due consideration was given to the potential of young people in the program to experience discomfort or distress, either in response to content in the program, interactions in the group work context, or in the context of extraneous factors co-occurring with their participation in the program. Due consideration was also given to the fact that for young people who identified as Aboriginal, any potential discomfort or distress could be compounded due to cultural considerations and additional socioeconomic and systemic challenges and disadvantage posed due to colonisation. A collaborative approach to risk mitigation was taken, with strategies addressing issues of safety, accessibility, and literacy developed with input from the NNN stakeholder consortium. Measures of cultural responsivity were embedded within the program and were Aboriginal practice-led, with input and support from the cultural reference group and NNN. This included the development of detailed distress and cultural safety protocols as well as practice approaches that focused on co-creating tools for safety within the group setting.

Conclusion

This chapter has provided an overview of the NNN program for young people. It has described the CBPR processes and stakeholder collective of people involved in its development as well as the underpinning theory of change and evidence base that inform its aims and objectives. The chapter has provided an overview of the practice principles for NNN, its structure, and core components and has outlined how the program collects and analyses data to inform its continuous improvement. Details of an evaluation of the program were also presented alongside ethical considerations. Having sketched the NNN program, which will serve as a case study focus for this text, the following chapters explore what it means for a program to be trauma-informed and culturally safe and what we learn about youth violence from working in this way.

References

Adams, K., Burns, C., Liebzeit, A., Ryschka, J., Thorpe, S., & Browne, J. (2012). Use of participatory research and photo-voice to support urban Aboriginal healthy eating. *Health & Social Care in the Community*, *20*(5), 497–505. https://doi.org/10.1111/j.1365-2524.2011.01056.x

Baidawi, S. (2020). Crossover children: Examining initial criminal justice system contact among child protection-involved youth. *Australian Social Work*, *73*(3), 280–295. https://doi.org/10.1080/0312407X.2019.1686765

Bessarab, D., & Ng'andu, B. (2010). Yarning about yarning as a legitimate method in Indigenous research. *International Journal of Critical Indigenous Studies*, *3*(1), 37–50. https://doi.org/10.5204/ijcis.v3i1.57

Blakemore, T., Agllias, K., Howard, A., & McCarthy, S. (2019). The service system challenges of work with juvenile justice involved young people in the Hunter Region, Australia. *Australian Journal of Social Issues*, *54*(3), 341–356. https://doi.org/10.1002/ajs4.69

Blakemore, T., Rak, L., Agllias, K., Mallett, X., & McCarthy, S. (2018). Crime and context: Understandings of youth perpetrated interpersonal violence among service providers in regional Australia. *Journal of Applied Youth Studies*, *2*(5), 53–69.

Blakemore, T., Randall, E., Rak, L., & Cocuzzoli, F. (2021). Deep listening and relationality: Cross-cultural reflections on practice with young women who use violence. *Australian Social Work*, *75*(3), 304–316. https://doi.org/10.1080/0312407X.2021.1914697

Bochner, A., & Ellis, C. (2016). *Evocative autoethnography: Writing lives and telling stories*. Routledge. https://doi.org/10.4324/9781315545417

Boxall, H., Morgan, A., & Brown, R. (2020). The prevalence of domestic violence among women during the COVID-19 pandemic. *Australasian Policing*, *12*(3), 38–46.

Bradley, R. G., & Follingstad, D. R. (2003). Group therapy for incarcerated women who experienced interpersonal violence: A pilot study. *Journal of Traumatic Stress*, *16*(4), 337–340. https://doi.org/10.1023/A:1024409817437

Bromfield, L. M., Gillingham, P., & Higgins, D. J. (2007). Cumulative harm and chronic child maltreatment. *Developing Practice: The Child Youth and Family Work Journal*, *19*, 34–42.

Brooks, C. M., & Poudrier, J. (2014). Anti-oppressive visual methodologies: Critical appraisal of cross-cultural research design. *Qualitative Sociology Review*, *10*(4), 32–51. https://doi.org/10.18778/1733-8077.10.4.02

Browne, A. J., & Fiske, J. A. (2001). First Nations women's encounters with mainstream health care services. *Western Journal of Nursing Research*, *23*(2), 126–147. https://doi.org/10.1177/019394590102300203

Budig, K., Diez, J., Conde, P., Sastre, M., Hernán, M., & Franco, M. (2018). Photovoice and empowerment: Evaluating the transformative potential of a participatory action research project. *BMC Public Health*, *18*(1), 1–9. https://doi.org/10.1186/s12889-018-5335-7

Cargo, M., & Mercer, S. L. (2008). The value and challenges of participatory research: Strengthening its practice. *Annual Review of Public Health*, *29*, 325–350. https://doi.org/10.1146/annurev.publhealth.29.091307.083824

Chang, H. (2008). *Autoethnography as method: Developing qualitative inquiry*. Left Coast Press.

Chenhall, R. D., Senior, K., Cole, D., Cunningham, T., & O'Boyle, C. (2010). Individual quality of life among at risk Indigenous youth in Australia. *Applied Research in Quality of Life*, *5*, 171–183. https://doi.org/10.1007/s11482-010-9101-y

Chesney-Lind, M., & Eliason, M. (2006). From invisible to incorrigible: The demonization of marginalized women and girls. *Crime, Media, Culture*, *2*(1), 29–47.

Cox, E., Leung, R., Baksheev, G., Day, A., Toumbourou, J. W., Miller, P., Kremer, P., & Walker, A. (2016). Violence prevention and intervention programmes for adolescents in Australia: A systematic review. *Australian Psychologist*, *51*(3), 206–222. https://doi.org/10.1111/ap.12168

Creighton, G., Oliffe, J. L., Ferlatte, O., Bottorff, J., Broom, A., & Jenkins, E. K. (2018). Photovoice ethics: Critical reflections from men's mental health research. *Qualitative Health Research*, *28*(3), 446–455. https://doi.org/10.1177/1049732317729137

Davidson, R. J. (2003). Alterations in brain and immune function produced by mindfulness meditation. *Psychosocmatic Medicine*, *65*(4), 564–570. https://doi.org/10.1097/01.PSY.0000077505.67574.E3

Davis, R., Campbell, R., Hildon, Z., Hobbs, L., & Michie, S. (2015). Theories of behaviour and behaviour change across the social and behavioural sciences: A scoping review. *Health Psychology Review*, *9*(3), 323–344. https://doi.org/10.1080/17437199.2014.941722

Dierkhising, C. B., Ko, S. J., Woods-Jaeger, B., Briggs, E. C., Lee, R., & Pynoos, R. S. (2013). Trauma histories among justice-involved youth: Findings from the national child traumatic stress network. *European Journal of Psychotraumatology*, *4*(1), Article 20274. https://doi.org/10.3402/ejpt.v4i0.20274

Edwards, E. R., Dichiara, A., Epshteyn, G., Snyder, S., Linzer, S., Riglietti, K., Weishoff, N., Lee, A., Tsai, J., Marcano, E., Geraci, J., & Goodman, M. (2022). Dialectical behavior therapy for justice-involved veterans (DBT-J): Feasibility and acceptability. *Psychological Services*. https://doi.org/10.1037/ser0000691

Egan, G. (2010). *Exercises in helping skills: A manual to accompany The Skilled Helper. A problem-management and opportunity-development approach to helping* (9th ed.). Brooks/Cole Cengage Learning.

Ellis, C., & Bochner, A. (2000). Autoethnography, personal narrative, reflexivity: Researcher as subject. In N. Denzin & Y. Lincoln (Eds.), *Handbook of qualitative research* (2nd ed.). SAGE Publications.

Evans-Chase, M. (2015). If they like it they can take with them: A mixed methods look at the use of Internet based instruction of mindfulness meditation with incarcerated youth. *Advances in Social Work*, *16*(1), 93–106. https://doi.org/10.18060/17973

Fitzgibbon, W. (2022). *Applied photovoice in criminal justice: Voices made visible*. Taylor & Francis. https://doi.org/10.4324/9781003017127

Fitzgibbon, W., & Healy, D. (2019). Lives and spaces: Photovoice and offender supervision in Ireland and England. *Criminology & Criminal Justice*, *19*(1), 3–25. https://doi.org/10.1177/1748895817739665

Fitzgibbon, W., & Stengel, C. M. (2018). Women's voices made visible: Photovoice in visual criminology. *Punishment & Society*, *20*(4), 411–431. https://doi.org/10.1177/1462474517700137

Fox, A. M., Miksicek, D., Veele, S., & Rogers, B. (2020). An evaluation of dialectical behavior therapy for juveniles in secure residential facilities. *Journal of Offender Rehabilitation*, *59*(8), 478–502. https://doi.org/10.1080/10509674.2020.1808557

George, M., Lim, H., Lucas, S., & Meadows, R. (2015). Learning by doing: Experiential learning in criminal justice. *Journal of Criminal Justice Education*, *26*(4), 471–492. https://doi.org/10.1080/10511253.2015.1052001

Gross, C. R., Krietzer, M. J., Reilly-Spong, M., Winbush, N. Y., Schomaker, E. K., & Thomas, W. (2009). Mindfulness meditation training to reduce symptom distress in transplant patients: Rationale, design, and experience with a recycled waitlist. *Clinical Trials*, *6*(1), 76–89. https://doi.org/10.1177/1740774508100982

Guest, G., MacQueen, K. M., & Namey, E. E. (2011). *Applied thematic analysis*. SAGE Publications. https://doi.org/10.4135/9781483384436

Halkola, U. (2013). A photograph as a therapeutic experience. In D. Lowenthal (Ed.), *Phototherapy and therapeutic photography in a digital age* (pp. 21–33). Routledge.

Harper, D. (2002). Talking about pictures: A case for photo elicitation. *Visual Studies*, *17*(1), 13–26.

Himelstein, S., Hastings, A., Shapiro, S., & Heery, M. (2012). A qualitative investigation of the experience of a mindfulness-based intervention with incarcerated adolescents. *Child and Adolescent Mental Health*, *17*, 231–237. https://doi.org/10.1111/j.1475-3588.2011.00647.x

Iverson, K. M., Shenk, C., & Fruzzetti, A. E. (2009). Dialectical behaviour therapy for women victims of domestic abuse: A pilot study. *Professional Psychology: Research and Practice*, *40*(3), 242–248. https://doi.org/10.1037/a0013476

Jain, S., Shapiro, S. L., Swanick, S., Roesch, S. C., Mills, P. J., Bell, I., & Schwartz, G. E. R. (2007). A randomized controlled trail of mindfulness meditation versus relaxation training: Effects on distress, positive states of mind, rumination, and distraction. *Annals of Behavioral Medicine*, *33*(1), 11–21. https://doi.org/10.1207/s15324796abm3301_2

Johnson, A. L., & LeMaster, B. (Eds.). (2020). *Gender futurity, intersectional autoethnography: Embodied theorizing from the margins*. Routledge. https://doi.org/10.4324/9781003043683

Johnson, S. D., Tilley, N., & Bowers, K. J. (2015). Introducing EMMIE: An evidence rating scale to encourage mixed-method crime prevention synthesis reviews. *Journal of Experimental Criminology*, *11*(3), 459–473. https://doi.org/10.1007/s11292-015-9238-7

Kabat-Zinn, J. (2015). Mindfulness. *Mindfulness*, *6*, 1481–1483. https://doi.org/10.1007/s12671-015-0456-x

Kabat-Zinn, J., Massion, A. O., Kristeller, J., Peterson, L. G., Fletcher, K. E., Pbert, L., Lenderking, W. R., & Santorelli, S. F. (1992). Effectiveness of a mediation-based stress reduction program in the treatment of anxiety disorders. *American Journal of Psychiatry*, *149*(7), 936–943. https://doi.org/10.1176/ajp.149.7.936

Karger, J., & Currie-Rubin, R. (2013). Addressing the educational needs of incarcerated youth. *Journal of Special Education Leadership*, *26*(2), 106–116.

Kolb, D. A. (2015). *Experiential learning: Experience as the source of learning and development* (2nd ed.). Pearson Education.

Ledwith, M., & Springett, J. (2010). *Participatory practice: Community-based action for transformative change*. Policy Press. https://doi.org/10.2307/j.ctt1t89038

Linehan, M. M. (2015). *DBT skills training manual* (2nd ed.). The Guilford Press.

Loewenthal, D. (2013). Introducing phototherapy and therapeutic photography in a digital age. In D. Loewenthal (Ed.), *Phototherapy and therapeutic photography in a digital age* (pp. 5–20). Routledge.

Mazza, J. J., Dexter-Mazza, E. T., Miller, A. L., Rathus, J. H., & Murphy, H. E. (2016). *DBT skills in schools: Skills training for emotional problem solving for adolescents (DBT Steps-A)*. The Guilford Press. https://doi.org/10.1093/oxfordhb/9780198758723.013.21

Miller, S. D., & Duncan, B. L. (2000). *The outcome and session rating scales: Administration and scoring manual*. Institute of the Study of Therapeutic Change.

Minkler, M., & Wallerstein, N. (2003). Part one: Introduction to community-based participatory research. In M. Minkler & N. Wallerstein (Eds.), *Community-based participatory research for health*. Jossey-Bass/Wiley.

Moffitt, P., & Vollman, A. R. (2004). Photovoice: Picturing the health of Aboriginal women in a remote northern community. *Canadian Journal of Nursing Research*, *36*(4), 189–201.

National Statement on Ethical Conduct in Human Research. (2018). *The national health and medical research council, the Australian research council and universities Australia*. Commonwealth of Australia.

Nelson-Gray, R. O., Keane, S. P., Hurst, R. M., Mitchell, J. T., Warburton, J. B., Chok, J. T., & Cobb, A. R (2006). A modified DBT skills training for oppositional defiant adolescents: Promising preliminary findings. *Behaviour Research and Therapy*, *44*(12), 1811–1820. https://doi.org/10.1016/j.brat.2006.01.004

Owen-Smith, A., Black, H., Emerson, D., Cofner, M., Smith, H., Jackson, D., Ford, J. D., DeBar, L., Di Clemente, R., & Hayat, M. (2021). A pilot study to adapt a trauma-informed mindfulness based yoga intervention for justice-involved youth. *International Journal of Yoga Therapy*, *31*(1). https://doi.org/10.17761/2021-D-21-00032

Pawson, R., Tilley, N., & Tilley, N. (1997). *Realistic evaluation*. SAGE Publications.

Pederson, L. D. (2015). *Dialectical behavior therapy: A contemporary guide for practitioners*. John Wiley & Sons. https://doi.org/10.1002/9781118957882

Pradhan, E. K., Baumgarten, M., Langenberg, P., Handwerger, B., Gilpin, A. K., Magyari, T., Hochberg, M. C., & Berman, B. M. (2007). Effect of minfulness-based stress reduction in rheumatoid arthritis patients. *Arthritis and Rheumatism*, *57*(7), 1134–1142. https://doi.org/10.1002/art.23010

Rak, L., & Warton, T. (2023). His, hers and theirs: Comparative narratives from young people who use violence. *Safer Communities*, *22*(1), 42–55. https://doi.org/10.1108/SC-08-2022-0033

Rayment-McHugh, S., McKillop, N., Adams, D., & Hull, I. (2021). *Name.Narrate.Navigate: A prevention initiative for youth violence: Evaluation report*

[Unpublished report]. Sexual Violence Research and Prevention Unit, University of the Sunshine Coast.
Rose, D. (2000). Universal design for learning. *Journal of Special Education Technology*, *15*(1), 67–70.
Rose, D., & Meyer, A. (2006). *A practical reader in universal design for learning.* Harvard Education Press.
Sarnat, J. E. (2019). What's new in parallel process? The evolution of supervision's signature phenomenon. *The American Journal of Psychoanalysis*, *79*(3), 304–328. https://doi.org/10.1057/s11231-019-09292-5
Sheehan, R., & Baidawi, S. (2022). Children and young people in court. In M. Camilleri & A. Harkness (Eds.), *Australian courts*. Palgrave Macmillan. https://doi.org/10.1007/978-3-031-19063-6_13
Shelton, D., Kesten, K., Zhang, W., & Trestman, R. (2011). Impact of a dialectic behavior therapy – Corrections Modified (DBT-CM) upon behaviorally challenged incarcerated male adolescents. *Journal of Child and Adolescent Psychiatric Nursing*, *24*(2), 105–113. https://doi.org/10.1111/j.1744-6171.2011.00275.x
Shelton, D., Sampl, S., Kesten, K. L., Zhang, W., & Trestman, R. L. (2009). Treatment of impulsive aggression in correctional settings. *Behavioural Sciences and the Law*, *27*(5), 787–800. https://doi.org/10.1002/bsl.889
Speca, M., Carlson, L. E., Goodey, E., & Angen, M. (2000). A randomized, wait-listed controlled clinical trial: The effect of a mindfulness meditation-based stress reduction program on mood and symptoms of stress in cancer outpatients. *Psychosomatic Medicine*, *62*(5), 613–622. https://doi.org/10.1097/00006842-200009000-00004
Staff, J., & Kreager, D. A. (2008). Too cool for school? Violence, peer status and high school dropout. *Social Forces*, *87*(1), 445–471.
Stuart, G. (2019). *4 types of power: What are power over; power with; power to and power within?* Sustaining Community. https://sustainingcommunity.wordpress.com/2019/02/01/4-types-of-power/
Sutton-Brown, C. A. (2014). Photovoice: A methodological guide. *Photography and Culture*, *7*(2), 169–185. https://doi.org/10.2752/175145214X13999922103165
Swan, S. C., Gambone, L. J., Caldwell, J. E., Sullivan, T. P., & Snow, D. L. (2008). A review of research on women's use of violence with male intimate partners. *Violence and Victims*, *23*(3), 301–314.
Sweet, P. L. (2020). Who knows? Reflexivity in feminist standpoint theory and Bourdieu. *Gender & Society*, *34*(6), 922–950. https://doi.org/10.1177/0891243220966600
Turney, D. (2012). A relationship-based approach to engaging involuntary clients: The contribution of recognition theory. *Child & Family Social Work*, *17*(2), 149–159. https://doi.org/10.1111/j.1365-2206.2012.00830.x
Wallerstein, N., Duran, B., Oetzel, J. G., & Minkler, M. (Eds.). (2017). *Community-based participatory research for health: Advancing social and health equity*. John Wiley & Sons.
Wang, C. C. (1999). Photovoice: A participatory action research strategy applied to women's health, *Journal of Women's Health*, *8*(2), 185–192. https://doi.org/10.1089/jwh.1999.8.185
Wang, C. C., & Burris, M. A. (1997). Photovoice: Concept, methodology, and use for participatory needs assessment. *Health Education & Behavior*, *24*(3), 369–387. https://doi.org/10.1177/109019819702400309

Warton, T. J. (2020). *The development of a criminal identity amongst adolescent males* [Doctoral dissertation]. Monash University.

Watts, L. (2019). Reflective practice, reflexivity, and critical reflection in social work education in Australia. *Australian Social Work*, *72*(1), 8–20. https://doi.org/10.1080/0312407X.2018.1521856

Williams, J. M. G. (2008). Mindfulness, depression and modes of mind. *Cognitive Therapy and Research*, *32*(6), 721–733. https://doi.org/10.1007/s10608-008-9204-z

Winters, D. E., & Beerbower, E. (2017). Mindfulness and meditation as an adjunctive treatment for adolescents involved in the justice system: Is repairing the brain and nervous system possible? *Social Work in Health Care*, *56*(7), 615–635. https://doi.org/10.1080/00981389.2017.1316341

5 Trauma, culture, and youth violence

Tamara Blakemore, Louise Rak, and Chris Krogh

Acknowledgement

This chapter includes reflections shared by Felicity Cocuzzoli and Auntie Elsie Randall. Felicity is a proud descendant of the Wiradjuri Nation, an artist, and practitioner. Auntie Elsie is a Yagel/Bundjalung woman currently living on Awabakal Country. Auntie Elsie is an acknowledged Aboriginal Elder, chair of the NNN cultural reference group, professional artist, business owner, and co-founder and director of Justiz community social justice agency. We acknowledge the contributions and leadership of Felicity and Elsie in this work.

Trauma, culture, and youth violence

The Name.Narrate.Navigate (NNN) program works with young people who have used and experienced violence. So far, we have worked with almost equal numbers of young men and young women, around 40% of whom were of Aboriginal and Torres Strait Islander descent. For many, intersecting experiences of violence, abuse, and trauma mean they have been kept out of much needed systems of support, as their *use* of violence has outweighed remediation of their *experience* of violence. This chapter explores the importance of a trauma-informed and culturally safe practice for this cohort. It explores evidence and theory relating to trauma, culture, and youth violence and shares narratives of young people involved in the NNN program. Collected with appropriate ethics approval via practitioner reflections, these de-identified narratives provide an important insight into the realities of justice-involved young people impacted by trauma.

In Australia, robust evidence suggests many young people before the Children's Court for criminal matters have experienced violence, abuse, and trauma (AIHW, 2018; Baidawi & Sheehan, 2019; Baidawi, 2020). Malvaso et al. (2022) identify that for incarcerated youth, this rate can be upwards of 90%. Young people involved with both child protection

DOI: 10.4324/9781003177883-5

and youth justice systems have variously been referred to as a "crossover", "dual order", or "dual jurisdiction" cohort (Herz et al., 2010) and are found to experience poor outcomes associated with early adversity often compounded by structural disadvantage and experiences of care and/or custody. Baidawi (2020) reports crossover cohorts encounter the criminal justice system earlier and are more often charged with violent offences. The Australian Institute of Health and Welfare (AIHW, 2018) reports Aboriginal young people are 17 times more likely than non-Aboriginal peers to be represented in crossover cohorts and 18 times more likely to be incarcerated, representing up to 59% of the population of incarcerated youth despite only comprising around 5% of the overall youth population. Similar findings are reported for Indigenous young people in other countries carrying historic legacies of settler-colonialism, such as Canada (Turpel-Lafond & Kendall, 2009).

It is important to emphasise that the consequences of trauma are varied, and the vast majority of young people impacted by trauma do not become involved in crime (Malvaso et al., 2017). Rather, both the occurrence and outcomes of trauma are multidetermined; situated, enacted, experienced, and sometimes reproduced through sociopolitical and historical landscapes and moderated by individual and collective strengths and resilience. An understanding of young people's histories and recognition of the complex interplay between overlapping experiences of marginalisation and inherent strengths is fundamental to trauma-informed and culturally safe work with youth violence. In the following sections, we unpack trauma research and theory, including a discussion on trauma's associations with violence. We then describe relationships between culture, trauma, and violence before discussing what trauma-informed and culturally safe practice looks like and how this is embedded within NNN.

What is trauma?

In our work, we refer to trauma as the experience (and its ongoing consequences) not the event itself. We recognise that trauma describes our embodied response to something outside of our normal experience, that in isolation, or accumulation, overwhelms our capacity to cope (Herman, 1992; Krupnik, 2019). Examples of overwhelming traumatic events for young people can include actions (child maltreatment; parental illness, incarceration, or substance use; or acrimonious divorce); incidents (natural disaster, war, terror attacks, or community violence); and accidents (associated with vehicles, transport, or sports) but also disadvantage, marginalisation, and racism (Norris, 1992; Paton et al., 2009; Taylor & Weems, 2009). Regardless of origin, events that lead to trauma have three key elements: the event is unexpected, the person is unprepared, and the person feels powerless to stop the event from happening. (Harms, 2015). Understanding trauma as an experience recognises that even when faced with the same event, people can respond differently.

Typologies of trauma

Typologies of trauma commonly focus on how often trauma is experienced (differentiated as acute, chronic, or complex trauma) and who experiences trauma (described as developmental, intergenerational, collective, and/or historic trauma). The following summaries describe understandings of trauma important to our work with youth violence.

Acute trauma results from a single (extreme) incident that threatens our internal sense of emotional and physical safety. Acute trauma can result from experiencing or witnessing natural disasters, robberies, terror attacks, assaults, and accidents (Herman, 1992). Symptoms can arise quickly and can include exhaustion, confusion, sadness, anxiety, guilt, dissociation, re-experiencing, or avoiding cues associated with the traumatic event (Bremmer, 1999). If these symptoms persist and go unaddressed, they can contribute to acute or post-traumatic stress disorder (PTSD) (Bremmer, 1999).

Chronic trauma happens when we experience or are exposed to repeated or multiple traumatic events over a prolonged period. Chronic trauma is associated with child maltreatment, domestic and family violence (DFV), refugee experiences, and life in some religious or lifestyle cults (De Deckker, 2018; Rahim, 2014). Compared to acute trauma, symptoms of chronic trauma can take longer to present (Kezelman & Stavropoulos, 2012).

Complex trauma results from experience or exposure to multiple and repeated traumatic stressors in contexts that compromise secure attachment with primary caregivers (Cook et al., 2005; Ford, 2005). Complex trauma can be associated with child maltreatment, bullying, forced adoptions, DFV, racism, and discrimination (Finkelhor et al., 2009; Porter & Haslam, 2005). Because complex trauma is associated with planned, extreme, and repeated actions, it is suggested to have severe and persistent impacts on self-regulatory competencies, including attention and learning, working and autobiographical memory, emotional regulation, and social relatedness (Cloitre et al., 2009; Ford, 2005).

Developmental trauma occurs during childhood and commonly in the context of child maltreatment and the loss of important attachments and connections (Denton et al., 2017). Early relational trauma can adversely impact emotional and behavioural regulation, cognition, and the development of self-concept and identity (van der Kolk, 2009).

Intergenerational trauma was first used to explain the experiences of Holocaust survivors post–World War 2 and describes how memories, emotions, and lived experiences are passed on to subsequent generations through biological and social processes (Herman, 1992; Kellerman, 2001). In Australia, intergenerational trauma among many Aboriginal communities is slowly being recognised by the broader community.

Collective trauma relates to shared experiences of traumatic events, such as natural disasters, war, conflict, acts of terror, and pandemics (Stanley et al., 2021) and refers to how these events are experienced psychologically and how these impacts live on as a reminder of the collective experience of the event (Hirschberger, 2018).

Historical trauma compounds individual trauma (Mitchell & Arseneau, 2019) and results from dominant groups taking direct or indirect actions to attack or disrupt culture and extinguish shared and symbolic experiences that imbue lives with collective meaning (Subica & Link, 2022). Members of an affected culture may experience trauma-related symptoms without having been exposed to traumatic events (Mohatt et al., 2014, p. 128).

Type I versus Type II trauma was differentiated by Lenore Terr (1991) in her seminal work on the experience of trauma. *Type I trauma* is sometimes described as "simple" trauma, experienced in relation to one-off traumatic events, and *Type II trauma* is considered "complex" trauma, experienced in relation to prolonged or repeated traumatic events (Franco, 2021; McCormack & Thomson, 2017).

Big T versus Little t trauma represents a differentiation between trauma experienced in relation to extraordinary or catastrophic events and those experienced in relation to traumatic experiences of disadvantage, disruptive change, and loss (Draper & Brown, 2022; Oglesby, 2005). *Big T trauma* is associated with significant events that leave us feeling powerless (Draper & Brown, 2022), whereas *Little t trauma* is associated with events of everyday life that overwhelm our capacity to cope (Draper & Brown, 2022).

Trauma and adverse childhood experiences

The term "adverse childhood experiences" (ACEs) was coined by Felitti et al. (1998) to describe the cumulative impacts of childhood experiences of maltreatment (including physical, sexual, and emotional abuse; physical and emotional neglect; and domestic violence) and household dysfunction (including parental separation or divorce, mental illness or substance abuse, or incarceration). Felitti et al.'s (1998) study established ACEs are incredibly common, with more than half the study respondents reporting at least one ACE and a quarter reporting two or more. Reporting experience of one ACE was found to be associated with between a 65% and 93% probability of reporting the experience of another (Felitti et al., 1998). Report of larger numbers of ACEs was associated with report of poorer health and wellbeing and greater behavioural problems (Felitti et al., 1998). Reporting four or more ACEs was associated with between a 4- and 12-fold increase in reported health-related risks for substance abuse, depression, and suicide attempts (Felitti et al., 1998). These findings have been replicated across cohorts and contexts, substantiating the association between cumulative exposure to traumatic events in childhood and a range of issues in later life.

ACEs among justice-involved youth

More than 90% of justice-involved young people are reported to have experienced at least one ACE (e.g., Abram et al., 2004; Baglivio et al., 2014; Charak et al., 2018). In Australia, Malvaso et al. (2019) report just under a third of a sample of almost 3,000 justice-involved young people identify experiencing six or more with the greater number of ACEs reported by young women. Reported rates of ACEs for justice-involved young people are three times greater than those people reported in the original study (Baglivio et al., 2014) and up to eight times greater than those reported in the community (Abram et al., 2004). Crossover youth are more likely to report multiple ACEs. In a review of 300 court files for crossover youth, Baidawi and Sheehan (2019) found that 68% experienced five or more traumatic events prior to their involvement with the justice system. More than three-quarters had been exposed to family violence and almost two-thirds had experienced neglect (Baidawi & Sheehan, 2019). Relative to non-Aboriginal young people, higher proportions of Aboriginal young people had been exposed to family violence, substance abuse, and the incarceration of a family member (Baidawi & Sheehan, 2019).

Higher numbers of ACEs and prior experiences of maltreatment have each been associated with young people's use of violence (De Lisi & Beauregard, 2018; Fox et al., 2015; Malvaso et al., 2019). In Baidawi and Sheehan's (2019) study, 86% of crossover youth had been charged with "offences against the person" – a rate approaching four times that reported for all children sentenced in Victoria (VIC) at the time. Malvaso et al. (2021) likewise note 63% of young people in their study had convictions for violent offences, with over two-thirds having a prior experience of maltreatment. In this study, cumulative ACEs were significantly higher amongst those charged with violent offences, a higher proportion of whom were young women (Malvaso et al., 2021). Justice-involved young people we have worked with in NNN have been exposed to family violence, child maltreatment, placement in out-of-home care, mental illness, substance abuse, and incarceration of family members. All the justice-involved young women we have worked with have experienced interpersonal violence, commonly perpetrated by a male.

Box 5.1 What we've learned . . .

Some young people have shared raw accounts of their past or contemporaneous ACEs, almost as an unimportant detail in accounts of everyday life, never linking these experiences to their current circumstances, an example of this follows:

> "So, he was off his face on ice [drugs] and was flogging me around the kitchen. And I was pregnant at the time. I was so angry at him because he and [his partner] weren't planning shit for my little brother's birthday so I had to go out and rack [steal] him a bunch of party shit like streamers and shit". (Kylie, 16)

The violence Kylie described was experienced at the hands of her father. It wasn't the focal point of her story nor was the fact that she was pregnant at the time. At the time of telling her story, it was just months after this event, and she was no longer pregnant and didn't have a child. Her reason for sharing this story was to highlight how angry she was that her father was not giving her 1-year-old brother a first birthday party.

The association between ACEs, trauma, and youth violence

Neuroscience explains the association between ACEs, trauma, and youth violence via the impact of adversity and trauma on our bodies, brains, and behaviour. It is useful here to distinguish between what we expect to see in positive, healthy human development and what we tend to see in development impacted by trauma. In the former, we expect to see young people interacting with the world around them in ways that are safe and reinforced by consistent messages of support. Instead, what we see in the latter is young people, particularly those confronted by multiple, severe, or persistent traumatic events, interacting with the world around them with a preoccupation with detecting and surviving threats (Pine, 2007). Operating in "survival mode" for prolonged periods of time can affect structural and functional changes in the body's central and autonomic nervous system (Neumeister et al., 2007; Teicher et al., 2003). Neuro-imaging studies of young people impacted by early relational trauma identify structural differences in the corpus callosum (responsible for problem-solving), hippocampus (involved in forming and retrieving memories), and amygdala (involved in detecting threat and triggering fear) and decreased activity in the prefrontal cortex (responsible for problem-solving and regulating emotions and behaviours) (McCrory et al., 2010; Teicher & Samson, 2016). These changes can impact a young person's cognitive, psychological, and behavioural functioning, shaping how they see themselves and how they interact with others in the world around them.

Different kinds of traumatic events can be associated with different impacts (Boxer & Terranova, 2008; Duron et al., 2022). Traumatic events that occur in the context of interpersonal relationships, especially early, pivotal relationships, can be associated with complex trauma and more severe symptoms and greater impacts, including PTSD and complex-PTSD (C-PTSD) (Briere & Scott, 2015; Cloitre et al., 2009; Kerig, 2013). In the United States, rates of PTSD among justice-involved young people are comparable to those of soldiers returning from war and are highest among young women and young people from racial and ethnic minorities (Wolpaw & Ford, 2004). In Japan, 33% of justice-involved young women report experiencing PTSD (Ariga et al., 2008), a rate comparable to that reported for justice-involved young men in Switzerland (27%) (Urbaniok et al., 2007). Diagnosis of PTSD has been predicated on evidence or reported experience of hyperarousal (a persistent expectation of danger), intrusion (flashbacks), and constriction (numbing or dissociation) (Herman & Harvey, 1997). C-PTSD, is more associated with enduring changes to personality and behaviour, often involving difficulties with emotion and behaviour regulation, identity, and relationality (Briere & Scott, 2015; Kerig, 2013).

Young people who have experienced complex trauma may experience heightened sensitivity and reactivity to perceived threats but, as a consequence of traumatic impacts, have less ability to regulate their responses (Ford et al., 2012). Contributing to this can be interconnected difficulties in appreciating facial expressions, retrieving memories to infer meaning about them, and regulating emotions and behaviours experienced in response (Kar, 2019). Difficulties with emotional regulation have been linked to violence, both towards others (Finkel, 2007) and the self (Pisani et al., 2013). This may be linked to traumatic impacts on cognitive-information processing that make young people more vulnerable to self-criticism and shame (Sachs-Ericsson et al., 2006), prone to endorse aggression (Bradshaw & Garbarino, 2006), seek connection with antisocial peers (Ford et al., 2010), and use violence in situations involving substance use/misuse (Finkelhor et al., 2007). Difficulties with behavioural regulation have been linked to externalising problems, including impulsivity, oppositionality, hostility, and aggression (Farrington, 1993; Ford et al., 2008). Ford et al. (2012) explain aggression and aggressive acts vary in function (i.e., some are proactive attempts to harm and control, whereas others are reactive attempts to protect oneself or others) and form (e.g., physical violence is overt, whereas coercive control is often covert). Some evidence suggests that when young people have experienced violence, they are more likely to use reactive but not proactive aggression (Ford et al., 2010). This is consistent with observations that what appears to be proactive violence may be reactive and trauma-related (Jaffee et al., 2004).

The criminalisation of trauma

In our work, we have often worried that apparent increases in youth violence, particularly young female violence, might more accurately reflect an increase in the criminalisation of traumatic impacts. Buckingham (2016), citing the work of Bloom and Covington (2001), suggests early, persistent, and multiple experiences of violence and abuse can lead to young women reacting criminally to their trauma. This has been explained as a function of misperceived threats (McCrory et al., 2011) and acts of safeguarding or self-protection (Gershoff, 2002; Kerig & Becker, 2010; White & Habibis, 2005). Young women's use of violence is often relational, and sometimes reciprocal, oscillating between offending and trauma (Azad et al., 2018; Odgers et al., 2005). Reciprocated trauma may stem from difficulties in engaging, tolerating, and narrating emotions (Pearlman & Courtois, 2005). When the outcome of trauma-related behaviours are criminal charges, a "double penalty" is issued, whereby the behaviours are criminalised as is the individual's experience/s of trauma (Blakemore et al., 2021; Segrave & Carlton, 2010; Stubbs, 2011). Young women we work with have shared stark examples of their experiences of violence, abuse, and trauma and its impacts being disregarded, denied, or criminalised.

Box 5.2 What we've learned . . .

In one incident, police were called to a witnessed assault on Jazz. She became distressed in dealing with police and was taken to hospital under a mental health schedule.

> "These two seccies[guards] came. They stand at the door like this, with their arms crossed, didn't even say one word to me,

just standing there like they're trying to intimidate me or whatever . . . I was asking to see my mum and if can I make a phone call, and the nurse she was like, 'nah, you're not allowed to until you speak to the doctor' . . . and then I start getting agitated. When the doctor came he was like, 'it's 8.30 now, you can't see your mum' . . . after I'd been sitting there for the last three hours saying I wanted to see my mum. I was like, 'can you get out? can you just leave me alone please', like, and he was like, "yeah that's fine rah rah rah" and just kept talking. I was like, "can you just move away from me" . . . as soon as he moved away from me I just lost it". (Jazz)

Jazz was charged by the police with criminal damage to a patient information board.

While all young women are vulnerable to societal judgements about what constitutes (gender-normed) appropriate and acceptable behaviour, young women who have experienced violence, abuse, and trauma seem particularly susceptible to the heavy gaze of systems and structures (Terry, 2018). It has been observed that when these young women encounter the U.S. justice system, their behaviour is rarely seen as trauma-related but rather the result of poor choices or criminogenic, to be remediated by harsh penalties, including incarceration (Chesney-Lind, 2003; Sherman & Balck, 2015). Media coverage of female violence (e.g., "Women can be as violent as men"; Zimmerman, 2018), perpetuates support for tough-on-crime approaches resulting in women becoming the fastest growing incarcerated population cohort (Chesney-Lind, 2006).

Culture (trauma) and youth violence

Notions of the criminalisation of trauma may find no stronger example than the experiences of Aboriginal young people, who live with the aftershocks of violent colonisation, the state-sanctioned removal of Aboriginal children, and complex intersections of systemic and structural racism, discrimination, and marginalisation (Barnes & Motz, 2018; Cunneen & Tauri, 2019). Past exposures are added to by current high rates of separation of children and young people from families through involvement with child protection and youth justice systems and through high rates of adult imprisonment and premature mortality (Ball & Baidawi, 2021; Raphael et al., 2007). Despite making up only 5% of the

Australian youth population, Aboriginal young people are taken into youth detention at a rate more than 18 times their non-Aboriginal peers. As a result, they represent 59% of incarcerated youth (AIHW, 2020). Child protection systems were also involved in the lives of half of these young people. These traumatic experiences impact individuals, families, communities, and culture through cumulative and interconnected experiences of complex, intergenerational, historical, and collective trauma (Menzies, 2019; Miller & Berger, 2020; Raphael et al., 2007).

Dominant systems of knowledge building and reporting have generated deficit discourses where Aboriginal individuals, families, and communities are viewed through a lens of "negativity, deficiency and failure" (Fogarty et al., 2018a, p. 2). In many cases, this has led to policies and interventions to solve individual problems and fix Aboriginal communities (Fogarty et al., 2018b) while avoiding examination of the systems and processes that cause the harm Aboriginal people live with each day. In these contexts, there has been limited attention to family, kinship, and connectedness that are central to Aboriginal understandings of social and emotional wellbeing (Gee, 2016). There has also been limited recognition of cultural identity and continuity of connection to culture and country, which have been demonstrated to have a protective and healing effect for trauma-related outcomes for Aboriginal people (Chandler & Lalonde, 2008). In NNN, young Aboriginal women have commonly told stories of nested disconnection within characteristically connected contexts. These young women have described familial violence, grief, loss, and separation through removal and incarceration. They also share stories of positive connection with a family member, usually an Auntie or grandmother, who they learnt from and could rely on. Sadly, positive connections are often outnumbered by negative relationships not of the young women's doing but artefacts of familial breakdown between older relatives. This splintering of connections within families and communities meant some young women had limited opportunities to connect with their culture, affecting new or additional experiences of disconnection and loss.

Box 5.3 What we've learned . . .

Ciara (age 14) reflected:

> "I want to know my Uncle more but he and Nan [grandmother] don't get along and Nan is the boss so I don't get to". (Ciara)

Ciara (not her real name) had a strong connection with her Nan and did not want to risk going against her wishes. Ciara did not know why the relationship had broken down but did know her sense of obligation and direction as set by her Nan as an Elder in her family.

The centrality of deep interconnectedness in Aboriginal life may also amplify the experience of trauma. Experiences of grief and loss can be compounded through relationships, impacting Aboriginal young people's social and emotional wellbeing from a young age, situating them at perilous intersections of disconnection, disadvantage, vulnerability, and risk (Ralph & Ryan, 2017).

Understandings of youth violence in this context must consider how collective trauma impacts the individual and what role family, culture, and connection can play in mediating and moderating outcomes. Youth violence cannot be understood in the absence of contextual factors relating to the continuing violence of colonisation, including silencing expressions of culture and the invisibility of Aboriginal voices in giving violence meaning (Cunneen & Tauri, 2019). Atkinson (2002, 2013) contends collective trauma manifests across generations as expressions of violence against self and others, as both experience and activity. Raphael et al. (2007) suggest patterns of behaviour, including cycles of violence and abuse, risk-taking, substance use, and actions adverse to looking after the self, health, and wellbeing (Halloran, 2004), are expressions of complex and collective trauma. Data suggest Aboriginal young people report psychological distress and emotional and behavioural challenges at rates almost three times higher than their non-Aboriginal peers (Calma et al., 2017; Ralph & Ryan, 2017). These rates are exacerbated for justice-involved Aboriginal young people, where 90% are estimated to have a psychological disorder of some kind (Kalucy et al., 2019). These symptoms of trauma are suggested to be transmitted through traumatic memories, emotional contagion, or secondary impacts associated with the traumatisation of a loved one (Raphael et al., 2007).

Trauma-informed and culturally safe practice with youth violence

Evidence regarding the intersections of trauma, culture, and youth violence substantiate the need for trauma-informed and culturally safe ways of working with young people who use and experience violence. To date, this need has not been met, and trauma-informed and culturally safe ways of working with youth violence are typically thought of separately and rarely converge in meaningful ways. These observations echo those of Menzies (2020), who found none of the 55 statutory child protection workers surveyed reported using trauma theory (and hence trauma-informed approaches) in their work with Aboriginal families. Reflecting on these findings, Menzies and Grace (2022) note culturally meaningful approaches to practice are important to address issues of overrepresentation in child protection and justice systems and that historic and sociopolitical contexts of violent colonisation, forcible removal, and assimilation mean that it is critical that our approach to practice recognises the experience and impacts of intergenerational and collective trauma for Aboriginal people. From a contrasting (but complementary) perspective, a further impetus for thinking about trauma-informed and culturally safe approaches to practice in unison is the incredible opportunity to learn from Aboriginal people – privileging and respecting their knowledge systems and practices (Tujague & Ryan, 2023). Hewlett et al. (2023) note Aboriginal wisdom and practices are inherently strengths-based and healing-informed, emphasising connection as intrinsic to wellbeing (Garvey et al., 2021; Hine et al., 2023; Parter & Wilson, 2021) and have much to offer trauma-informed approaches to practice with all young people who use violence. In the following sections, we explore what it means for practice to be trauma-informed and culturally safe before describing what that looks like for us in NNN.

What does it mean to be trauma-informed?

Being trauma-informed seems to mean different things to different people. Rather than a specific intervention to implement and evaluate, a trauma-informed approach involves adopting a "trauma lens" in our work. Yatchmenoff et al. (2017) note despite differences in how this lens is described, there is consistent agreement that being trauma-informed means being aware of the prevalence of trauma, understanding its impact(s), and committing to incorporate these understandings in policy, procedure, and practice (Guarino et al., 2009; Hopper et al., 2010; SAMHSA, 2014). Practice that is trauma-informed is guided by principles that emphasise safety; trustworthiness and transparency; peer support; collaboration and mutuality; empowerment, voice, and choice; and responsivity to cultural, historical, and gender issues (SAMHSA, 2014). Trauma-informed practice is person-centred, strengths-based, and sensitive to universal needs for safety, belonging, and self-efficacy (Levine & Kline, 2006; Scott et al., 2021). The most widely accepted framework for trauma-informed practice is that issued in the US by the Substance Abuse and Mental Health Services Administration (SAMHSA) (2014). This framework characterises trauma-informed practice as existing across a continuum, progressing from realising the widespread experience and impact(s) of trauma and understanding the potential pathways to recovery, to recognising the signs and symptoms of trauma in clients, families, staff, and others involved in the service system; to responding by fully integrating knowledge about trauma into all aspects of policy, procedure and practice; and finally by seeking to actively avoid re-traumatisation (SAMHSA, 2014). The SAMHSA (2014) model's predominant focus on recognition and response has been extended with the suggestion of two further goals to characterise trauma-informed practice: "replenishment" (Atkinson, 2013) and "regenerate and revive" (Cubillo, 2021). These refer to cultural practices of care, connection, and healing.

What does it mean to be culturally safe?

Irihapeti Ramsden (Papps & Ramsden, 1996: Ramsden, 2002), a Māori nurse and scholar, first used the term "cultural safety" to urge more responsive, respectful, and self-aware practice in New Zealand health care. Tujague and Ryan (2023) note that valuable contemporary understandings of cultural safety privilege the experiences of Aboriginal people over those of non-Aboriginal practitioners and situate the experience of cultural safety from the perspective of Aboriginal people. Cultural safety can be thought of as a lens which views individuals in their location related to experience of colonial oppression and marginalisation (Wood & Schwass, 1993). Tujague and Ryan (2023) argue culturally safe and trauma-informed approaches are indivisible – practice cannot be culturally safe if it is not trauma-informed.

As with trauma-informed approaches, culturally safe approaches to practice exist across a continuum. In this case, they move from cultural awareness, through cultural competence, to cultural safety (Ramsden, 1992, 2002; Tujague & Ryan, 2023). Cultural awareness training aims to increase awareness of the historic and sociocultural factors that contextualise Aboriginal people's experiences – often urging self-reflection on worldviews and possible bias (Thomson, 2005). Critiques of cultural awareness reason that awareness alone rarely translates to meaningful changes for those most affected (Fredericks et al., 2011). Notions of cultural competency and culturally sensitive practice are similarly critiqued for any real associated change, perhaps because of their underpinning construction of culture as "other" and "different" (Browne & Varcoe, 2006). Greater promise is associated with culturally appropriate and culturally responsive practice that reflects local traditions, meets local needs, and acknowledges experiences of colonisation and oppression (Danso, 2018). Culturally responsive practice requires self-awareness but suggests this involves an ongoing process of recognising and renegotiating one's own positionality (Bennett & Gates, 2019). Browne and Fiske (2001) explain cultural safety goes beyond the approaches described to include "an analysis of power imbalances, institutional discrimination, and the nature of relationships between the colonized and colonizers as they apply to interactions at the macro and micro levels" (pp. 8–9).

Trauma-informed and culturally safe practice in NNN

Consistent with a trauma-informed lens, NNN takes a person-centred, strengths-based approach (Levine & Kline, 2006; Scott et al., 2021), recognising that young people bring knowledge, skills, and experience to inform practice. We explain that we want to better understand violence, positioning them as experts in a relational and collaborative process of knowing and growing. Informed by a culturally safe ethos, this process is led by young people's perspectives, unpacking social constructions of identity, culture, and Othering. Similarly, we avoid assumptions about class, cultural and racialised identities that often inform dominant ideas about risk, and (criminogenic) needs related to violence, instead focusing on the young person's "whole story," considering the wider determinants of experience at the intersections of trauma, class, culture, and gender.

Integral to the development and continuous improvement of NNN is that Aboriginal knowledges and ways of doing are respected and foregrounded in the program, for all young people, not just those of Aboriginal heritage. We respect the intrinsic fit between what the neuroscience of trauma tells us about impacts of trauma and what we need to heal and Aboriginal knowledges and practices that prioritise connection and story (Perry, 2008). This is consistent with Atkinson's (2013) recommendation that the synergies between Aboriginal healing and neuroscience-informed approaches be realised. The work of influential clinician Dr Bruce Perry and his development of the neurosequential model of therapeutics (NMT) has been important in this regard. NMT is a neuroscience and trauma-informed approach to practice that focuses on identifying strengths and sequencing interventions that target regulation and relationality (Perry, 2008, 2009). NMT approaches are relational, relevant, repetitive, rewarding, rhythmic, and respectful of people and culture (Barfield et al., 2012). Perry (2008) notes that the characteristic qualities of NMT respond to lessons from Aboriginal culture on what it takes to heal from trauma. He points out the importance, therein, of experiential retelling or re-enactment through song, story, or dance; the patterned repetitive representation of experience through art;

and the position of both within intensely relational connections to family, culture, and country (Perry, 2008).

Trauma-informed and culturally safe practice in NNN is established through a sensitive, relational, and strengths-based way of working. We tend to take a low-key, non-threatening approach in our work with young people. We are clear about our roles as practitioners, acknowledging that while we know some things (Bessarab & Ng'andu, 2010), we are there to learn from young people. We are transparent about the program, its aims, and its objectives, acknowledging that contexts of justice-involvement can constrain choices about participation. We encourage young people to decide how they will participate, thereby recognising young people's agency to make choices about what works for them. Particular attention is given to considering space, materials, and time. Where possible, we work alongside young people, sitting parallel to them (while not intruding on personal space), avoiding too direct eye contact, while using visual and tactile exhibits as a focus of conversation.

Our approach to practice is deeply relational and embraces the importance of reciprocity in building relational connection. Working in this way requires the program to have a carefully balanced structure content and pace. Reflection and feedback on processes of beginnings and endings in the pilot phase of NNN motivated us to do things differently in the program. This has meant largely surrendering controlled, actuarial approaches in the content, instead drawing from practice wisdom imbued within decolonising and creative methodologies to stimulate narrative story telling by the young person about their experience. This has challenged us to sit with discomfort of unforetold stories and to have patience while allowing processes of connection, knowing, and understanding to unfold.

In developing our understanding of the role and place of violence (and trauma) in the lives of the young people we work with, we are conscious to recognise and validate the experience of harm and to recognise young people's strengths and resilience. Consistent with Westerman (2004), our communication styles are open-ended and positively phrased and focus on the narratives young people provide. We are genuinely interested in young people's perspectives and the things that matter most to them. In the following section, we describe how these practices are enacted in our development, testing, and trialling of the Now.See. Hear! (NSH) card set in beginning sessions of NNN.

Now.See.Hear!

NSH is a card-based tool currently "under construction" by the NNN program. NSH uses photographic images, conversational prompts, card sort, and narrative scoring cues to provide a tactile, engaging, and

Figure 5.1 A young person contemplating photo prompts for the Now.See.Hear! tool

accessible way of giving voice to young people's exposure to trauma, its impacts, and the subsequent experience (see Figure 5.1). The visual and narrative format of the tool is consistent with Aboriginal knowledges and practices as well as being trauma-informed. Culturally safe trauma screening is a critical, yet often overlooked, first step towards improving justice-involved young people's experiences and outcomes in programs. Currently, no culturally safe trauma screening tool exists for this cohort. We consider the tool to have wider applicability across practice settings for sensitively screening and stimulating storied narratives about traumatic experiences and their impacts.

Development

The NSH tool is being developed with the support of the NSW Government Justice Innovation Fund. The project team is guided by Aboriginal leadership from Auntie Elsie Randall, Dr Karen Menzies, and the NNN cultural reference group; lived-experience leadership from the NNN youth consortium; and subject matter expertise from Dr Susan Rayment-McHugh and Dr Tim Warton. With appropriate ethics approval, developing the tool has involved testing and trialling various sample photographs of people, places, events, and interactions alongside an evolving set of conversational prompts.

Photographs are a common way of documenting and describing the social world (Carrabine, 2012; Fitzgibbon & Stengel, 2018; Pauwels, 2017). They are at once a familiar and shared way of seeing and showing, but their interpretation and meaning embodies a way of seeing that is uniquely our own (Berger, 1992). Photographs have been used by researchers to prompt memories and stimulate discussions about past or present experiences and events. Harper (2002) suggests photographs can support a deeper understanding of human experience than words alone. Copes et al. (2018) observe photographs can allow a person to tell their story in ways that allow for emotions to contextualise the meanings made about it. When used carefully and with considered application, visual methods such as photo elicitation and Photovoice have been identified to be culturally appropriate (Brooks et al., 2008) and trauma-informed (Golden, 2020). We appreciate that while this approach is distinct, it is not unique. Visual methods have also long been used with justice-involved young people, primarily in the form of projective psychological techniques. The Roberts Apperception Test for Children (RATC) (McArthur & Roberts, 1982) has been used with justice-involved young people to assess behavioural, social, and emotional functioning and concerns, conflicts, and emotional management strategies (Almiro et al., 2023). The RATC is administered using 16 cards featuring line drawings of interpersonal situations of everyday life. Young people are asked to develop a story with a beginning, middle, and end about each card (McArthur & Roberts, 1982). It is theorised that young people will project their own thoughts, concerns, conflicts, and problem-solving styles onto these stories, with findings suggesting that responses are less distorted by defensiveness or social desirability than they are for self-report surveys or scales (Aiken, 1999).

Delivery

Informed by such approaches, we have tested and trialled the NSH tool by presenting young people with a range of photos and asking them to select ones they think best represent their experiences as they relate to conversational prompts exploring (1) how the young person perceives and describes themselves, including what matters to them and what their strengths are; (2) what's happening for them now, what's happened in the past, and what might have happened in between; (3) how the young person experiences and uses power and control; (4) their experiences of systems and services; and (5) their meaningful relationships with family, friends, community, and culture. To describe this in more detail, the practitioner begins by presenting the young person with a range of photos and inviting them to select two or three they think best represent them. The practitioner lets the young person know that they'll do the same so that in getting to know a bit more about the young person, the young person can get to know a bit more about the practitioner. The practitioner notes that if there isn't a photo that either of them feels suits, they can describe what one would look like, acknowledging the card set can always be improved with the advice of young people we work with. After both have selected their photos, the practitioner explains that next we'll share what these photos represent for us. The practitioner may offer to go first, showing the photos they've selected and sharing the stories that explain them. The practitioner should take care to select and story photos to match a level of interpersonal sharing with the young person while prioritising concrete examples rather than esoteric ponderings. To provide a concrete example, Figure 5.2 is a photograph used in pilot work for this tool. The photo captures the legs and feet of a person, focusing on their distinctive red shoes. This brand and style of shoe is observed in the local community to be associated by some people with a particular subculture of young people; however, even those who identify with the subculture are also divided on these particular shoes, normally because of their colour. The narrative following the photo shows the story the practitioner shares.

Figure 5.2 A photo of distinctive red shoes used in development of the Now.See. Hear! tool

Box 5.4 NNN practitioner reflection . . .

The following quote represents a typical reflection the practitioner makes in selecting this photo and storying its relevance.

> "I've selected this photo because I really like shoes, I love a good pair of sneakers, especially ones that stand out from the crowd! These shoes really interest me because of their colour, but also . . . because I notice they're a shoe that seems to divide people, like you're either team red TN, or you're not, and then even if you are team TN sometimes you're not into the red ones! What do you think about them? Are you team TN? Do you like the red?"

By going first, choosing a relatable photo, and sharing personal information in this way the practitioner establishes the activity as a non-threatening experience. The professional's story is personal but not too intimate. For subsequent prompts thereafter, the young person's stories are prioritised, and their perspectives validated.

Feedback from the field

We have found the Now.See.Here! process to be an engaging way to work with young people who have used and experienced violence. It establishes a space for shared conversation by practitioners modelling an authentic response in selecting photos and sharing stories for the first conversation prompt. We have found that some young people have shared rich and nuanced narratives that contextualise their experiences and would have otherwise been unknown. Feedback loops (Castleden & Garvin, 2008) between test and trial, the cultural reference group, and the youth consortium are continuing to shape and refine the photos used, the wording of conversational prompts, and how the tool should be implemented and interpreted.

Conclusion

This chapter has explored the importance of a trauma-informed and culturally safe approach to working with youth violence. It commenced with an overview of what we mean by trauma, how trauma has been linked to the use of violence, and the complexities of interconnected experiences of culture (trauma) and violence. The chapter outlined our understandings of what it means to be trauma-informed and culturally safe in our practice and how this is conceptualised in the NNN program and foregrounded in beginning sessions by using visual methods and narrative storytelling. These methods are expanded on in the following chapter where they are used to explore emotional recognition and regulation.

References

Abram, K. M., Teplin, L. A., Charles, D. R., Longworth, S. L., McClelland, G. M., & Dulcan, M. K. (2004). Posttraumatic stress disorder and trauma in youth in juvenile detention. *Archives of General Psychiatry*, *61*(4), 403. https://doi.org/10.1001/archpsyc.61.4.403

Aiken, L. R. (1999). *Personality assessment methods and practice* (3rd rev.). Hogrefe & Huber Publishers.

Almiro, P. A., Marques, P. R., Duarte, M. C., Alberto, I. M., & Simões, M. R. (2023). Validation study of the Roberts Apperception Test for children (RATC) in an adolescents' forensic sample. *Acta Psychologica*, *235*, Article 103900. https://doi.org/10.1016/j.actpsy.2023.103900

Ariga, M., Uehara, T., Takeuchi, K., Ishige, Y., Nakano, R., & Mikuni, M. (2008). Trauma exposure and posttraumatic stress disorder in delinquent female adolescents. *Journal of Child Psychology and Psychiatry*, *49*(1), 79–87. https://doi.org/10.1111/j.1469-7610.2007.01817

Atkinson, J. (2002). *Trauma trails, recreating song lines: The transgenerational effects of trauma in Indigenous Australia*. Spinifex Press.

Atkinson, J. (2013). *Trauma-informed services and trauma-specific care for Indigenous Australian children* (Resource Sheet No. 21). Produced for the Closing the Gap Clearinghouse. Australian Institute of Family Studies.

Australian Institute of Health and Welfare. (2018). *Young people in child protection and under youth justice supervision: 1 July 2013 to 30 June 2017* (AIHW Cat. No. CSI 26). www.aihw.gov.au/reports/child-protection/young-people-in-youth-justice-supervision-2013-17/

Australian Institute of Health and Welfare. (2020). *Young people under youth justice supervision and in child protection 2018–19*. https://doi.org/10.25816/ech1-dg08

Azad, A., Hau, H. G., & Karlsson, M. (2018). Adolescent female offenders' subjective experiences of how peers influence norm-breaking behavior. *Child and Adolescent Social Work Journal*, *35*(3), 257–270. https://doi.org/10.1007/s10560-017-0526-0

Baglivio, M. T., Epps, N., Swartz, K., Huq, M. S., Sheer, A., & Hardt, N. S. (2014). The prevalence of adverse childhood experiences (ACE) in the lives of juvenile offenders. *Journal of Juvenile Justice, 3*(2), 1–17. www.prisonpolicy.org/scans/Prevalence_of_ACE.pdf

Baidawi, S. (2020). Crossover children: Examining initial criminal justice system contact among child protection-involved youth. *Australian Social Work*, *73*(3), 280–295. https://doi.org/10.1080/0312407x.2019.1686765

Baidawi, S., & Sheehan, R. (2019). *"Crossover kids": Offending by child protection-involved youth* (Trends and Issues in Crime and Criminal Justice No. 582). Australian Institute of Criminology. https://doi.org/10.52922/ti04138

Ball, R., & Baidawi, S. (2021). Aboriginal crossover children's characteristics, service needs and service responses: The views of Australian key stakeholders. *Children and Youth Services Review*, *129*, Article 106176. https://doi.org/10.1016/j.childyouth.2021.106176

Barfield, S., Dobson, C., Gaskill, R., & Perry, B. D. (2012). Neurosequential model of therapeutics in a therapeutic preschool: Implications for work with children with complex neuropsychiatric problems. *International Journal of Play Therapy*, *21*(1), 30–44. https://doi.org/10.1037/a0025955

Barnes, J. C., & Motz, R. T. (2018). Reducing racial inequalities in adulthood arrest by reducing inequalities in school discipline: Evidence from the school-to-prison pipeline. *Developmental Psychology*, *54*(12), 2328–2340. https://doi.org/10.1037/dev0000613

Bennett, B., & Gates, T. G. (2019). Teaching cultural humility for social workers serving LGBTQI Aboriginal communities in Australia. *Social Work Education*, *38*(5), 604–617. https://doi.org/10.1080/02615479.2019.1588872

Berger, J. (1992). *Keeping a rendezvous*. Vintage International.

Bessarab, D., & Ng'andu, B. (2010). Yarning about Yarning as a legitimate method in Indigenous research. *International Journal of Critical Indigenous Studies*, *3*(1), 37–50. https://doi.org/10.5204/ijcis.v3i1.57

Blakemore, T., Randall, E., Rak, L., & Cocuzzoli, F. (2021). Deep listening and relationality: Cross-cultural reflections on practice with young women who use violence. *Australian Social Work*, *75*(3), 304–316. https://doi.org/10.1080/0312407x.2021.1914697

Bloom, B., & Covington, S. (2001). *Effective gender-responsive interventions in juvenile justice: Addressing the lives of delinquent girls*. Paper presented at the 2001 Annual Meeting of the American Society of Criminology.

Boxer, P., & Terranova, A. M. (2008). Effects of multiple maltreatment experiences among psychiatrically hospitalized youth. *Child Abuse & Neglect*, *32*(6), 637–647. https://doi.org/10.1016/j.chiabu.2008.02.003

Bradshaw, C. P., & Garbarino, J. (2006). Social cognition as a mediator of the influence of family and community violence on adolescent development: Implications for intervention. *Annals of the New York Academy of Sciences*, *1036*(1), 85–105. https://doi.org/10.1196/annals.1330.005

Bremmer, D. (1999). *Effects of childhood abuse on the HPA axis and hippocampus in women with and without posttraumatic stress disorder*. Paper presented at 38th Annual Meeting of American College of Neuropsychopharmacology, Acapulco.

Briere, J., & Scott, C. (2015). Complex trauma in adolescents and adults: Effects and treatment. *Psychiatric Clinics*, *38*(3), 515–527. https://doi.org/10.1016/j.psc.2015.05.004

Brooks, C., Poudrier, J., & Thomas-MacLean, R. (2008). Creating collaborative visions with Aboriginal women: A photovoice project. In P. Liamputtlong (Ed.), *Doing cross-cultural research: Ethical and methodological perspectives* (pp. 193–211). Springer International Publishing. https://doi.org/10.1007/978-1-4020-8567-3_13

Browne, A. J., & Fiske, J.-A. (2001). First Nations women's encounters with mainstream health care services. *Western Journal of Nursing Research*, *23*(2), 126–147. https://doi.org/10.1177/019394590102300203

Browne, A. J., & Varcoe, C. (2006). Critical cultural perspectives and health care involving Aboriginal peoples. *Contemporary Nurse*, *22*(2), 155–168. https://doi.org/10.5172/conu.2006.22.2.155

Buckingham, S. (2016). Trauma informed juvenile justice. *American Criminal Law Review*, *53*(3), 641–692.

Calma, T., Dudgeon, P., & Bray, A. (2017). Aboriginal and Torres Strait Islander social and emotional wellbeing and mental health. *Australian Psychologist*, *52*(4), 255–260. https://doi.org/10.1111/ap.12299

Carrabine, E. (2012). Just images: Aesthetics, ethics and visual criminology. *British Journal of Criminology*, *52*(3), 463–489. https://doi.org/10.1093/bjc/azr089

Castleden, H., & Garvin, T. (2008). Modifying photovoice for community-based participatory Indigenous research. *Social Science & Medicine*, *66*(6), 1393–1405. https://doi.org/10.1016/j.socscimed.2007.11.030

Chandler, M. J., & Lalonde, C. E. (2008). Cultural continuity as a protective factor against suicide in first nations youth. *Horizons*, *10*, 68–72.

Charak, R., Ford, J. D., Modrowski, C. A., & Kerig, P. K. (2018). Polyvictimization, emotion dysregulation, symptoms of posttraumatic stress disorder, and behavioral health problems among justice-involved youth: A latent class analysis. *Journal of Abnormal Child Psychology*, *47*(2), 287–298. https://doi.org/10.1007/s10802-018-0431-9

Chesney-Lind, M. (2003, October). *Gender and justice: What about girls?* Presentation at the National Girls' Initiative Symposium, Washington, DC.

Chesney-Lind, M. (2006). Patriarchy, crime, and justice: Feminist criminology in an era of backlash. *Feminist Criminology*, 1(1), 6–26. https://doi.org/10.1177/1557085105282893

Cloitre, M., Stolbach, B. C., Herman, J. L., van der Kolk, B., Pynoos, R., Wang, J., & Petkova, E. (2009). A developmental approach to complex PTSD: Childhood and adult cumulative trauma as predictors of symptom complexity. *Journal of Traumatic Stress*, 22(5), 399–408. https://doi.org/10.1002/jts.20444

Cook, A., Spinazzola, P., Ford, J., Lanktree, C., Blaustein, M., Cloitre, M., DeRosa, R., Hubbard, R., Kagan, R., Liautaud, J., Mallah, K., Olafson, E., & van der Kolk, B. (2005). Complex trauma in children and adolescents. *Psychiatric Annals*, *35*, 390–398. https://doi.org/10.3928/00485713-20050501-05

Copes, H., Tchoula, W., Brookman, F., & Ragland, J. (2018). Photo-elicitation interviews with vulnerable populations: Practical and ethical considerations. *Deviant Behavior*, *39*(4), 475–494. https://doi.org/10.1080/01639625.2017.1407109

Cubillo, C. (2021). *Trauma-informed care: Culturally responsive practice working with Aboriginal and Torres Strait Islander communities.* https://psychology.org.au/for-members/publications/inpsych/2021/august-special-issue-3/trauma-informed-care

Cunneen, C., & Tauri, J. M. (2019). Indigenous peoples, criminology, and criminal justice. *Annual Review of Criminology*, 2(1), 359–381. https://doi.org/10.1146/annurev-criminol-011518-024630

Danso, R. (2018). Cultural competence and cultural humility: A critical reflection on key cultural diversity concepts. *Journal of Social Work*, *18*(4), 410–430. https://doi.org/10.1177/1468017316654341

De Deckker, K. (2018). Understanding trauma in the refugee context. *Journal of Psychologists and Counsellors in Schools*, *28*(2), 248–259. https://doi.org/10.1017/jgc.2018.12

De Lisi, M., & Beauregard, E. (2018). Adverse childhood experiences and criminal extremity: New evidence for sexual homicide. *Journal of Forensic Sciences*, *63*(2), 484–489. www.doi.org/10.1111/1556-4029.13584

Denton, R., Frogley, C., Jackson, S., John, M., & Querstret, D. (2017). The assessment of developmental trauma in children and adolescents: A systematic review. *Clinical Child Psychology and Psychiatry*, *22*(2), 260–287. https://doi.org/10.1177/1359104516631607

Draper, C., & Brown, I. (2022). *Effective treatment for trauma – skills for EA professionals*. https://archive.hshsl.umaryland.edu/handle/10713/18574

Duron, J. F., Williams-Butler, A., Mattson, P., & Boxer, P. (2022). Trauma exposure and mental health needs among adolescents involved with the juvenile justice system. *Journal of Interpersonal Violence*, *37*(17–18), NP15700–NP15725. https://doi.org/10.1177/08862605211016358

Farrington, D. P. (1993). Childhood origins of teenage antisocial behaviour and adult social dysfunction. *Journal of the Royal Society of Medicine*, *86*, 13–17.

Felitti, V. J., Anda, R. F., Nordenberg, D., Williamson, D. F., Spitz, A. M., Edwards, V., Koss, M. P., & Marks, J. S. (1998). Relationship of childhood abuse and household dysfunction to many of the leading causes of death in adults. The Adverse Childhood Experiences (ACE) study. *American Journal of Preventive Medicine*, *14*(4), 245–258. https://doi.org/10.1016/s0749-3797(98)00017-8

Finkel, E. J. (2007). Impelling and inhibiting forces in the perpetration of intimate partner violence. *Review of General Psychology*, *11*(2), 193–207.

Finkelhor, D., Ormrod, R. K., & Turner, H. A. (2007). Polyvictimization and trauma in a national longitudinal cohort. *Development and Psychopathology*, *19*(1), 149–166. https://doi.org/10.1017/S0954579407070083

Finkelhor, D., Ormrod, R. K., & Turner, H. A. (2009). The developmental epidemiology of childhood victimization. *Journal of Interpersonal Violence*, *24*, 711–731. https://doi.org/10.1177/0886260508317185

Fitzgibbon, W., & Stengel, C. M. (2018). Women's voices made visible: Photovoice in visual criminology. *Punishment & Society*, *20*(4), 411–431. https://doi.org/10.1177/1462474517700137

Fogarty, W., Bulloch, H., McDonnell, S., & Davis, M. (2018a). *Deficit discourse and Indigenous health: How narrative framings of Aboriginal and Torres Strait Islander people are reproduced in policy*. The Lowitja Institute.

Fogarty, W., Lovell, M., Langenberg, J., & Heron, M.-J. (2018b). *Deficit discourse and strengths-based approaches: Changing the narrative of Aboriginal and Torres Strait Islander health and wellbeing*. The Lowitja Institute.

Ford, J. D. (2005). Treatment implications of altered neurobiology, affect regulation and information processing following child maltreatment. *Psychiatric Annals*, *35*, 410–419. https://doi.org/10.3928/00485713-20050501-07

Ford, J. D., Chapman, J., Connor, D. F., & Cruise, K. R. (2012). Complex trauma and aggression in secure juvenile justice settings. *Criminal Justice and Behavior*, *39*(6), 694–724. https://doi.org/10.1177/0093854812436957

Ford, J. D., Hartman, J. K., Hawke, J., & Chapman, J. C. (2008). Traumatic victimization posttraumatic stress disorder, suicidal ideation, and substance abuse risk among juvenile justice-involved youths. *Journal of Child and Adolescent Trauma*, *1*, 75–92.

Ford, J. D., Hawke, J., & Chapman, J. C. (2010). *Complex psychological trauma among juvenile justice-involved youth*. University of Connecticut.

Fox, B. H., Perez, N., Cass, E., Baglivio, M. T., & Epps, N. (2015). Trauma changes everything: Examining the relationship between adverse childhood experiences and serious, violent and chronic juvenile offenders. *Child Abuse & Neglect*, *46*, 163–173. https://doi.org/10.1016/j.chiabu.2015.01.011

Franco, F. (2021). Understanding and treating C-PTSD. *Journal of Health Service Psychology*, *47*(2), 85–93. https://doi.org/10.1016/j.chiabu.2015.01.011

Fredericks, B., Adams, K., Finlay, S., Fletcher, G., Andy, S., Briggs, L., & Hall, R. (2011). Engaging the practice of Indigenous yarning in action research. *ALAR: Action Learning and Action Research Journal*, *17*(2), 12–24.

Garvey, G., Anderson, K., Gall, A., Butler, T. L., Whop, L. J., Arley, B., Cunningham, J., Dickson, M., Cass, A., Ratcliffe, J., Tong, A., & Howard, K. (2021). The fabric of Aboriginal and Torres Strait Islander Wellbeing: A conceptual model. *International Journal of Environmental Research and Public Health*, *18*(15), Article 7745. https://doi.org/10.3390/ijerph18157745

Gee, G. (2016). *Resilience and recovery from trauma among Aboriginal help-seeking clients in an urban Aboriginal community controlled health organisation*. University of Melbourne.

Gershoff, E. T. (2002). Corporal punishment by parents and associated child behaviors and experiences: A meta-analytic and theoretical review. *Psychological Bulletin*, *128*(4), 539–579. https://doi.org/10.1037/0033-2909.128.4.539

Golden, T. (2020). Reframing photovoice: Building on the method to develop more equitable and responsive research practices. *Qualitative Health Research*, *30*(6), 960–972. https://doi.org/10.1177/1049732320905564

Guarino, K., Soares, P., Konnath, K., Clervil, R., & Bassuk, E. (2009). *Trauma-informed organizational toolkit*. Center for Mental Health Services, Substance Abuse and Mental Health Services Administration, the Daniels Fund, the National Child Traumatic Stress Network, and the W. K. Kellogg Foundation. www.air.org/resource/trauma-informed-organizational-toolkit

Halloran, M. (2004). Cultural maintenance and trauma in Indigenous Australia. *Murdoch University Electronic Journal of Law*, *11*(4).

Harms, L. (2015). *Understanding trauma and resilience*. Bloomsbury Publishing.

Harper, D. (2002). Talking about pictures: A case for photo elicitation. *Visual Studies*, *17*(1), 13–26. https://doi.org/10.1080/14725860220137345

Herman, J. L. (1992). Complex PTSD: A syndrome in survivors of prolonged and repeated trauma. *Journal of Traumatic Stress*, *5*(3), 377–391. https://doi.org/10.1002/jts.2490050305

Herman, J. L., & Harvey, M. R. (1997). Adult memories of childhood trauma: A naturalistic clinical study. *Journal of Traumatic Stress*, *10*, 557–571. https://doi.org/10.1002/jts.2490100404

Herz, D. C., Ryan, J. P., & Bilchik, S. (2010). Challenges facing crossover youth: An examination of juvenile-justice decision making and recidivism. *Family Court Review*, *48*(2), 305–321.

Hewlett, N., Hayes, L., Williams, R., Hamilton, S., Holland, L., Gall, A., Doyle, M., Goldsbury, S., Boaden, N., & Reid, N. (2023). Development of an Australian FASD Indigenous framework: Aboriginal healing-informed and strengths-based ways of knowing, being and doing. *International Journal of Environmental Research and Public Health, 20*(6), Article 5215. http://doi.org/10.3390/ijerph20065215

Hine, R., Krakouer, J., Elston, J., Fredericks, B., Hunter, S.-A., Taylor, K., Stephens, T., Couzens, V., Manahan, E., DeSouza, R., Boyle, J., Callander, E., Cunningham, H., Miller, R., Willey, S., Wilton, K., & Skouteris, H. (2023). Identifying and dismantling racism in Australian perinatal settings: Reframing the narrative from a risk lens to intentionally prioritise connectedness and strengths in providing care to First Nations families. *Women and Birth*, *36*(1), 136–140. https://doi.org/10.1016/j.wombi.2022.04.007

Hirschberger, G. (2018). Collective trauma and the social construction of meaning. *Frontiers in Psychology*, *9*, Article 1441. https://doi.org/10.3389/fpsyg.2018.01441

Hopper, E. K., Bassuk, E. L., & Olivet, J. (2010). Shelter from the storm: Traumainformed care in homelessness services settings. *The Open Health Services and Policy Journal*, *3*(2), 80–100. https://doi.org/10.2174/1874924001003020080

Jaffee, S. R., Caspi, A., Moffitt, T. E., & Taylor, A. (2004). Physical maltreatment victim to antisocial child: Evidence of an environmentally mediated process. *Journal of Abnormal Psychology*, *113*(1), 44.

Kalucy, D., Nixon, J., Parvizian, M., Fernando, P., Sherriff, S., McMellon, J., D'Este, C., Eades, S. J., & Williamson, A. (2019). Exploring pathways to mental healthcare for urban Aboriginal young people: A qualitative interview study. *BMJ Open*, *9*, e025670–e025670. https://doi.org/10.1136/bmjopen-2018-025670

Kar, H. L. (2019). Acknowledging the victim to perpetrator trajectory: Integrating a mental health focused trauma-based approach into global violence programs. *Aggression and Violent Behavior*, *47*, 293–297. https://doi.org/10.1016/j.avb.2018.10.004

Kellerman, N. P. (2001). Psychopathology in children of Holocaust survivors: A review of the research literature. *Israel Journal of Psychiatry and Related Sciences*, *38*(1), 36–46.

Kerig, P. K. (2013). *Trauma-informed assessment and intervention*. National Center for Child Traumatic Stress.

Kerig, P. K., & Becker, S. P. (2010). From internalizing to externalizing: Theoretical models of the processes linking PTSD to juvenile delinquency. In S. J. Egan (Ed.), *Postraumatic stress disorder (PTSD): Causes, symptoms, and treatment* (pp. 33–78). Nova Science Publishers.

Kezelman, C., & Stavropoulos, P. (2012). *'The last frontier'–practice guidelines for treatment of complex trauma and trauma informed care and service delivery*. Adults Surviving Child Abuse.

Krupnik, V. (2019). Trauma or adversity? *Traumatology*, *25*(4), 256–261. https://doi.org/10.1037/trm0000169

Levine, P. A., & Kline, M. (2006). *Trauma through a child's eyes: Awakening the ordinary miracle of healing*. North Atlantic Books.

Malvaso, C. G., Cale, J., Whitten, T., Day, A., Singh, S., Hackett, L., Delfabbro, P. H., & Ross, S. (2021). Associations between adverse childhood experiences and trauma among young people who offend: A systematic literature review. *Trauma, Violence, & Abuse*, *23*(5), 1677–1694. https://doi.org/10.1177/15248380211013132

Malvaso, C. G., Day, A., Hackett, L., Cale, J., Delfabbro, P., & Ross, S. (2022). *Adverse childhood experiences and trauma among young people in the youth justice system* (Trends & Issues in Crime and Criminal Justice No. 651). Australian Institute of Criminology.

Malvaso, C. G., Delfabbro, P. H., & Day, A. (2017). The child protection and juvenile justice nexus in Australia: A longitudinal examination of the relationship between maltreatment and offending. *Child Abuse & Neglect*, *64*, 32–46. https://doi.org/10.1016/j.chiabu.2016.11.028

Malvaso, C. G., Delfabbro, P. H., & Day, A. (2019). Adverse childhood experiences in a South Australian sample of young people in detention. *Australian & New Zealand Journal of Criminology*, *52*(3), 411–431.

McArthur, D. S., & Roberts, G. E. (1982). *Roberts apperception test for children*. Western Psychological Services.

McCormack, L., & Thomson, S. (2017). Complex trauma in childhood, a psychiatric diagnosis in adulthood: Making meaning of a double-edged phenomenon. *Psychological Trauma: Theory, Research, Practice, and Policy*, *9*(2), 156–165. https://doi.org/10.1037/tra0000193

McCrory, E. J., De Brito, S. A., Sebastian, C. L., Mechelli, A., Bird, G., Kelly, P. A., & Viding, E. (2011). Heightened neural reactivity to threat in child victims of family violence. *Current Biology*, *21*(23), R947–R948. https://doi.org/10.1016/j.cub.2011.10.015

McCrory, E. J., De Brito, S. A., & Viding, E. (2010). Research review: The neurobiology and genetics of maltreatment and adversity. *Journal of Child Psychology and Psychiatry*, *51*(10), 1079–1095. https://doi.org/10.1111/j.1469-7610.2010.02271.x

Menzies, K. (2019). Understanding the Australian Aboriginal experience of collective, historical and intergenerational trauma. *International Social Work*, *62*(6), 1522–1534. https://doi.org/10.1177/0020872819870585

Menzies, K. (2020). *And it's not history. It's now: Embedding a trauma framework into the practice of welfare practitioners who work with Aboriginal families in the NSW child protection sector* [PhD thesis]. University of Western Sydney.

Menzies, K., & Grace, R. (2022). The efficacy of a child protection training program on the historical welfare context and Aboriginal trauma. *Australian Social Work*, *75*(1), 62–75. https://doi.org/10.1080/0312407X.2020.1745857

Miller, J., & Berger, E. (2020). A review of school trauma-informed practice for Aboriginal and Torres Strait Islander children and youth. *The Educational and Developmental Psychologist*, *37*(1), 39–46. https://doi.org/10.1017/edp.2020.2

Mitchell, T., & Arseneau, C. (2019). Colonial trauma: Complex, continuous, collective, cumulative and compounding effects on the health of Indigenous peoples in Canada and beyond. *International Journal of Indigenous Health*, *14*(2), 74–94. https://doi.org/10.32799/ijih.v14i2.32251

Mohatt, N. V., Thompson, A. B., Thai, N. D., & Tebes, J. K. (2014). Historical trauma as public narrative: A conceptual review of how history impacts present-day health. *Social Science & Medicine*, *106*, 128–136. https://doi.org/10.1016/j.socscimed.2014.01.043

Neumeister, A., Henry, S., & Krystal, J. H. (2007). Neurocircuitry and neuroplasticity in PTSD. In M. J. Friedman, T. M. Keane, & P. A. Resick (Eds.), *Handbook of PTSD: Science and practice* (pp. 151–165). The Guilford Press.

Norris, F. H. (1992). Epidemiology of trauma: Frequency and impact of different potentially traumatic events on different demographic groups. *Journal of Consulting and Clinical Psychology*, *60*(3), 409–418. https://doi.org/10.1037/0022-006X.60.3.409

Odgers, C. L., Moretti, M. M., & Dickon, N. R. (2005). Examining the science and practice of violence risk assessment with female adolescents. *Law and Human Behavior*, *29*, 7–27. https://doi.org/10.1007/s10979-005-1397-z

Oglesby, C. A. (2005). Coping with trauma: Staying the course. In P. Markula (Ed.), *Feminist sport studies: Sharing experiences of joy and pain* (pp. 101–109). State University of New York Press.

Papps, E., & Ramsden, I. (1996). Cultural safety in nursing: The New Zealand experience. *International Journal for Quality in Health Care*, *8*(5), 491–497. https://doi.org/10.1093/intqhc/8.5.49

Parter, C., & Wilson, S. (2021). My research is my story: A methodological framework of inquiry told through storytelling by a Doctor of Philosophy student. *Qualitative Inquiry*, *27*(8–9), 1084–1094. https://doi.org/10.1177/1077800420978759

Paton, J., Crouch, W., & Camic, P. (2009). Young offenders' experiences of traumatic life events: A qualitative investigation. *Clinical Child Psychology and Psychiatry*, *14*(1), 43–62. https://doi.org/10.1177/1359104508100135

Pauwels, L. (2017). Key methods of visual criminology: An overview of different approaches and their affordances. In M. Brown & E. Carrabine (Eds.), *Routledge international handbook of visual criminology* (pp. 62–73). Routledge. https://doi.org/10.4324/9781315713

Pearlman, L. A., & Courtois, C. A. (2005). Clinical applications of the attachment framework: Relational treatment of complex trauma. *Journal of Traumatic Stress*, *18*(5), 449–459. https://doi.org/10.1002/jts.20052

Perry, B. D. (2008). Forward. In C. A. Malchiodi (Ed.), *Creative interventions with traumatised children*. The Guilford Press.

Perry, B. D. (2009). Examining child maltreatment through a neurodevelopmental lens: Clinical applications of the neurosequential model of therapeutics. *Journal of Loss and Trauma*, *14*(4), 240–255. https://doi.org/10.1080/15325020903004350

Pine, D. S. (2007). Research review: A neuroscience framework for pediatric anxiety disorders. *Journal of Child Psychology and Psychiatry*, *48*(7), 631–648. https://doi.org/10.1111/j.1469-7610.2007.01751.x

Pisani, A. R., Wyman, P. A., Petrova, M., Schmeelk-Cone, K., Goldston, D. B., Xia, Y., & Gould, M. S. (2013). Emotion regulation difficulties, youth – adult relationships, and suicide attempts among high school students in underserved communities. *Journal of Youth and Adolescence*, *42*(6), 807–820. https://doi.org/10.1007/s10964-012-9884-2

Porter, M., & Haslam, N. (2005). Predisplacement and postdisplacement factors associated with mental health of refugees and internally displaced persons-A meta-analysis. *Journal of the American Medical Association*, *294*(5), 602–612. https://doi.org/10.1001/jama.294.5.602

Rahim, M. (2014). Developmental trauma disorder: An attachment-based perspective. *Clinical Child Psychology and Psychiatry*, *19*(4), 548–560. https://doi.org/10.1177/1359104514534947

Ralph, S., & Ryan, K. (2017). Addressing the mental health gap in working with Indigenous youth: Some considerations for non-Indigenous psychologists working with Indigenous youth. *Australian Psychologist*, *52*(4), 288–298. https://doi.org/10.1111/ap.12287

Ramsden, I. (1992). *Kawa Whakaruruhau: Guidelines for nursing and midwifery education*. Nursing Council of New Zealand.

Ramsden, I. (2002). *Cultural safety and nursing education in Aotearoa and Te Waipounamu* [PhD thesis]. Victoria University of Wellington.

Raphael, B., Delaney, P., & Bonner, D. (2007). Assessment of trauma for Aboriginal people. In J. P. Wilson & C. So kum Tan (Eds.), *Cross-cultural assessment of psychological trauma and PTSD* (pp. 337–358). Springer. https://doi.org/10.1007/978-0-387-70990-1_14

Sachs-Ericsson, N., Verona, E., Joiner, T., & Preacher, K. J. (2006). Parental verbal abuse and the mediating role of self criticism in adult internalizing disorders. *Journal of Affective Disorders*, *93*(1–3), 71–78. https://doi.org/10.1016/j.jad.2006.02.014

Scott, J., Jaber, L. S., & Rinaldi, C. M. (2021). Trauma-informed school strategies for SEL and ACE concerns during COVID-19. *Education Sciences*, *11*(12), 796. https://doi.org/10.3390/educsci11120796

Segrave, M., & Carlton, B. (2010). Women, trauma, criminalisation and imprisonment. *Current Issues in Criminal Justice*, 22(2), 287–305. https://doi.org/10.1080/10345329.2010.12035887

Sherman, F., & Balck, A. (2015). *Gender injustice: System-level juvenile justice reforms for girls*. National Crittenton Foundation.

Stanley, B. L., Zanin, A. C., Avalos, B. L., Tracy, S. J., & Town, S. (2021). Collective emotion during collective trauma: A metaphor analysis of the COVID-19 pandemic. *Qualitative Health Research*, *31*(10), 1890–1903. https://doi.org/10.1177/10497323211011589

Stubbs, J. (2011). Indigenous women in Australian criminal justice: Over-represented but rarely acknowledged. *Australian Indigenous Law Journal*, *15*(1), 47–61.

Subica, A. M., & Link, B. G. (2022). Cultural trauma as a fundamental cause of health disparities. *Social Science & Medicine*, *292*, 1–8. https://doi.org/10.1016/j.socscimed.2021.114574

Substance Abuse and Mental Health Services Administration. (2014). *Trauma-informed care in behavioral health services*. Treatment Improvement Protocol Series 57. Substance Abuse and Mental Health Services Administration. www.samhsa.gov/nctic/trauma-interventions

Taylor, L. K., & Weems, C. F. (2009). What do youth report as a traumatic event? Toward a developmentally informed classification of traumatic stressors. *Psychological Trauma: Theory, Research, Practice, and Policy*, *1*(2), 91–106. https://doi.org/10.1037/a0016012

Teicher, M. H., Andersen, S. L., Polcari, A., Anderson, C. M., Navalta, C. P., & Kim, D. M. (2003). The neurobiological consequences of early stress and childhood maltreatment. *Neuroscience & Biobehavioral Reviews*, *27*(1), 33–44. https://doi.org/10.1016/S0149-7634(03)00007-1

Teicher, M. H., & Samson, J. A. (2016). Annual research review: Enduring neurobiological effects of childhood abuse and neglect. *Journal of Child Psychology and Psychiatry*, *57*(3), 241–266. https://doi.org/10.1111/jcpp.12507

Terr, L. C. (1991). Acute responses to external events and posttraumatic stress disorders. In M. Lewis (Ed.), *Child and adolescent psychiatry: A comprehensive textbook* (pp. 755–763). Williams & Wilkins Co.

Terry, A. N. (2018). *Dirt roads to justice and heartland girls: Coercive sexual environments in non-metropolitan communities* [Doctoral dissertation].

Thomson, N. (2005). Cultural respect and related concepts: A brief summary of the literature. *Australian Indigenous Health Bulletin*, *5*(4), 1–11. https://healthinfonet.ecu.edu.au/uploads/resources/2034_2034.pdf

Tujague, N., & Ryan, K. (2023). Yarning at the campsite: Understanding trauma. In *Cultural safety in trauma-informed practice from a First Nations perspective: Billabongs of knowledge*. Springer International Publishing.

Turpel-Lafond, M., & Kendall, P. (2009). *Kids, crime and care—health and well-being of children in care: youth Justice experiences and outcomes*. Representative for Child and Youth Care and Office of the Provincial Health Officer.

Urbaniok, F., Endrass, J., Noll, T., Vetter, S., & Rossegger, A. (2007). Posttraumatic stress disorder in a Swiss offender population. *Swiss Medical Weekly*, *137*(9–10), 151–156.

Van der Kolk, B. A. (2009). Developmental trauma disorder: Towards a rational diagnosis for chronically traumatized children. *Praxis Der Kinderpsychologie Und Kinderpsychiatrie*, *58*(8), 572–586. https://doi.org/10.13109/prkk.2009.58.8.572

Westerman, T. (2004). Engagement of Indigenous clients in mental health services: What role do cultural difference play? *Australian E-Journal for the Advancement of Mental Health*, *3*(3), 88–93. https://doi.org/10.5172/jamh.3.3.88

White, R., & Habibis, D. (2005). *Crime and society*. Oxford University Press.

Wolpaw, J. W., & Ford, J. D. (2004). *Assessing exposure to psychological trauma and post-traumatic stress in the juvenile justice population*. National Child Traumatic Stress Network. www.ojp.gov/ncjrs/virtual-library/abstracts/assessing-exposure-psychological-trauma-and-posttraumatic-stress

Wood, P. J., & Schwass, M. (1993). Cultural safety: A framework for changing attitudes. *Nursing Praxis in New Zealand*, *8*(1), 4–15. https://doi.org/10.36951/NgPxNZ.1993.009

Yatchmenoff, D. K., Sundborg, S. A., & Davis, M. A. (2017). Implementing trauma-informed care: Recommendations on the process. *Advances in Social Work*, *18*(1), 167–185. https://doi.org/10.18060/21311

Zimmerman, A. (2018). Women can be as violent as men. *Quadrant Online*. https://quadrant.org.au/magazine/2018/09/women-can-violent-men/

6 Emotional recognition, regulation, and relationality

Tamara Blakemore and Louise Rak

Emotional recognition, regulation, and relationality

The reality of our work is that many young people who use violence also experience violence, and the emotional experience of both seem inextricably intertwined. We observe violence as an emotionally laden experience, and working with young people who use and experience violence can likewise feel emotionally laden in complex ways. Some young people we work with are dealing with big, hard, and heavy emotions, some describe being emotionally numb, others seem to oscillate between high highs and low lows without ever achieving a sense of emotional equilibrium. How practitioners engage with these emotional states seems a critical factor in whether young people feel heard, seen, validated, and sufficiently supported to achieve meaningful goals. How we, as practitioners, do this (and how well we do this) seems to be linked to our own capabilities for emotional recognition and regulation, ironically the same skill set we might be trying to support in young people we work with. In this chapter, we consider what we know about emotions and what we know about the role of emotions in youth violence. With appropriate ethics approval, we draw on practitioner reflections to present insights on how young people in NNN express, experience, and engage with emotions and the implications of this for relational practice.

What do we know about emotions?

Emotions characterise, colour, and contextualise our lives; what frightens, bores, and impassions us – what we love and hate – can all define, and sometimes disrupt, our lives (Solomon, 2002). Because emotions are such a central part of our lives, we have spent a long time contemplating their nature, origins, and outcomes. What we know about emotions represents the evolution of old ideas being replaced by new enthusiasms stretching back many centuries (Solomon, 2002). In the following

DOI: 10.4324/9781003177883-6

sections, we present a selective review of this evidence, briefly sketching understandings of emotion and its expression and experience.

What are emotions?

Emotions are elusive. As surmised by Fehr and Russell (1984), "Everybody knows what an emotion is, until asked to give a definition" (p. 464). William James posed the question, "What is an emotion?" in a paper of the same name in 1884. In the 100 years since, more than 100 alternate and increasingly complex theories of emotion have emerged (Kleinginna & Kleinginna, 1981). There is still no consensus in scientific circles about how emotion should be defined, categorised, or measured (Crivelli & Fridlund, 2019). If we retrace our steps to James' (1884) response to the question "What are emotions?", we find he theorised that emotions were discrete responses to perceptions of patterned changes in the body – hence feelings. Key propositions underpinning this theory are the ideas that emotions/feelings involve neural events (conscious perceptions) and somatic events (responses to changes in the body) (Immordino-Yang et al., 2016). Efforts to understand emotions since have scrutinised links between neural and somatic events, theorising whether these are biologically determined, (e.g., Tomkins & McCarter, 1964) or mediated by sociocultural processes (e.g., Averill, 1980), or both (e.g., Ekman, 1972) and how they might be dynamically shaped by culture and context (e.g., Mesquita, 2003, 2010; Scherer, 2009). These efforts have interrogated aspects of form (including expression or physical indicators of experience) and function (purpose and potential contribution to evolutionary goals) (Holodynski & Friedlmeier, 2006).

The neurocultural theory of emotion (Ekman, 1972) has been particularly influential in shaping the way we have come to understand emotion. Origins of this theory are found in the basic emotions' framework, informed by Darwin's (1872) thesis that universality of facial expressions infer that primary (basic) emotions are biologically innate and evolutionarily adaptive (TenHouten, 2021). Theories informed by this ethos are underpinned by logic that facial *expression* is equated to *experience* (or the feeling) and is definitive of the *emotion*. The neurocultural theory originally described six iconic facial expressions, each produced by a basic emotion. These included happiness, sadness, anger, fear, surprise, and disgust (Ekman, 1972). All other emotions are most often referred to as a blend of primary (basic) emotions (Plutchik, 1980).

Numerous critiques of this approach exist, focusing on method, validity, reliability, and generalisability (Barrett et al., 2019; Durán et al., 2017; Ortony & Turner, 1990). In response to these critiques and with advances in technology enabling deeper investigation of neural and somatic experience, theories of emotion have become more complex over time. Contemporary understandings of emotion suggest it is a multifaceted and dynamic process arising from and influencing change in the interactions between a person and their environment (Mulligan & Scherer, 2012). This is suggested to involve interconnected *components* of appraisal, action preparation, physiological response, expressive behaviour, and subjective feeling, with schematics explaining processes and pathways involved (Scherer & Moors, 2019). These theories reject the idea that emotions *are* feelings; instead, feelings are seen more as a cog in the multimodal process-driven machine of emotions. Despite developments such as these, Colombetti (2014) observes understandings informed by the basic emotions' framework have acquired a life of their own and, consequently, continue to shape (particularly commonplace) understandings of what emotion is and how it is expressed (Barrett et al., 2019).

How are emotions expressed?

Emotions are expressed verbally and nonverbally through words, voice, body posture, gesture, touch, and movement. We each demonstrate relatively constant patterns of emotional expression across different modalities, characterising us as either more or less emotionally expressive (Lee & Wagner, 2002). These patterns are mediated by sociocultural context (Mesquita, 2003, 2010). Across contexts, the expression and exchange of emotional cues are both reflexive and relational and reliant on skills we develop very early including, importantly, the ability to perceive facial expressions of emotion (Barrett et al., 2019). Infants and toddlers are observed to recognise their parents' expressions (Charlesworth & Kreutzer, 1973) and respond in kind to express emotional needs (Flin & Dziurawiec, 1989). From this time on, we look to faces as rich and interesting sources of information to decide who is trustworthy, loveable, need worthy, guilty, or innocent (Todorov, 2017; Zebrowitz, 2017; Zhang et al., 2018). How accurate these decisions are depends on how well we appreciate, discriminate, and respond to emotional cues associated with facial expressions (Carr & Lutjemeier, 2005; Marsh & Blair, 2008). Early studies suggest people *universally* produce and recognise *basic emotions* in fairly consistent ways (Ekman & Davidson, 1994; Ekman & Friesen, 1971; Russell, 1994). For example, anger might be expressed by clenching the large muscles around the jaw, tightly pressing the lips together or having a square open mouth (often with teeth bared), eyes tightly focused and wrinkles between the brows (Collins, 2009). Whereas fear might be expressed by a slack or weak jaw, eyes wide open, and upturned brows causing wrinkles across the forehead (Collins, 2009).

Critiques of this idea of universal basic emotions observe the same emotion may be expressed in different ways (Elfenbein, 2017), and we use a variety of facial expressions to convey emotions, sometimes using the same expression for multiple conflicting or even the absence of emotion (Barrett et al., 2019). As such, its suggested that the idea of universal basic emotions describes stereotypes not prototypes of facial expressions of emotion. An important implication of this critique is that context can shape not only how we express emotions but also the likelihood of these emotions being accurately perceived and appropriately responded to (Barrett et al., 2019). More recent research has characterised emotional expression as multimodal, dynamic patterns of behaviour involving facial action, vocalisation, bodily movement, gesture, touch, and cultural dialects (Cordaro et al., 2018; Keltner & Cordaro, 2016). Dialect theories of emotional expression (Elfenbein et al., 2007) suggest emotion has common elements shared by everyone as well as dialects, or specific variations particular to certain groups or locations. Studies of cultural dialects of emotional expression (Cordaro et al., 2018; Elfenbein et al., 2007; Laukka et al., 2016) find almost every emotion is expressed in ways specific to the culture in some contexts. Elfenbein et al. (2007) suggest that cultural dialects are particularly relevant to emotions that people express in everyday social interactions (e.g., happiness, anger, or shame), with emotions less directly or frequently used (e.g., fear or disgust) more prototypical in their expression. Across cultures, how we express emotions will convey information to others and shape our own experiences via interactive processes and pathways (Keltner, 2003).

How do we experience emotions?

We experience emotions in intrapersonal and interpersonal ways, both involving us accurately recognising and appropriately responding to emotional cues and both shaping our subsequent interactions with the world around us. Cultural worldviews related to emotions tell us which emotions are acceptable and which are not, providing guidelines for how we make sense of and respond to emotional cues (Tsai et al., 2006). These norms provide predictability and order in our social interactions. Indeed, our experience of emotion can serve important adaptive functions for the health and happiness of our interpersonal interactions as well as our safety and survival. Science explains that we effectively perceive, appreciate, and respond to emotional cues, informed by our own experience of that emotion and our understanding of what it requires from us. For instance, when paying attention to the facial expressions of others can trigger facial mimicry (Dimberg et al., 2000). Our own facial expressions in response trigger concordant changes in the autonomic nervous system (ANS), mirror neuron system (MNS), and amygdala that can translate to us feeling the corresponding emotion (Blair et al., 1999; Drevets et al., 2000). Hence, perception stimulates emotional synchronisation and, in turn, emotional recognition (Stel & van Knippenberg, 2008; Van Baaren et al., 2009). Our accurate recognition of an emotional cue shapes the likelihood of appropriate response.

The processes suggested to underpin emotional recognition might prepare us for response, but they don't necessarily guarantee a response or, if a response is enacted, that it is the right one. This depends on the healthy coordinated function of systems involving perception, attention, inference, learning, memory, goal choice, motivation, physiological reactions, motor behaviours, and decision-making (Cosmides & Tooby, 2000; Tooby & Cosmides, 2008). There are many points in this process where emotional cues can be misperceived and misunderstood. An important implication of this is that how we experience emotions can influence our thoughts, attitudes, and beliefs and, by association, our behaviours (Hwang & Matsumoto, 2019). Where we have difficulties accurately recognising, or appropriately responding to, the negative or distress signals of others, we're more likely to experience the world as unpredictable and chaotic. Synchronisation processes suggest this can contribute to antisocial or harmful behaviours (Blair et al., 2001; Blair 2005).

What do we know about the role of emotions in youth violence

The role of emotions in youth violence centres around capacities for emotional recognition and emotional regulation. Both are part of a system of influence that involves awareness, understanding, and acceptance of emotions; skills to inhibit or control emotional or behavioural responses; and capacities to flexibly use strategies to manage distress (Gratz & Roemer, 2004). These skills develop in the context of safe, consistent, and supportive attachment relationships between infants, children, and their parents/caregivers (Calkins et al., 2004; Pollack et al., 2001). Disruptions to these relationships (in the absence of other protective factors) can infer less opportunity to develop skills for emotional recognition and emotional regulation and necessitate alternate patterns of coping (Syngelaki et al., 2013). Both emotional recognition and emotional regulation are independently associated with aggression, suggesting they likely represent two separate, but overlapping constructs (Roberton et al., 2015). A body of research suggests justice-involved young people (and particularly those who use violence) experience difficulties recognising and regulating emotions. Notably, much of this literature is focused on the experiences of justice-involved young men. There is relatively less attention in the literature to the role of emotion in young female violence. This seems important given understandings of young female violence as often relational and embedded in emotional ties and connections (Azad et al., 2018).

Emotional recognition

Emotional recognition refers to our abilities to accurately anticipate, appreciate, and assess emotional cues in the facial expressions of others (Schönenberg et al., 2013). These skills underpin our capacity to find and form healthy relationships, participate in society, and keep ourselves safe. Studies suggest development of these skills for young people who use violence is often compromised, resulting in difficulties discerning facial expressions, especially for cues of fear, sadness, and anger (Bowen et al., 2014; Robinson et al., 2012; Sato et al., 2009). The pattern of results across studies suggests this cohort may be simultaneously more sensitive to negative cues of anger and less sensitive to distress signals of fear and sadness (Fairchild et al., 2008, 2010; Sato et al., 2009; Schönenberg et al., 2013). Other studies qualify that the intensity of emotional cues also matters, with justice-involved young men noted to be especially sensitive to high-intensity anger but significantly less able to identify low-intensity anger (Bowen et al., 2014). Instead, and perhaps both the result of and responsive to contexts characterised by uncertainty and unpredictability, justice-involved young men are found to privilege contextual cues, especially body posture, when interpreting the emotional content of a social situation, often overvaluing them as likely threats (Santamaría-García et al., 2019).

Explanations for these findings suggest interconnected biological, behavioural, and social factors and processes may be involved. Biological explanations commonly reference Blair's (1999) integrated emotions system model, theorising challenges to neural pathways involving the limbic system and the amygdala (our centres for fear detection) can result in difficulties accurately processing others' distress. This neural system is also responsible for regulating and coordinating how we perceive and process information from attentive eye gaze, so impacts to the system might explain what we appreciate and the assessments we make about it (Adolphs & Spezio, 2007). Other explanations reference sociocognitive processing models and poor *fear conditioning* (Fairchild et al., 2008, 2010; Syngelaki et al., 2013). Fear conditioning is a form of learning where fear becomes associated with a previously neutral stimulus (Syngelaki et al., 2013). Confronted with fearful or sad facial expressions, children might fear punishment or retribution deterring them from behaviours potentially associated with causing distress in the other person. Children less sensitive to these cues will be less punished by them and less likely to be deterred from acts that cause fear or sadness (Blair, 1999;

Dodge, 1986, 2014). In one of the few studies to examine experiences for justice-involved young women, Fairchild et al. (2010) report this cohort show less responsivity to fear stimulation and are less able to recognise fear in facial expressions compared to their non-justice involved peers

Social and behavioural explanations suggest environmental factors and experiences shape emotional regulation and can situate violence as normative or necessary social strategy. Bowen et al. (2014), for example, argue environments of justice-involved young men offer less opportunity for appropriate socialisation of fear and sadness and greater socialisation and familiarity with anger. Increased experience of hostile interactions can heighten awareness of hostile cues – an identified criminogenic risk factor for violence (Crick & Dodge, 1994). In these contexts, young men may develop a hostility bias which may cause them to (over) anticipate hostile threats, even in ambiguous situations (Bowen et al., 2014; Carr & Lutjemeier, 2005; Dodge, 1993, 2003). Bowen et al. (2014) suggest this can create a ripple effect where a greater exposure to anger may be associated with a greater likelihood of using aggression (including violence), which, in turn, can increase a bias towards hostility by virtue of negative evaluations by others, which can evoke retaliatory anger.

Adverse childhood experiences and associated traumatic impacts are relevant to both biological and social/behavioural explanations of the link between emotional recognition and young people's use of violence. Yet few studies have expressly interrogated this intersecting experience (Leist & Dadds, 2009). Developmental trauma can increase a sense of uncertainty and unpredictability in a young person's environment (Dadds & Salmon, 2003), making certain cues, particularly anger, more salient indicators of threat (Pollack et al., 2001). A growing body of evidence informed by the neuroscience of trauma points to changes in the centres of the brain responsible for the awareness and processing of emotional experience (Barrett et al., 2007; Van der Kolk, 2003). Studies suggest that under conditions of persistent perceived or actual threat, neural disconnection can occur, disrupting the person's awareness of emotional cues and their capacity to access strategies ordinarily used to de-escalate emotional arousal (Briere & Spinazzola, 2005; Siegel, 2003). This process has been implicated in the experience of alexithymia, defined as a compromised ability to process emotions that can give rise to dysregulated behavioural and emotional responses including violence (Dimaggio et al., 2009; Siegel, 2013).

Emotional regulation

Emotional regulation is "the process of initiating, maintaining, modulating or changing the occurrence, intensity or duration of internal feeling states and emotion-related physiological processes" (Eisenberg et al.,

2000, p. 137). Emotional regulation supports self-efficacy in coping with stress and distress, enhanced problem solving, and stronger relationships. While separate, the skills and abilities of emotional recognition and emotional regulation overlap in ways that reinforce each other's effectiveness (or limits thereof). Skills for emotional recognition are critical for emotional regulation (i.e., an emotion needs to be recognised for it to be regulated) (Dvir et al., 2014), but, in turn, emotional regulation strengthens emotional competencies including recognition of our own and others' emotion states (Saarni, 1999).

Regulating our emotions is generally thought of as effortful and intentional. It involves processes variously aimed at decreasing, maintaining, or increasing one or more aspects of emotion that can occur either in readiness or response to an emotional experience. Gross and Thompson (2007) observe emotional regulation processes of situation selection, situation modification, diverting attention, and cognitive change are antecedent-focused, that is, used before an anticipated emotional response. By contrast, response-modulation is a response-focused emotional regulation process, occurring after the emotional response (Gross & Muñoz, 1995; Gross & Thompson, 2007). Strategies involving cognitive reappraisal or change and those associated with problem-solving, such as situation selection and modification, are found to be more effective, and those associated with avoidance, suppression, distraction, or rumination are less effective (Gross & John, 2003).

Processes for emotional regulation can achieve goals of increasing or amplifying positive emotional states, maintaining current states, or decreasing or dampening negative emotional states. Studies suggest in individualistic cultures people generally seek out positive, high-arousal emotional states, whereas in collectivist cultures people generally seek out positive but low-arousal emotional states (Tsai et al., 2006). Sheppes et al. (2011) also found the intensity of situations we are confronted with influence the regulation process we use. They found low-intensity situations were associated with cognitive reappraisal strategies, but in high-intensity situations, processes of distraction or diverting attention were more common. This last finding, while counter to evidence of effectiveness, may make sense if thinking about high-intensity distress for children and young people. Aldao (2013) observes that in contexts of persistent perceived or actual risk, cognitive reappraisals are unlikely to be an effective strategy for emotional regulation, whereas threat vigilance (perhaps analogous to rumination) and avoidance may foster immediate safety and coping, though possibly at the cost of longer-term vulnerability (Thompson, 2019).

This vulnerability can be expressed in terms of emotional dysregulation, defined as patterns of emotional experience that interfere with goal-directed activity towards distress tolerance, problem-solving, and interpersonal connection (Beauchaine, 2015; Thompson, 2019). Importantly, emotional dysregulation is not just the absence of emotional regulation but also the development of patterns of emotional expression associated with a different set of goals – namely safety and survival. Four kinds of emotional dysregulation are described by Cole et al. (2017): (1) emotions that endure ineffective attempts at regulation; (2) emotions that interfere with appropriate behaviour; (3) emotions that are expressed or experienced are context inappropriate; and/or (4) emotions change either too quickly or too slowly. Emotional dysregulation can reflect to cope in circumstances when more adaptive strategies aren't possible and emotional regulation is difficult (Thompson, 2019).

Studies find young men who use violence report difficulties with emotional regulation, display high levels of emotional arousal, and are highly reactive to the distress of others (Charak et al., 2019; D'Andrea et al., 2012; de Castro et al., 2005). De Castro et al. (2005), for example, found young men who use violence reported less effective emotional regulation strategies, noting that when confronted with situations of stress or distress, they tended to use distraction or, alternatively, further aggression in response. In an Australian study (Roberton et al., 2015), problems with emotional regulation were associated with greater use of violence across the lifespan. Emotional dysregulation is more commonly associated with reactive aggression than instrumental aggression (Card & Little, 2006), though the two forms of aggression are acknowledged to be highly interrelated (Poulin & Boivin, 2000). Capacities for emotional regulation can be contextual; for instance, Petering et al. (2021) found the risk for young people using violence decreases by 60% if they don't experience difficulties with emotional regulation *and* they are situated in typically well-regulated social networks. The authors note the protective benefit of emotional regulation skills is enhanced when these are replicated (and reinforced) in your social environment (Petering et al., 2021).

Explanations of the role of emotional regulation in violence reference broader constructs of self-regulation and self-control and the latter's theorised importance in Gottfredson and Hirschi's (1990) general theory of crime. This theory explains low self-control (characterised by impulsivity, risk-seeking, and low distress tolerance) contributes to violence used to gain instant gratification, retribution, or self-protection. This theory is supported by evidence that low self-control is associated with increased involvement in crime and improved self-control can lead to reduced recidivism – especially for young women (Hay et al., 2018; Vazsonyi et al., 2017). Alternative conceptions suggest violence emerges from unhelpful ways of coping with emotional turmoil and aversive experiences that might be amenable to change through increased emotional recognition and regulation (Lubell & Vetter, 2006; Petering et al., 2021).

Emotions in NNN

Emotions are the focus of the first session in the NNN program for young people. Key objectives of the session include making welcomes and introductions and establishing safety in the group setting. Activities in the session target emotional recognition and beginning steps towards emotional regulation. Photo elicitation and Photovoice practices are introduced in this session.

Practice approach

Our practice approach in NNN is trauma-informed and culturally safe. It is implemented through relational practice (Fletcher, 1998), focused on creating significant connections with young people and placing them at the centre of the work. The importance of the relationship between practitioners and the people they work with has long been recognised as important to how people experience the work and its outcomes (Horvarth & Symonds, 1991). Often conceptualised as a *working alliance* between practitioner and client, these relationships exist as an emotional connection built on trust and respect (Ayotte et al., 2017). Relational practice supports our work with youth violence in three interconnected ways: (1) creating conditions of safety and support, (2) validating trauma, and (3) understanding violence in context. These conditions provide a foundation for working with complex processes associated with violence, including emotional recognition and regulation.

Relationality requires and inspires regulation, enhancing the experience of safety and support. Work with youth violence can involve and instigate challenging emotions. A relational approach understands practitioners and young people we work with as intertwined in generating and experiencing these emotions. Rather than dampening down negative emotions or enhancing positive ones, effective work in these contexts involves reflexive processes of negotiation (Campos et al., 2011).

Table 6.1 Program structure, session focus: Emotions

Program structure	*Session*	*Focus*
		Beginnings
	1	**Emotions**
	2	Voice
	3	Empathy
	4	Power and Control
	5	Shame
	6	Choice
		Endings

This continuous process involves considering how and why our goals and those of young people may differ and then relinquishing, modifying, or persevering (Campos et al., 2011) towards a safe and supportive experience of consistent, trust-based, and respectful relationships.

Learning from Aboriginal ways of knowing and doing, we recognise that connecting and building a relationship with the young people we work with is "more than just establishing rapport it is about understanding and honoring history, setting context, and whole-heartedly *hearing* the story" (Bessarab & Ng'andu, 2010, p. 42). Bennett et al. (2011) stress the importance of time, stillness, and silence in being able to effectively hear peoples' stories. Brearley (2014) describes this as *deep listening*, a way of learning and togetherness, involving listening, being present, and developing relationships where listening happens respectfully, responsibly, and with reciprocity. Working in a relational way that prioritises connection informed by deep listening has supported us to acknowledge the unrecognised, normalised, or delegitimised experiences of trauma for young people we work with.

Relationality is "central to Indigenous understandings of kinship" (Dudgeon & Bray, 2019, p. 3) and understood as the "the process of connecting" and ties between people and place (Rose et al., 2003, p. 61). We situate understandings of young people's use of violence in its (sociocultural, historical, and relational) contexts, locating them at the centre of the work and as author of their own stories. Our approach to practice embraces story, stories, and storying as a way to give voice to contextualised experience. Story is universally central to Aboriginal knowledge systems (Kovach, 2021) and, in Western practice, recognised in work influenced by Paulo Freire (1970) and his notion that action (and change) occur through reflection inspired by self-awareness, the awareness of others, and the capacity for perspective-taking. As such, it was important to us that the activities we chose to use in the NNN reflected an ethos of reflection and reflexivity, listening, and learning.

Photo elicitation

Photo-elicitation activities are used in this session to explore what emotions look like and invite stories that explain their expression and experience. Photo elicitation is a research interview technique using visual images (photographs) to stimulate discussion and reflection (Harper, 2002). Photo-elicitation activities can elicit less pressure to find the "right" answer, avoid the awkwardness of having to maintain (or tolerate) eye contact, and can be empowering when sharing personal perspectives (Banks, 2007). Applied to a therapeutic setting, this method has been referred to as photo therapy (Halkola, 2013) and has been used to facilitate recognising and expressing emotions and promoting

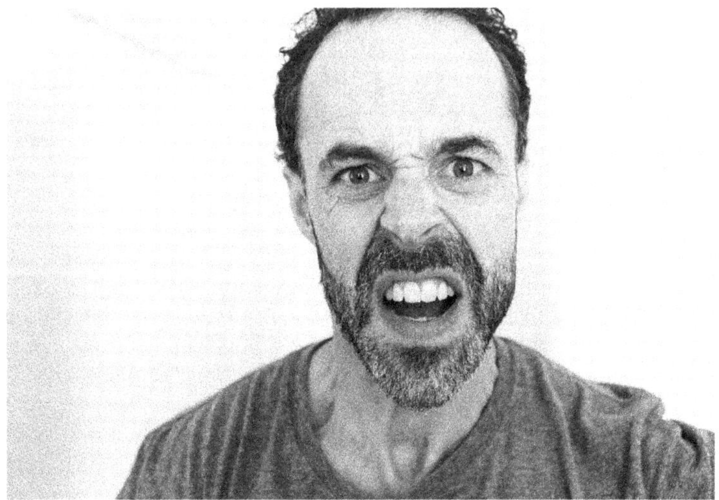

Figure 6.1 Angry face

self-awareness. It has been used effectively with justice-involved young people (Loewenthal, 2013). Photo-elicitation activities in this session focus on how we identify the emotional states of others through close inspection of facial features. Using various photo prompts, non-directive discussion explores what emotions young people associate with different photos, whether some facial expressions are difficult to make sense of, which they class as more/less familiar, and what intensity of emotion they might associate with various photos. Young people engage easily with these activities, and we observe spontaneous instances of perspective-taking and collaborative decision-making as they (unprompted) sort and categorise the photos. One activity examines prototypical images of angry faces and has explored anticipated responses to such emotional expressions (see Figure 6.1). We share here what we've learned from young people in this activity.

Box 6.1 What we've learned . . .

Working with young men in youth detention we explored how they would likely experience someone coming towards them with this kind of facial expression. Wondering how they might respond; young men told us:

> "You step up, step in, cause like he's asking for it yeah?"

Asked what sorts of things they might think or feel when confronted by a face like this, the young men said:

> "Step up/save face", "Excitement", "Match his energy".

When prompted, none of the young men anticipated they would be feeling fear or a desire to avoid the man or considering what might happen next.

Photovoice

Photovoice activities are included in all but the last group work session of NNN as an opportunity for hands-on visual storytelling about emotions, invalidation, empathy, power and control, and shame and what they mean for young people who use violence. We use Photovoice because it is a trauma-informed and culturally safe way to learn about youth violence from young people intimately involved in its experience and use. As discussed in explication of the NNN program in Chapter 4, Photovoice has been alternately viewed as a method of intervention or prevention and a tool of both practice and research (Fitzgibbon & Healy, 2019). Applied in therapeutic settings, it is sometimes referred to as therapeutic photography (Loewenthal, 2013).

Photovoice provides opportunities for young people to tell stories, either about themselves, their communities, and their past, present, or future (Irby et al., 2018; Chonody et al., 2013). It is usually, but not always, a group activity (Latz, 2017). With guidance from a practitioner/researcher, participants are invited to reflect on a topic and take a photo to capture a focus idea, topic, or concept (Latz, 2017). Photovoice sessions aimed at engaging with young people often guide participants to reflect on their community documenting representations of strengths and challenges (Strack et al., 2004). Photos take on meaning as they illustrate the importance of community, interpersonal relationships, and resource distribution in community-based issues (Keller et al., 2008). This step is important in the process to articulate the positionality of individuals in the context of their community (Chonody et al., 2013). Participants then reconvene as a group to view their photos, sharing stories and meanings, writing captions, and reflecting on experiences and any similarities and differences between theirs and the photos of their fellow participants (Fitzgibbon & Healy, 2019). It is through this process that rich narratives about life experiences begin to be shared and explored (Fitzgibbon & Healy, 2019; Latz, 2017).

A consistent goal of Photovoice is to "flatten out" power relations that might exist between the practitioner/researcher and the participant (Creighton et al., 2018). An emphasis on equalising power and striving for empowerment and change means that Photovoice is often noted for its alignment with feminist, Marxist, and critical/realist pedagogy. Photovoice reflects both the participant's experience and the practitioner/researcher's perception of their experience (Irby et al., 2018). Each are relevant to contextualising the issues examined, especially as both parties work collaboratively to select, theme, and add stories to the resulting photos (Irby et al., 2018; Shannon & Hess, 2019). In addition to naming and narrating personal and interpersonal experiences, Photovoice also provides opportunities for participants to speak back to the policies and practices that directly impact upon them, in ways that are very rarely offered (Shannon & Hess, 2019). As an example, justice-involved young people may have limited or significantly constrained opportunities to contribute to decision-making that directly impacts them (Shannon & Hess, 2019). Photovoice offers a process for young people to challenge stereotypes and expand practice understandings of key drivers of violence (Shannon & Hess, 2019). The following practice note outlines the purpose, presentation, and rationale for Photovoice activities in NNN.

What we've learned

Consistent with the observations of Fitzgibbon and Healy (2019), we have observed that Photovoice seems to "speed up" the process of engagement with young people we work with. The photos elicit reflection, and as sessions progress, we see young people become more confident in selecting and storying their photo work, quickly moving into roles as "experts" on experiences and their social, cultural, and contextual meanings and enjoying "educating" the practitioners in the room. As Fitzgibbon and Healy (2019) point out, this differs fundamentally from traditional research or practice in this space where power often lies solely with the researcher/practitioner.

Photovoice provided us with important insights into how young people experience each of the themes investigated: emotions, invalidation, empathy, power and control, and shame. Further it provided the catalyst for us as practitioners to see the community through the lens of the young people we were walking alongside. We saw the role of

Table 6.2 Practice note: Photovoice

Practice note: Photovoice	
Description:	Photovoice
Time:	30 minutes
Resources:	Cameras (can be digital or Instamax – we prefer digital), a camera allocation chart, a location/community map, guidelines for photography.
Purpose:	A creative and expressive way of engaging, Photovoice encourages narrative exploration within and amongst participants, promoting co-creation, joint observation, and participatory action. Photovoice is the primary method for NNN.
Presentation:	• Discuss the photo excursion and, as a group, determine guidelines on how, what, when, and where to take photographs. • Allocate cameras and give participants time and opportunity to orient themselves to the cameras. • Discuss destination and use community map to plot a route with participants. • Outline the purpose of the photo excursion is to take photos. While on the excursion, we should all note what catches and holds our attention, the things that may make us feel particular way, or anything that may spark curiosity or conversation.
Rationale:	Photovoice is a creative methodology that operates on the premise that images and concepts can symbiotically work together to visually express the needs, problems, and objectives of people and their wider community (Fitzgibbon & Healy, 2019). Photovoice's primary aim is to produce a deeper, more critical reflection and consciousness between and within participants (Fitzgibbon & Stengel, 2018). Participants are encouraged to document and record parts of their lives through use of photography, providing a coinciding story to narrate their meaning. Photovoice acts as an impetus for group discussion, assisting participants to tell their stories where they may have been otherwise unable to find the words (Fitzgibbon & Healy, 2019). The three main goals of Photovoice are to (1) assist participants to document and contemplate issues, (2) promote group conversation, and (3) provide the basis of an approach to influence policy/practice change (Wang & Burris, 1997). Photovoice has been found to be a suitable tool for working with young people who use violence, as it encourages them to act as participatory co-developers of new knowledge (Chonody et al., 2013; James & Olausson, 2018). The young people are supported to learn more about their community and themselves, developing insight into the how social structures and systems, beliefs, behaviours, and personal associations can reinforce and influence interpersonal violence (Chonody et al., 2013).

violence in their daily lives, gender differences in the way public spaces were utilised, how young people engaged with their community, and the way their community responded in turn. We witnessed firsthand how social structures like the police interacted with the young people and how mutual distrust could easily flourish.

It was as though there were two sets of young people: the ones we saw in the group setting and the ones who existed outside in the community. Within the four walls of the group setting, the young people were contemplative and collaborative. Outside, while walking to take photos, we noticed they were louder, more abrupt, and, at times, showed outward aggression. They still showed care towards each other and the practitioners, for example, by surreptitiously waiting or checking over their shoulders to make sure we (the practitioners) were not too far behind and slowing down if we were. Their care was covert and, potentially, came at more of a cost to them if it were to be seen as a weakness by others.

While neuroscience would suggest we are hard-wired for exchanging emotional cues that enrich our everyday lives, the ease and effect of this process is not the same for all of us, in all circumstances. Justice-involved young people, perhaps because of adverse early life experiences in their homes and their communities, often report negative educational experiences and problems with literacy and often demonstrate a lack of confidence and ability to articulate experiences and feelings (McNeill et al., 2011).

Box 6.2 What we've learned . . .

Reflecting on the difficulties young people can experience with recognising and regulating emotions, Ray (a young person who completed NNN) was keen to share his thoughts on his own and his peers' experiences:

> "Oh yeh yeh they don't know, like, they can tell when they're happy or sad, but they can't tell what feeling love looks like, (well, they can, but they don't know it). They can't tell when someone's exhausted or scared or disappointment or any of that . . . more just happy sad . . . yeh, black and white . . . yeh, that used to be me". (Ray)

Across deliveries of the program, we have consistently observed that emotions are difficult to live with, even symbolically, as Jazz (a young

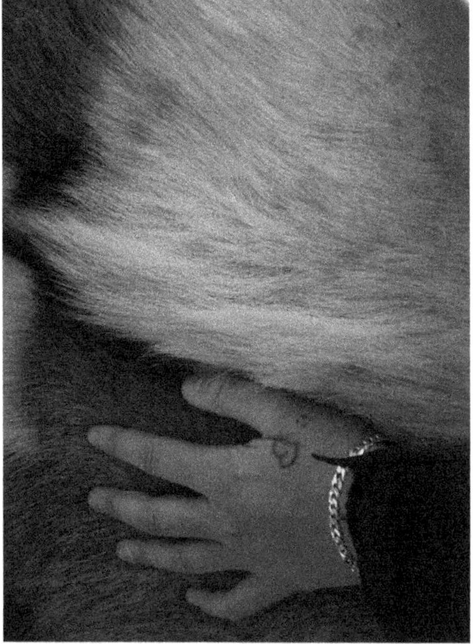

Figure 6.2 Jazz hands

person who had completed NNN) notes commenting on her photo in Figure 6.2.

Box 6.3 What we've learned . . .

"I hate it – it's the first thing people see". (Jazz)

Jazz explained the thing she dislikes most about her tattoo was that it symbolised love.

It's notable that Ray and Jazz both allude to difficulties in relation to the idea or feeling of love. As an organising response related to attachment and survival, love plays a significant role in our adaptive development, health, and happiness (Hatfield & Rapson, 2000). For young people struggling with traumatic impacts and prioritising survival, the idea or feeling of love may be the last thing they are able to embrace whilst perhaps being their greatest need (Freeman, 2015). Apart from its connotation with romantic partnership, love is an important aspect of generosity, care, belonging, and connection (Brendtro et al., 2001), all protective factors for development. Yet, for many of these young people, it seemed barriers and conflicting feelings about love were related to repeated experiences of being let down and left behind, leading to attributions and expectations that tended to exacerbate a tendency towards hypervigilance of possible threats (Gregorowski & Seedat, 2013). Accordingly, while emotions of love were uneasy and unfamiliar for some young people, we've found anger to be a consistently familiar one.

Box 6.4 What we've learned . . .

Through a photo-elicitation exercise that used faces conveying different emotional states, Jazz reported that she believed anger was easy to identify in others, unlike other emotions:

> "He's upset and angry, she's angry, she's upset . . . I just see it as angry . . . people can hide sadness and fear, [but] anger is pretty easy to pick up on. Disgust I'm not sure . . . you just know.
>
> I don't look at people. I mean, I do if they give me a filthy look, but I don't look at their eyebrows, their eyes, and stuff, I just look straight at their face". (Jazz)

How we experience emotions involves us exchanging emotional cues with others and making meaning of these cues. This helps us achieve a sense of predictability and order in our interpersonal interactions. Our perception and understanding of others' emotions is thought to be linked to our awareness and insights into our own emotions (Bird et al., 2010).

Box 6.4 What we've learned . . .

Ray's insights into his emotions articulate what studies might suggest about a bias towards anger (hostility bias), explaining he feels anger is like a cycle he can get stuck in.

> "Like you don't know what you're feeling till it comes again, and if you take notice of it, like, whatever you're feeling ends up turning into sadness or anger because you end up getting frustrated with yourself without knowing it. It's like a cycle".
>
> "Sometimes you see in the way they talk or in their faces".
>
> "While you're angry you just think everyone else is angry as well . . . That's what I used to feel anyway".
>
> "I'd like see everyone like talking, and like, when they were talking, they'd use a tone or something, and I'd like take mad offence to it and like blow up". (Ray)

Often, we assume anger is the primary emotion involved in the use of violence, and it is common to hear young people who use violence referred to as *angry*!

Box 6.5 What we've learned . . .

Interestingly, Ray offers an insight into anger that portrays it as a more complicated experience, possibly hinting at theorised relationships with anxiety and fear.

> "When you're angry at the world, you're angry at yourself. When you're angry at the world, like, everything you think is about you and what you're thinking, I guess, about the world, but when you're screaming it out, you're letting everyone know who you are and what you are, yeh . . . like, when you're angry I don't think you're telling the full truth . . . you sort of lie to yourself and everyone else around it". (Ray)

Our observations from practice and comments about lived experience show a richer picture, reflecting more nuanced theories and understandings about the role of emotions in young people's use of violence. For example, an alternative position proposed by the micro-sociological theory of violence suggests the relationship of anger to violence is interwoven with experiences of fear (Collins, 2008, 2009). Examining hundreds of photos of situational violence, Collins (2008) found, rather than anger, the most common emotion displayed by people using violence was fear, or its milder version – tension. Collins (2009) suggests "confrontational tension/fear" (p. 567) is triggered by anger, usually contextualised by finding yourself provoked or affronted to such a degree that rather than the sustained attention involved in promoting attunement and connection, it turns to confrontational tension and fear (Collins, 2009). While this theory might be at odds with evidence about poor fear conditioning in young people who use violence, it does give us pause for thought about the complexity of emotional experience and the likely role of emotions in youth violence.

Takeaways for practice

1. We live our lives through our emotional engagement with the world around us. When the world in which we have grown is hostile and uncertain, our emotional responses can reflect what it has taken to survive in that context.
2. Recognition and regulation of emotions are contextualised actions that are as important for practitioners as they are for young people who use and experience violence.
3. Visual methods like Photovoice can increase self-awareness and self-confidence in identifying and sharing emotions and experiences and strengthen self-reflection.
4. Relational practice and collaborative activities like Photovoice can inspire the kind of bridge-building necessary to re-legitimate meaningful connections to services and supports.

Conclusion

This chapter has considered the role of emotions in young people's use of violence. It provided an overview of evidence suggesting young people who use violence may experience difficulties with emotional recognition and regulation and raised the proposition that these same skills are important for practitioners to work effectively with youth violence. The chapter shared our relational approach to practice and how we use visual methods including Photovoice to stimulate narrative storytelling to explore emotions and their experience. Narratives from young people highlighted the complexity of emotional experience and the importance of context in understanding the role of emotion in the use of violence.

References

Adolphs, R., & Spezio, M. (2007). The neural basis of affective and social behavior. In J. Cacioppo, L. Tassinary, & G. Berntson (Eds.), *Handbook of psychophysiology* (3rd ed., pp. 540–554). Cambridge University Press.

Aldao, A. (2013). The future of emotion regulation research: Capturing context. *Perspectives on Psychological Science*, *8*, 155–172. https://doi.org/10.1177/1745691612459518

Averill, J. R. (1980). A constructivist view of emotion. In R. Plutchik & H. Kellerman (Eds.), *Emotion theory, research, and experience* (Vol. 1., pp. 305–339). Academic Press.

Ayotte, M. H., Lanctot, N., & Touriguy, M. (2017). The association between the working alliance with adolescent girls in residential care and their trauma-related symptoms in emerging adulthood. *Child Youth Care Forum*, *46*, 601–620. https://doi.org/10.1007/s10566-017-9398-x

Azad, A., Hau, H. G., & Karlsson, M. (2018). Adolescent female offenders' subjective experiences of how peers influence norm-breaking behavior. *Child and Adolescent Social Work Journal*, *35*(3), 257–270. https://doi.org/10.1007/s10560-017-0526-0

Banks, M. (2007). *Using visual data in qualitative research*. SAGE Publications.

Barrett, L. F., Adolphs, R., Marsella, S., Martinez, A. M., & Pollak, S. D. (2019). Emotional expressions reconsidered: Challenges to inferring emotion from human facial movements. *Psychological Science in the Public Interest*, *20*(1), 1–68. https://doi.org/10.1177/1529100619832930

Barrett, L. F., Mesquita, B., Ochsner, K. N., & Gross, J. J. (2007). The experience of emotion. *Annual Review Psychology*, *58*, 373–403.

Beauchaine, T. P. (2015). Future directions in emotion dysregulation and youth psychopathology. *Journal of Clinical Child & Adolescent Psychology*, *44*, 875–896. https://doi.org/10.1080/15374416.2015.1038827

Bennett, B., Zubrzycki, J., & Bacon, V. (2011). What do we know? The experiences of social workers working alongside Aboriginal people. *Australian Social Work*, *64*(1), 20–37. https://doi.org/10.1080/0312407x.2010.511677

Bessarab, D., & Ng'andu, B. (2010). Yarning about Yarning as a legitimate method in Indigenous research. *International Journal of Critical Indigenous Studies*, *3*(1), 37–50.

Bird, G., Silani, G., Brindley, R., White, S., Frith, U., & Singer, T. (2010). Empathic brain responses in insula are modulated by levels of alexithymia but not autism. *Brain*, *133*, 1515–1525. www.doi.org/10.1093/brain/awq060

Blair, R. J. R. (1999). Responsiveness to distress cues in the child with psychopathic tendencies. *Personality and Individual Differences*, *27*, 135–145. www.doi.org/10.1016/S0191-8869(98)00231-1

Blair, R. J. R. (2005). Applying a cognitive neuroscience perspective to the disorder of psychopathy. *Development and Psychopathology*, *17*(3), 865–891. www.doi.org/10.1017/S0954579405050418

Blair, R. J. R., Colledge, E., Murray, L., & Mitchell, D. G. (2001). A selective impairment in the processing of sad and fearful expressions in children with psychopathic tendencies. *Journal of Abnormal Child Psychology*, *29*, 491–498.

Bowen, K. L., Morgan, J. E., Moore, S. C., & van Goozen, S. H. M. (2014). Young offenders' emotion recognition dysfunction across emotion intensities: Explaining variation using psychopathic traits, conduct disorder and offense severity. *Journal of Psychopathology and Behavioral Assessment*, *36*, 60–73.

Brearley, L. (2014). Deep listening and leadership: An Indigenous model of leadership and community development in Australia. In C. Voyageur, L. Brearley &

B. Calliou (Eds.), *Restoring Indigenous leadership: Wise practices in community development* (pp. 91–128). Banff Centre Press.

Brendtro, L., Brokenleg, M., & Van Bockern, S. (2001). *Reclaiming youth at risk: Our hope for the future*. Solution Tree.

Briere, J., & Spinazzola, J. (2005). Phenomenology and psychological assessment of complex posttraumatic states. *Journal of Traumatic Stress*, *18*(5), 401–412.

Calkins, S. D., Howse, R. B., & Philippot, P. (2004). Individual differences in self-regulation: Implications for childhood adjustment. In P. Philippot & R. S. Feldman (Eds.), *The regulation of emotion* (pp. 307–332). Taylor & Francis.

Campos, J. J., Walle, E. A., Dahl, A., & Main, A. (2011). Reconceptualizing emotion regulation. *Emotion Review*, *3*(1), 26–35. https://doi.org/10.1177/1754073910380975

Card, N. A., & Little, T. D. (2006). Proactive and reactive aggression in childhood and adolescence: A meta-analysis of differential relations with psychosocial adjustment. *International Journal of Behavioral Development*, *30*, 466–480.

Carr, M. B., & Lutjemeier, J. A. (2005). The relation of facial affect recognition and empathy to delinquency in young offenders. *Adolescence*, *40*(159), 601–619.

Charak, R., Ford, J. D., Modrowski, C. A., & Kerig, P. K. (2019). Polyvictimization, emotion dysregulation, symptoms of posttraumatic stress disorder, and behavioral health problems among justice-involved youth: A latent class analysis. *Journal of Abnormal Child Psychology*, *47*(2), 287–298. https://doi.org/10.1007/s10802-018-0431-9

Charlesworth, W. R., & Kreutzer, M. A. (1973). Facial expressions of infants and children. In P. Ekman (Ed.), *Darwin and facial expression: A century of research in review* (pp. 91–168). Academic Press.

Chonody, J., Ferman, B., Amitrani-Welsh, J., & Martin, T. (2013). Violence through the eyes of youth: A photovoice exploration. *Journal of Community Psychology*, *41*(1), 84–101. https://doi.org/10.1002/jcop.21515

Cole, P. M., Hall, S. E., & Hajal, N. J. (2017). Emotion dysregulation as a vulnerability to psychopathology. In T. P. Beauchaine & S. P. Hinshaw (Eds.), *Child and adolescent psychopathology* (3rd ed., pp. 346–386). John Wiley & Sons.

Collins, R. (2008). *Violence: A micro-sociological theory*. Princeton University Press.

Collins, R. (2009). The micro-sociology of violence. *The British Journal of Sociology*, *60*(3), 566–576. https://doi.org/10.1111/j.1468-4446.2009.01256

Colombetti, G. (2014). *The feeling body: Affective science meets the enactive mind*. MIT Press. https://doi.org/10.7551/mitpress/9780262019958.001.0001

Cordaro, D. T., Sun, R., Keltner, D., Kamble, S., Huddar, N., & McNeil, G. (2018). Universals and cultural variations in 22 emotional expressions across five cultures. *Emotion*, *18*(1), 75–93. https://doi.org/10.1037/emo0000302

Cosmides, L., & Tooby, J. (2000). Evolutionary psychology and the emotions. In M. Lewis & J. M. Haviland-Jones (Eds.), *Handbook of emotions* (2nd ed., pp. 91–115). The Guilford Press.

Creighton, G., Oliffe, J. L., Ferlatte, O., Bottorff, J., Broom, A., & Jenkins, E. K. (2018). Photovoice ethics: Critical reflections from men's mental health research. *Qualitative Health Research*, *28*(3), 446–455.

Crick, N. R., & Dodge, K. A. (1994). A review and reformulation of social information-processing mechanisms in children's social adjustment. *Psychological Bulletin, 115*, 74–101.

Crivelli, C., & Fridlund, A. J. (2019). Inside-out: From basic emotions theory to the behavioral ecology view. *Journal of Nonverbal Behavior, 43*(2), 161–194. https://doi.org/10.1007/s10919-019-00294-2

D'Andrea, W., Ford, J. D., Stolbach, B., Spinazzola, J., & van der Kolk, B. A. (2012). Understanding interpersonal trauma in children: Why we need a developmentally appropriate trauma diagnosis. *American Journal of Orthopsychiatry, 82*, 187–200. https://doi.org/10.1111/j.1939-0025.2012.01154.x

Dadds, M. R., & Salmon, K. (2003). Punishment insensitivity and parenting: Temperament and learning as interacting risks for antisocial behaviour. *Clinical Child and Family Psychology Review*, 6, 69–86. www.doi.org/10.1023/A:1023762009877

Darwin, C. (1872). *The expression of emotion in man and animals*. Oxford University Press.

de Castro, B. O., Merk, W., Koops, W., Veerman, J. W., & Bosch, J. D. (2005). Emotions in social information processing and their relations with reactive and proactive aggression in referred aggressive boys. *Journal of Clinical Child and Adolescent Psychology, 34*, 105–116.

Dimaggio, G., Vanheule, S., Lysaker, P. H., Carcione, A., & Nicolo, G. (2009). Impaired self-reflection in psychiatric disorders among adults: A proposal for the existence of a network of semi-independent functions. *Consciousness and Cognition, 18*, 653–664.

Dimberg, U., Thunberg, M., & Elmehed, K. (2000). Unconscious facial reactions to emotional facial expressions. *Psychological Science, 11*, 86–89. www.doi.org/10.1111/1467-9280.00221

Dodge, K. A. (1986). Social information-processing variables in the development of aggression and altruism in children. In *Altruism and aggression: Biological and social origins* (pp. 280–302). Cambridge University Press.

Dodge, K. A. (1993). Social-cognitive mechanisms in the development of conduct disorder and depression. *Annual Review of Psychology, 44*, 559–584. www.doi.org/10.1146/annurev.ps.44.020193.003015

Dodge, K. A. (2003). A biopsychosocial model of the development of chronic conduct problems in adolescence. *Developmental Psychology, 39*, 349–371. www.doi.org/10.1037/0012-1649.39.2.349

Dodge, K. A. (2014). A social information processing model of social competence in children. In *Cognitive perspectives on children's social and behavioral development* (pp. 85–134). Psychology Press.

Drevets, W. C., Lowry, T., Gautier, C., Perrett, D. I., & Kupfer, D. J. (2000). Amygdalar blood flow responses to facially expressed sadness. *Biological Psychiatry, 47*, S160. www.doi.org/10.1016/S0006-3223(00)00796-4

Dudgeon, P., & Bray, A. (2019). Indigenous relationality: Women, kinship and the law. *Genealogy, 3*(2), 23. https://doi.org/10.3390/genealogy3020023

Durán, J. I., Reisenzein, R., & Fernández-Dols, J. M. (2017). Coherence between emotions and facial expressions. In J. M. Fernández-Dols & J. A. Russell (Eds.), *The science of facial expression* (pp. 107–129). Oxford University Press.

Dvir, Y., Ford, J. D., Hill, M., & Frazier, J. A. (2014). Childhood maltreatment, emotional dysregulation, and psychiatric comorbidities. *Harvard Review of Psychiatry*, *22*(3), 149–161.

Eisenberg, N., Fabes, R. A., Guthrie, I. K., & Reiser, M. (2000). Dispositional emotionality and regulation: Their role in predicting quality of social functioning. *Journal of Personality and Social Psychology*, *78*, 136–157.

Ekman, P. (1972). Universals and cultural differences in facial expression of emotion. In J. R. Cole (Ed.), *Nebraska symposium on motivation* (pp. 207–283). University of Nebraska Press.

Ekman, P., & Davidson, R. J. (1994). *The nature of emotion: Fundamental questions*. Oxford University Press.

Ekman, P., & Friesen, W. V. (1971). Constants across cultures in the face and emotion. *Journal of Personality and Social Psychology*, *17*(2), 124–129. https://doi.org/10.1037/h0030377

Elfenbein, H. A. (2017). Emotional dialects in the language of emotion. In J.-M. Fernández-Dols & J. A. Russell (Eds.), *The science of facial expression* (pp. 479–496). Oxford University Press.

Elfenbein, H. A., Beaupre, M., Levesque, M., & Hess, U. (2007). Toward a dialect theory: Cultural differences in the expression and recognition of posed facial expressions. *Emotion*, *7*(1), 131–146.

Fairchild, G., Stobbe, Y., van Goozen, S. H. M., Calder, A. J., & Goodyer, I. M. (2010). Facial expression recognition, fear conditioning, and startle modulation in female subjects with conduct disorder. *Biological Psychiatry*, *68*(3), 272–279. https://doi.org/10.1016/j.biopsych.2010.02.019

Fairchild, G., Van Goozen, S. H., Stollery, S. J., & Goodyer, I. M. (2008). Fear conditioning and affective modulation of the startle reflex in male adolescents with early-onset or adolescence-onset conduct disorder and healthy control subjects. *Biological Psychiatry*, *63*(3), 279–285. https://doi.org/10.1016/j.biopsych.2007.06.019

Fehr, B., & Russell, J. A. (1984). Concept of emotion viewed from a prototype perspective. *Journal of Experimental Psychology: General*, *113*(3), 464–486. https://doi.org/10.1037/0096-3445.113.3.464

Fitzgibbon, W., & Healy, D. (2019). Lives and spaces: Photovoice and offender supervision in Ireland and England. *Criminology & Criminal Justice*, *19*(1), 3–25. https://doi.org/10.1177/1748895817739665

Fitzgibbon, W., & Stengel, C. M. (2018). Women's voices made visible: Photovoice in visual criminology. *Punishment & Society*, *20*(4), 411–431.

Fletcher, J. K. (1998). Relational practice. *Journal of Management Inquiry*, *7*(2), 163–186. https://doi.org/10.1177/105649269872012

Flin, R., & Dziurawiec, S. (1989). Developmental factors in fact processing. In A. W. Young & H. D. Ellis (Eds.), *Handbook of research on face processing*. Elsevier.

Freeman, J. (2015). Trauma and relational care: Integrating an awareness of trauma into the characteristics of relational child and youth care. *Journal of Child and Youth Care Work*, *25*, 120–132.

Freire, P. (1970). *Pedagogy of the oppressed*. Herder & Herder.

Gottfredson, M. R., & Hirschi, T. (1990). *A general theory of crime*. Stanford University Press.

Gratz, K. L., & Roemer, L. (2004). Multidimensional assessment of emotion regulation and dysregulation: Development, factor structure, and initial validation of the difficulties in emotion regulation scale. *Journal of Psychopathology and Behavioral Assessment*, 26, 41–54. https://doi.org/10.1023/B:JOBA.0000007455.08539.94

Gregorowski, C., & Seedat, S. (2013). Addressing childhood trauma in a develop-mental context. *Journal of Child & Adolescent Mental Health*, *25*(2), 105–118.

Gross, J. J., & John, O. P. (2003). Individual differences in two emotion regulation processes: Implications for affect, relationships, and well-being. *Journal of Personality and Social Psychology*, *85*, 348–362. https://doi.org/10.1037/0022-3514.85.2.348

Gross, J. J., & Muñoz, R. F. (1995). Emotion regulation and mental health. *Clinical Psychology: Science and Practice*, 2, 151–164.

Gross, J. J., & Thompson, R. A. (2007). Conceptual foundations for the field. In J. Gross (Ed.), *Handbook of emotion regulation* (pp. 3–24). The Guilford Press.

Halkola, U. (2013). A photograph as a therapeutic experience. In *Phototherapy and therapeutic photography in a digital age* (pp. 33–42). Routledge.

Harper, D. (2002). Talking about pictures: A case for photo elicitation. *Visual Studies*, *17*(1), 13–26.

Hatfield, E., & Rapson, R. L. (2000). Love and attachment processes. In M. Lewis & J. M. Haviland-Jones (Eds.), *Handbook of emotions* (2nd ed., pp. 654–662). The Guilford Press.

Hay, C., Widdowson, A., & Young, B. C. (2018). Self-control stability and change for incarcerated juvenile offenders. *Journal of Criminal Justice*, *56*, 50–59. https://doi.org/10.1016/j.jcrimjus.2017.08.008

Holodynski, M., & Friedlmeier, W. (2006). *Development of emotions and emotion regulation*. Springer International Publishing.

Horvath, A. O., & Symonds, B. D. (1991). Relation between working alliance and outcome in psychotherapy: A meta-analysis. *Journal of Counseling Psychology*, *38*(2), 139–149. https://doi.org/10.1037/0022-0167.38.2.139

Hwang, H., & Matsumoto, D. (2019). Functions of emotions. *Noba Textbook Series: Psychology*, *44*(6), 849–873.

Immordino-Yang, M. H., Yang, X.-F., & Damasio, H. (2016). Cultural modes of expressing emotions influence how emotions are experienced. *Emotion*, *16*(7), 1033–1039. https://doi.org/10.1037/emo0000201

Irby, M. B., Hamlin, D., Rhoades, L., Freeman, N. R., Summers, P., Rhodes, S. D., & Daniel, S. (2018). Violence as a health disparity: Adolescents' perceptions of violence depicted through photovoice. *Journal of Community Psychology*, *46*(8), 1026–1044.

James, F., & Olausson, S. (2018). Designing for care: Employing ethnographic design methods at special care homes for young offenders – a pilot study. *Design for Health*, 2(1), 127–141.

James, W. (1884). What is an emotion? *Mind*, *os-IX*(34), 188–205. https://doi.org/10.1093/mind/os-ix.34.188

Keller, C., Fleury, J., Perez, A., Ainsworth, B., & Vaughan, L. (2008). Using visual methods to uncover context. *Qualitative Health Research*, *18*(3), 428–436.

Keltner, D., & Cordaro, D. T. (2016). Understanding multimodal emotional expressions: Recent advances in basic emotion theory. In A. Scarantino (Ed.), *Emotion researcher*. http://emotionresearcher.com/

Keltner, D., & Haidt, J. (2003). Approaching awe, a moral, spiritual, and aesthetic emotion. *Cognition and Emotion*, *17*(2), 297–314.

Kleinginna, P. R., & Kleinginna, A. M. (1981). A categorized list of emotion definitions, with suggestions for a consensual definition. *Motivation and Emotion*, *5*(4), 345–379. https://doi.org/10.1007/bf00992553

Kovach, M. (2021). *Indigenous methodologies: Characteristics, conversations, and contexts*. University of Toronto Press.

Latz, A. O. (2017). *Photovoice research in education and beyond: A practical guide from theory to exhibition*. Taylor & Francis.

Laukka, P., Elfenbein, H. A., Thingujam, N. S., Rockstuhl, T., Iraki, F., Wanda, C., & Althoff, J. (2016). The expression and recognition of emotions in the voice across five nations: A lens model analysis based on acoustic features. *Journal of Personality and Social Psychology*, *11*(5), 686–705.

Lee, V., & Wagner, H. (2002). The effect of social presence on the facial and verbal expression of emotion and the interrelationships among emotion components. *Journal of Nonverbal Behavior*, *26*, 3–25. https://doi.org/10.1023/A:1014479919684

Leist, T., & Dadds, T. R. (2009). Adolescents' ability to read different emotional faces relates to their history of maltreatment and type of psychopathology. *Clinical Child Psychology and Psychiatry*, *14*, 237–250. www.doi.org/10.1177/1359104508100887

Loewenthal, D. (2013). Introducing phototherapy and therapeutic photography in a digital age. In D. Loewenthal (Ed.), *Phototherapy and therapeutic photography in a digital age* (pp. 5–20). Routledge.

Lubell, K. M., & Vetter, J. B. (2006). Suicide and youth violence prevention: The promise of an integrated approach. *Aggression and Violent Behavior*, *11*(2), 167–175.

Marsh, A. A., & Blair, R. J. (2008). Deficits in facial affect recognition among antisocial populations: A meta-analysis. *Neuroscience and Biobehavioral Reviews*, *32*, 454–465. www.doi.org/10.1016/j.neubiorev.2007.08.003

McNeill, F., Anderson, K., Colvin, S., Overy, K., Sparks, R., & Tett, L. (2011). Inspiring desistance? Arts projects and "what works?" *Justitiele Verkenningen*, *37*(5), 80–101.

Mesquita, B. (2003). Emotions as dynamic cultural phenomena. In R. Davidson, H. Goldsmith, & K. R. Scherer (Eds.), *Handbook of affective sciences* (pp. 871–890). Oxford University Press. http://dx.doi.org/10.1192/bjp.185.1.84-a

Mesquita, B. (2010). Emoting: A contextualised process. In B. Mesquita, L. F. Barrett., & E. R. Smith (Eds.), *In mind context* (pp. 83–104). The Guilford Press.

Mulligan, K., & Scherer, K. R. (2012). Toward a working definition of emotion. *Emotion Review*, *4*(4), 345–357. https://doi.org/10.1177/1754073912445818

Ortony, A., & Turner, T. J. (1990). What's basic about basic emotions? *Psychological Review*, *97*(3), 315–331. https://doi.org/10.1037/0033-295x.97.3.315

Petering, R., Barr, N., & Rice, E. (2021). Can better emotion regulation protect against interpersonal violence in homeless youth social networks?

Journal of Interpersonal Violence, *36*(11–12), 5209–5228. https://doi.org/10.1177/0886260518804183

Plutchik, R. (1980). A general psychoevolutionary theory of emotion. In R. Plutchik & H. Kellerman (Eds.), *Emotion: Theory, research, and experience: Volume 1: Theories of emotion* (pp. 3–34). Academic Press.

Pollack, S. D., Klorman, R., Thatcher, J. E., & Cicchetti, D. (2001). P3b reflects maltreated children's reactions to facial displays of emotion. *Psychophysiology*, *38*, 267–274. www.doi.org/10.1111/1469-8986.3820267

Poulin, F., & Boivin, M. (2000). Reactive and proactive aggression: Evidence of a two-factor model. *Psychological Assessment*, *12*, 115–122.

Roberton, T., Daffern, M., & Bucks, R. S. (2015). Beyond anger control: Difficulty attending to emotions also predicts aggression in offenders. *Psychology of Violence*, *5*(1), 74–83.

Robinson, L., Spencer, M. D., Thomson, L. D. G., Sprengelmeyer, R., Owens, D. G. C., Stanfield, A. C., Hall, J., Baig, B. J., MacIntyre, D. J., McKechanie, A., & Johnstone, E. C. (2012). Facial emotion recognition in Scottish prisoners. *International Journal of Law and Psychiatry*, *35*(1), 57–61. https://doi.org/10.1016/j.ijlp.2011.11.009

Rose, D. B., James, D., & Watson, C. (2003). *Indigenous kinship with the natural world in New South Wales*. NSW National Parks and Wildlife Service.

Russell, J. A. (1994). Is there universal recognition of emotion from facial expression? A review of the cross-cultural studies. *Psychological Bulletin*, *115*(1), 102–141. https://doi.org/10.1037/0033-2909.115.1.102

Saarni, C. (1999). *The development of emotional competence*. The Guilford Press.

Santamaría-García, H., Ibáñez, A., Montaño, S., García, A. M., Patiño-Saenz, M., Idarraga, C., Pino, M., & Baez, S. (2019). Out of context, beyond the face: Neuroanatomical pathways of emotional face-body language integration in adolescent offenders. *Frontiers in Behavioral Neuroscience*, *13*. https://doi.org/10.3389/fnbeh.2019.00034

Sato, W., Uono, S., Matsuura, N., & Toichi, M. (2009). Misrecognition of facial expressions in delinquents. *Child and Adolescent Psychiatry and Mental Health*, *3*, Article 27. www.doi.org/10.1186/1753-2000-3-27

Scherer, K. R. (2009). The dynamic architecture of emotion: Evidence for the component process model. *Cognition & Emotion*, *23*(7), 1307–1351. https://doi.org/10.1080/02699930902928969

Scherer, K. R., & Moors, A. (2019). The emotion process: Event appraisal and component differentiation. *Annual Review of Psychology*, *70*(1), 719–745. https://doi.org/10.1146/annurev-psych-122216-011854

Schönenberg, M., Louis, K., Mayer, S., & Jusyte, A. (2013). Impaired identification of threat-related social information in male delinquents with antisocial personality disorder. *Journal of Personality Disorders*, *27*, 496–505. www.doi.org/10.1521/pedi_2013_27_100

Shannon, C. R., & Hess, R. S. (2019). Out but in: Exploring juvenile reentry through photovoice. *International Journal of School & Educational Psychology*, *7*(1), 28–41.

Sheppes, G., Scheibe, S., Suri, G., & Gross, J. J. (2011). Emotion-regulation choice. *Psychological Science*, *22*(11), 1391–1396.

Siegel, D. J. (2003). An interpersonal neurobiology of psychotherapy: The developing mind and the resolution of trauma. In M. F. Solomon & D. J. Siegel (Eds.), *Healing trauma: Attachment, mind, body and brain* (pp. 1–56). W. W. Norton & Company.

Siegel, J. P. (2013). Breaking the links in intergenerational violence: An emotional regulation perspective. *Family Process*, *52*(2), 163–178. https://doi.org/10.1111/famp.12023

Solomon, R. C. (2002). Back to basics: On the very idea of "basic emotions". *Journal for the Theory of Social Behaviour*, *32*(2), 115–144. https://doi.org/10.1111/1468-5914.00180

Stel, M., & van Knippenberg, A. (2008). The role of facial mimicry in the recognition of affect. *Psychological Science*, *19*, 984–985. www.doi.org/10.1111/j.1467-9280.2008.02188.x

Strack, R. W., Magill, C., & McDonagh, K. (2004). Engaging youth through photovoice. *Health Promotion Practice*, *5*(1), 49–58.

Syngelaki, E. M., Fairchild, G., Moore, S. C., Savage, J. C., & van Goozen, S. H. M. (2013). Fearlessness in juvenile offenders is associated with offending rate. *Developmental Science*, *16*(1), 84–90. https://doi.org/10.1111/j.1467-7687.2012.01191.x

TenHouten, W. D. (2021). Basic emotion theory, social constructionism, and the Universal Ethogram. *Social Science Information*, *60*(4), 610–630. https://doi.org/10.1177/05390184211046481

Thompson, R. A. (2019). Emotion dysregulation: A theme in search of definition. *Development and Psychopathology*, *31*(3), 805–815. https://doi.org/10.1017/s0954579419000282

Todorov, A. (2017). *Face value: The irresistible influence of first impressions*. Princeton University Press.

Tomkins, S. S., & McCarter, R. (1964). What and where are the primary affects? Some evidence for a theory. *Perceptual and Motor Skills*, *18*(1), 119–158. https://doi.org/10.2466/pms.1964.18.1.119

Tooby, J., & Cosmides, L. (2008). The evolutionary psychology of the emotions and their relationship to internal regulatory variables. In M. Lewis, J. M. Haviland-Jones, & L. Feldman Barrett (Eds.), *Handbook of emotions* (3rd ed., pp. 114–137). The Guilford Press.

Tsai, J. L., Knutson, B., & Fung, H. H. (2006). Cultural variation in affect valuation. *Journal of Personality and Social Psychology*, *90*(2), 288–307.

Van Baaren, R., Decety, J., Dijksterhuis, A., Van der Leij, A., & Van Leeuwen, M. (2009). Being imitated: Consequences of nonconsciously showing empathy. In J. Decety & W. Ickes (Eds.), *The social neuroscience of empathy* (pp. 31–42). MIT Press.

Van der Kolk, B. A. (2003). The neurobiology of childhood trauma and abuse. *Child and Adolescent Psychiatric Clinics*, *12*, 293–317.

Vazsonyi, A. T., Mikuˇska, J., & Kelley, E. L. (2017). It's time: A meta-analysis on the self-control-deviance link. *Journal of Criminal Justice*, *48*, 48–63. https://doi.org/10.1016/j.jcrimjus.2016.10.001

Wang, C. C., & Burris, M. A. (1997). Photovoice: Concept, methodology and use for participatory needs assessment. *Health Education and Behavior*, *24*(3), 369–387.

Zebrowitz, L. A. (2017). First impressions from faces. *Current Directions in Psychological Science*, 26(3), 237–242. https://doi.org/10.1177/0963721416683996

Zhang, Q., Chen, L., & Yang, Q. (2018). The effects of facial features on judicial decision making. *Advances in Psychological Science*, 26(4), 698–709. https://doi.org/10.3724/sp.j.1042.2018.006

7 Invalidation, voice, and connection

Louise Rak, Chris Krogh, and Tamara Blakemore

Invalidation, voice, and connection

Young people too often experience their interests, their hopes, their views, and their concerns not listened to or not taken seriously. What young people think and who they are are regularly invalidated. While this can happen at the interpersonal level, within family or with peers, it can also happen within services and systems they engage with. Schools, health services, and justice systems are places that spend much time directing young people and little time relating to them. This chapter explores the invalidation that young people face and the ways that invalidation can be connected to using violence. It also discusses ways of working to address invalidation, with particular attention to reciprocal communication and giving young people an opportunity to express what they know and what they feel. How these different elements are woven into the Name.Narrate.Navigate (NNN) program are then discussed, with particular attention to the Postcards to Practice activities that are a regular feature of each NNN group work session. Young people's narratives about invalidation, collected with appropriate ethics approval through practitioner reflections on NNN group work sessions and through young people's anonymous Postcard to Practice feedback are also presented. The following sections of the chapter situate our understanding of invalidation in relation to current literature and practice experience.

Invalidation

Invalidation is the process by which a person in a position of power ignores or disavows another person's lived experience and communication. While this is generally harmful, it is even more significant for people living with trauma as it can compound existing experiences of being excluded, ignored, and oppressed. Earlier chapters of this book have presented in detail the NNN understanding that trauma is the embodied

DOI: 10.4324/9781003177883-7

consequence of overwhelming, negative experiences that can affect the way the world is felt, seen, and understood, leading to behaviours that can be surprising and destructive. For young people who are excluded within mainstream social systems and structures such as schools and the justice system, invalidation is a common experience that may compound and exacerbate the effects of trauma and may precede their use of violence.

Psychological attention to invalidation and validation arose in the context of the development of dialectical behavioural therapy (DBT) – a clinical therapeutic practice with people who lived with chronic suicidality and met the diagnostic criteria for borderline personality disorder. Discussed in Chapter 4 in relation to the informing evidence base for NNN, DBT started in the early 1980s and grew out of behaviour-focused therapeutic approaches, seeking to provide solutions to clients' persistent, life-threatening responses to distress (Linehan & Wilks, 2015). DBT's foundational model for the development of borderline personality disorder is biosocial theory, positing that borderline personality disorder is the result of a child with pre-disposing individual traits growing up in a close personal environment (e.g., family home) that is pervasively "invalidating" (Grove & Crowell, 2017; Musser et al., 2018). Through clinical application and a dedicated program of research, DBT evolved to incorporate behavioural and learning theories, radical acceptance, mindfulness, and dialectics to create a model of practice that straddled a tension between change and acceptance in an ever-shifting "dance" of client and practitioner (Linehan & Wilks, 2015).

Invalidation can be experienced by young people from a range of different sources such as parents (Adrian et al., 2018); individual service providers such as counsellors, psychologists, and clinicians (Wasson Simpson et al., 2022); systems and institutions such as schools (Fasulo et al., 2015) or the justice system (CREATE Foundation, 2018); or from broader social structures such as laws and socially sanctioned discrimination against particular groups (Cardona et al., 2022). The combination of power imbalance within an adult/young person relationship and the invitation for the young person to make themselves vulnerable within that relationship are oftentimes central to invalidation's powerfully corrosive processes. The young person's wish to be seen for who they are and have their knowledge or abilities, interests, individuality, and uniqueness recognised are ignored in invalidating environments with the adults' priorities being centred. In service-delivery contexts, when professionals put their agenda before the interests, needs, and worldview of the person they are working with, the person can experience that as invalidating (Fasulo et al., 2015). As Linehan (1997) originally observed, therapists "focusing on client change, either of motivation or by enhancing capabilities, is often experienced as invalidating by clients who are in intense emotional pain" (p. 354). In the therapeutic context, such invalidation can lead to a range of responses including disengagement and/or lashing out (Linehan, 1997).

Research has continued to examine (in)validation of young people in a range of contexts and life circumstances. For example, a study with students from one university in the United States identified that invalidation is experienced negatively regardless of gender and responses to that invalidation include sadness, guilt, and hostility (Weber & Herr, 2019). Writing about youth experiences in the Canadian mental health system, Wasson Simpson et al. (2022) identified validation and invalidation as key contributors to more encouraging or more discouraging journeys through help-seeking and service use. Importantly, invalidation led to changes in feeling, thinking, and acting, including internalising a sense of self-deficit. This was particularly the case where communication was lacking. The authors wrote:

> Without open communication about the invalidation, youth were often left to make their own assumptions about the mental health system, leading some to internalize systemic barriers as personal shortcomings (e.g., not trying hard enough) or deservingness for help (e.g., not sick enough).
>
> (Wasson Simpson et al., 2022, p. 485)

Feelings of anger and frustration were the most common emotional reactions to invalidation for the 31 participants in the qualitative study by Wasson Simpson et al. (2022). Additionally, young women (20 to 25 years of age) in an Australian study of help-seeking in the face of relationship violence (Tarzia et al., 2017) reported that the potential for professionals to be invalidating or judgemental is a reason they might choose a website or app as a source of information about their situation rather than seeking information directly from a professional. Invalidation has been examined as a dimension of, and contributor to, "minority stress" for gender and sexually diverse people (Cardona et al., 2022), with the authors arguing for the need to recognise invalidation embedded in social structures and for invalidation to lead to post-traumatic symptoms of intrusive thoughts and memories as well as ongoing negative changes to a person's relationships with their emotions. These authors propose the need to recognise "traumatic invalidation" when working with people who belong to gender and sexually diverse minority groups. In a U.S. study of young people and their parents in a treatment program for youth self-harm, parental invalidation was found to be highly correlated with young people's self-harming behaviours and to be a way of relating that was very difficult for parents to change (Adrian et al., 2018).

It is possible that invalidation is a driver of youth violence. The previously mentioned sources report that responses to invalidation include lashing out (Linehan, 1997), hostility (Weber & Herr, 2019), frustration (Wasson Simpson et al., 2022), and self-harm (Adrian et al., 2018). Ryan (1999) indicated invalidating developmental environments could be one of the etiological dimensions for young people who go on to act sexually abusively. In one experiment with college young people in the US, invalidating comments were found to interact with other dimensions of personality, such that some young people were likely to react aggressively when faced with invalidation (Herr et al., 2017). Despite these strong indicators of relationship between invalidation and young people's involvement in crime, invalidation has been minimally explored in studies of the drivers of young people's use of violence or their broader justice-involvement.

Invalidation and voice in NNN

NNN explores the role of violence in young people's life stories. An important part of any story is how it is told and how it is heard. Concepts of invalidation and voice are explored in the second group work session. This session explores how "voice" factors into experiences of violence by examining what helps and hinders expressive and receptive communication of emotions and experience. The practice approach for this session involves the use of validation and reciprocal communication. This chapter highlights the Postcard to Practice activity used throughout the program to prioritise and potentiate young people's voices in shaping understandings of youth violence and best practice response.

Table 7.1 Program structure, session focus: Voice

Program structure	*Session*	*Focus*
		Beginnings
	1	Emotions
	2	**Voice**
	3	Empathy
	4	Power and Control
	5	Shame
	6	Choice
		Endings

Practice Approach: Validation in NNN

Practice experience combined with the indicators in the literature about the possible link between invalidation and use of violence have led the NNN team to ensure that validation is a key dimension of communication with young people in the program. Validation strategies seek to communicate to the young person that their responses and reactions to different situations can or may make sense within their frame of reference and the circumstances in which they were operating at the time (Becker & Stinson, 2011). Distinct from the approach described by Becker and Stinson (2011), though, validation in NNN does not serve a functional purpose such as facilitating or increasing participant engagement in a program for change. It is part of a comprehensive ethic of trust in the young person and that their response or actions in a particular moment were what was possible for them at the time, based on their experience of the situation and their existing skills and knowledge, reflecting the approach of Fasulo et al. (2015).

Validation practices do not mean, though, that other actions or other outcomes might not have been possible or would not have been preferable. The program does not encourage, endorse, or turn a blind eye to the violence a young person has used. The program works with a complex and important tension of validating the young person and understanding their actions as contextually situated and significant for the young person at the time at the same time as making space for the possibility for change. Through the eight weeks of the program, the young people are offered new knowledge to be able to experience situations differently in the future and new skills to be able to act differently should they face a similar situation again. NNN, through the principles and practices of validation, though, starts from not trying to convince the young person of the error of their ways nor from seeking to convince the young person they could or should have acted differently. NNN believes that these could be experienced as just another moment of professional judgement and invalidation by the young person. Practices of validation start from standing alongside the young person, seeking to see the world from inside their experience and not pointing out perceived errors in their thinking or the harm caused by their actions. Reflecting examples from other DBT-informed group programs with young people in justice system contexts (Banks & Gibbons, 2016; Fasulo et al., 2015; Sewell et al., 2019), NNN allows the young people to take from the program's activities as they will rather than telling them what they should be thinking, feeling, doing, or learning.

Validating practices require the worker to avoid an attitude of "I know best" and avoid telling the young person (or even implying) that they should have done something differently. It is that approach that young people find particularly invalidating. Within the NNN program, practitioners assume that the young person knows their life, their situation, and their context better than that worker does and that given time, space, and positive relational conversations, as well as effective learning activities, the young person will come to try out the new knowledge and skills the program offers to see if, and when, these might be possible in their life. From this starting point, practitioners can take a position of learning from and learning with the young person and avoid giving unrealistic advice or trying to direct the young person to change. This approach aims to avoid the pitfalls of challenging or confronting the young person as a pathway to change, which can impact significantly on engagement and reinforce negative experiences of professionals and systems (Linehan, 1997). Illustrating this point, research has reported that adults' suggestions to young people they should "just walk away" from trouble such as fighting is disconnected from their lived experiences (Quinn et al., 2017), can be found laughable by young people (Phillips & Phillips, 2010), or contribute to disengagement in therapy (Barrett & Rappaport, 2011). When a program does connect well with young people and present information in a way that they can engage with, though, being able to walk away from compromising situations is something they report doing and valuing (Sewell et al., 2019). In this context, NNN practitioners actively steer clear of giving advice to young people about what they should have done in different situations. Instead, practitioners focus on learning more about what was happening for the young person in those moments and how they were experiencing the situation. This can then make the space for the young person to try out the activities and ideas the program is offering.

Validation is not a simple act. It is not easy to attend to the perspective of the young person when they appear not to care about or even recognise that they have hurt other people. In this situation, NNN practitioners walk a fine line of validating the young person's reality and their experience of their context while not diminishing the harm their actions have caused as well as also not aligning themselves with justifications for the violence and not legitimising harmful actions (such as using violence) and worldview (such as suggesting the acceptability of revenge). In such situations, practitioners may validate the depth of emotion the young person was feeling in their circumstance or validate their attempt to connect but not validate the violence they used or the harm they caused.

Linehan (1997) presents a detailed discussion of validation with DBT. Included in this are the potential targets for validation – thoughts, emotions, actions – as well as a hierarchy of six levels of validation she discerned. While basic interpersonal skills of listening to and observing the person and then accurate reflection of content provide the foundational levels of validation practices, the highest and distinctly different level is that of "radical genuineness". Mirroring the Rogerian humanistic psychology stance of the therapist being genuinely present and open to the client, radical genuineness' may include visible, honest, empathic responses to the client's circumstances or situations in which they have been (Linehan, 1997).

In their chapter discussing validation practices within DBT, Fruzzetti and Ruork (2015) restate and extend Linehan's (1997) earlier six levels of validation, where each level is "more complex and complete" (Fruzzetti & Ruork, 2015, p. 13) than the one preceding it. The extension provided by Fruzzetti and Ruork is "validating through self-disclosure". In this process, the professional may judiciously choose to illustrate their own vulnerabilities by disclosing genuine examples of similar experiences from their own life that serve to validate the client experience through normalising their experience as well as treating the client as a person of equal status with the clinician (Fruzzetti & Ruork, 2015). It is this that these authors call "reciprocal communication".

Practice Approach: Reciprocal Communication in NNN

The term "reciprocal communication" has been used to mean different things. For example, it has been used in research to describe basic, two-way, real-time communication over the internet (Rollman et al., 2000). Within the DBT framework, however, reciprocal communication combines both radical genuineness and careful, client-serving self-disclosure (Banks & Gibbons, 2016). The practices of reciprocal communication involve workers responding to the young person in genuinely warm and accepting, emotion-inclusive ways, supported by relevant observations about the young person and the careful use of self-disclosure. It is in direct service of the young person and their experience, rather than in the service of the worker or the changes the worker hopes to see. It requires genuine care about the lived experience of each of the young people in the program, recognising that this is fundamental to the validation required before effective change work can proceed.

Reciprocal communication requires practitioners to be contemplative and self-disclose to induce deeper learning and connection (Linehan & Wilks, 2015; Pederson, 2015; Sarnat, 2019). Practitioners are not seen as the experts, rather as (optimally) authentic, curious people in the encounter (Linehan & Wilks, 2015; Pederson, 2015). In NNN, practitioners share their experiences in relation to the skills and concepts being discussed. Shared next are reflections on what the skill of reciprocal communication can look like. These reflections are drawn from the practitioner's own notes on this aspect of her work.

Box 7.1 NNN Practitioner reflection . . .

"We were facilitating a session on shame, the young women in our group were struggling to connect with the content, likely because the shame session is always challenging especially due to the vulnerability it can elicit.

I had witnessed my 6-year-old daughter be publicly shamed a few days earlier and decided to take a chance and share the story. I say chance because sharing the story was a risk for several reasons, one because it was my daughter's story and not mine and because I would be talking about taking my children out for a meal with other families, a scenario that we knew based on the stories of the young women, they were not experienced in.

I told the story of how my daughter, along with other children, was eating nuggets and chips when a father of another child loudly proclaimed that 'jeez you must be hungry, look at how much you are eating'. My daughter looked at me with confusion on her face. She knew a point was being made but not what the point was. I shared with the NNN group that I encouraged my daughter to keep eating and enjoy her meal while giving her a smile and a squeeze.

I then said not much else to the NNN group other than to point out that the scrutiny, shaming, and invalidation of women, especially regarding their bodies, starts early. The effect of this story was immediate, with all group members becoming outraged on behalf of my daughter.

They asked:

> "What did you do?"
> "Did you hit him?"
> "How did you sort him out?"

I said that inside I was raging, but I knew that to say anything to him would be pointless (based on what I knew of him) and would possibly make my daughter more embarrassed. My only objective, I said, was to make sure my daughter felt safe and comfortable.

This shared story opened the gates to multiple experiences from each of the young women in the group, which would not have happened had I not decided to practice reciprocal communication in that moment".

In social work literature, self-disclosure is a multi-dimensional, learned skill that includes both in the moment reflections and observations about the worker/client interaction as well as the professional sharing information about historical or recent life experiences (Segev & Hochman, 2022). In a study of young people on the cusp of adulthood with very difficult life circumstances, such as complex trauma, system involvement, homelessness, and substance use by McCormick et al. (2022), the authors found that when done effectively, self-disclosure can increase trust, reduce power imbalances, and increase the young person's feelings of being understood by a worker.

This is a highly skilled aspect of practice that requires a balance of genuineness and judicious decision-making. Effective self-disclosure is "natural" not forced, calculated, or deliberate. At the same time, it involves assessing and deciding what information about themselves is appropriate to share, how much and when to share, and being clear about whose needs are being met through that sharing – the young person's or their own. The consequences of poor practitioner self-disclosure may include the misinterpretation of information and situations which may make the person receiving the service to feel uncomfortable or at risk of harm (Levenson, 2017).

Reciprocal communication focuses on the quality of the working relationship between the professionals and the young people in the program. Reciprocal communication provides an alternative to distancing practices, often associated with "professional boundaries" that erect "restrictive artificial barriers" (O'Leary et al., 2013, p. 136) between the worker and the client, reducing trust and equality. As shown by Brown et al. (2019), young people in care feel the difference between workers who have a personal investment in their care and those for whom the young person is "just a piece of paperwork" (p. 224). The young people in this study showed a need for workers to have a contextualised appreciation of their behaviours (validation) as well as demonstrate persistent and unconditional care (genuineness). Other research has reported that social workers who share a little of their own vulnerabilities (self-disclosure) contributed to building positive and more equal working relationships with clients (Kam, 2020). Practice that integrates an understanding of the unequal power relationships between "helper" (the worker/professional) and "helpee" (client/service user) is essential when working with trauma and can be demonstrated through relational practices that include worker "transparency, authenticity and [a commitment to building] an understanding of what both people see as helpful" (Sweeney et al., 2018, p. 324). These authors, who include people with lived experience of trauma and the U.K. psychiatric care system, recommend "developing relationships that are non-judgemental, empathic, respectful and use honest and direct communication" (Sweeney et al., 2018, p. 328).

Reciprocal communication may contribute to participants in a program experiencing the practitioners in a positive way and increase their willingness to participate and remain in a group as well as to participate in its activities. Qualitative research examining barriers to, or enablers of, participation in group treatment program for "long-term depressed, low-income mothers" in the US found that the participants need genuine, warm, empathic professionals who attend to relationship-building over formulaic, technique-driven approaches (DeCou & Vidair, 2017). These authors propose DBT reciprocal communication as an approach that can meet these needs. The participants in the study identified that along with a genuine and trustworthy professional, they want effective strategies for change (DeCou & Vidair, 2017). In their exploration of DBT-informed validation within a group program with long-term incarcerated young people, Fasulo et al. (2015) illustrate use of reciprocal communication in an interaction with a young person about their artwork. When each of the young people had risked sharing their creative self-expression with the group, they displayed high levels of anxiety reflecting how vulnerable they felt during the process. The authors reported that using responses that included careful, limited reference to their own artistic inabilities and genuine appreciation for the young person's effort and skill shifted the young person's anxiety as well as brought the group closer together. Building relationship through validating and reciprocal communication can open the doors to conversations about change strategies that would have been dismissed or argued against without that foundation.

Open and reciprocal communication may serve not only to build relationship but also be a basis for learning in therapeutic contexts. Radically Open DBT incorporates this into a broader therapeutic framework. Illustrating this point, Hempel et al. (2018) propose that in the context of Radically Open DBT with people with anorexia nervosa, the client learning to reveal opinions, thoughts, and emotions can contribute to relationship building as well as generate useful learning for themselves and those around them.

Postcards to Practice

In addition to practitioner validation of the young people, there are strategies within NNN that seek to hear the voice of the young person and learn from their knowledge of their life and experience. This reflects the fundamental ethic of NNN of complete respect for the young person as the expert in their own life and experience. From this perspective, it is the young person's knowledge of their world that needs to be heard, respected, and privileged by people working in this program. It is distinct from approaches that have decided the young person doesn't know what is important to know or has distorted understandings of the world and, therefore, requires either (re)educating or informing. As shown by Munford and Sanders (2015), not being listened to or not having their views accounted for are often the experiences of young people in controlling systems such as juvenile justice and out-of-home care. Some of the young people interviewed by Munford and Sanders (2015) reported that their problematic actions stemmed from not being listened to and that when they did meet workers who really listened, their confidence and motivation increased and behaviours started to change.

The long-standing, though sometimes marginal, approach to seeing the person as the expert in their life and experience grew out of humanistic psychology (e.g., Carl Rogers) and was extended through constructivist therapeutic practice such as that described by Anderson and Goolishian (1992) and narrative therapy as described by White and Eptson (see Hales, 1992). Central to Anderson and Goolishian's approach is that of the therapist "not knowing" the meanings the client is making of their realities and not starting with "preconceived opinions and expectations about the client, the problem, or what must be changed" (1992, p. 29). The approach seeks to avoid asking the client questions which are pedagogic – questions that imply the "correct" answer – or questions that are rhetorical – those that contain their own answer (Anderson & Goolishian, 1992). Rather, questions must be based on genuine curiosity, asking something about which the worker has not already made up their mind.

Within the Postcards to Practice exercise, we invite participants to explain things from their lives they want us and other practitioners to know, to highlight things practitioners miss, don't know, or don't hear. The questions seek to communicate to the young person "I cannot know this", "I would like to know about this", and "I believe it's important for me to understand this". The answers to the questions are designed to be anonymous; however, some of the young people elected to put a name to their postcards. The questions are asked to all the group and then the young people "post" their cards into a box; the answers are anonymous. The program wants to know what young people know about these questions but does not need to know what was said by any one participant. In this way, the program hopes to communicate that the answers to the questions will not be used against the young people as has been reportedly experienced by others in the context of controlling systems (see, for example, Gillett-Swan & Sargeant, 2018). The Universal Declaration of Human Rights elaborated for children through the United Nations Convention on

Table 7.2 Practice note: Postcards to Practice

Practice note: Postcards to Practice	
Description:	Postcards to Practice provides a weekly chance for participants to write, draw, and communicate ideas and information to practitioners.
Time:	5–10 minutes
Resources:	Postcards with printed prompts Selected prompts include: "If you walked a day in my shoes, you would know", "I feel invalidated when", "What I know about being controlled is" A letterbox
Presentation:	• Share postcards and demonstrate use of letterbox. • Introduce and describe the postcard activity, noting that it will be repeated weekly. • Outline that the postcard activity is a way for participants to provide feedback to practice and practitioners of some of the experiences shared in the session. • Of importance is highlighting that practitioners do not have all the answers and that this activity is a way of us looking to the young people as experts to teach us things that we don't know, miss, or don't hear. • Practitioners may need to support participants who have issues with literacy.
Rationale:	The Postcards to Practice method is a way of embedding reciprocal communication in the program participation and process. Reciprocal communication is part of the relational way of working that is central to NNN. Reciprocal communication is about sharing with the young person. It involves honest, genuine reactions and responses to the experience of the young person and the sharing of relevant observations, experiences, and insights that provide a real example of a concept or idea. Reciprocal communication involves treating the young person as an equal. Self-disclosure requires considered thought and appreciating difference and deeply hearing the experience of the other. It is always in the service of the interests of the young person and not the practitioner. Reciprocal communication does not involve advice-giving or problem-solving, especially based on opinion, or extraneous information. Reciprocal communication skills help with balancing power between parties and in establishing conditions for open dialogue and exchange.

the Rights of the Child determined that children and young people had a right to have their opinions about their education heard and incorporated into their schooling. In reality, teachers and school systems dictate when children can and can't speak and what they can do and often punish children and young people when they speak out, in practice stifling children young people's communication freedoms and contravening their right to be express an opinion and be heard (Gillett-Swan & Sargeant, 2018). At the same time, the questions and the process imply that there is a much wider audience to the knowledge the young person is sharing. These answers are designed to inform practice much more widely. Through this activity, young people in the program are experts, helping to educate the kinds of people who have so often not listened to their voice. Postcards to Practice is explored in the following practice note.

What we've learned

In the first sessions of NNN, a core focus is the joint exploration of communication skills and capacities, where we analyse what it looks like to be and feel heard (validated) and talk about what it is like to not be heard (invalidated). Young people shared stories of being invalidated throughout their lives, by family and friends and, also, by the practitioners and systems supposedly there to supported them. These system-based interactions have often intersected with trauma and relate to cultural violence, justice involvement, child abuse, neglect, and removal from birth families. These sessions are illuminating, and, as practitioners, we repeatedly saw consistency in participant experiences of invalidation. Through sharing about these consistent but largely unspoken experiences, deep connections and links formed in this session cross-culturally and within the different gender groups.

In the following discussion of what we've learned so far, we will share the voices and experiences of young people who have participated in NNN. This information, presented in textboxes, demonstrates how common and significant invalidation is for them. Information presented was collected with appropriate ethics approval through practitioner reflections on group work sessions, referencing narratives shared as part of group work activities as well as those narratives shared by young people in anonymous Postcards to Practice. Sitting outside the textboxes are perspectives we have heard from practitioners who are part of the NNN cultural reference group, steering committee, and practitioner working party. This information was collected with appropriate ethics approval through focus group discussions. In all instances pseudonyms are used to protect the identity of those involved.

Invalidation is common and destructive

Participants shared consistent examples of not being heard and the subsequent fallout when their feelings and experiences were not validated (see Figure 7.1).

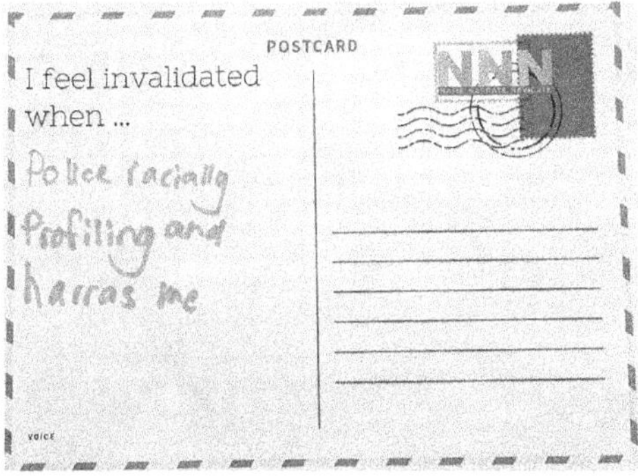

Figure 7.1 Postcard to practice

Box 7.2 What we've learned . . .

Lara, a young woman whose use of violence could be described as reactive and explosive explained how she felt she was perceived by the community and practitioners through her response to the postcard prompt: "If you walked a day in my shoes you would know. . ." Her response was reflective of some of the challenges she faced daily:

> "Why I am who I am and act like I do. You's all would know how I feel and what I have to go through and what I have been though. Life's Fucked. 100%.

Not being heard was further illuminated by Jason who articulated the following in response to the prompt "I wish you knew how it feels when . . .".

> "Y'all say I'm talking back when I am giving an opinion".

Jason was emotional in his engagement with the postcard process, reflecting through a conversation with a practitioner that he had never been asked to tell his story or share his opinions.

Illustrating a young person's perspective on the invalidating experience of not being listened to, one young male's postcard in relation to the prompt "Some advice from me to you . . ." read:

> "Listen when I tell you what's going on or I'll never want to speak to you again".

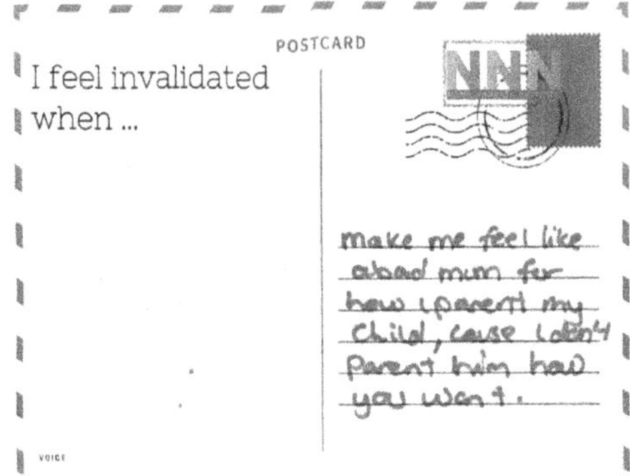

Figure 7.2 Postcard to practice

As practitioners we witnessed how common it was for the young people's experiences of victimisation to be disregarded, dismissed, and ignored by caseworkers, youth workers, police, and other support workers. On one occasion, when following up with a caseworker about a disclosure from a 15-year-old female NNN participant regarding a previous pregnancy, we were told "not to worry, she's had heaps of miscarriages, 4–5 at least". It is these types of invalidating dismissals of experiences that potentially reinforce cyclic patterns of the use of violence and poor self-identity (Bubolz & Lee, 2019). This was illustrated in focus group discussions with practitioners where one practitioner said: "[the young people tell us] why bother trying, if this is who I am, and what I'm dealing with, and people are telling me that those things don't fit in here?" (see Figure 7.2).

Box 7.3 What we've learned . . .

Reflections on how young people felt they were perceived and treated by workers was common, especially in the invalidation session. This is demonstrated in the postcard of a young male who in response to the prompt "I wish you knew how it feels when . . ." stated:

> "You grew up a different way to others and staff expect you to behave like others without help".

Showing how young people experience adults (presumably workers) and the importance of building connection, a different young male wrote, in response to the same prompt:

> "Is that when I feel comfortable around you, I'll open up more".

Invalidation and violence

NNN practitioners have heard ways in which invalidation can play a multifaceted role in youth-perpetrated violence. It can act as an antecedent to violence, and when young people disclose experiences of abuse and trauma, if their experience is met with invalidation, it can intensify the original trauma (Bollinger et al., 2017), potentially leading to more violence. Through stories shared, young people described their choices to use violence as a form of communication, a way to be-heard when they felt invalidated by systems. For example, young women reported feeling frustrated with workers who were not hearing or were judging them, such as telling the young women outright that they would they inevitably re-offend and, in response some of the young women, would "go on a riff", including actions such as shoplifting/stealing, assaulting someone, or doing a break-and-enter offence, fulfilling the original prophecy of their caseworkers.

The participants also described using violence as a way of being like family members and/or peers, and that in these situations, their violence was validated and helped to form connections or bonds with others. As practitioners, we saw examples of this in the stories of young people who enacted violence on behalf of siblings or friends. This was demonstrated in the stories shared by Jazz and Kylie, who reflected on their mutual dislike of most of the girlfriends their brothers had had over the years. They discussed the role they played in keeping the girlfriends in check, remarking they frequently "wait for the day your brother calls you to come and bash his missus". This example was a stark reflection of how Jazz and Kylie perceived violence, as they were at pains to assure us that their brothers would never hit a woman, but they could not, or would not, recognise that their brothers were enacting violence on their partners through them. For their parts, Jazz and Kylie spoke with pride about the bond they had with their brothers through their role of pseudo-behaviour enforcers.

This example indicates a distinctly gendered dimension to violence and invalidation, something observed regularly by NNN practitioners.

Speaking more broadly, the practitioners saw that while there was a high level of consistency and shared experiences of invalidation and validation among participants, there were ways in which the experience and the response were particular to different genders and cultural groups. Both genders experienced parental (mainly maternal) invalidation and systemic invalidation through how they were treated by police, teachers, and case workers. Yet, as practitioners, we witnessed invalidation playing a strong and evident role in the use of violence in interpersonal relationships for young women but less so for young men.

Invalidation, gender, and violence

As practitioners, we witnessed the gendered direction of young people's use of violence, particularly its relationship with the necessity for self-reliance. This is exemplified in the quote from Kylie: "You know a man will hurt you, but a woman will always let you down". The need to be able to do for oneself and not overly rely on other people has been a pervasive theme for young females who use violence (Batchelor, 2005; Blakemore et al., 2021). For the young female participants of NNN, having a sense of being "let down" by other females included caseworkers, carers, teachers, family, and kin; however, this feeling was most referenced regarding mothers. Often young female NNN participants would describe their mums as being disinterested, unavailable, or absent, sharing examples through their stories of being unheard or having their experiences and needs unmet or invalidated. This is in line with the work of Thompson and McGrath (2012), which indicates that young women who use violence in their interpersonal relationships also have poor and broken relationships with a female caregiver as well as having experienced erratic discipline in childhood.

We not only heard and witnessed stories from young people about them not feeling seen and not being heard, but also, as practitioners, we directly experienced occasions where their lives were devalued and their very real concerns about health and homelessness were dismissed and minimised by the workers and service structures put in place to support them. The results of these dismissals were negative, often leading to injury to others as young people reacted, using violence to communicate and be heard and often to feel a sense of connection – to their peers or with themselves.

The sense of not feeling seen and heard extended to the production of invalidating assumptions about motivations of female violence with some practitioners indicating that female violence is less serious than male use of violence or that it is only ever used for self-defence purposes. While it is undoubtably true that self-defence may be one factor in the use of violence by young women, it is not the only reason young women use violence. The young women in NNN provided several reasons why they used violence, which included but went beyond existing invalidating assumptions that violence used by women is only for self-defence purposes (Hamby & Jackson, 2010).

Box 7.4 What we've learned . . .

When we asked young women why they used violence, they provided the following narratives:

Boredom, having nothing to do so going out and starting fights. This is comparative with literature that indicates that young women are involved with violence due to displacement and boredom (Batchelor, 2005; Havard et al., 2021; Jones, 2004).

Getting others before you "get got". This refers to pre-emptive violence, such as young women hearing a rumour that someone had an issue with them and wanted to fight, so the young women perceived they needed to act first. This is consistent with Batchelor's (2005) findings that young women are caught in a difficult tension of needing female relationality but, at the same time, are incredibly hard on other women to the point of hypervigilance.

Acts of obligation for family, friends, and community. Instances here related to another person being physically hurt or embarrassed by someone. This included having goods stolen and the young women felt duty-bound to retaliate. This is mirrored in Brown's (2011) work, where women indicated they had roles in defending fellow gang and community members.

Contributing to the policing of behaviours deemed un/acceptable within their communities. This is consistent with Jones (2004), who found young women negotiating and contributing to violence in their communities. Often young women in NNN describe acts of "snitching", speaking out of turn, or telling a story not theirs to tell. Snitching was met with swift action, often in the form of violence or community mistrust and shunning.

Retribution. This relates to when violence was used to rectify a situation. The young women in NNN shared stories of times where they felt they needed to step in on behalf of someone or to "right a wrong". This is reiterated in the work of Jones (2004) where it was indicated that young women felt they had a role in retribution.

Self-protection. It was common for young women to use violence to defend themselves. This is reiterated in the existing research (Seamans et al., 2007).

For control over others such as coercive violence. This has been rarer among young women in NNN but includes example where practitioners noted a young woman's actions being monitored by another female friend who dictated who the young woman could associate with. The work of Havard et al. (2021) speaks to the use of coercive control by young women; however, it is in the context of gang violence and use of coercive control for geographic dominance in the drug trade.

As a commodity. This is an emerging theme where violence was deployed in exchange for something – often this was friendship or to secure a place to sleep. While there is research that talks to the associations between violence as a commodity and gender (Yeh et al., 2021), there is a dearth of research on young women's use of violence as a commodity.

Unknown reasons. Sometimes young women couldn't remember why they used violence, experienced blackout rages, or only recalled violence if it was recorded and shown to them or people recounted the story to them. Work by Ness (2004) indicates similar findings, where young women shared times where pre-violence buildup was so great that it caused memory blackouts.

In recognising the role of invalidation in the use of violence, we are not validating the use of violence itself, rather, as with all components of our work, we are seeking to better understand the complex components contributing to youth interpersonal violence. The young women tended to brush over or ignore the violence perpetuated against them by their male caregivers and kin. While no less valid, there may be an element of gender perception bias in the young women's reflections given all the young women in NNN had violence used against them by men, but their anger and hypervigilance was directed at women.

Reflecting on our work with young men suggests experiences of maternal invalidation are perhaps more common or at least more impactful for justice-involved young women. Young men we have worked with have commonly recounted experiences of invalidation, but these were often in the context of their interactions with teachers, caseworkers, and police. This is echoed in the work of Warton (2020) on criminal identity formation in adolescent males where his findings suggest that the way in which police, caseworkers, and teachers interact with young males may have great impact on identity formation and criminal trajectory. Through NNN work, young men discussed experiences of racial profiling and abuse, which was like the work of Ravulo (2016), who identified in work with young Pasifika men that over half of those interviewed had weekly contact and/or interaction with police.

The young men in NNN commonly recalled these experiences as fueling anger and, sometimes, reactive or explosive violence. However, the experience of maternal invalidation has been discussed by relatively few young men involved in NNN, with few identifying it as an impetus for their use of violence. Many young men we have worked with have talked about their mothers, grandmothers, aunts, sisters, and girlfriends in protective ways. Some even talked about using violence in defence of their mothers, sisters, and girlfriends, citing slights or violence against females in their life as a call to arms to defend and protect their own. Where young men were estranged from their mothers, this was often in contexts where they perceived their mothers as having let them down, often by prioritising the needs of others over theirs and, in doing so, failing to see, hear, and respond to them in protective and positive ways. Caseworkers reported that in these situations, some mothers had made concerted efforts to repair relationships with their sons without success. Similar reflections were identified through the work of Sattler and Thomas (2016), where juvenile justice caseworkers spoke about the challenge they saw parents having in engaging and interacting with their children due to feelings of disadvantage, community violence, and low social, financial, and cultural capital.

For all the young men with estranged relationships with their mothers, a generalised sense of contempt for women was commonly observed. This was confirmed by caseworkers as well as female NNN practitioners working with these young men. It was as if their experiences with their mothers had generated to a worldview where women were a potential source of pain. Noting the preliminary research by Byrd et al. (2023), who have identified a relationship among maternal invalidation, mothers with emotional dysregulation, and aggression in preschool-aged children, there is minimal research on the role of maternal invalidation and youth use of violence. Contemplating reported and perceived experiences of maternal invalidation gave us pause for thinking about family composition for the young people we work with. We note that many live in sole-parent families, mainly headed by mothers. We wonder, then, whether reported maternal invalidation for these young people might overemphasise the maternal role and, perhaps, falsely infer a gendered component to invalidation. We do not have enough insight into what experiences might look like in sole-father headed families and whether these same experiences might more accurately be described as primary parent invalidation.

Invalidation, voice, and controlling systems

Most children and young people have experiences of being in institutions (particularly school) where their activities are directed to a greater or lesser degree by adults who hold power over what they do and what they express. For young people in NNN, they have more experiences of this than most. They have often spent time in out-of-home care system, hospitals, and health care systems, and all have had some level of contact with the justice system. In such contexts, it is difficult for young people to experience having a legitimate voice, and the effects of this can be volatile. Research with young people with a history of out-of-home care and interactions with the criminal system found that roughly 17% reported "frustration and anger" as the precipitating circumstances that led to their contact with this system (Tillack et al., 2018). For these young people, their use of violence related to seeking to restore a sense of justice in a circumstance where they felt wronged. The young people reported being stigmatised, devalued, and pre-judged by workers. They experienced not being seen, not being asked about their actions, and not being listened to (Tillack et al., 2018). As shown in the practice material, this experience of systemic invalidation and not being listened to is common for young people in NNN.

Box 7.5 What we've learned . . .

As a body of program research data, the postcards provide a catalogue of perspectives on daily life of young people in the program and their experiences of interactions with peers, adults, and systems. They can also indicate developing perspectives on issues the program has invited them to think about.

For example, Brodie shared one of her negative experiences with police through the postcard prompt "Some advice from me to you" in her response:

> "When I was talking to the police . . . They didn't hear it because they could see I was agitated. If I was talking calmly and non-threatening, they would listen to me ".

Brodie's postcard was in the latter stages of the program, demonstrating her growing insights into changing behaviours indicating that she had learnt new skills of engagement with police and those around her.

While they might not be being listened to, young people in these situations are not without voice or the capacity to respond to what is happening around them. Considering young people's place in contemporary society, Gardner (2010) argues that working class young Brown and Black men in the US face shrinking opportunities for socially sanctioned achievements alongside increasing expectations regarding their alignment with social expectations, which is all occurring under the watchful gaze of disciplining institutions such as corrections and welfare systems. At the same time, these young people are not passive recipients of the state's responses to their ways of being. They are agents actively responding to and making sense of the world around them. As Gardner (2010) states, "If adults warily scrutinize young people struggling through the process of becoming, many young people in turn take a hard look at the society in which they are asked to participate as adults and find it wanting" (p. 83). Given the opportunity to express their perspectives on the circumstances of their lives, young people who are the subjects of interventions by state and non-state actors provide an articulate critique of the growing social expectations, on one hand, and the failures of systems to support their broad development, on the other (Gardner, 2010).

Takeaways for practice

1. Our work highlights that experiences of invalidation may have a potentiating effect on young people's use of violence.
2. Invalidation is also intimately intertwined with young people's experiences of violence, highlighting the synergistic ways in which the dynamics of power and disempowerment involved in invalidation are perhaps implicated in both the experience and use of violence.
3. Sources of invalidation can be structural and systemic, community and kin, peers, partners, and, importantly, parents.
4. Practice with young people who have used and experienced violence can perpetuate cycles of invalidation through language used, misguided attempts at humour and connection, and practitioner dysregulation and/or a discomfort with sitting with the perspective of the young person.
5. The Postcards to Practice tool provided unique insights into what we might think of as unseen and unheard experiences. In this way, it is a useful tool to validate experience if the insights gained from the activity are used to inform continuing practice.

Conclusion

This chapter has considered invalidation as an all-too-common feature of NNN program participants' experiences. It has described why and how validation is a critical skill for program practitioners and, also, the way reciprocal communication complements and extends validation as a bedrock interpersonal skill. Finally, the chapter considered young people's voice and being listened to in the context of systems they interact with, showing how the Postcards to Practice activities provide one demonstration of young people having voice in NNN. The intersection of invalidation and power is discussed in the following chapter. This next chapter unpacks theoretical and conceptual models of power and control and their relationship to violence. The chapter also provides a critical review of the current evidence base which is linked to the shared narratives of participants and practitioners associated with NNN.

References

Adrian, M., Berk, M. S., Korslund, K., Whitlock, K., McCauley, E., & Linehan, M. (2018). Parental validation and invalidation predict adolescent self-harm. *Professional Psychology, Research and Practice*, *49*(4), 274–281. https://doi.org/10.1037/pro0000200

Anderson, H., & Goolishian, H. (1992). The client as the expert: A not-knowing approach to therapy. In S. McNamee & K. J. Gergen (Eds.), *Therapy as social construction* (pp. 25–39). Sage Publications.

Banks, B. P., & Gibbons, M. M. (2016). Dialectical behavior therapy techniques for counseling incarcerated female adolescents: A case illustration. *Journal of Addictions & Offender Counseling*, *37*(1), 49–62. https://doi.org/10.1002/jaoc.12015

Batchelor, S. (2005). "Prove me the bam!" Victimisation and agency in the lives of young women who commit violent offences. *The Journal of Community and Criminal Justice*, *52*(4), 358–375. https://doi-org./10.3167/ghs.2019.120207

Becker, J. V., & Stinson, J. D. (2011). *Extending rehabilitative principles to violent sexual offenders*. Oxford University Press. https://doi.org/10.1093/acprof:oso/9780195384642.003.0061

Blakemore, T., Randall, E., Rak, L., & Cocuzzoli, F. (2021). Deep listening and relationality: Cross-cultural reflections on practice with young women who use violence. *Australian Social Work*, *75*(3), 304–316. https://doi.org/10.1080/0312407X.2021.1914697

Bollinger, J., Scott-Smith, S., & Mendes, P. (2017). How complex developmental trauma, residential out-of-home care and contact with the justice system intersect. *Children Australia*, *42*(2), 108–112. https://doi.org/10.1017/cha.2017.9

Brown, M. (2011). The sad, the mad and the bad: Co-existing discourses of girlhood. *Child & Youth Care Forum*, *40*, 107–120. https://doi.org/10.1007/s10566-010-9115-5

Brown, R., Alderson, H., Kaner, E., McGovern, R., & Lingam, R. (2019). "There are carers, and then there are carers who actually care": Conceptualizations of care among looked after children and care leavers, social workers and carers. *Child Abuse & Neglect*, 92, 219–229. https://doi.org/10.1016/j.chiabu.2019.03.018

Bubolz, B. F., & Lee, S. (2019). Putting in work: The application of identity theory to gang violence and commitment. *Deviant Behavior*, *40*(6), 690–702. https://doi.org/10.1080/01639625.2018.1437655

Byrd, A. L., Frigoletto, O. A., Vine, V., Vanwoerden, S., Jennings, J. R., Zalewski, M., & Stepp, S. D. (2023). Maternal invalidation and child RSA reactivity to frustration interact to predict teacher-reported aggression among at-risk preschoolers. *Psychological Medicine*, 1–10.

Cardona, N. D., Madigan, R. J., & Sauer-Zavala, S. (2022). How minority stress becomes traumatic invalidation: An emotion-focused conceptualization of minority stress in sexual and gender minority people. *Clinical Psychology*, *29*(2), 185–195. https://doi.org/10.1037/cps0000054

DeCou, S. E., & Vidair, H. B. (2017). What low-income, depressed mothers need from mental health care: Overcoming treatment barriers from their perspective. *Journal of Child and Family Studies*, *26*(8), 2252–2265. https://doi.org/10.1007/s10826-017-0733-5

Fasulo, S. J., Ball, J. M., Jurkovic, G. J., & Miller, A. L. (2015). Towards the development of an effective working alliance: The application of DBT validation and stylistic strategies in the adaptation of a manualized complex trauma group treatment program for adolescents in long-term detention. *American Journal of Psychotherapy*, *69*(2), 219–239. https://doi.org/10.1176/appi.psychotherapy.2015.69.2.219

Fruzzetti, A. E., & Ruork, A. (2015). *Validation principles and practices in dialectical behavior therapy*. Oxford University Press.

Barrett, J., & Rappaport, N. (2011). Keeping it real: Overcoming resistance in adolescent males mandated into treatment. *Adolescent Psychiatry*, *1*(1), 28–34.

Gardner, J. (2010). Democracy's orphans: Rights, responsibility, and the role of the state in the lives of incarcerated youth. *Youth & Society*, *42*(1), 81–103. https://doi.org/10.1177/0044118X09336268

Gillett-Swan, J., & Sargeant, J. (2018). Assuring children's human right to freedom of opinion and expression in education. *International Journal of Speech Language Pathology*, *20*(1), 120–127. https://doi.org/10.1080/17549507.2018.1385852

Grove, J. L., & Crowell, S. E. (2017). *Invalidating environments and the development of borderline personality disorder*. Oxford University Press.

Hales, J. (Ed.). (1992). *Experience, contradiction, narrative & imagination: Selected papers of David Epston and Michael White, 1989–1991*. Dulwich Centre Publications.

Hamby, S., & Jackson, A. (2010). Size does matter: The effects of gender on perceptions of dating violence. *Sex Roles*, *63*, 324–331. https://doi.org/10.1007/s11199-010-9816-0

Havard, T. E., Densley, J. A., Whittaker, A., & Wills, J. (2021). Street gangs and coercive control: The gendered exploitation of young women and girls in county lines. *Criminology & Criminal Justice*. https://doi.org/10.1177/17488958211051513

Hempel, R., Vanderbleek, E., & Lynch, T. R. (2018). Radically open DBT: Targeting emotional loneliness in Anorexia Nervosa. *Eating Disorders*, *26*(1), 92–104. https://doi.org/10.1080/10640266.2018.1418268

Herr, N. R., Meier, E. P., Weber, D. M., & Cohn, D. M. (2017). Validation of emotional experience moderates the relation between personality and aggression. *Journal of Experimental Psychopathology, 8*(2), 126–139. https://doi.org/10.5127/jep.057216

Jones, N. (2004). "It's not where you live, it's how you live": How young women negotiate conflict and violence in the inner city. *The Annals of the American Academy of Political and Social Science, 595*(1), 49–62.

Kam, P. K. (2020). "Social work is not just a job": The qualities of social workers from the perspective of service users. *Journal of Social Work, 20*(6), 775–796. https://doi.org/10.1177/1468017319848109

Levenson, J. (2017). Trauma-informed social work practice. *Social Work, 62*(2), 105–113. https://doi.org/10.1093/sw/swx001

Linehan, M. M. (1997). *Validation and psychotherapy*. American Psychological Association.

Linehan, M. M., & Wilks, C. R. (2015). The course and evolution of dialectical behavior therapy. *American Journal of Psychotherapy, 69*(2), 97–110. https://doi.org/10.1176/appi.psychotherapy.2015.69.2.97

McCormick, K. A., Chatham, A., Klodnick, V. V., Schoenfeld, E. A., & Cohen, D. A. (2022). Mental health service experiences among transition-age youth: Interpersonal continuums that influence engagement in care. *Child & Adolescent Social Work Journal*, 1–12. https://doi.org/10.1007/s10560-022-00890-0

Munford, R., & Sanders, J. (2015). Young people's search for agency: Making sense of their experiences and taking control. *Qualitative Social Work: Research and Practice, 14*(5), 616–633. https://doi.org/10.1177/1473325014565149

Musser, N., Zalewski, M., Stepp, S., & Lewis, J. (2018). A systematic review of negative parenting practices predicting borderline personality disorder: Are we measuring biosocial theory's "invalidating environment"? *Clinical Psychology Review, 65*, 1–16. https://doi.org/10.1016/j.cpr.2018.06.003

Ness, C. D. (2004). Why girls fight: Female youth violence in the inner city. *The Annals of the American Academy of Political and Social Science, 595*(1), 32–48.

O'Leary, P., Tsui, M.-S., & Ruch, G. (2013). The boundaries of the social work relationship revisited: Towards a connected, inclusive and dynamic conceptualisation. *The British Journal of Social Work, 43*(1), 135–153. https://doi.org/10.1093/bjsw/bcr181

Pederson, L. D. (2015). *Dialectical behavior therapy: A contemporary guide for practitioners*. John Wiley & Sons.

Phillips, B., & Phillips, D. A. (2010). Learning from youth exposed to domestic violence: Decentering DV and the primacy of gender stereotypes. *Violence Against Women, 16*(3), 291–312. https://doi.org/10.1177/1077801209359193

Quinn, K., Pacella, M. L., Dickson-Gomez, J., & Nydegger, L. A. (2017). Childhood adversity and the continued exposure to trauma and violence among adolescent gang members. *American Journal of Community Psychology, 59*(1–2), 36–49. https://doi.org/10.1002/ajcp.12123

Ravulo, J. (2016). Pacific youth offending within an Australian context. *Youth Justice, 16*(1), 34–48.

Rollman, J. B., Krug, K., & Parente, F. (2000). The chat room phenomenon: Reciprocal communication in cyberspace. *CyberPsychology and Behavior, 3*(2), 161–166. https://doi/abs/10.1089/109493100316003

Ryan, G. (1999). Treatment of sexually abusive youth: The evolving consensus. *Journal of Interpersonal Violence*, *14*(4), 422–436. https://doi.org/10.1177/088626099014004005

Sarnat, J. E. (2019). What's new in parallel process? The evolution of supervision's signature phenomenon. *The American Journal of Psychoanalysis*, *79*, 304–328. https://doi.org/10.1057/s11231-019-09202-5

Sattler, L. J., & Thomas, K. A. (2016). "Parents need a village": Caseworkers' perceptions of the challenges faced by single parents of system-involved youth. *Children and Youth Services Review*, *70*, 293–301.

Seamans, C. L., Rubin, L. J., & Stabb, S. D. (2007). Women domestic violence offenders: Lessons of violence and survival. *Journal of Trauma & Dissociation*, *8*(2), 47–68. https://doi.org/10.1300/J229v08n02_04

Segev, E., & Hochman, Y. (2022). Teaching note – The hidden key: Opening the door to self-disclosure in social work education. *Journal of Social Work Education*. https://doi.org/10.1080/10437797.2022.2039822

Sewell, K. M., Woods, S., Bélisle, E., Walsh, M., & Augimeri, L. K. (2019). SNAP youth justice: Youth perceptions of their learning during a pilot of an evidence-informed intervention. *Journal of Evidence-Based Social Work*, *16*(5), 478–496. https://doi.org/10.1080/26408066.2019.1629139

Sweeney, A., Filson, B., Kennedy, A., Collinson, L., & Gillard, S. (2018). A paradigm shift: Relationships in trauma-informed mental health services. *BJPsych Advances*, *24*(5), 319–333. https://doi.org/10.1192/bja.2018.29

Tarzia, L., Iyer, D., Thrower, E., & Hegarty, K. (2017). "Technology doesn't judge you": Young Australian women's views on using the internet and smartphones to address intimate partner violence. *Journal of Technology in Human Services*, *35*(3), 199–218. https://doi.org/10.1080/15228835.2017.1350616

Thompson, A. P., & McGrath, A. (2012). Subgroup differences and implications for contemporary risk-need assessment with juvenile offenders. *Law and Human Behavior*, *36*(4), 345–355. https://doi.org/10.1037/h0093930

Tillack., K., Raineri, T., Cahill, A., & McDowall, J. J. (2018). *Youth justice report: Consultation with young people in out-of-home care about their experiences with police, courts and detention*. CREATE Foundation.

Warton, T. J. (2020). *The development of a criminal identity amongst adolescent males* [Doctoral dissertation]. Monash University.

Wasson Simpson, K. S., Gallagher, A., Ronis, S. T., Miller, D. A. A., & Tilleczek, K. C. (2022). Youths' perceived impact of invalidation and validation on their mental health treatment journeys. *Administration and Policy in Mental Health and Mental Health Services Research*, *49*(3), 476–489. https://doi.org/10.1007/s10488-021-01177-9

Weber, D. M., & Herr, N. R. (2019). The messenger matters: Invalidating remarks from men provoke a more negative emotional reaction than do remarks from women. *Psychological Reports*, *122*(1), 180–200. https://doi.org/10.1177/0033294117748618

Yeh, M. A., Eilert, M., Vlahos, A., Baker, S. M., & Stovall, T. (2021). Toward a "human being to commodity model" as an explanation for men's violent, sexual consumption of women. *Journal of Consumer Affairs*, *55*(3), 911–938.

8 Empathy expressed and experienced

Tamara Blakemore and Louise Rak

Empathy, connection, and youth violence

This chapter explores the construct of empathy and its relevance to youth violence. In the Name.Narrate.Navigate (NNN) program, we explain empathy as *walking in someone else's shoes . . . to understand how they think and feel.* Other practitioners we work with refer to it as *feeling with* as opposed to *feeling for* or seeing the world through someone else's eyes. The value of these analogies is that they represent empathy as both an embodied and relational experience and a skilled and intentional act of connection, an experience central to the trauma-informed and culturally safe ethos of NNN. In this chapter, we provide an overview of the evidence base informing our work, describe our practice approach, and share examples of experiential learning activities we have used. Narratives shared by young people in response to these activities are presented in textboxes across the chapter. These de-identified narratives were collected with appropriate ethics approval through practitioner reflections on group work sessions. The perspectives of practitioners on these narratives are also presented. Practitioner input was collected as part of the ethics-approved action research associated with the design and continuous improvement of NNN. This involved focus group discussions with members of the NNN cultural reference group, practitioner working party, and steering committee. We start this chapter by describing how empathy and its expression and experience are understood.

Understandings of empathy

Empathy is described as the cornerstone of genuine and reciprocal human relationships (Bons et al., 2013), constituting both the *ability* and *inclination* to recognise, understand, and vicariously share the emotional state and experience of another (Decety & Moriguchi, 2007; Eisenberg et al., 2006). Across competing conceptualisations, empathy

DOI: 10.4324/9781003177883-8

is commonly understood as a function of interactions between cognitive processes and emotional (or affective) responses. The affective aspect of empathy refers to feelings we experience in response to another's affective state (Feshbach, 1975). Whereas the cognitive aspect refers to processes we use to make sense of emotional experiences (Hoffman, 1977). While some conceptualisations describe affective and cognitive aspects as separate but interrelated *components* of empathy, others describe them as different *types* of empathy in and of themselves.

Cognitive empathy relates to our capacity to understand another person's experience and associated mental states (their thoughts, feelings, beliefs) from their perspective. Batson (1991) qualifies that perspective-taking allows us to understand the mental states of another *like* they were our own while distinguishing them *from* our own. Other cognitive strategies involved in empathy relate to the idea of a *theory of mind*, which suggests we explain and predict other people's behaviour by theorising about how their mental states inform behaviour (Spaulding, 2017). This has also been referred to as *mentalising* (Hooker et al., 2008). Proponents of this idea explain that we infer someone's mental state from their behaviour (Carruthers & Smith, 1996). We then use this inference to predict their subsequent behaviours and/or inform what is required of us in response (Davies & Stone, 1995).

Affective empathy relates to our appreciation of and response to the emotions or experiences of others. Maibom (2017) suggests affective empathy involves an interconnected array of emotional states including sympathy (empathic concern), emotional contagion, and personal distress. Discussions of affective empathy variously draw attention to our appreciation of the consequences of our actions on the feelings of others (sometimes referred to as *emotional empathy* (Mehrabian et al., 1988)); the supportive responses we issue to others (sometimes referred to as *behavioural empathy* (Stepien & Baernstein, 2006); and, increasingly, the neurophysiological processes via which we attune with the emotional states of others (sometimes referred to as *motor empathy* (Blair, 2005)).

Our common-world notion of empathy as "walking in someone else's shoes" is informed by the thinking of Gerdes and Segal (2009), who define empathy as a multifaced process involving (1) the reflexive exchange of mirrored emotions; (2) appreciation of the meaning and context of these emotions via self/other awareness and perspective-taking; and (3) conscious decisions to take emotionally regulated, empathic action. This perspective draws on growing evidence from social-cognitive research using neural imaging to understand links between our bodies, brains, and behaviour and empathy. Jean Decety and colleagues (Decety & Jackson, 2004; Decety & Lamm, 2006; Decety & Moriguchi, 2007) use this evidence to suggest that four distinct functional components dynamically interact to generate empathy, via both unconscious and conscious processes. The perception–action model of empathy proposes the first component (affective response) is a largely unconscious or automatic experience, evoked when another's emotions or experience stimulate neural networks in our brain to produce a mirrored feeling (Decety & Moriguchi, 2007). The other three components (self/other awareness, perspective-taking, emotion regulation) are not automatic but rather sophisticated cognitive skills that are learned and consciously enacted to appreciate the experience of others (Decety & Lamm, 2006).

The expression and experience of empathy

As practitioner/academics working across fields of violence, abuse, and trauma for much of our careers, we felt we intuitively knew what empathy was but, more so, what its presence or absence looked and felt like in our work. Expressions of empathy have been described as involving thoughts and/or actions that are at their core altruistic and that usually result in positive and prosocial outcomes (Batson & Coke, 1981; Eisenberg & Miller, 1987). Carl Rogers (1964) suggested empathy was a *way of knowing* involving subjective, interpersonal, and objective strategies to make sense of the experiences of others, initially through a self-oriented frame of reference, then an other-oriented frame sometimes referenced to broader information. This person-centred approach aligns with understandings of empathy that highlight its deep roots in our evolutionary history (Arceneaux, 2017).

Empathy serves adaptive functions; it impels care for future generations (MacLean, 1985), helps us get along with others, and aids in problem-solving collaboratively to achieve common goals (Buck, 2002). Thought to be universal across cultures, empathy develops with age, its quantity and quality argued to be associated with characteristics of the environment in which development occurs (Owen & Fox, 2011). Environments conducive to the development of empathy are suggested to be ones that: (1) are consistently safe and stable; (2) encourage children to experience and express a range of emotions; and (3) provide exposure to the modelling of emotional sensitivity, regulation, and responsiveness (Barnett, 1990). Empathy is not fixed but rather a learned capacity that grows over time and which can vary among people (Eysenck et al., 1985; Grühn et al., 2008).

Variable capacities for empathy mean that some people are highly attuned to emotional cues, others almost oblivious, and many in between (Baron Cohen, 2004). Gender is suggested by some to make a difference to empathy. Some studies report females score higher on indices and tests of empathy than males (Baron-Cohen & Wheelwright, 2004), while others qualify that where this difference exists it is relatively small (Eisenberg & Lennon, 1983). A perceptible difference between male and female experiences of empathy is confirmed by some neurophysiological studies (Rueckert & Naybar, 2008). This is reasoned to manifest in females being more likely to approach dilemmas from a relational approach that prioritises others, compared to men who may, instead, emphasise issues of justice and fairness (Ford & Lowery, 1986; Galotti et al., 1991).

Narratives of the self and other

Rogers (1957) described empathy as the ability "to sense the other's private world as if it were your own but never losing the '*as if*' quality" (p. 829). From this, empathy involves both self-other association *and* self-other distinction. While self-other *distinction* is emphasised in Rogers' (1957) account – the cogent power of self-other *association* is worth considering. Batson (1991) argues taking the perspective of another person is always referenced back to and understood in the context of our own perspective. May (2017) observes, "Empathy tends to make us locate (not our identities) but shared properties or qualities in others" (p. 175). This often results in positive outcomes for both the person experiencing (receiving) empathy and the person expressing empathy. May (2017) notes empathy seems to increase our sense of agency and by "sharing the pain, or joy of others, we are reminded that we too have our own concerns relationships and values" (p. 175). Consistent with social cognition approaches to social comparison, it seems – *we find ourselves in others* (Buunk & Gibbons, 2007).

An implication of this is that we tend to empathise more with those we perceive as *like* us (i.e., *ingroup*), rather than those we see as *unlike* us (i.e., *outgroup*) (Adams et al., 2010; de Waal, 2008). The gap in empathy between ingroup and outgroup members (hereafter; the *outgroup empathy gap*) could have arisen throughout human evolution to establish and maintain social hierarchies (Batson & Ahmad, 2001; Orbell et al., 2004). We seem to almost assign people automatically as ingroup or outgroup members and, in doing so, ascribe *stereotypes* to how we expect them to think, feel, and act (Reskin, 2000). These stereotypes can result in biased perceptions, interpretations, and evaluations that can skew our empathetic responses (Becker, 2001). The outgroup empathy gap can also be influenced by fundamental attribution errors whereby we think of outgroup members' experiences as the result of some personal fault, flaw, or deficit, not a result of circumstance or situation (Becker, 2001). Powerful cultural scripts and dominant beliefs and values across society can reinforce the outgroup empathy gap (Becker, 2001), particularly in situations of real or perceived threat (Petersen, 2015). In such contexts, anxiety alerts us to threat and shapes our responses, potentially triggering ingroup favouritism and outgroup bias as a protective measure (Hatemi et al., 2013). The notion of contextual threat and its links to empathy are particularly relevant to understanding the situation of young people who use and experience violence.

The role of empathy in youth violence

The role of empathy in youth violence has been the subject of many studies. Seminal authors in the field Jolliffe and Farrington (2004) explain (in a simplified way) the logic informing these studies reasons that: empathy exists within and varies between individuals (Eisenberg & Strayer, 1990) and has an influence on behaviour (Eisenberg et al., 1996). As studies have suggested, empathy can be associated with prosocial and altruistic behaviours (Batson et al., 1987). It is assumed that a *lack of empathy* may be associated with antisocial and aggressive behaviours (Burke, 2001; Miller & Eisenberg, 1988). While this logic may over-simplify the complexity of empathy and youth violence and the interrelated factors associated with occurrence and outcome, the resulting evidence base has been influential in shaping accepted understandings of youth violence and empathy-focused intervention.

A body of evidence consistently finds young people who use violence score lower on indices and tests of empathy than other young people (Broidy et al., 2003), a finding reported for both males and females (Jolliffe & Farrington, 2007). Meta-analysis studies (statistically analysing the results of multiple studies) suggest displaying less empathy may be linked to greater aggression, including violence (Jolliffe & Farrington, 2004; Miller & Eisenberg, 1988). While young people who use violence are a heterogenous group, Robinson et al. (2007) propose common early experiences of adversity, inconsistency, hardship, and disadvantage may underscore the cohort's reported lower levels of empathy and higher levels of anger and aggression (see Chapter 5). Apart from its possible roots in trauma, the association between empathy and aggression (including violence) has been explained in several ways. Narvey et al. (2021) suggest lower levels of empathy may mean young people are less inhibited to use harmful behaviour since they don't appreciate the experience of harm from the perspective of the other person (Jolliffe & Farrington, 2006; Miller & Eisenberg, 1988). Robinson et al. (2007) propose lower levels of empathy are associated with cognitive distortions (including hostile attributions and beliefs justifying the use and efficacy of violence) and emotions (anger) that make aggression more likely. The authors also suggest that lower levels of empathy can interfere with young people finding and forming prosocial connections with non-aggressive peers, forcing them to associate with *antisocial* peers (Robinson et al., 2007). These associations, often characterised as abrasive and unsatisfying, are argued to increase risk for more frequent and diverse antisocial behaviour (Dishion et al., 1995; Thornberry et al., 1993).

Although these findings and reasonings indicate empathy plays a role in youth violence, the empirical evidence inconsistently describes what that role is and whether it's the same for all young people and all kinds of violence (Jolliffe & Farrington, 2004). Meta-analyses report a significant negative (inverse) association between cognitive dimensions of empathy and violence but a relatively weak one between affective dimensions of empathy and violence (Jolliffe & Farrington, 2004; Van Langen et al., 2014). These findings suggest the role of empathy in youth violence probably relates to differences in how young people access and use cognitive strategies known to support empathy (Lauterbach & Hosser, 2007). This might be especially true for young men, where it is suggested that difficulties appreciating emotional states of others and taking another's perspective can be associated with more frequent and reactive displays of anger and aggression (Jolliffe & Farrington, 2004; van Langen et al., 2014). Robinson et al. (2007) suggest this may be a consequence of selective or misinterpretation of social cues. They report young people who use violence over-attend to cues of anger, aggression, hostility, and potential humiliation, perceiving threat in neutral or ambiguous social cues or even cues of distress (fear and sadness) (Robinson et al., 2007). Further they suggest young people who use violence respond to these faulty assumptions from a limited range of response options and a compromised capacity to regulate or inhibit impulsive and/or aggressive responses (Robinson et al., 2007). Other cognitive strategies may also play a role in youth violence by effectively "neutralizing" empathy by dissociating the young person's self-concept from their actions (Barriga et al., 2009; McCrady et al., 2008). In these situations, young people may use strategies such as self-centredness, blaming others, minimising/mislabelling, and assuming the worst with the effect of "turning off" empathic responses to the victim(s) of their violence (Barriga et al., 2009).

It may also be the case that not all young people who use violence experience difficulties appreciating the mental states of others, and, for some, a developed sense of social competence may play a part in manipulative or coercive violence (Caravita et al., 2009; Björkqvist et al., 2000). These young people are described as having less affective empathy, demonstrating less sensitivity to impacts of their actions on the feelings of others and less awareness of their own inner experiences (Jolliffe & Farrington, 2004). Consistent with this, Robinson et al. (2007) found justice-involved young people, compared to their non-justice-involved peers, described themselves as less emotionally responsive to evocative cues, responding less often in empathic ways, and reasoning their responses in more self-referencing ways. Low scores on affective empathy have been associated with high school violence, including physical and relational violence for young men (Jolliffe & Farrington, 2006; Topcu & Erdur-Baker, 2012), and physical violence for young women (Jolliffe & Farrington, 2006). However, other studies have reported young women who use violence report *high* scores on personal distress indicating heightened emotional responses and greater sensitivity to affective cues (e.g., Lindsey et al., 2001; Jonason & Kroll, 2015). The need to escape these feelings and the association between personal distress, irritability, and hostility are suggested to explain the links between heightened emotional responsivity and aggression (Davis, 1996; Pechorro et al., 2021). Dinić et al. (2016) observe, while young women are, overall, more empathic, there appears to be more variability in their ability to resonate and sit with the emotional distress of another person than their ability to appreciate and understand another person's emotional state. The conflicting nature of these findings, combined with a reliance on self-report measures, has led some to question whether the apparent influence of gender on the association between empathy and youth violence instead represents differences in expressed empathy rather than felt empathy (O'Neill, 2020; Eisenberg, 2000).

Myths and misconceptions

Reflecting on our sketch of key propositions relating to empathy and its expression and experience, we are inspired by Warden (2018) to clarify what seem to be persuasive myths and misconceptions about empathy as it relates to young people who use violence.

First, empathy is not fixed or static (Duan & Hill, 1996), especially in adolescence where capacities for empathy are still emerging (Grühn et al., 2008). Gerdes and Segal (2011, p. 143) emphasise that empathy can be "taught, increased, refined and mediated". During adolescence, and later, low scores on indices or tests of empathy don't necessarily reflect a lack of capacity to empathise (Lummer & Hageman, 2015). As Warden (2018) reminds us, readiness and willingness to empathise are likely contextualised by prior experience. Young people will make protective assessments about the consequences of empathising with others, especially in contexts of real or perceived threat (Petersen, 2015).

Second, young people's expressions of empathy may or may not be reflective of their experiences of empathy. We often hold culturally defined expectations about what empathy should look like and how it should be expressed. While communicated through affect (Luna, 2003), empathy itself is an internal process, so we shouldn't conflate the absence or presence of emotional expression with empathy (Buckingham, 2012). Warden (2018) observes that expectations of justice-involved cohorts to demonstrate empathic understanding of the consequences of their actions often fail to take into account the many factors that situate, constrain, and facilitate expressions of empathy.

Third, as Warden (2018) notes, while related, empathy is *not* remorse. Remorse is a feeling (Davis & Gold, 2011). Empathy is far more complex, involving recognition and pivoting on mental processes governing appreciation and response. While empathy may elicit remorse (Davis & Gold, 2011), the two are not the same and are not necessarily associated with the same outcomes. As Warden (2018) notes, empathy is distinguished by the explanatory and transformative power it can have over relationships and, through them, opportunities for change.

Empathy in NNN

Empathy is the focus of the third session in the NNN program for young people. Building on prior content, this session explores what happens when we feel invalidated and how that might impact empathy (or, putting ourselves in someone else's shoes). It also explores what it would be like for someone to put themselves in the shoes of the young people we work with (i.e., show them empathy). Key objectives of the session include continuing to model reciprocal communication (discussed in Chapter 7) and validating the young people's perspectives, recognising that contextual factors shape their experiences. Activities in the session consider the consequences of invalidation and explore the experience and expression of empathy.

Table 8.1 Program structure, session focus: Empathy

Program structure	*Session*	*Focus*
		Beginnings
	1	Emotions
	2	Voice
	3	**Empathy**
	4	Power and Control
	5	Shame
	6	Choice
		Endings

Practice approach

Interventions for youth violence have long focused on developing or strengthening empathy (e.g., Gibbs et al., 1995; Richardson et al., 1994). They have been trans-theoretically informed, variously targeting both emotional empathy (how we understand impacts of our actions) and behavioural empathy (how we express empathy). Some interventions have been based on cognitive retraining, others on experiential learning. Most have a focus on holding narratives of the self and other separate but together in one's awareness. Our practice approach shares this focus. Consistent with our ethos of trauma-informed, culturally safe, and relational ways of working, we adopt a person-centred approach that is sensitive to dynamics of power, privilege, and place.

Person-centred

We recognise synergies between our way of working and the person-centred *approach*. This approach involves the application of principles derived from the work of Carl Rogers and others since that are suggested to give rise to a way of being in our relationship to others (Wood, 1996). It is beyond the scope of this chapter to provide an in-depth discussion of the person-centred approach. Instead, we provide a brief discussion of core concepts of the approach that are instructive to our work. The person-centred approach is commonly associated with Rogers' (1957) notion that there are necessary and sufficient aspects of practice that, when present, facilitate change. These are often summarised as: (1) unconditional positive regard; (2) empathic regard; and (3) congruence (or genuineness) (Rogers, 1957). The assertion is made that when practice creates conditions where people feel recognised and respected and they experience practitioners as empathic and genuine, positive change occurs, irrespective of the intervention used (Rogers, 1986). There is good support for these claims, particularly regarding the importance of empathy. Bohart et al. (2002) conducted a large meta-analysis of studies on practice outcomes, finding a significant and meaningful correlation between people's perceived experience of practitioner empathy and positive therapeutic outcomes.

Clark and Butler (2020) remind us that empathic responses are necessary to demonstrate that we recognise and understand the explicit and implicit experiences of the people we work with. Tacit here is an acknowledgement that the people we work with are unique and *unknown* and that our task involves better *knowing* them, their situation, and their circumstance. This positions the person at the centre of practice, recognising them as experts in their experience and active agents in their own growth and development (Wilkins, 2015). Studies show when we better understand people we work with and they feel understood, they are more likely to fully engage with interventions and report better outcomes (Corey, 2017; Wilson et al., 2011). Enacting this in practice embodies Rogers' (1964) notion of empathy as a *way of knowing*. Arthur Clark's (2004) translation of this theory to an integral model of social work practice has been instructive to our work. He notes *subjective empathy* involves the internal responses we have when we are engaged in work with others (Clark, 2004; Clark & Butler, 2020). For us, this is the feel of the work, the vibe of the room, and the unspoken, *sensed knowledge* we take on in our work. It informs the pace of our practice, the pitch and tone of our voice, how we place our bodies, and where we focus our attention. It also informs *interpersonal empathy*, which Clark (2004; Clark & Butler, 2020) describes as our understanding of the felt experience of the people we work with and our accurate communication of that understanding to them. We think of this as shared knowledge co-created with, but led by, the expertise of young people we work with. Objective empathy relates to knowledge borne out of theory and evidence (Clark, 2004; Clark & Butler, 2020). An important distinction for us is that evidence that informs our work is knowledge for and from practice. By triangulating and moving between each of these three ways of knowing, we get to know the young people we work with in richer, deeper, and more meaningful ways.

Social empathy

Our practice approach to work with empathy is also informed by Elizabeth A. Segal's (2011) notion of *social empathy*. This refers to the ability to understand people relative to their situation and experience and the impacts of structural inequalities and disparities. Recognising the potent influence of power and context, social empathy (Segal, 2007a, 2007b, 2011) is a useful complement to a person-centred approach, noting critiques that warn it can be culturally bound in individualising experience (Cooper, 2007; Mearns & Cooper, 2005). From a trauma-informed and culturally safe ethos, it is important that while being person-centred, our practice approach is also sensitive to dynamics of power, privilege, and place. Segal (2011) explains the exercise of social empathy is built on normal conceptions of individual empathy but expands to include deep insight and knowledge of contextual experiences that can prompt, facilitate, and constrain experience and outcomes. Consistent with this, the premise and objective of exploring empathy in NNN has been reflecting on how we might put ourselves in the shoes of another. In this task, we use experiential learning methods to bridge the space between cultural and societal assumptions and actual lived realities (Adelman et al., 2016).

Experiential learning

A meaningful activity for exploring empathy in NNN is referred to as *putting yourself in someone else's shoes*. The design and delivery of this activity adopts an *experiential learning* approach. Experiential learning is defined by Chan et al. (2021) as a process that "facilitates learners to transform and create knowledge, skills, attitudes, and ways of thinking" (p. 2). Experiential learning involves action-reflection and experience-abstraction (Chan et al., 2021), accommodating different learning styles and abilities by integrating aspects of experience, perception, cognition, and behaviour (Lewis & Williams, 1994; Kolb & Kolb, 2009; Kolb, 2014).

In the activity, young people are presented with curated shoeboxes themed to different genders and life stages. Each shoebox contains a pair of shoes and an assortment of found objects representing the miscellanea of everyday life (see Figures 8.1, 8.2). Young people are encouraged to inspect, play with, and try on the contents of the box. Practitioners provide conversational prompts to explore values, beliefs, and assumptions

Figure 8.1 Football boots shoebox

Figure 8.2 Fancy lady shoebox

about the imagined owners of these shoes, considering context, situation, feelings, thoughts, actions, and needs. Narratives provided by the young people in response can support critically reflective conversations about the meanings they have made about the imagined owner of the shoes and what informs them. Young people can present conflicting points of view, creating opportunities to consider alternative understandings of the same stimulus. The activity engages young people with important skills for empathy including recognising, appreciating, perspective-taking, mentalising and considered response.

Experiential learning supports new ways of thinking, being, and doing by engaging and connecting with different ways of knowing in the learning process (Kolb & Kolb, 2009). Influential in this field, Kolb (1984) proposes four stages of learning involving: "concrete experience, reflective observation, abstract conceptualisation, and active experimentation" (p. 40). Studies suggest experiential learning can help develop critical thinking skills (Lisko & O'dell, 2010) and self-awareness (Burch et al., 2016). Of specific interest to our work, Chan et al. (2021), in a systematic review of empathy-focused interventions, found that those delivered from an experiential learning approach were more effective than other forms of intervention. We find that young people can engage deeply with this activity, with narratives emerging from conversations had during the activity exploring ingroup/outgroup identities, gender and age-related stereotypes, and the experience of violence across the life course. We detail the *putting yourself in someone else's shoes* activity in Table 8.2.

What we've learned

Young people we have worked with have demonstrated an ongoing willingness to share their stories and experiences in a mutually trusting, reciprocal relationship with us as practitioners. Organic examples of this behavioural type of expressed empathy began emerging as the participants became more comfortable with each other and through the ongoing group co-creation processes. As practitioners, we witnessed countless demonstrations of acts of care between group members as well as the tendency to think about and reflect on the personal circumstances of peers and practitioners. In groups of young women, this has often played out in concern over peer participants' wellbeing in areas such as self-harm, housing arrangements, violence at home, and state of relationships. We similarly saw acts of concern expressed between young men, though often in more action-oriented ways, for example, waiting for one another, sharing *war stories* to initiate conversation, and ensuring each other got their desired food during shared snack breaks. In both male and female groups, we have consistently seen young people start to overtly extend acts of empathy towards the practitioners from this session onwards.

Empathy gender, grief, and loss

One of the first observations we made as practitioners was that young men and women engaged with empathy differently but not always in the ways we would have expected. Broidy et al. (2003, p. 503) explain:

> implicit in most theoretical understandings of sex differences in offending is the notion that females are less likely to engage in violent crime, in part because of their comparatively higher levels of concern for others and stronger affiliative ties.

Yet, at face value, our work with young people who have used violence, gendered ways of exploring and engaging with empathy were quite different. Young men in NNN readily connected with the shoebox activity, particularly engaging with a shoebox filled with stereotypical "little boy" or male-gendered items such as football boots, a small toy car, and tickets to the football match (see Figure 8.1).

Table 8.2 Practice note: Putting yourself in someone else's shoes

Practice note: "Putting yourself in someone else's shoes" – the shoebox activity	
Description:	The aim of the "shoebox" activity is to provide an experiential, visual, and tactile stimulus to support the idea of empathy as "putting yourself in someone else's shoes".
Time:	15 minutes
Resources:	Each young person is presented with a curated shoebox with a pair of shoes and found items from everyday life. No narrative is provided to the owner of the shoes or their story.
Purpose:	The purpose of the activity is to present young people with the opportunity to imagine alternate realities and to explore what another person might think, feel, experience, need, and know in a safe space free from judgement or immediate connection to their own experience.
Presentation:	Young people are asked to contemplate the shoeboxes and touch, feel, and sort through their contents and consider: • Who owns these shoes? • What's their story? • What's happening for them? • What might they be feeling? • What might have made them feel this way? • What might they do about that? • What do you think they need? Young people are prompted to reflect on what it takes to put yourself in someone else's shoes (risks, vulnerabilities, skills) and what it feels like for the participants when someone puts themselves in their shoes.
Rationale:	This activity provides young people with opportunities for exposure, experience, and exploration of different life narratives and imagining themselves in the lives of people they understand as different to them (Adelman et al., 2016; Segal, 2007a). The design and delivery of this activity adopts an *experiential learning* approach. Experiential learning is defined by Chan et al. (2021) as a process that "facilitates learners to transform and create knowledge, skills, attitudes, and ways of thinking" (p. 2). Theory and practice underpinnings for the activity include the person-centred approach and social empathy. The activity situates the young people at the centre of the activity and seeks to better understand, with more sensitivity, their experiences and perspectives. Experiential techniques are consistent with person-centred approaches (Sanders et al., 2013). The activity also draws on Segal's (2007b) pedagogical model for supporting the development of "social empathy", or the *application* of empathic understanding by drawing attention to ways contexts can prompt, facilitate, and constrain experience.

Box 8.1 What we've learned . . .

Young men often present sentimental or nostalgic narratives to explain the life of the imagined owner of this shoebox, often referenced to their own experiences:

> "I bet he has parents who took him to football every weekend".
>
> "And drumsticks, probably has a drumkit too".
>
> "These boots are really clean; he's really looked after them".
>
> "That's out of a speedracer Lego set . . . decent".

The narratives young men have shared in relation to this shoebox confirm that in an experiential learning activity, they can place themselves in the shoes of another (per Gerdes et al., 2011; Segal, 2007a, 2007b) and do reference back to their own experiences to inform their understanding of this (imagined) person's experience. An intriguing new learning for us was that engaging with this shoebox has consistently evoked narratives of grief, loss, and sadness for young men. These narratives are often about being left out, left behind, missing out, or missing a time when they felt connected to others or as belonging. Some young men have considered the items in the box with awe and even a little envy, others with a melancholic nostalgia or sentimentality, others with frank sadness. One young man, who said he couldn't relate to the items in the shoebox (they weren't things he would have had as a child), then said, "*But . . . it's what I'd want my kid to have*" (Ash). We think these findings are important. They have highlighted for us the potential of this activity to elicit narratives of the self and other and to both stimulate affective and cognitive empathy. They also identify opportunities for strengthening self-awareness and the claiming of needs – particularly in relation to grief and loss. While Lansing et al. (2018) has reported on the disproportionate experience of grief among justice-involved young men, these findings relate more to bereavements than cumulative loss associated with historical and intergenerational trauma, disadvantage, and disruptive change. To date, there has been little focus on exploring the role of grief and loss in youth violence.

Empathy, gender, antagonism, and avoidance

Young women, by contrast, have been less willing or able to engage with the stories of others in this activity often citing that to do so would be akin to "snitching" (i.e., telling someone else's story). This seems to particularly relate to the shoebox we tend to refer to as the *fancy lady* box (see Figure 8.2). While young women seem to pay cursory attention to the other shoeboxes, where they do engage, this shoebox seems to evoke antagonism and even contempt.

Box 8.2 What we've learned . . .

Young women have presented narratives of the imagined owner of this shoebox that stereotype her age, parenting abilities, lifestyle behaviours, morality, and personality:

> Tash (14) said, "Look at this slut, out drinking when she should have been home with her kids . . . why does she even need to list to remember milk . . . and she lost her keys, stupid bitch".

Of note, there is nothing in the shoebox that suggests the owner has children or that she has been out drinking; however, these are frequently made assumptions.

We have been surprised by the level and consistency of antagonism young women have displayed towards the imagined owner of this shoebox. Young men, in comparison seem superficially interested in this shoebox, sometimes saying it reminds them of a sister or cousin, but not expressing any negativity or judgement towards the imagined owner's imagined actions or character. As we will discuss in Chapter 9, the way young women reacted to this shoebox was consistent with the hypervigilance to female presence, potential judgement, or threat we observed when out in the community with them. As noted in Chapter 7, many of these young women reported fractured relationships with females in their life and openly voiced the sentiment that "women will let you down" (Kylie). These sentiments reflect findings that young women who use violence frequently report a lack of emotional support from family and a general unhappiness with the function of the family life (Molidar, 1996). The primacy of relationships in the lives of young women cannot be underestimated. In the context of fractured families, kinship, and connection, relationships with peers and partners can define and reinforce young women's identities while also serving to protect against isolation and violence (Letendre, 2007).

These gendered differences in reaction to women were also observed in response to photo-elicitation activities. As discussed in Chapter 6, these activities involved young people being shown a large range of photos capturing diverse populations engaged in everyday activities across cultures and socioeconomic cohorts both similar and dissimilar to the NNN participants. In this activity, young men tended to respond with high levels of compassion, demonstrating a level of insight into the imagined stories of the people in the photos. In one photo of a woman with a baby, a young man noted: "She looks sad. Her partner probably just left her, and she is worried about how she is going to care for her baby" (Jake). By contrast, young women tended to demonstrate a hostility towards other females in the photos labelling them as "junkies", "skanks", and "sluts" depending on how they physically presented. Young women, while engaged in the activity, appeared unable or unwilling to engage with the people in the photos, particularly any females in the photos, in the same way as their male counterparts. Young women's antagonism towards the *fancy lady* and even photographic images of other women may relate to Adelman et al.'s (2016) observation that, as humans, we are more likely to identify (and empathise) with those most like us and contemplating and understanding difference can be an internally difficult, if not threatening, experience.

When we presented these observations to fellow practitioners, it was suggested that visceral reactions by young women to photographs of other women could be viewed as an act of resistance and self-preservation: "It's like this projection of hatred onto whoever is perceived as having what I don't have" (Practitioner A). Understanding this as an act of self-preservation relies on recognising that, in difference, we can see threat – particularly in contexts of learned hypervigilance to risk and where trusting others may leave you vulnerable and at risk of exploitation or harm (Bollinger et al., 2017; Thompson & McGrath, 2012). This sentiment was echoed by our practitioner peers who, when reflecting on empathy and youth violence, highlight:

> [For young people life can be] pretty taxing, they live in cultures, contexts and communities where there's lots of dimensions of harm and violence, so I think that there can often be a really strong protective drive and that can lead to the use of violence . . . protecting self or siblings/others.
>
> (Practitioner B)

Indeed, Broidy et al. (2003) suggest that empathy may moderate the relationship between trauma and the involvement in serious crime (including violence). Reporting on a comparison-cohort study of incarcerated young people (n=232) and non-incarcerated peers (n=425), the authors found all young women reported going out of their way to help others, but incarcerated young women were less inclined to think about the emotional impact of their actions on others (Broidy et al., 2003).

These findings are consistent with the argument that greater empathy deficits are required for females compared to males for them to engage in serious crime, but also, paradoxically, with the fact that, for females, serious crime can often be motivated by empathic concern for others, for relationships, and for emotional commitments (Steffensmeier & Broidy, 2000).

Empathy and vulnerability

Our observations of how challenging it was for some young women to sit with and contemplate the experience of another reminds us that, at its core, empathy is a vulnerable-making experience (Stout, 2019). When young women were at first reluctant to engage with the activity, they explained, "You can't tell someone else's story" and made links between telling someone else's story and "snitching", a serious social infraction with real consequences for their safety. For these young women, the act of empathy, even symbolically, presented a personal risk and/or may have required a loosening of their tight hold on power and control in their relationships and interactions with others. The vulnerability associated with exploring empathy was observed as a potential point of disconnect and disengagement in the NNN program. Regardless of gender, young people who self-reported communication styles and strategies consistent with coercive control rather than transactional, impulsive, explosive, or reactive violence tended to find activities exploring empathy uncomfortable. This is consistent with Holt (2016), who notes that particular therapeutic work is challenging and there are certain touch points that cause people to disconnect and disengage. This vulnerability is about unconscious truths, self-awareness, and emerging narratives of the self coming into clearer focus for participants. It is important to note that the majority of young people who experienced the exploration of empathy difficult, continued to participate, even if missing a session in between. This indicated that the value proposition of the program overrode the discomfort experienced.

Empathy as an embodied experience

As practitioners, when we reflect on our work exploring empathy with young people who use violence, we caution others to appreciate context and complexity. Conscious of our positionality and privilege, we acknowledge that our constructs of empathy may not align with those of the young people we work with, especially those who have experienced and who continue to live in chronic and cumulative states of trauma. Practitioner peers highlight that for many young people, "Violence is almost a normal part of their day to day, and they don't understand that it's not for everyone around them". In these contexts, practitioners consulted highlight that for some young people, anger on behalf of another can be a demonstration of empathy, "Then empathy in that situation would look like you're angry, and you want to punch him . . . you can't so we are punching for you". Empathy can, hence, be prosocial and antisocial and, as another practitioner highlights, self-protective: "For young people empathy is a big scary word . . . I feel like they do their very best to protect themselves . . . trying to show empathy to themselves".

The implications of our work for practice reiterate the need for a challenging of assumptions and a healthy dose of optimism. Understanding the role of empathy in youth violence is complex and is often community and culturally bound (Narvey et al., 2021). Use of violence does not mean young people are devoid of empathy; the capacity for empathy is there for most, as it is for almost all people. It may just present differently, emerge later, or be hidden. We must also recognise that empathy may come at a cost, or risk, to the individual displaying it, especially for young women.

Takeaways for practice

1. Empathy is complex and contextualised.
2. In work with young people who use violence, empathy is rarely simply present or absent but, rather, mediated, moderated, or supressed by factors including prior experience(s) and associated impact(s).
3. Differences in empathy are observed across gender. We noted empathy to evoke feelings of deep grief and loss for young men and to present significant vulnerability for young women.
4. For both genders, engaging with empathy can be a point of disconnect, presumably due to implicit and unconscious processes of self-reflection it may stimulate.

Conclusion

This chapter has explored the relevance of empathy to youth violence. It provided a selective overview of the ways in which empathy has been conceptualised and how young people who use violence articulate empathy through experiential learning activities. The chapter explored the value of a person-centred, social empathy–informed approach to practice, finding that efforts to better understand youth violence with more sensitivity to context resulted in new and emerging findings that challenge previously held assumptions. Following chapters explore related experiences of power and shame.

References

Adams, R. B., Rule, N. O., Franklin, R. G., Wang, E., Stevenson, M. T., Yoshikawa, S., Nomura, M., Sato, W., Kveraga, K., & Ambady, N. (2010). Cross-cultural reading the mind in the eyes: An Fmri investigation. *Journal of Cognitive Neuroscience*, 22(1), 97–108. https://doi.org/10.1162/jocn.2009.21187

Adelman, M., Rosenberg, K. E., & Hobart, M. (2016). Simulations and social empathy. *Violence Against Women*, 22(12), 1451–1462. https://doi.org/10.1177/1077801215625850

Arceneaux, K. (2017). Anxiety reduces empathy toward outgroup members but not ingroup members. *Journal of Experimental Political Science*, *4*(1), 68–80. https://doi.org/10.1017/xps.2017.12

Barnett, N. (1990). Empathy and related responses in children. In N. Eisenberg & J. Strayer (Eds.), *Empathy and its development* (pp. 146–162). Cambridge University Press.

Baron-Cohen, S. (2004). *Essential difference: Male and female brains and the truth about autism*. Basic Books.

Baron-Cohen, S., & Wheelwright, S. (2004). The empathy quotient: An investigation of adults with Asperger syndrome or high functioning autism, and normal sex differences. *Journal of Autism and Developmental Disorders*, *34*(2), 163–175.

Barriga, A. Q., Sullivan-Cosetti, M., & Gibbs, J. C. (2009). Moral cognitive correlates of empathy in juvenile delinquents. *Criminal Behavior and Mental Health*, *19*, 253–264. https://doi.org./10.1002/cbm.740

Batson, C. D. (1991). *The altruism question: Toward a social-psychological answer*. Lawrence Erlbaum Associates, Inc.

Batson, C. D., & Ahmad, N. (2001). Empathy-induced altruism in a prisoner's dilemma II: What if the target of empathy has defected? *European Journal of Social Psychology*, *31*(1), 25–36. https://doi.org/10.1002/ejsp.26

Batson, C. D., & Coke, J. S. (1981). Empathy: A source of altruistic motivation for helping? In J. P. Rushton & R. M. Sorrentino (Eds.), *Altruism and helping behavior: Social, personality and developmental perspectives* (pp. 167–211). Lawrence Erlbaum Associates, Inc.

Batson, C. D., Fultz, J., & Schoenrade, P. A. (1987). Distress and empathy: Two qualitatively distinct vicarious emotions with different motivational consequences. *Journal of Personality*, *55*(1), 19–39.

Becker, M. (2001). The passions of battered women: Cognitive links between passion, empathy, and power. *William & Mary Journal of Women and the Law*, *8*(1), 1–72.

Björkqvist, K., Österman, K., & Kaukiainen, A. (2000). Social intelligence–empathy= aggression? *Aggression and Violent Behavior*, *5*(2), 191–200.

Blair, R. J. R. (2005). Responding to the emotions of others: Dissociating forms of empathy through the study of typical and psychiatric populations. *Consciousness and Cognition*, *14*, 698–718. https://doi.org./10.10161/j.concog.2005.06.004

Bohart, A. C., Elliott, R., Greenberg, L. S., & Watson, J. C. (2002). Empathy. In J. C. Norcross (Ed.), *Psychotherapy relationships that work: Therapist contributions and responsiveness to patients* (pp. 89–108). Oxford University Press.

Bollinger, J., Scott-Smith, S., & Mendes, P. (2017). How complex developmental trauma, residential out-of-home care and contact with the justice system intersect. *Children Australia*, *42*(2), 108–112. https://doi.org./10.1017/cha.2017.9

Bons, D., van den Broek, E., Scheepers, F., Herpers, P., Rommelse, N., & Buitelaaar, J. K. (2013). Motor, emotional, and cognitive empathy in children and adolescents with autism spectrum disorder and conduct disorder. *Journal of Abnormal Child Psychology*, *41*(3), 425–443. https://doi.org./10.1007/s10802-012-9689-5

Broidy, L., Cauffman, E., Espelage, D. L., Mazerolle, P., & Piquero, A. (2003). Sex differences in empathy and its relation to juvenile offending. *Violence and Victims*, *18*(5), 503–516. https://doi.org./10.1891/088667003780928143

Buck, R. (2002). The genetics and biology of true love: Prosocial biological affects and the left hemisphere. *Psychological Review*, *109*(4), 739–744. https://doi.org/10.1037/0033-295x.109.4.739

Buckingham, S. (2012). Reducing incarceration for youthful offenders with a developmental approach to sentencing. *Loy. LAL Review*, *46*, 801.

Burch, G., Giambatista, R. C., Batchelor, J., Hoover, J. D., Burch, J., Heller, N., & Shaw, J. (2016). Do experiential learning pedagogies effect student learning? A meta-analysis of 40 years of research. *Academy of Management Proceedings*, 16838. https://doi.org/10.5465/ambpp.2016.127

Burke, D. M. (2001). Empathy in sexually offending and nonoffending adolescent males. *Journal of Interpersonal Violence*, *16*(3), 222–233.

Buunk, A. P., &; Gibbons, F. X. (2007). Social comparison: The end of a theory and the emergence of a field. *Organizational Behavior and Human Decision Processes*, *102*(1), 3–21. https://doi.org/10.1016/j.obhdp.2006.09.007

Caravita, S. C. S., Di Blasio, P., & Salmivalli, C. (2009). Unique and interactive effects of empathy and social status on involvement in bullying. *Social Development*, *18*, 140–163. www.doi.org/10.1111/j.1467-9507.2008.00465.x

Carruthers, P., & Smith, P. K. (1996). *Theories of theories of mind*. Cambridge University Press.

Chan, H. H.-K., Kwong, H. Y., Shu, G. L., Ting, C. Y., & Lai, F. H.-Y. (2021). Effects of experiential learning programmes on adolescent prosocial behaviour, empathy, and subjective well-being: A systematic review and meta-analysis. *Frontiers in Psychology*, *12*. https://doi.org/10.3389/fpsyg.2021.709699

Clark, A. J. (2004). Empathy: Implications of three ways of knowing in counseling. *Journal of Humanistic Counseling, Education and Development*, *43*, 141–151.

Clark, A. J., & Butler, C. M. (2020). Empathy: An integral model in clinical social work. *Social Work*, *65*(2), 169–177. https://doi.org/10.1093/sw/swaa009

Cooper, M. (2007). Developmental and personality theory. In M. Cooper, M. O'Hara, P. F. Schmid, & G. Wyatt (Eds.), *The handbook of person-centred psychotherapy and counselling*. Palgrave Macmillan.

Corey, G. (2017). *Theory and practice of counseling and psychotherapy* (10th ed.). Thompson Brooks/Cole, Cengage Learning.

Davies, M., & Stone, T. (1995). *Folk psychology: The theory of mind debate*. Blackwell Publishers.

Davis, J. R., & Gold, G. J. (2011). An examination of emotional empathy, attributions of stability, and the link between perceived remorse and forgiveness. *Personality and Individual Differences*, *50*(3), 392–397. https://doi.org/10.1016/j.paid.2010.10.031

Davis, M. H. (1996). *Empathy: A social psychological approach*. Brown & Benchmark Publishers.

de Waal, F. B. M. (2008). Putting the altruism back into altruism: The evolution of empathy. *Annual Review of Psychology*, *59*(1), 279–300. https://doi.org/10.1146/annurev.psych.59.103006.093625

Decety, J., & Jackson, P. L. (2004). The functional architecture of human empathy. *Behavioral and Cognitive Neuroscience Reviews*, *3*(2), 71–100. https://doi.org/10.1177/1534582304267187

Decety, J., & Lamm, C. (2006). Human empathy through the lens of social neuroscience. *Scientific World Journal*, *6*, 1146–1163.

Decety, J., & Moriguchi, Y. (2007). The empathic brain and its dysfunction in psychiatric populations: Implications for intervention across different clinical conditions. *Biopsychosocial Medicine*, *1*(22), 1–21. https://doi.org./10.1186/1751-0759-1-22

Dinić, B. M., Kodžopeljić, J. S., Sokolovska, V. T., & Milovanović, I. Z. (2016). Empathy and peer violence among adolescents: Moderation effect of gender. *School Psychology International*, *37*(4), 359–377. https://doi.org/10.1177/0143034316649008

Dishion, T., Andrews, D., & Crosby, L. (1995). Antisocial boys and their friends in early adolescence: Relationship characteristics, quality, and interactional process. *Child Development*, *66*, 139–151.

Duan, C., & Hill, C. E. (1996). The current state of empathy research. *Journal of Counseling Psychology*, *43*(3), 261–274. https://doi.org/10.1037/0022-0167.43.3.261

Eisenberg, N. (2000). Empathy and sympathy. In M. Lewis & J. M. Haviland-Jones (Eds.), *Handbook of emotions* (2nd ed., pp. 677–691). Guilford Press.

Eisenberg, N., Fabes, R. A., Murphy, B., Karbon, M., Smith, M., & Maszk, P. (1996). The relations of children's dispositional empathy-related responding to their emotionality, regulation, and social functioning. *Developmental Psychology*, *32*(2), 195–209. https://doi.org/10.1037/0012-1649.32.2.195

Eisenberg, N., & Lennon, R. (1983). Sex differences in empathy and related capacities. *Psychological Bulletin*, *94*, 100–131. https://doi.org./10.1037/0033-2909.94.1.100

Eisenberg, N., & Miller, P. A. (1987). The relation of empathy to prosocial and related behaviors. *Psychological Bulletin*, *101*, 91–119.

Eisenberg, N., Spinrad, T. L., & Sadovsky, A. (2006). Empathy related responding in children. In M. Killen & J. Smetana (Eds.), *Handbook of moral development* (pp. 517–549, 712–718). Lawrence Erlbaum Associates, Inc.

Eisenberg, N., & Strayer, J. (1990). *Empathy and its development*. Cambridge University Press.

Eysenck, S. B., Eysenck, H. J., & Barrett, P. (1985). A revised version of the psychoticism scale. *Personality and Individual Differences*, *6*(1), 21–29.

Feshbach, N. D. (1975). Empathy in children: Some theoretical and empirical considerations. *The Counseling Psychologist*, *5*(2), 25–30. https://doi.org/10.1177/001100007500500207

Ford, M., & Lowery, C. (1986). Gender differences in moral reasoning: A comparison of the justice and care orientations. *Journal of Personality and Social Psychology*, *50*, 777–783.

Galotti, K., Kozberg, S., & Appleman, D. (1991). Younger and older adolescents' thinking about commitments. *Journal of Experimental Child Psychology*, *50*, 324–339.

Gerdes, K. E., & Segal, E. A. (2009). A social work model of empathy. *Advances in Social Work*, *10*(2), 114–127. https://doi.org/10.18060/235

Gerdes, K. E., & Segal, E. A. (2011). Importance of empathy for social work practice: Integrating new science. *Social Work*, *56*(2), 141–148. https://doi.org./10.1016/j.cpr.2006.03.003

Gerdes, K. E., Segal, E. A., Jackson, K., & Mullins, J. L. (2011). Teaching empathy: A framework rooted in social cognitive neuroscience and social justice. *Journal of Social Work Education*, *47*, 109–131. https://doi.org/10.5175/JSWE.2011.200900085

Gibbs, J. C., Potter, G., & Goldstein, A. (1995). *The EQUIP program: Teaching youth to act responsibly through a peer-helping program*. Research Press.

Grühn, D., Rebucal, K., Diehl, M., Lumley, M., & Labouvie-Vief, G. (2008). Empathy across the adult lifespan: Longitudinal and experience-sampling findings. *Emotion*, *8*(6), 753.

Hatemi, P. K., McDermott, R., Eaves, L. J., Kendler, K. S., & Neale, M. C. (2013). Fear as a disposition and an emotional state: A genetic and environmental approach to out-group political preferences. *American Journal of Political Science*, *57*(2), 279–293. https://doi.org/10.1111/ajps.12016

Hoffman, M. L. (1977). Moral internalization: Current theory and research. In L. Berkowitz (Ed.), *Advances in experimental social psychology* (Vol. 10, pp. 85–133). Academic Press.

Holt, A. (2016). Adolescent-to-parent abuse as a form of "domestic violence" a conceptual review. *Trauma, Violence, & Abuse*, *17*(5), 490–499. https://doi.org/10.1177/1524838015584372

Hooker, C.I., Verosky, S.C., Germine, L.T., Knight, R.T., & D'Esposito, M. (2008). Mentalizing about emotion and it's relationship to empathy, *Social Cognitive and Affective Neuroscience*, *3*(3), 204–217. https://doi.org/10.1093/scan/nsn019

Jolliffe, D., & Farrington, D. P. (2004). Empathy and offending: A systematic review and meta-analysis. *Aggression and Violent Behavior*, *9*(5), 441–476. https://doi.org/10.1016/j.avb.2003.03.001

Jolliffe, D., & Farrington, D. P. (2006). Examining the relationship between low empathy and bullying. *Aggressive Behavior*, *32*(6), 540–550. https://doi.org./10.1002/ab.20154

Jolliffe, D., & Farrington, D. P. (2007). Examining the relationship between low empathy and self-reported offending. *Legal and Criminological Psychology*, *12*, 265–286. https://doi.org./10.1348/135532506X147413

Jonason, P. K., & Kroll, C. H. (2015). A multidimensional view of the relationship between empathy and the dark triad. *Journal of Individual Differences*, *36*, 150–156. https://doi.org./10.1027/1614-0001/a000166

Kolb, A. Y., & Kolb, D. A. (2009). Experiential learning theory: A dynamic, holistic approach to management learning, education and development. *SAGE*

Handbook of Management Learning, Education and Development, *42*, 68. https://doi.org/10.4135/9780857021038.n3

Kolb, D. A. (1984). *Experiential learning: Experience as the source of learning and development*. Prentice-Hall.

Kolb, D. A. (2014). *Experiential learning: Experience as the source of learning and development*. FT Press.

Lansing, A. E., Plante, W. Y., Beck, A. N., & Ellenberg, M. (2018). Loss and grief among persistently delinquent youth: The contribution of adversity indicators and psychopathy-spectrum traits to broadband internalizing and externalizing psychopathology. *Journal of Child & Adolescent Trauma*, *11*(3), 375–389. https://doi.org/10.1007/s40653-018-0209-9

Lauterbach, O., & Hosser, D. (2007). Assessing empathy in prisoners – a shortened version of the interpersonal reactivity index. *Swiss Journal of Psychology*, *66*(2), 91–101. https://doi.org./10.1024/1421-0185.66.2.91

Letendre, J. (2007). "Sugar and spice but not always nice": Gender socialization and its impact on development and maintenance of aggression in adolescent girls. *Child and Adolescent Social Work Journal*, *24*(4), 353–368. https://doi.org/10.1007/s10560-007-0088-7

Lewis, L. H., & Williams, C. J. (1994). Experiential learning: Past and present. *New Direction for Adult and Continuing Education*, *1994*, 5–16. https://doi.org/10.1002/ace.36719946203

Lindsey, R. E., Carlozzi, A. F., & Eells, G. T. (2001). Differences in the dispositional empathy of juvenile sex offenders, non-sex-offending delinquent juveniles, and nondelinquent juveniles. *Journal of Interpersonal Violence*, *16*(6), 510–522. https://doi.org./10.1177/088626001016006002

Lisko, S. A., & O'dell, V. (2010). Integration of theory and practice: Experiential learning theory and nursing education. *Nursing Education Perspectives*, *31*, 106–108. https://doi.org./10.1043/1536-5026-31.2.106

Lummer, R., & Hagemann, O. (2015). Victim empathy within prison walls: Experiences from pilot projects in Schleswig-Holstein. *Ljetopis socijalnog rada*, *22*(1), 37–60.

Luna, E. (2003). Punishment theory, holism, and the procedural conception of restorative justice. *Utah Law Review*, 205.

MacLean, P. D. (1985). Brain evolution relating to family, play, and the separation call. *Archives of General Psychiatry*, *42*(4), 405. https://doi.org/10.1001/archpsyc.1985.01790270095011

Maibom, H. L. (2017). Affective empathy. In H. Maibom (Eds.), *The Routledge handbook of philosophy of empathy* (pp. 22–32). Routledge. https://doi.org./10.4324/9781315282015

May, J. (2017). Empathy and intersubjectivity. In H. Maibom (Ed.), *The Routledge handbook of philosophy of empathy* (pp. 169–179). Routledge. https://doi.org./10.4324/9781315282015

McCrady, F., Kaufman, K., Vasey, M. W., Barriga, A. Q., Devlin, R. S., & Gibbs, J. C. (2008). It's all about me: A brief report of adolescent sex offenders' generic and sex-specific cognitive distortions. *Sexual Abuse: A Journal of Research and Treatment*, *20*(3), 261–271. https://doi.org./10.1177/1079063208320249

Mearns, D., & Cooper, M. (2005). *Working at relational depth in counselling and psychotherapy*. SAGE Publications.

Mehrabian, A., Young, A. L., & Sato, S. (1988). Emotional empathy and associated individual differences. *Current Psychology*, *7*(3), 221–240. https://doi.org/10.1007/bf02686670

Miller, P. A., & Eisenberg, N. (1988). The relation of empathy to aggressive and externalizing/antisocial behavior. *Psychological Bulletin*, *103*(3), 324–344. https://doi.org/10.1037/0033-2909.103.3.324

Molidar, C. E. (1996). Female gang members: A profile of aggression and victimization. *Social Work*, *41*, 251–257.

Narvey, C., Yang, J., Wolff, K. T., Baglivio, M., & Piquero, A. R. (2021). The interrelationship between empathy and adverse childhood experiences and their impact on juvenile recidivism. *Youth Violence and Juvenile Justice*, *19*(1), 45–67. https://doi.org/10.1177/1541204020939647

O'Neill, K. K. (2020). Adolescence, empathy, and the gender gap in delinquency. *Feminist Criminology*, *15*(4), 410–437. https://doi.org/10.1177/1557085120908332

Orbell, J., Morikawa, T., Hartwig, J., Hanley, J., & Allen, N. (2004). "Machiavellian" intelligence as a basis for the evolution of cooperative dispositions. *American Political Science Review*, *98*(1), 1–15. https://doi.org/10.1017/s0003055404000966

Owen, T., & Fox, S. (2011). Experiences of shame and empathy in violent and non-violent young offenders. *Journal of Forensic Psychiatry & Psychology*, *22*(4), 551–563. https://doi.org/10.1080/14789949.2011.602096

Pechorro, P., Jolliffe, D., & Nunes, C. (2021). Correlates of affective and cognitive empathy among incarcerated male and female youth offenders. In D. Jolliffe & D. Farrington (Eds.), *Empathy versus offending, aggression, and bullying* (pp. 113–125). Routledge.

Petersen, M. B. (2015). Evolutionary political psychology: On the origin and structure of heuristics and biases in politics. *Political Psychology*, *36*, 45–78. https://doi.org/10.1111/pops.12237

Reskin, B. F. (2000). The proximate causes of employment discrimination. *Contemporary Sociology*, *29*(2), 319–328.

Richardson, D. R., Hammock, G. S., Smith, S. M., Gardner, W., & Signo, M. (1994). Empathy as a cognitive inhibitor of interpersonal aggression. *Aggressive Behavior*, *20*(4), 275–289. https://doi.org./10.1002/1098-2337(1994)20:43/0.CO:2-4

Robinson, R., Roberts, W. L., Strayer, J., & Koopman, R. (2007). Empathy and emotional responsiveness in delinquent and non-delinquent adolescents. *Social Development*, *16*(3), 555–579. https://doi.org/10.1111/j.1467-9507.2007.00396.x

Rogers, C. R. (1957). The necessary and sufficient conditions of therapeutic personality change. *Journal of Consulting Psychology*, *21*(2), 95.

Rogers, C. R. (1964). Toward a science of the person. In T. W. Wann (Ed.), *Behaviorism and phenomenology: Contrasting bases for modern psychology* (pp. 109–140). University of Chicago Press.

Rogers, C. R. (1986). Reflection of feelings. *Person-Centered Review*, *1*, 375–377.

Rueckert, L., & Naybar, N. (2008). Gender differences in empathy: The role of the right hemisphere. *Brain and Cognition*, *67*(2), 162–167.

Sanders, P., Cooper, M., O'Hara, M., & Schmid, P. F. (2013). The "family" of person-centred and experiential therapies. In M. Cooper, M. O'Hara, & P. F. Schmid (Eds.), *The handbook of person-centred psychotherapy and counselling* (pp. 46–65). Palgrave Macmillan.

Segal, E. A. (2007a). Social empathy: A new paradigm to address poverty. *Journal of Poverty, 11*(3), 65–81. https://doi.org/10.1300/J134v11n03_06

Segal, E. A. (2007b). Social empathy: A tool to address the contradiction of working but still poor. *Families in Society: The Journal of Contemporary Social Sciences, 88*, 333–337.

Segal, E. A. (2011). Social empathy: A model built on empathy, contextual understanding, and social responsibility that promotes social justice. *Journal of Social Service Research, 37*(3), 266–277. https://doi.org./10.1080/01488376.2011.564040

Spaulding, S. (2017). Cognitive empathy. In H. Maibom (Ed.), *The Routledge handbook of philosophy of empathy* (pp. 13–21). Routledge. https://doi.org./10.4324/9781315282015

Steffensmeier, D., & Broidy, L. M. (2000). Explaining female offending. In L. Goodstein (Ed.), *Women, crime and criminal justice: Contemporary issues*. Roxbury Press.

Stepien, K. A., & Baernstein, A. (2006). Educating for empathy: A review. *Journal of General Internal Medicine, 21*, 524–530.

Stout, R. (2019). Empathy, vulnerability and anxiety. *International Journal of Philosophical Studies, 27*(2), 347–357. http://doi.org/10.1080/09672559.2019.1612626

Thompson, A. P., & McGrath, A. (2012). Subgroup differences and implications for contemporary risk-need assessment with juvenile offenders. *Law and Human Behavior, 36*(4), 345–355. https://doi.org./10.1037/h0093930

Thornberry, T., Krohn, M., Lizotte, A., & Chard-Wierschem, D. (1993). The role of juvenile gangs in facilitating delinquent behavior. *Journal of Research in Crime and Delinquency, 30*, 55–87.

Topcu, C., & Erdur-Baker, O. (2012). Affective and cognitive empathy as mediators of gender differences in cyber and traditional bullying. *School Psychology International, 33*(5), 550–561. https://doi.org./10.1177/0143034312446882

Van Langen, M. A., Wissink, I. B., Van Vugt, E. S., Van der Stouwe, T., & Stams, G. (2014). The relation between empathy and offending: A meta-analysis. *Aggression and Violent Behavior, 19*(2), 179–189.

Warden, R. (2018). Where is the empathy: Understanding offenders' experience of empathy and its impact on restorative justice. *UMKC Law Review, 87*(4), 953–978.

Wilkins, P. (2015). *Person-centred therapy: 100 key points*. Routledge.

Wilson, K., Ruch, G., Lymberg, M., & Cooper, A. (2011). *Social work: An introduction to contemporary practice* (2nd ed.). Longman.

Wood, J. K. (1996). The person-centered approach: Towards an understanding of its implications. In R. Hutterer, G. Pawlowsky, P. F. Schmid, & R. Stipsits (Eds.), *Client-centered and experiential psychotherapy: A paradigm in motion*. Peter Lang.

9 Power, control, and agency

Tamara Blakemore, Louise Rak, and Graeme Stuart

Power, control, and youth violence

Power and control represent a pervasive context of our work with youth violence. We understand power and control as dynamics of behaviour that strengthen the achievement of personal and political goals either through negative or positive means. Power and control can be resources and assets, the access to and control over which can determine people's agency, self-efficacy, and locus of control. Power and control can also be used to inflict harm on others, diminishing their sense-of-self and creating fear or uncertainty, which may be the basis for limiting, constraining, or controlling their choices. This chapter outlines the concepts, theory, and evidence that inform these understandings and our work with young people who use and experience violence in the Name. Narrate.Navigate (NNN) program. It describes our practice approach and what we've learned from young people about how they experience power and control and what role power and control might play in youth violence. Deidentified narratives from the young people we have worked with are presented in textboxes and discussed in relation to the evidence for practice with youth violence and how we understand and work with power. These narratives were collected with appropriate ethics approval via practitioner reflections on group work activities.

Understandings of power and control

In its simplest form, power is about one person or group's ability to influence behaviours or outcomes of another. Seminal work by Raven and colleagues (French & Raven, 1959; Raven, 1965, 2008) explains influence involves drawing on available resources which collectively represent informational, reward, coercion, legitimate, expertise, and referent bases of power and understanding that people select strategies of influence depending on need and perceived cost benefits (McClelland, 1975; Winter, 1973). Synthesising the individual, structural, and

DOI: 10.4324/9781003177883-9

ideological relations of influence, Lukes (2005) suggests power can take differing forms, effecting different functions, including: *power to* (i.e., the capacity or agency to act), *power over* (i.e., exerting control over others), and *power through* (i.e., ideological influence of dominant systems). Spencer (2013) offers a fourth conceptual distinction of *power within*, explained as the person's belief in their control over events and actions. To a greater or lesser extent, everyone has access to power of some sort, but some have access to greater amounts of more socially acceptable, sanctioned, and useable power, while the forms of power that are available to others are not socially legitimate. Access to socially sanctioned power is likely influenced by intersectional experiences and is not distributed evenly across society. We can gain access to power by virtue of a variety of characteristics including age, size, role, education, position, wealth, and privilege (Hamby, 2017; Sell et al., 2016).

Control is understood as both an outcome of power and a form or function of power. Having power provides people with a greater sense of, and capacity for, control. Haidt and Rodin (1999) note "people like to control their environments" (p. 317) and do better when they feel like they have greater control over important aspects of their life (Langer & Rodin, 1976; Rodin & Langer, 1977). Related to control (and power) is the notion of agency. Spencer and Doull (2015) observe agency is the capacity (or power) for conscious and intentional action and choice. Hitlin and Long (2009) note agency allows us to "exert influence on situations in our lives" (p. 141). The capacity for agency is thought to be universal (Watkins, 2012) but variable within and between individuals as a function of time, situation, and social location (Bay-Cheng, 2012; Threadgold, 2011). An important distinction and point of debate in the literature is the relationship between our subjective beliefs about our capacity for choice and control and our objective opportunities to exert control or act freely on our choices (Hitlin & Long, 2009). Some authors suggest social and structural forces likely impact both the feelings people have about power, control, agency, and choice *and* whether and how a person can act on these feelings (Albanesi, 2009; Bay-Cheng, 2012). Others suggest people may believe they have significant agency and control yet be quite circumscribed by structural and social forces in their exercise of this agency, a phenomenon referred to as *bounded agency* (Evans, 2002; Shanahan & Hood, 1998).

Enacting power and control

Munford and Sanders (2015) reflect the notion of *bounded agency* is instructive in drawing our attention to how young people seek to voice and enact power and control, particularly where they have limited options and resources to draw upon. Ungar (2022) describes people as motivated to gain access to and control over resources that sustain health and wellbeing, including emotional states of self-efficacy, self-esteem, and coping; physical assets of housing, finances, and care; and sociopolitical resources of rights as recognised and represented. Evoking understandings of bounded agency, the author notes that while interconnected and interdependent, the capacity to access and use these resources is constrained by social and structural forces and their influence on perceptions of personal control in specific situations (Ungar, 2022).

Self-control theory suggests that young people's use of violence relates to a sense of powerlessness in regulating or controlling behavioural responses to emotions or events, resulting in impulsive, risk-taking behaviour and less ability to delay gratification or the urge to redress grievances or hurts (Gottfredson & Hirschi, 1990). Locus-of-control theories, by comparison, are concerned with whether the outcomes of behaviour are seen as within or outside a person's control. Ahlin (2014) explains young people with an internal locus of control might attribute being arrested as the result of their use of violence, something they understand as *within their control*, whereas a young person with an external locus of control might attribute the same outcome to bad luck or other actions or events they perceive as *outside their control.* An external locus of control has been described as a state of mind that is learned (Rotter, 1966) and endorsed by socialisation and acculturation in contexts of uncertainty and inconsistency, where actions don't always result in desired, intended, or fair outcomes.

While parenting, families, and neighbourhoods have been linked to the likelihood of developing an internal locus of control, where actions and outcomes are seen as predictable consequences of choice (Kelley, 1996; Lefcourt, 1982), experiences of structural and systemic marginalisation may instead influence individual, social, and collective expectations and experiences of powerlessness over outcomes (Dalgard et al., 2006). In this way, social disadvantage contributes to developing an external locus of control. This, in turn, contributes to the potential for using violence as studies suggest that even controlling for contextual factors, the relationship between locus of control and the use of violence by young people remains remarkably stable, with young people with an internal locus of control far less likely to use violence than those with an external locus of control (Ahlin, 2014). In turn, young people's actions towards change will also depend on whether they believe they have the power or control to change and whether they believe they themselves are responsible for making that change happen (Ungar, 2022).

Experiencing power and control

We note young people we work with commonly report experiences of disempowerment, constrained agency, and oppression. These experiences arise in their interactions with school, family, youth-focused services, public spaces, and social media and seem intensified for those with marked vulnerability (e.g., those experiencing poverty, sustained justice involvement, food scarcity, housing insecurity, poor mental health, involvement with the child protection system, or whose identities have been marginalised) (World Health Organisation (WHO), 2020). Practices informed by social control theory, where young people become subject to increased surveillance and control measures (Hirschi, 1969; Huebner & Betts, 2002), can disproportionately impact vulnerable cohorts (Gabriel et al., 2022). For example, in education settings, young people who display challenging or unacceptable behaviours (which may be related to traumatic impacts), frequently face disciplinary sanctions, detention, or exclusion. Despite "a substantial body of research demonstrating an association between the experience of school exclusion and short- and long-term negative outcomes" (Skiba et al., 2014, p. 557), control-based approaches to behaviour management remain commonplace and can contribute to education systems disengaging from young people most in need (Chu & Ready, 2018; Welsh & Little, 2018). Responses to challenging behaviour in youth services (including out-of-home care settings) can range from non-controlling strategies (e.g., creating a positive environment, meeting the needs of young people, and negotiation) to control-based strategies (e.g., physical restraint, calling the police, and exclusion) (Stuart, 2004). Similarly, in youth justice settings, despite a need to balance "control and treatment" (Rains et al., 2001, p. 5), it is observed that many responses are experienced by justice-involved youth as punitive, repressive, and controlling (Case, 2016). Through our work, we are continually reminded that the use of violence by young people needs to be considered in the context of structural, systemic, racial, gendered, and direct violence, where young people themselves experience and are exposed to violence.

Reaction and resistance to power and control

Bounds and Posey (2022) suggest multidirectional and cyclical relationships can exist between systems and structures of power and control and the experience of marginalisation. The authors explain that marginalised young people may rely on alternate or nondominant developmental pathways to navigate complex circumstances by using the types of resources available to them, sometimes "coping with powerlessness by finding power through violent, aggressive, and risk-taking behaviours"

(Ungar, 2022, p. 147). In response and consistent with social control imperatives, systems and structures may then impose sanctions that increase marginalisation. Lohmeyer (2018) contends such acts of governance, power, and control are themselves a form of violence and that "violence done to young people shapes the violence done by young people" (p. 1071). The author notes that vulnerable young people are often hyper-governed and experience violence in its many forms, as ubiquitous across their interactions with social structures (Lohmeyer, 2018). Central to these understandings of young people's reactions to power and control is the idea that youth violence is often underscored by significant vulnerability.

The recognition that we, as people, are never outside of relationships and systems of power and that "where there is power, there is resistance" (Foucault, 1978, p. 95) has been highly productive for research and contributed to broader understandings of relationships between social systems and the people subject to their controls. This is particularly the case for service users in contexts with a substantial imbalance of legitimate power, including justice-involved young people. Bounds and Posey (2022) argue that systemic methods of normalising operate at all levels of the social ecology – from the macro level of politics, social attitudes, and policy, through to the micro level of interpersonal interactions. Young people do not undertake these identity projects alone but, rather, do so within their communities, which can vary and take on different forms. Young people in the justice system, whether incarcerated or on community orders, are the subjects of multiple oppressions – oppression understood here as formal and informal social systems that confer benefits upon dominant groups through the exclusion and control of nondominant groups (Wray-Lake et al., 2022). These young people are also actively engaged in resistance of those formal and informal social controls.

A wider conceptualisation of the role of power and control in youth violence?

Through our work, we are continually reminded that young people's use of violence should be considered as contextualised by exposures to and experiences of structural, systemic, cultural, gendered, direct, and symbolic violence. This gives us pause to consider how practice-based responses have approached the role of power and control in youth violence, where we see a concentrated focus on domestic and family violence (DFV) or intimate partner violence (IPV), separate to considerations of interconnected experiences of other forms of violence. We wonder whether this reflects a generalisation in our understandings of violence and whether we assume young people use violence in the same way that adults do. In turn, do we generalise dominant feminist thinking about DFV/IPV as underpinned by dynamics of power and control to explain the role of power and control in youth violence? On this theme, Carlisle et al. (2022) found that while young people are familiar with different types of DFV/IPV and the harm it causes, they were less familiar with power and control as underpinning its occurrence and outcome. The authors suggest perhaps these terms are too technical for young people to understand (Carlisle et al., 2022), but we wonder whether concentrating our understanding of power and control in youth violence as a dynamic that occurs in relationships without acknowledging the social and structural dynamics of violence may also cause confusion.

The relationships between power, control, and DFV/IPV are complex and even more so when considering young people who use violence in their interpersonal relationships (Aghtaie et al., 2018; Moulds et al., 2016). Since the early 1990s, one of the most influential understandings of DFV is the *Duluth model* (Domestic Abuse Intervention Programs, 2017), which describes the types of behaviours that men use to gain, maintain, enact, and exert power and control over women, all of which are reinforced by actual or threatened physical and sexual violence. Conceptualised and operationalised by a *power and control wheel* (Duluth Model, 2021), the model hypothesises DFV is a pattern of behaviour arising from male privilege and patriarchal power involving coercion, intimidation, isolation, and emotional and financial abuse and which may involve the exploitation of children. The developers of the model are very clear that this conceptualisation is only intended to explain the use of violence by men towards women and that "making the Power and Control Wheel gender neutral would hide the power imbalances in relationships between men and women that reflect power imbalances in society (Domestic Abuse Intervention Programs, 2017, para. 7). Where young people use DFV, it can be towards partners but also parents, carers, or siblings and other family members.

We are further challenged by how existing conceptions understand the role of power and control in young women's use of violence. Consistent with prior research (e.g., Sears et al., 2006), Tagesson and Gallo (2021) found practitioners largely rejected the idea of young women's use of IPV, finding it difficult to even talk about. In our practice, we commonly find young women use violence towards other females, who may or may not be known to them (Blakemore et al., 2021; Rak & Warton, 2023). This often takes the form of lateral violence, described by the Australian Human Rights Commission (AHRC, 2011) as the tendency of people from oppressed groups to direct internalised and embodied frustrations and anger towards members of their own group. It can involve physical violence as well as acts of bullying, scapegoating, shaming, backstabbing, undermining, malicious gossip, social isolation, and exclusion (Dudgeon et al., 2014; Korff, 2019).

Power and control in NNN

The role of power and control in youth violence is the focus of the fourth group work session in the NNN program. This session explores what power and control (can) look like in relationships and how it is experienced in community life. The session generates discussion about how we can react to experiences of power and control and how our reactions are linked to our socialised and acculturated thoughts and feelings about the experience.

The approach to practice in NNN recognises inherent imbalances in power between practitioners and young people as well as between and among group members and practitioners.

Practice approach

Consistent with a critical youth perspective (Carlisle et al., 2022), our practice approach to working with power and control centres on two key principles: (1) prioritising young people's perspectives in co-constructed understandings of their experience (Allen, 2009) and (2) acknowledging and attending to power differentials that may contribute to the occurrence and outcomes of these experiences (Corney et al., 2021). This can be challenging where systemic and structural practices outside of, but contextualising, our work can infer a pervasive sense of sanction and surveillance for justice-involved youth.

Young people we work with relate this in terms of real or perceived fears of being "breached" for non-compliance with youth-justice community supervision orders, seeing this as *power-over* them by workers

Table 9.1 Program structure, session focus: Power and Control

Program structure	*Session*	*Focus*
		Beginnings
	1	Emotions
	2	Voice
	3	Empathy
	4	**Power and Control**
	5	Shame
	6	Choice
		Endings

and systems. Yet many workers tell us they don't see it this way, instead suggesting young people have *power-to* choose whether they comply with orders they are accountable to, though some recognise orders often involve unachievable conditions. Other workers identify that they regularly use the power available to them in their role and suggest that breaching young people early and/or often reinforces consequences and accountability. Our thinking about power involves an awareness of the subordinated and disenfranchised social position (Best, 2007) of many young people we work with and a curiosity about how power differentials in practice privilege adult-centred dynamics of knowledge and power (Carlisle et al., 2022). As such, our approach to practice with power and control is influenced by transformative and empowerment-oriented notions of power, particularly *power-with* (Follet, 1940) and *power-within* (Townsend, 1999).

Working in this way, we are commonly asked how we *manage* or *control* behaviour. Our response relates to how we understand young people's behaviour, how we conceive our role, and how we see both as intertwined with notions of power and agency. Our conception of power in our practice is consistent with Gallagher's (2008) interpretation of Foucault that power "is a form of action, that transforms and influences other actions" (p. 144). We recognise challenging behaviour can be an invitation to vie for power and control over the use of time, what is done, and how it is done. From a trauma-informed perspective, we understand these invitations to be informed by expectation and experience, anxiety and fear, and a self-protective need to establish safety and separation from any source of potential threat, coercion, or control. From a culturally safe lens, we appreciate how dominant social and structural contexts shape experience in ways that can perpetuate marginalisation.

We are clear that our way of working requires practitioners to sit outside of the need to advise, instruct, coach, or "manage" and, instead, step into a reciprocal and relational way of working where power is understood to flow between practitioners and young people in ways that are interdependent and negotiated (Duck, 2007; Poggi, 2005). In the small moments of interaction in practice, what we find works is unsettling expectations of domination and control in favour of relational responses. This can involve recognising and naming what we see, resonating with feelings expressed, or redistributing and sharing power in the moment. This is always done with due consideration of risk to safety or potential harm for self and others. We also see this as quite different to "relinquishing" power as discussed by Plows (2012), reflecting instead an intent and objective to flatten power imbalances by embracing the relational nature of power and agency.

Mapping power and control

This activity starts with an externalised focus, describing types of behaviours that people use to gain and maintain power and control over others. Priority is given to capturing the words and language that young people use and exploring their meaning and narrated experience.

Table 9.2 Practice note: Mapping power and control

Practice note: Mapping power and control	
Description:	This activity involves a discursive intervention of "mapping" young people's perspectives on power and control and its role in youth violence.
Time:	15 minutes
Purpose:	The task prioritises the perspectives of young people and seeks to make conscious links between individual experiences and broader social contexts which explain the origins and outcomes of power and control.
Resources:	Canvas sheet, marker pens, photo-elicitation prompts
Presentation:	Using a large canvas, young people are asked to explore, reflect, and record the types of behaviours (e.g., words and actions) that people use to gain and maintain power and control over others. Photo-elicitation cards are used to match visual prompts to narratives provided. Practitioners facilitate discussion about possible sources of power, who has (more/less) power, whether in their experience using power and control over people works (why/why not), and what it feels like to (have/not have) power and control.
Rationale:	This activity draws on ideas of systems mapping informed by "soft systems methods" for inquiry into complex social problems (Checkland & Poulter, 2006). These methods use visual means to capture and contrast different perspectives on dynamic and variable experiences (Bailey & Gamman, 2022) by giving voice to those with direct experience of the phenomenon of interest. Maps highlight common themes as well as exceptions, consistency with established ideas, and new knowledge and contradictions to existing ideas. Importantly, the maps externalise ideas about and experiences of power and control as it relates to youth violence, providing a safe distance from which young people can contemplate their own and others' experiences and reflect on the meanings made about it. Bailey and Gamman (2022) propose system maps represent discursive objects that can reframe narratives and generate new knowledge on taken-for-granted assumptions about youth violence. The authors also suggest mapping can counter or decentralise individualist conceptions by highlighting youth violence as a social practice, suggesting it is learned, repeated, and meaningful to particular groups in certain contexts (Reckwitz, 2002; Shove et al., 2012).

Photo-elicitation prompts aid discussion and provide a visual representation of narratives provided. This removes a reliance on words and writing and allows participants to represent ideas and experience through visual means. Practitioners facilitate discussion, making conscious links between possible sources of power, individual experience, and social and structural understandings of power and control. The map created is treated as an externalised narrative object to prompt reflection on the utility and experience of power and control.

Of particular interest to us is the observation that in mapping understandings or experiences of an issue, the activity itself involves dynamics of power, control, agency, and choice. Kitchin et al. (2011) observe that the maps produced "embody a perspective, certain things are shown, others omitted, they are vested in the interests of their creators" (p. 441). We note maps made by young people we work with heavily reference the role of power and control in youth violence to social and structural interactions and experiences rather than behaviours of young people themselves. Narratives provided by young people often highlight sophisticated knowledge of systemic processes and strategies used to navigate and resist imposed experiences of power and control. These findings are consistent with work by Bailey and Gamman (2022), who reflect this brings the structuring contexts back into view, hence intervening or interjecting with dominant discourses about youth violence.

What we've learned

Young people we have worked with in NNN demonstrate knowledge and understanding of the constructs and dynamic of power and control, its use, experience, and outcomes. We observe that when we ask young people to tell us what they know about power and control, they commonly tell us what it is like to be disempowered and controlled. We note a heavy gaze in these reflections to their interactions and experiences with social structures and systems, highlighting for us that applying adult-centric understandings of the role of power and control in IPV and DFV may obscure a more nuanced understanding of youth violence. For the young people we work with, reflections on their use of power and control and its potential role in their use of violence varied depending on their intersectional experiences and were impacted by temporal and spatial contexts. In the following section, we share these reflections, with information collected with appropriate ethics approval through practitioner reflections on group work sessions, referencing narratives shared as part of group work activities. In all instances, pseudonyms are used to protect the identities of those involved.

Young people are familiar with power and control

Young people we've worked with have been readily able to identify examples of behaviours that people use to gain power and control over others, though often discussing this in contexts and dynamics much broader than just IPV or DFV. We note the depth of meaning and the ways young people articulate power and control in their own lives is contextualised comparative to their own experiences and current situations. In the Postcards to Practice activity, some young people have shared succinct understandings of being controlled which mostly describe dislike of the experience: "It's not good"; "It is annoying"; "It's not fun". Other young people made clear links between the experience of power and control and violence: "It normally comes with mental and physical abuse and can lead to problems"; "It's a form of abuse". What is interesting in these examples is that young people's familiarity with and understanding of power and control seem firmly grounded in what it feels like as an experience. Perhaps unsurprisingly, across settings and regardless of gender and age, young people use different types of language to describe power and control than we find in practice models related to adult's use of power and control in contexts of IPV and DFV. For example, whereas young people tell us how power and control make them feel, the Duluth model outlines and describes actions men take with the intent of exerting power and control over women. For many young people we've worked with, it was the felt experience of power and control that mattered, to which they associated their own interpretations of motive and intent. Young men in detention did offer more action-oriented descriptions of power and control, often referencing their own experiences of structures and systems where practices and policies further marginalised them. These young men also articulated what gave people power, equating this to role, authority, position, size, and strength, clearly referencing system-relevant actors, not just themselves or fellow peer participants.

Young people use power and control

In our work, we have experienced or heard stories of young people using or enacting power, control, and agency in a range of situations. Some young people we work with have used power and control to gain access to and control over resources and sometimes this has involved or constituted violence to others. Consistent with the observations of Walby (2013), we are careful here to recognise the relationship between power and control and violence but not to confound the constructs as necessarily one and the same. We also recognise that when young people use power and control as part of violence towards others, it is not always (at least initially) conceived of or spoken about in ways that are consistent with adult-centric understandings of power and control in IPV or FDV. For example, consistent with existing evidence (e.g., Moulds et al., 2016; Routt & Anderson, 2014), we've found young men who use power and control against mothers in contexts of adolescent violence in the home often present this as being motivated by wanting access to their phone, money, or Xbox or having a greater say in how they spend their time. Yet, in richer discussions, some of these young men also spoke of deeper hurts driving their behaviours, including perceived and real injustices and sustained experiences of invalidation.

At other times, we were witness to young people using their expert and referent power (Raven, 2008) to share knowledge in ways that exerted influence on us as practitioners and induced changes in our behaviours in positive ways. In these instances, young people chose to share specific contextualised information about their experiences with practitioners, often taking on the role of teaching and educating us. For example, while working with young men in detention, loud disturbances outside the group work room unsettled the practitioner who commented on this, and two young men empathised with her, noting how it must be confronting and taking time to explain what was happening and sharing how they'd "gotten used to" these occurrences over time. Some young people with positional privilege and power demonstrated sharing this with others. For example, while working with Aboriginal young women living on traditional lands of their ancestors, where the connection to culture and Country was strong, the practitioner observed that young women held a position of power through their knowledge of Country, women's business, and women's only areas. The young women shared their knowledge with the non-Aboriginal practitioner, disrupting what many may perceive as traditional power dynamics.

Young people's experience of power and control

In our work so far across contexts, both young men and young women of differing ages commonly tell us about their experience of having power and control used over them, of being disempowered and controlled. How young people make sense of these experiences and the meaning and importance they attribute to them has reflected socialised and acculturated learnings of what's probable and permissible in their communities, for their genders, and amongst peers.

Young women we have worked with have described experiences of having power and control used over them by other young women, often in the context of female friendships. Simmons (2002, p. 21) explains that relational aggression, often used between young women, can involve "acts that harm others through damage (or the threat of damage) to relationships or feelings of acceptance, friendship or inclusion". Talbot (2002) notes the importance of establishing and maintaining friendships for young women, as both a situation and process of psychosocial connection and identity development, means relationships are often more intense, and young women can leverage this intimacy against each other.

For young women we have worked with, sometimes, in recounting these experiences, there was a sense that some behaviours are just what people do, and the relevance of that to the quality (or health) of the relationship was not always readily apparent and, sometimes, came as a revelation when pointed out by others.

Box 9.1 What we've learned . . .

Reflecting on behaviours that give people power and control over others, Jazz related her experiences with a female friend:

Jazz: "You know how you have a friend who gets angry with you when you spend times with other people, when you tell them your secrets and not her?"

Group members: "Ummm no?"

Jazz: "You know, like when you don't call her back straight away and she gets angry and doesn't talk to you for like a day or two?"

Group member: "No dude, that sounds toxic as shit . . . that's not a good friend".

As Jazz was talking and hearing the responses of the group, her facial expression transitioned into shock then understanding as she realised that her friendship was not a positive one.

Jazz: "Oh God, you're right, she isn't a good friend, is she?"

The narratives provided by young women highlight the, at times, difficult nature of their female friendships and how power and control can be present across contexts and relationships, though recognising coercion in action is a process that can require support to understand. Currie et al. (2007) suggest relational aggression used by young women is a symptom of the systemic oppression of women through sexist practices, whereby acts of self-interest are inconsistent with accepted ways of being, generating alternative dynamics of action, response, and meaning.

Young people we have worked with consistently share stories and produce Photovoice work where the police are situated as agents of power and control and, often, as structural actors who have disempowered and controlled them. Young people present narratives where police are described as using excessive force and racist language, making incorrect assumptions, and disregarding or denying them due care. As practitioners, we have experienced the hyper-localised way in which young people interact with the police in what Nava (2007, p. 135) describes as the "microterritories of the local". On a Photovoice excursion, practitioners and young people were followed by the police, who asked the group what we were doing. When the practitioners replied that they worked at the university and were running a group program, they were met with a "Yeah, sure you are" and were followed for another 15 minutes. Young people in the group were not surprised by the interaction, recounting it as a common interaction and experience, but for the practitioners, it was uncharacteristic and challenging to their assumed sense of self and position in place. The experience highlighted for us not only how structural actors can use power and control and how this can contribute to the marginalisation of young people but also how place and space factor into this dynamic. As Harris and Wyn (2009) explain, manifestations of place represent key sites of young people's self-making, and where young people have limited capacity to physically move beyond the locale, greater scrutiny and control shape opportunities for seeing themselves as having legitimate power and agency.

Gendered experiences of power and control

In our work, narratives shared by young people suggested gendered experiences of power and control exist, underscored by differences in how power and control are discussed and how the use and experience of power and control are understood. Young women we have worked with have described experiencing gender-based violence involving coercive control, threats, intimidation, and abuse; we haven't heard these same narratives from young men. This is consistent with evidence that suggests an almost unidirectional use of control and surveillance by young men towards young women. Aghtaie et al. (2018) for example, report data from a study of five European countries finding the exercise of power and control is common and nearly all the young women had experienced control and surveillance from male partners and, in most cases, control and surveillance (both online and offline) were combined with sexual coercion or physical violence. This has been exemplified in our work where one young woman shared how she had (on several occasions) had male friends and boyfriends pressure her to send nude photos of herself to them, threatening to end relationships if she didn't. On the times that she did send photos, she was then threatened that the photos would be shared if she did not do what the young men were asking of her. In an example of what Galtung (1990, p. 292) might describe as "cultural violence" (involving the symbolic legitimisation of structural violence through gendered or class norms), the young woman described how when she disclosed this to caseworkers and educators, their responses were not of concern for her but rather to lecture her on why she should not have sent the photos.

While young women recognised dynamics of power and control in gendered violence involving sexual coercion, these same dynamics were less recognised and less meaningful to young women as they related to financial coercion. For example, we observed some young women we worked with to be routinely "hum-bugged" (the concept of what's yours is mine) or harassed by family members for cash on "payday". We did not observe this for young men. While noticeably annoyed by the intrusion on their time and space, young women appeared unsurprised and largely unperturbed by these frequent requests and insinuated obligation to share their money. Discussion indicated that from the young women's perspective, giving away money was an accepted reality where they also rarely got the money back. When practitioners reflected the difficulty of this situation, we were met with shrugs and comments like "*That's just the way it is*". These findings resonate with Storer et al.'s (2020) observation that young people can find it hard to distinguish between more subtle types of coercive control, but importantly and consistent with Edwards et al. (2022), young people use cultural scripts to construct boundaries about what behaviours are permissible and, in turn, what constitutes "real" violence or abuse.

The importance of cultural scripts in defining what is labelled (or mislabelled) as acceptable acts of power and control was similarly made apparent to us as practitioners as we witnessed female "policing" of other women's behaviour in the community. On one occasion, practitioners and young women on a Photovoice excursion encountered a group of young men of a similar age. One of the young women swore at the young men and told them in no uncertain terms to leave them alone. The young men hurried away, and between the incident occurring and the following week, the young men shared details of the exchange with their female cousins, sisters, and friends, who had sought out the young women, threatening retribution if they spoke to the young men in the same way again. This incident seemed to present as the monitoring of actions that could be described as staying or not staying in one's lane. Currie et al. (2007) explains that within female peer culture, power comes from being able to invoke unspoken "rules" that police the boundaries of what's acceptable behaviour and that young women's agency comes from a culturally mandated conception of girlhood or femininity. Among the many things that were interesting about this incident was that the young men knew that they could rely on the females in their lives to deal with female-related interactions. Fine (1988) perceives this as cultural duplicity, pointing out that while it may be young women who police the boundaries of what's deemed acceptable behaviour for other young women, they do so through a male gaze.

While it was apparent that young men undoubtedly benefit from this absolution of role and responsibility in female peer-on-peer violence, it was unclear to what extent they enacted active agency in this process. Indeed, the experience of working with young men on power and control and its role in youth violence was one of perplexing contrasts and contradictions bound up in complex intersections of heteronormative (Totten, 2000) and hegemonic masculinities (Barter, 2009) as well as contested dualities between having been exploited and exploiting others (Ringrose & Renold, 2011). We note that young men we have worked with sometimes display outwardly negative gendered behaviours in group or more public settings that seem at odds with their behaviours in one-on-one interactions. This included graphic swearing and derogatory language towards women or comments that normalised violence towards women, like "I'd hit her if she didn't do as she was told" or group talk about it being okay for men to cheat on their partners but not for women to do the same. Yet, in one-on-one discussions, one young man disclosed that loyalty was very important to him, saying how he could never cheat on his girlfriend, and many talked protectively and respectfully about their mothers, grandmothers, and sisters. These findings are generally consistent with those of Wood et al. (2010), who reported gender differences in how young people discussed the role of power and control in relationships and in the use of violence. In this study, most of the young women believed that young men were more likely to try to control their partner, and this was often connected to beliefs that males should be more dominant than females (Wood et al., 2010). The authors found, however, that young men were less explicit about their use of power and control, with many of them in discussion noting they were aware of the imbalance in physical power between young men and women and stating it was unacceptable to use physical violence against their partner (Wood et al., 2010). However, perceiving a need to maintain a public image of power and violence meant that "violence was routinely and publicly used both to control their partners and demonstrate their power" (Wood et al., 2010, p. 97). Some young men used violence against a real or perceived rival for their partner in order to "save face" and to "reaffirm power in their relationship" (Wood et al., 2010, p. 39).

Figure 9.1 Power and control map

The contradictions in young men's thinking and discussion about power and control and its role in violence, particularly as it relates to gendered violence, became apparent in the mapping power and control activity delivered with young men in detention (see Figure 9.1). The following example draws on the first author's own practice reflections from this activity.

Box 9.2 NNN practitioner reflection . . .

"Working with young men in detention on power and control and its role in youth violence has highlighted the performative qualities of power and control as both a dynamic and a personal characteristic.

In activities where young men demonstrated their agreement or disagreement with statements about types of behaviour in relationships, there was obvious conforming to group norms or deliberate dissent around notions of equality and choice. Yet, when we moved to map what power and control looked like, the process of naming behaviours that give people power and control over others seemed to shift thinking and discussion towards their own experiences of being disempowered and controlled.

Young men in detention described acts, including racial profiling, stereotyping, surveillance, discrimination, isolation, and confinement, as being used by people (by discussion; in their current circumstance) to get and hold power and control over people. Discussion on who has more or less power and control quickly established that young men thought adults and people in roles of authority or government (or who had access to keys) had more power.

Using techniques of reciprocal communication, I pondered whether this was always the case and reflected that yesterday I'd taken my son to watch a soccer game, and he had remarked he thought his friend's team would have won, only they had a female referee. He said, 'I think she's good, but she would have been intimidated by the boys and that will have swayed the results'. I asked the young men what they thought about this. They replied they thought my son's reasoning was wrong because 'Everyone has equal power and control', and 'She's the ref – she's in charge'.

Questioning what gives them power in their current circumstances, young men emphasised acts of 'standing over' and attributes of 'size' and lesser so 'threats' and 'physical violence'. Tentatively reflecting on the young female referee, I wondered how these different experiences of power and control might compare, leaving this as a weighty but unexplored observation I was able to note a shifting sense of awareness among the young men".

Power, control, and young people's use of violence

Based on the stories shared by young people we have worked with, it appears that most were, at least at times, acutely aware of the impact of power and control in their lives, especially when it was enacted by others over them. Depending on the age, maturity, and insights of the individual, whether they could apply those same reflections to the role of power and control in their use of violence was varied. For some young people, their use of violence was in reaction to experiences of power and control. Narratives of this kind indicated that, sometimes, when young people felt disempowered or controlled, invalidated, or threatened, they reacted with violence in ways that they described as uncontrollable or almost reflexive and quick to occur. Both young men and young women described experiencing power and control in this way and using violence as an almost unthought about reaction in response. This often happened in public and sometimes resulted in injury to others, with some young people describing experiences of being overcome with rage and often not recalling the specifics of what they'd done until after or because someone had filmed the incident. In other instances, feeling disrespected or as though their personal sense of power and social position had been threatened resulted in violent responses that were less spontaneously reactive and more thought out and planned. For example, a young woman discussed a story of a time someone stole her sister's shoes. As the young woman shared, "So I watched her, and I waited for about a week . . . then I waited around the corner from where I knew she'd be . . . I flogged her and I got those shoes back". In this case, the young woman's approach was planned and purposeful and suggested that she felt aggrieved on behalf of her sister and wanted to seek retribution and to regain "face" and a sense of power.

Young people described how violent reactions or resistance to disempowerment and repression are often met, in turn, by structurally endorsed acts of power and control perceived and experienced as state-sanctioned violence.

Box 9.3 What we've learned . . .

Recounting having been arrested by male police officers while swimming with friends, Jazz noted she didn't own swimmers so was swimming in her underwear and, hence, arrested in her underwear. She told us that after being arrested, she was placed in the "fishbowl" (police holding cells enabling a visual line of sight to and among people detained) and given nothing to cover herself with for hours afterward. Jazz said:

> "I thought I was going to die, I wanted to die in there, in the fishbowl it was so bad".

Jazz said this experience made her feel negatively about herself and the police though she spoke positively about the female officer who she said did give her a blanket, referring to her as "*one of the good ones*". As other young women listened on, nodding occasionally, shoulders and heads down looking at the floor, none appeared surprised by this example of power and control.

Recalling being subjected to violence at the hands of authorities in their exercise of power and control, Ray told us he was assaulted by police and witnessed his mum being assaulted.

> "I've had a cop hit me in the back of the head, like, while he was taking me to the paddy wagon and that. And then, that same time, I've had, the, another cop hit me mum. She just got out of hospital with me little brother. Like three days after it, she had him".

Ray named this experience as well as others as contributing to his poor relationship with police.

These examples extend Lohmeyer's (2018) contention that (largely symbolic) experiences of violence that disempower and control young people shape the violence done by young people. It highlights that marginalising policies and practices may also shape and endorse behaviours of direct violence in circumstances where powerful disincentives exist for disempowered young people to enact agency in ways that meet their needs for authentic voice.

Takeaways for practice

1. Young people provide rich examples of their experience of power in both overt and less overt ways that differ across genders and seem contextually bound.
2. Young people do not always name their actions and behaviours as acts of power and control or link the motives of their behaviour to intentions to gain power or exercise control though they do sometimes recognise that their behaviours have had this effect.
3. There is considerable tension in working towards objectives of ethical use of power from *power-over* practice perspectives.
4. Instead, a *power-with* for *power-within* approach is more likely to help us to better understand the experience and use of power and promote awareness and reflection on its efficacy and impacts.

Conclusion

This chapter has considered the role of power and control in youth violence. It described the understandings of power and control we found useful in shaping our work with young people who use and experience violence as well as the practice perspectives that informed the strategies we used in this work. It clarified our awareness of the subordinated and disenfranchised social position (Best, 2007) of many young people we work with and a curiosity about how power differentials in practice privilege adult-centred dynamics of knowledge and power (Carlisle et al., 2022). It described our approach to practice with power and control as influenced by transformative and empowerment-oriented notions of *power-with* (Follett, 1940) and *power-within* (Townsend, 1999), using processes of conscientisation to examine the inseparability of private and public experience. Learnings from our work detail how young people use and experience power and control in interconnected ways, where violence can be a reaction or resistance to this dynamic.

References

Aghtaie, N., Larkins, C., Barter, C., Stanley, N., Wood, M., & Øverlien, C. (2018). Interpersonal violence and abuse in young people's relationships in five European countries: Online and offline normalisation of heteronormativity. *Journal of Gender-Based Violence*, *2*(2), 293–310.

Ahlin, E. M. (2014). Locus of control redux. *Journal of Interpersonal Violence*, *29*(14), 2695–2717. https://doi.org/10.1177/0886260513520505

Albanesi, H. P. (2009). Eschewing sexual agency: A gender subjectivity approach. *Race, Gender & Class*, 102–132.

Allen, L. (2009). "Caught in the act": Ethics committee review and researching the sexual culture of schools. *Qualitative Research*, *9*, 395–410. https://doi.org/10.1177/1468794109337866

Australian Human Rights Commission. (2011). *Social justice report 2011*. Australian Human Rights Commission.

Bailey, J., & Gamman, L. (2022). The power in maps: Reviewing a "youth violence" systems map as discursive intervention. In D. Lockton, S. Lenzi, P. Hekkert, A. Oak, J. Sádaba, & P. Lloyd (Eds.), DRS2022: Bilbao, 25 June – 3 July, Bilbao, Spain. https://doi.org/10.21606/drs.2022.563

Barter, C. (2009). In the name of love: Exploitation and violence in teenage dating relationships. *British Journal of Social Work*, *39*, 211–232.

Bay-Cheng, L. Y. (2012). Recovering empowerment: De-personalizing and re-politicizing adolescent female sexuality. *Sex Roles*, *66*(11–12), 713–717. https://doi.org/10.1007/s11199-011-0070-x

Best, A. L. (Ed.). (2007). *Representing youth: Methodological issues in critical youth studies*. New York University Press.

Blakemore, T., Randall, E., Rak, L., & Cocuzzoli, F. (2021). Deep listening and relationality: Cross-cultural reflections on practice with Young Women who use violence. *Australian Social Work*, *75*(3), 304–316. https://doi.org/10.1080/0312407x.2021.1914697

Bounds, D. T., & Posey, P. D. (2022). A resistance framework for racially minoritized youth behaviors during the transition to adulthood. *Journal of Research on Adolescence*, *32*(3), 959–980. https://doi.org/10.1111/jora.12792

Carlisle, E., Coumarelos, C., Minter, K., & Lohmeyer, B. (2022). *It depends on what the definition of domestic violence is: How young Australians conceptualise domestic violence and abuse* [Research report, 09/2022]. ANROWS.

Case, S. (2016). Engaging youth justice: Children first, offenders second. *Dialogue in Praxis*, *3*(1), 1–15.

Checkland, P., & Poulter, J. (2006). *Learning for action: A short definitive account of soft systems methodology and its use for practitioners, teachers and students*. John Wiley & Sons.

Chu, E. M., & Ready, D. D. (2018). Exclusion and urban public high schools: Short-and long-term consequences of school suspensions. *American Journal of Education*, *124*(4), 479–509. https://doi.org/10.1086/698454

Corney, T., Cooper, T., Shier, H., & Williamson, H. (2021). Youth participation: Adultism, human rights and professional youth work. *Children & Society*. Advance online publication. https://doi.org/10.1111/chso.12526

Currie, D. H., Kelly, D. M., & Pomerantz, S. (2007). The power to squash people: Understanding girls' relational aggression. *British Journal of Sociology of Education*, *28*(1), 23–37. https://doi.org/10.1080/01425690600995974

Dalgard, O. S., Thapa, S. B., Hauff, E., McCubbin, M., & Syed, H. R. (2006). Immigration, lack of control and psychological distress: Findings from the Oslo Health Study. *Scandinavian Journal of Psychology*, *47*(6), 551–558. https://doi.org/10.1111/j.1467-9450.2006.00546.x

Domestic Abuse Intervention Programs. (2017). *Understanding the power and control wheel*. www.theduluthmodel.org/wheels/faqs-about-the-wheels/

Duck, S. (2007). *Human relationships* (4th ed.). SAGE Publications.

Dudgeon, P., Milroy, H., & Walker, R. (2014). *Working together: Aboriginal and Torres Strait Islander mental health and wellbeing principles and practice* (2nd ed.). Department of the Prime Minister and Cabinet.

Duluth Model. (2021, April 24). *Wheels: Domestic abuse intervention programs*. www.theduluthmodel.org/wheels/

Edwards, C., Bolton, R., Salazar, M., Vives-Cases, C., & Daoud, N. (2022). Young people's constructions of gender norms and attitudes towards violence against women: A critical review of qualitative empirical literature. *Journal of Gender Studies*. https://doi.org/10.1080/09589236.2022.2119374

Evans, K. (2002). Taking control of their lives? Agency in young adult transitions in England and the new Germany. *Journal of Youth Studies*, *5*(3), 245–269. https://doi.org/10.1080/1367626022000005965

Fine, M. (1988). Sexuality, schooling, and adolescent females: The missing discourse of desire. *Harvard Educational Review*, *58*(1), 29–53.

Follett, M.P. (1940). *Dynamic Administration: The Collected Papers of Mary Parker Follett*. London: Routledge.

Foucault, M. (1978). *The history of sexuality* (R. Hurley, Trans., Vol. 1). Pantheon Books.

French, J. R. P., Jr., & Raven, B. H. (1959). The bases of social power. In D. Cartwright (Ed.), *Studies in social power* (pp. 150–167). Institute for Social Research.

Gabriel, M. G., Brown, A., León, M., & Outley, C. (2022). Power and social control of youth during the COVID-19 pandemic. *Leisure Sciences*, *43*(1–2), 240–246. https://doi.org/10.1080/01490400.2020.1774008

Gallagher, M. (2008). "Power is not an evil": Rethinking power in participatory methods. *Children's Geographies*, 6(2), 137–150. https://doi.org/10.1080/14733280801963045

Galtung, J. (1990). Cultural violence. *Journal of Peace Research*, 27, 291–305.

Gottfredson, M. R., & Hirschi, T. (1990). *A general theory of crime*. Stanford University Press.

Haidt, J., & Rodin, J. (1999). Control and efficacy as interdisciplinary bridges. *Review of General Psychology*, 3(4), 317–337. https://doi.org/10.1037/1089-2680.3.4.317

Hamby, S. (2017). On defining violence, and why it matters. *Psychology of Violence*, 7(2), 167–180. https://doi.org/10.1037/vio0000117

Harris, A., & Wyn, J. (2009). Young people's politics and the micro-territories of the local. *Australian Journal of Political Science*, 44(2), 327–344. https://doi.org/10.1080/10361140902865308

Hirschi, T. (1969). A control theory of delinquency. In T. Hirschi, F. Williams, & M. McShane (Eds.), *Criminology theory: Selected classic readings* (pp. 289–305). Anderson Publishing.

Hitlin, S., & Long, C. (2009). Agency as a sociological variable: A preliminary model of individuals, situations, and the life course. *Sociology Compass*, 3(1), 137–160. https://doi.org/10.1111/j.1751-9020.2008.00189.x

Huebner, A. J., & Betts, S. C. (2002). Exploring the utility of social control theory for youth development: Issues of attachment, involvement, and gender. *Youth & Society*, 34(2), 123–145. https://doi.org/10.1177/0044118022 37860

Kelley, T. M. (1996). At-risk youth and locus of control: Do they really see a choice? *Juvenile and Family Court Journal*, 47(4), 39–54. https://doi.org/10.1111/j.1755-6988.1996.tb00759.x

Kitchin, R., Dodge, M., & Perkins, C. (2011). Power and politics of mapping. In M. Dodge, R. Kitchin, & C. Perkins (Eds.), *The map reader: Theories of mapping practice and cartographic representation* (pp. 439–446). John Wiley & Sons.

Korff, J. (2019, February 8). *Bullying & lateral violence*. Creative Spirits. www.creativespirits.info/aboriginalculture/people/bullying-lateralviolence

Langer, E. J., & Rodin, J. (1976). The effects of choice and enhanced personal responsibility for the aged: A field experiment in an institutional setting. *Journal of Personality and Social Psychology*, 34(2), 191–198. https://doi.org/10.1037/0022-3514.34.2.191

Lefcourt, H. M. (1982). *Locus of control: Current trends in theory and research* (2nd ed.). Lawrence Erlbaum Associates, Inc.

Lohmeyer, B. A. (2018). Youth as an artefact of governing violence: Violence to young people shapes violence by young people. *Current Sociology*, 66(7), 1070–1086. https://doi.org/10.1177/0011392117738040

Lukes, S. (2005). *Power: A radical view* (2nd ed.). Palgrave Macmillan.

McClelland, D. C. (1975). *Power: The inner experience*. John Wiley & Sons.

Moulds, L., Day, A., Mildred, H., Miller, P., & Casey, S. (2016). Adolescent violence towards parents – the known and unknowns. *Australian and New Zealand Journal of Family Therapy*, 37(4), 547–557. https://doi.org/10.1002/anzf.1189

Munford, R., & Sanders, J. (2015). Young people's search for agency: Making sense of their experiences and taking control. *Qualitative Social Work*, *14*(5), 616–633. https://doi.org/10.1177/1473325014565149

Nava, M. (2007). *Visceral cosmopolitanism: Gender, culture and the normalisation of difference*. Berg.

Plows, V. (2012). Conflict and coexistence: Challenging interactions, expressions of agency and ways of relating in work with young people in the minority world. *Children's Geographies*, *10*(3), 279–291. https://doi.org/10.1080/14733285.2012.693378

Poggi, G. (2005). Classical social theory, III: Max Weber and Georg Simmel. In A. Harrington (Ed.), *Modern social theory: An introduction* (pp. 63–86). Oxford University Press.

Rains, P., Teram, E., & Toutant, C. (2001). Special issue introduction young offenders: Balancing control and treatment. *Canadian Journal of Community Mental Health*, *20*(2), 5–9. www.cjcmh.com/doi/pdf/10.7870/cjcmh-2001-0010

Rak, L., & Warton, T. (2023). His, hers and theirs: Comparative narratives from young people who use violence. *Safer Communities*, *22*(1), 42–55. https://doi.org/10.1108/sc-08-2022-0033

Raven, B. H. (1965). Social influence and power. In I. D. Steiner & M. Fishbein (Eds.), *Current studies in social psychology* (pp. 371–382). Holt, Rinehart, Winston.

Raven, B. H. (2008). The bases of power and the power/interaction model of interpersonal influence. *Analyses of Social Issues and Public Policy*, *8*(1), 1–22. https://doi.org/10.1111/j.1530-2415.2008.00159.x

Reckwitz, A. (2002). Toward a theory of social practices a development in culturalist theorizing. *European Journal of Social Theory*, *5*(2), 243–263.

Ringrose, J., & Renold, E. (2011). Boys, girls and performing normative violence in schools: A gendered critique of bully discourses. In C. Barter & D. Berridge (Eds.), *Children behaving badly? Peer violence between children and young people* (pp 158–197). John Wiley & Sons.

Rodin, J., & Langer, E. J. (1977). Long-term effects of a control-relevant intervention with the institutionalized aged. *Journal of Personality and Social Psychology*, *35*(12), 897–902. https://doi.org/10.1037/0022-3514.35.12.897

Rotter, J. B. (1966). Generalized expectancies for internal versus external control of reinforcement. *Psychological Monographs: General and Applied*, *80*(1), 1–28. https://doi.org/10.1037/h0092976

Routt, G., & Anderson, L. (2014). *Adolescent violence in the home: Restorative approaches to building healthy, respectful family relationships*. Routledge.

Sears, H. A., Byers, E. S., Whelan, J. J., & Saint-Pierre, M. (2006). If it hurts you, then it is not a joke. *Journal of Interpersonal Violence*, *21*(9), 1191–1207. https://doi.org/10.1177/0886260506290423

Sell, A., Eisner, M., & Ribeaud, D. (2016). Bargaining power and adolescent aggression: The role of fighting ability, coalitional strength, and mate value. *Evolution and Human Behavior*, *37*(2), 105–116. https://doi.org/10.1016/j.evolhumbehav.2015.09.003

Shanahan, M. J., & Hood, K. E. (1998). Adolescents in changing social structures: Bounded agency in life course perspective. In R. Silbereisen & E. Crockett

(Eds.), *Negotiating adolescence in times of social change: Cross-national perspectives on developmental processes and social intervention* (pp. 123–134). Cambridge University Press.

Shove, E., Pantzar, M., & Watson, M. (2012). *The dynamics of social practice: Everyday life and how it changes*. SAGE Publications.

Simmons, R. (2002). *Odd girl out: The hidden culture of aggression in girls*. Harcourt, Inc.

Skiba, R. J., Arredondo, M. I., & Williams, N. T. (2014). More than a metaphor: The contribution of exclusionary discipline to a school-to-prison pipeline. *Equity & Excellence in Education*, *47*(4), 546–564. https://doi.org/10.1080/10665684.2014.958965

Spencer, G. (2013). Young people and health: Towards a new conceptual framework for understanding empowerment. *Health: An Interdisciplinary Journal for the Social Study of Health, Illness and Medicine*, *18*(1), 3–22. https://doi.org/10.1177/1363459312473616

Spencer, G., & Doull, M. (2015). Examining concepts of power and agency in research with young people. *Journal of Youth Studies*, *18*(7), 900–913. https://doi.org/10.1080/13676261.2014.1001827

Storer, H. L., Talan, A., Swiatlo, A., LeSar, K., Broussard, M., Kendall, C., & Madkour, A. S. (2020). Context matters: Factors that influence African American teens' perceptions and definitions of dating violence. *Psychology of Violence*, *10*(1), 79–90.

Stuart, G. (2004). Youth work and managing behaviour. *Youth and Policy*, (85), 19–36.

Tagesson, E. H., & Gallo, C. (2021). "When we talk about intimate partner violence we talk in an adult way" – social workers' descriptions of intimate partner violence between teenagers. *Qualitative Social Work*, *21*(2), 332–348. https://doi.org/10.1177/14733250211002890

Talbot, M. (2002, February 24). Girls just want to be mean. *The New York Times*, Section 6, 24.

Threadgold, S. (2011). Should I pitch my tent in the middle ground? On "middling tendency", beck and inequality in youth sociology. *Journal of Youth Studies*, *14*(4), 381–393. https://doi.org/10.1080/13676261.2010.538042

Totten, M. (2000). *Guys, gangs and girlfriend abuse*. Broadview Press.

Townsend, J. G. (1999). *Women and power: Fighting patriarchies and poverty*. Zed.

Ungar, M. (2022). *Nurturing hidden resilience in troubled youth*. University of Toronto Press.

Walby, S. (2013). Violence and society: Introduction to an emerging field of sociology. *Current Sociology*, *61*(2), 95–111.

Watkins, M. (2012). *Discipline and learn: Bodies, pedagogy and writing*. Sense Publishers.

Welsh, R. O., & Little, S. (2018). Caste and control in schools: A systematic review of the pathways, rates and correlates of exclusion due to school discipline. *Children and Youth Services Review*, *94*, 315–339. https://doi.org/10.1016/j.childyouth.2018.09.031

Winter, D. G. (1973). *The power motive*. Free Press.

Wood, M., Barter, C., & Berridge, D. (2010). *"Standing on my own two feet": Disadvantaged teenagers, intimate partner violence and coercive control.* NSPCC.

World Health Organization (WHO). (2020). *Adolescent health*. www.who.int/southeastasia/health-topics/adolescent-health

Wray-Lake, L., Halgunseth, L., & Witherspoon, D. P. (2022). Good trouble, necessary trouble: Expanding thinking and research on youth of color's resistance to oppression. *Journal of Research on Adolescence*, *32*(3), 949–995.

10 Shame named, known, and (re)negotiated

Chris Krogh and Tamara Blakemore

Acknowledgement

This chapter discusses the Shame Coat activity. This activity was developed in collaboration with Felicity Cocuzzoli, a proud descendant of the Wiradjuri Nation, equity practitioner, and artist who has been a NNN facilitator, cultural reference group member, and practitioner working party peer. We acknowledge Felicity's contribution to this work.

Shame and youth violence

This chapter presents a selective review of shame-related literature that has informed our thinking and practice in the Name.Narrate.Navigate (NNN) program. It considers how shame has been conceptualised and understood as a personal, interpersonal, and social experience. It also considers the role of shame in youth violence and how it has been addressed by different practice perspectives. Collected with appropriate ethics approval and drawing on practitioner reflections, de-identified insights into how young people who use violence name and know shame and their efforts to (re)negotiate its role in their lives are shared.

Conceptualising shame

In our work in the Name.Narrate.Navigate (NNN) program, we see shame as a motivator for young people's use of violence, an impact of the experience of violence, and a form of violence in and of itself. In this way, shame and responses to shame can be a compounding and cyclical experience for individuals and communities. Across the shame-related literature, there is agreement that not all shame is the same. This can be boiled down to a difference between feelings a person has about what they have *done* compared with feelings about who they *are*. For some authors, this is articulated as a difference between moral shame and image shame (Hamblet, 2010); for Braithwaite (2020), it is

DOI: 10.4324/9781003177883-10

disintegrative as opposed to reintegrative shame, and, for others still, it is the difference between shame and guilt (Tangney & Dearing, 2002). Our understanding of these complex emotions is informed by the work of Tangney and Dearing (2002). Put simply, these authors explain shame as negative evaluations of the self (*who I am*) and guilt as negative evaluations of behaviour (*what I've done*) (Tangney & Dearing, 2002). Guilt is seen as an emotion which is related to, but not the same as, shame. According to Morrison (2011), shame and guilt are distinct but not exclusive emotions – they can coexist and interact, each exacerbating the other. Generally, though, guilt can lead to actions to repair and seek forgiveness, while shame leads one to want to withdraw and hide, a feeling that would be resolved with forgiveness. Writing in the same psychodynamic tradition, Gilligan (2003) proposes that guilt requires a more complex set of emotional capacities and develops after the more reactive or "primitive" response of shame. Schalkwijk et al. (2016) find that within existing literature, guilt is linked to empathy and has been argued to restrain an individual from offending through regulation of behaviour or orientation towards repairing harm that has been done.

Shame at the personal level

Shame is a pervasive, potentially excruciating, and scarring emotion that challenges our overall self-concept (Morrison, 2011). In the face of shame, the self is "negatively evaluated and scrutinised", leading to feelings of "worthlessness and powerlessness" (Owen & Fox, 2011, p. 552). Shame can provoke feelings of bitterness, resentment, and blame of self or others (Tangney & Dearing, 2002) and lead us to want to shrink, disappear, or hide (Morrison, 2011). Shame can be expressed as sadness, remorse, regret, humiliation, social withdrawal, and anger (Scheff & Retzinger, 1991; Tomkins, 1987). Harris (2007) suggests shame can lead to powerful feelings of distress because it challenges our sense of self and, in particular, our ethical identity. We feel shame when a gulf emerges between our ideas of ourselves, including our values and beliefs, and our actions. Because shame is an uneasy feeling, we seek to discharge it through responses that distance and disconnect us from the targets of our behaviour and/or to restore dignity (Gilligan, 2003; Owen & Fox, 2011).

The development of the capacity for experiencing and then managing shame is understood slightly differently through different frameworks of development. Emotions-focused literature, for example, sees shame as one of the self-conscious emotions along with pride and guilt (Lewis, 2016; Schalkwijk et al., 2016). These emotions, based on a belief about how we are being seen by others (Muris & Meesters, 2014), arise later in childhood, following the development of underpinning cognitive achievements such as empathy and moral beliefs (Schalkwijk et al., 2016) or a sense of an independent self, a theory of mind, and understanding of rules and the opinions of others (Muris & Meesters, 2014). The constituent properties of self-conscious emotions and the ability to manage these arise in childhood and develop through adolescence and into adulthood. Eriksonian frameworks, influential in our thinking about shame, for instance, note the importance of the second stage of human development (toddlerhood) as a time where children are developing their sense of autonomy and control but first experience shame (Gross, 2020). Authors in this tradition highlight the developing child's early experiences of individual control over, and achievement of, basic processes, such as going to the toilet, provide a sense of self-sufficiency and build self-confidence to be able to use initiative in the next developmental stage. However, not achieving this can contribute to shame and doubt becoming prominent, contributing to an increased need for control (Gross, 2020). Alternative ideas about shame are those based on social theory, which see shame as connected with identities and with contravention of individually held values associated with those identities (De Boeck et al., 2018). From this perspective, Brown (2006) recognises shame as a psycho-social-cultural phenomenon. That is, it is an internal, emotional experience, tied to relationships and informed by cultural expectations. This is exemplified in the case of "criminalised women", where social expectations of being a "good woman" and "good mother" are socially-endorsed identities against which actions are evaluated and negative self-assessment is invited (Rutter & Barr, 2021).

Shame at the interpersonal level

While the emotion is experienced individually, shame is often triggered from our interactions with others (Herman, 2011) and our knowledge of, or beliefs about, how we will be seen by others. Indeed, from a developmental perspective, the capacities to experience and manage shame develop largely within familial/domestic relationships. Herman (2011, p. 265) proposes that relationships involving extreme power differentials, where dominance, coercion, and control are employed by one person or group over another are "inherently shaming". This can occur in a range of adult relationships, including domestic violence and modern slavery, as well as in some cases of abuse of children. While aspects of these relationships may be focused on instilling fear, other aspects are designed to humiliate and shame (Herman, 2011). Shame is also seen to regulate behaviour within relationships (Herman, 2011) and in society more broadly (Braithwaite, 1989) as individuals internalise interpersonal expectations and social norms. Stuewig and McCloskey (2005), for example, found that harsh or critical parenting was more likely than childhood maltreatment to lead to shame development, while warm and responsive parenting during adolescence led more to guilt responses. When it is not disabling, shame and guilt invoke a desire to repair harm that has been caused, while the associated emotion of pride can lead to aligning oneself with accepted standards in contexts that matter to the individual (Muris & Meesters, 2014).

Shame in social context

In addition to arising from transgressions of formal rules or agreed social norms, shame can be the consequence of having an "unwanted identity" (Brown, 2006) on the basis of belonging to an oppressed, ostracised, disapproved of, or marginalised group. These identities may be a wanted aspect of the person's sense of self, offering belonging and pride, or, alternatively, pressed upon individuals and not their preference or choice (Rutter & Barr, 2021). Illustrating the latter option, McWilliams (2017) identified the significance of stigma and shame associated with belonging to public schools in settings where charter schools are the chosen option for anyone able to secure entry. In this context, being one of the students or teachers left over "pooling" in a public school is seen as shameful in the community, with media reporting and local gossip contributing to that identity. In a different context, but with similar processes, Crewe et al. (2020) demonstrated that belonging to the identity category "murderer" was deeply shameful to long-term prison detainees because of the stigma that goes with that label. This stigma also flowed to family and close friends of the detainees to a greater or lesser extent.

Shame, through processes of humiliation, may also be institutionally embedded, deployed as a tactic of control against specific populations identified as socially unacceptable (Fattore & Mason, 2020). These authors identify that inculcation of shame is also a means of silencing individuals who might otherwise speak out against abuse they are being subject to. Theisen-Womersley (2021), writing about shame for displaced, refuge-seeking, and migrant populations, identifies both the contradictions within public shame experiences and the reinforcing nature of that shame saying: "Despite its omnipresence, shame is ashamed of itself. Shame activates shame" (p. 209). Theisen-Womersley (2021) notes systemic practices can contribute to this process where bureaucratic decisions can cancel one possible, hoped for identity, leaving space for it to be replaced with an unwanted identity. The powerlessness the individual feels in this process, as well as the scrutiny and judgement, is likely to have echoes of trauma experiences, and some of the consequences may mirror PTSD symptoms including flashbacks, emotional avoidance, and hyper-arousal (Theisen-Womersley, 2021).

Stigma-associated shame can be activated within an individual by deliberately attacking personally important identity categories and disrupting the individual's place within their family and community. Lewis (1998, p. 127) described stigma as "a public violation or action", which Goffman (1963) saw as related to injured ideas of identity. Sexual violence against men and making men witness sexual violence against their family members can be a tactic of war and used as a form of torture in conflict, such as in Uganda (Schulz, 2020). This form of torture is designed to be physically traumatic and to break down the man's sense of his masculinity. The multiple consequences of this include ongoing physical pain and scarring and deeply held shame, which leads, in turn, to being isolated from family and exclusion from community (Schulz, 2020).

People can actively work to reject or overturn shame-invoking identities put upon them. For example, people convicted of murder use the appeals process to try to overturn their convictions, seeking both the symbolic and practical possibilities this offers (Crewe et al., 2020). Members of stigmatised public schools in the US have sought to change the community view of them, with one interviewee saying (in part), "I don't think that it's the culture here that needs to be changed. I think it's the perception that needs rejecting out there" (McWilliams, 2017, p. 229). In contexts of enforced shaming, the distinction between shame and guilt may be less relevant if the individual has not acted in ways that transgress their personally held values (Brown, 2006).

The role of shame in youth violence

Understandings of the role of shame in youth violence and the relationship between shame, crime, and violence in general are not settled with different studies reporting different conclusions resulting in an equivocal evidence base (Mayer, 2019). Some studies suggest there is little difference in scores reported on shame scales for justice-involved and non-justice-involved youth (Schalkwijk et al., 2016). Others report justice-involved young people report lower levels of (shame-related) guilt (Stuewig & McCloskey, 2005), with those who use violence reporting lower levels of empathy (Fox et al., 2015). Routt and Anderson (2016), authors of the American "Step Up" program for adolescent family violence, suggest that when young people feel ashamed, they are less motivated to take responsibility and, instead, can become hostile and angry with the world around, and this can interfere with accountability, empathy, and behaviour change. This position is echoed by the authors Tangney and Dearing (2002), who note "in short, shamed individuals are inclined to assume a defensive posture, rather than take a constructive, reparative stance in their relationships" (pp. 180–181).

Anger seems to have the most tangible association between shame and young people's use of violence. Anger has been described as the "dark side of shame" (Bear et al., 2009, p. 229) and identified as a mediator between the experience of trauma and adverse outcomes (Bennett et al., 2005). Shame is suggested to lead to anger directed towards others, for example, when we blame others for the situations we find ourselves in (Tangney & Dearing, 2002; Tangney et al., 1992, 2007). According to attribution (Weiner, 2006) and cognitive dissonance (Gosling et al., 2006) theories, blaming others for our circumstances can be a self-protective measure that is learned through acculturation and socialisation (Kitayama et al., 1997). Anger may be used as an outlet to vent the internal pressure that shame creates, soothing the uncomfortable feelings in the process (Cairns & Howells, 2019). It can also, though, create a reinforcing cycle by provoking negative actions then feeling negatively about those actions, leading to further harmful/hurtful actions (Kerig et al., 2010); a process described as the "shame-rage spiral". This process can be interpersonal – turning shame-based rage towards others – or intrapersonal – turning shame-based rage in on oneself (Ryan, 1993).

The potential for violence to maintain one's identity and restore pride may be connected to the notion of "saving face". Cairns and Howells (2019, p. 356), for example, report that "expressions of anger may be seen as effective 'face-saving' strategies that promote a positive identity". An illustration of the potential for violence in the context of feeling shame in the eyes of others can be seen in Chapter 6 where the authors describe young men in youth detention's responses to the emotion recognition photo-elicitation activity using the stereotypically angry face. When asked about their potential feelings on seeing someone looking like that, one response was wanting to "Step up/**save face**" (emphasis added). The importance of not being diminished in the eyes of others (reflecting the notion of "image shame") can be seen here and is linked to actively stepping in to challenge the person and not "backing down". The potential for violence here is very high. Relatedly, highly developed sensitivity to the viewpoint of others and awareness of being judged was found to be associated with shame and anger in groups of men convicted of offending (Cairns & Howells, 2019).

There is some suggestion that anticipating shame may restrain a person from committing an offence. Studies, though, have shown this is not a simple equation. Schalkwijk et al. (2016), for example, studied the place of conscience (one component of which is shame and guilt) in offending of teenagers in the Netherlands. Approximately one-sixth of the study cohort of 334 young people had been involved in offending.

They found that anticipated shame was not used by the offending group as a moderator of offending. Rather, anticipated shame was a trigger for attacking others, whereas those who were not in the offending group were more likely to moderate their behaviour in the presence of anticipated shame. Gender differences in involvement in crime have also prompted some researchers to speculate whether different experiences of shame may be implicated as potential moderating or mediating processes. Rebellon et al. (2015) report "anticipated shaming" (an imagined view of the self, by others) was relevant but not sufficient to explain gender differences in offending. Paulo et al. (2020) found gender differences are notable in the use of internalising versus externalising shame-coping strategies with young women reporting coping mechanisms associated with higher levels of depression, interpersonal conflict, and self-harming behaviours, while young men were more likely to cope with shame through externalising, which led to the potential for more aggressive and "delinquent" responses.

Justice responses for working with shame

Shame has been woven into justice responses since ancient times. In ancient Greek society, for example, being offended by someone led those seeking justice to visit retributive vengeance, including humiliation and shame, on the person who had wronged them (Hamblet, 2010). This form of justice was designed to restore honour and to regain esteem in the eyes of one's peers, removing shame from the person harmed by shaming the offender. Shaming sentences are currently used in jurisdictions in the United States, where punishments can involve identifying a person as an offender and making them complete publicly humiliating punishments (Nussbaum, 2004). Foucault (1991) proposed that "shameful punishments are effective because they are based on the vanity that was at the root of the crime" (p. 107). Shame, from this perspective, is a two-way process where the shamed person is shown the disgrace they have brought upon themselves in the eyes of others and the others, in turn, are shown the suffering you can expect should you transgress. Foucault (1991) proposes that public witness to the fate of criminals is "a living lesson in the museum of order" (p. 112).

Nussbaum (2008), though, rejects the value of shaming sentences as a justice response on the basis of their being unreliable; the motives of the shamer may well be quite suspect; they represent a form of mob justice; and they stigmatise and ostracise the people against whom they are directed. Similar dispute comes from Mayer (2019), who suggests that while there are advocates who argue for shaming on the basis of it being cost-effective and preventing the offender becoming embroiled in crime culture, others argue that it is inhumane and includes an inappropriate involvement of the public in response to crime and, most importantly, that evidence for the effectiveness of such penalties is limited at best. Going further, Gilligan (2003) argues shaming a person who has used violence is a sure-fire way to increase their likelihood of using violence again.

Nussbaum (2004) also reminds us that shame is highly contextual and that what is shameful at one time and in one place won't be that way forever, hence highlighting the tenuous nature of shame as punishment. Similarly, in talking about the place of shame and shaming in different cultural contexts, Mayer (2019) writes, "What kind of crime is viewed as shameful usually relates to the culture, to the definition of power within a society and to value concepts" (p123). Highlighting this point, Blagg and Anthony (2019) suggest for Australian First Nations people, whose very identity has been stigmatised, being involved in the White criminal justice system may not shameful. Not denying the fear and shaming that is actively inflicted on First Nations adults and young people in detention, Blagg and Anthony (2019, p. 187) write, "One's status in Indigenous society is not threatened by involvement in the white justice system". Nussbaum (2004) also notes a contradiction in using shaming as a sentencing option at a time when many societies are working hard to reduce multiple stigmas (for example, on the grounds of discrimination against sexuality or disability). Instead, it is invoking stigma in this approach to sentencing.

Despite objections to systemic use of shaming, researchers recognise shame may have a behaviour-modifying effect that can lead us to act in some ways and not to act in other ways. Braithwaite (1989), for example, draws on the restraining qualities of shame to argue greater clarity and social reinforcement regarding behaviours that are unacceptable and, therefore, shameful will lead people not to do them. Braithwaite's thesis underpins a more practical application of shame in justice responses – restorative shaming (Braithwaite, 1989, 2020; Braithwaite & Mugford, 1994). Arguing that the rise of professionalised and bureaucratised models of criminal justice have disconnected community and offender from each other, such that the ruptures caused by offending are not experienced relationally by the offender, Braithwaite (1989) described a model for restorative, or reintegrative shaming. Reintegrative shaming requires the shame to be potent and for there to be formalised, ritualised processes to welcome the offender back into the community (Braithwaite, 1989). London (2011) describes the restorative shaming process as involving relationships of expectation between the victim(s), the offender(s), and the community, wherein the victim wants the offender to appreciate their suffering, society wants the offender to understand how their actions have broken social trust, and the offender is asked to feel individual shame for their actions and to make amends and restore trust for them to be re-included into society. This process is suggested to reduce crime, potentially make victims less fearful and feel they have been treated fairly in the process, and produce benefits for the community including increased capacity to respond to crime (Braithwaite, 2020). These ideas have been so central to the field of restorative justice that Benade (2015) sees reintegrative shaming as not just a part of restorative justice but as a foundational and necessary concept for the existence of the approach.

These approaches, however, are not without their complexities. For example, restorative or reintegrative shaming may be more effective in communitarian rather than individualistic settings (Benade, 2015; London, 2011). Benade (2015) also recognises that reintegrative shaming requires an individual offender to realign themselves with the norms of the community whose laws they have broken. This, in turn, requires that the norms of the community itself are experienced as just and worth returning to. For dispossessed, colonised, and otherwise disenfranchised populations, this potential is questionable at best (see, for example, Blagg, 1997, 2017; Blagg & Anthony, 2019). A great many of the young people who end up in the justice system have experienced multiple forms of injustice and oppression and have, therefore, been let down by the community to which they are expected to reintegrate. These ideas have been addressed by Jenkins (2009) in the context of working restoratively with men who have used violence in their families, noting this needs to involve acknowledging experiences of economic disadvantage, racial discrimination, and their own experiences of violence (Jenkins, 2009). Attempts at restoration that do not acknowledge these experiences add to existing injustice and may be experienced by these men as further moments of "being done to" by the community and justice system (Jenkins, 2009).

Practice responses for working with shame

Practice responses for working with shame variously and sometimes simultaneously position the practitioner as a supportive and nonjudgemental ally and an agent of provocation who invites critical reflection on actions and outcomes. The position of the practitioner can depend on the aspects or experiences of shame they are working with. Shame management theory (Ahmed, 2002, 2006) suggests that we deal adaptively with shame via acknowledgement or less adaptively via displacement. Acknowledgement involves recognising wrongdoing and harm caused and wishing to make amends, whereas displacement involves blaming others or external factors. These are not mutually exclusive conditions, and we are capable of both acknowledging and displacing shame, depending on context and our perceptions of threat. Often the task of the practitioner is to hold what Morrison (2011) describes as these bearable and unbearable aspects of shame in place until they become bearable and able to be worked with tolerably.

Sensitive, relational, and connection-based support is argued by some to be effective in this work as it counters the disconnected experience of shame. Sensitive support for the journey of facing experiences that invoke shame need not only come from therapists. Support groups of people with similar experiences can serve many purposes, including transforming the effects of shame through reducing isolation and breaking silence on the issue. Brown (2006), following elaboration of "shame resilience theory", proposes that psychoeducational groups can be a useful context for changing the impact of shame on women's lives when they are founded upon mutually respectful relationships, involve helping women to see shame for what it is and understand its processes, and empower women to challenge its effects.

Effective support has many components, with attention to practitioner ethics being one. Jenkin's (2009) formulation when working with men who have acted abusively within their family includes inviting the man into conversation about his actions as well as asking permission to question him more about potentially challenging topics. The approach also involves provocations (that is, a challenging question based on the dissonance within the man's stated ethics and his actions as well as understanding the broad context within which this is all happening) rather than the more commonly promoted practice of confrontation. This approach acknowledges that systemic and professional responses to abuse sit completely within the webs of power that are being worked with and must be as vigilant to their own use and abuse of power as to those of the man with whom they are working (Jenkins, 2009). Outlining that working with abuse is an ethical journey of the professional that runs in parallel with the ethical journey of the "client", Jenkins (2009, p. 20) writes, "Our work cannot be ethical if it employs shaming practices".

In the same way that abuse of power is not something from which professionals are immune, shame is also a feeling that can emerge for professionals in our work and requires conscious attention. Child protection social work, for example, is a context in which shame can be experienced by professionals. Gibson's (2016) review of existing studies in this field showed these workers can experience shame through being directly or indirectly devalued, through questioning their abilities or decisions made, and through "being torn" about what to do in different matters. Within the organisational and professional context of child protection social work, shame can also be activated for political ends, including to further the politically motivated reshaping of services and practice (Gibson, 2019). Shame may also be a resource in professional contexts. Powerfully, Asser (2022) demonstrates how a professional's well-developed attunement to their own shame can assist in defusing potentially violent group work situations. He writes, "As long as I can stay connected with my shame, this will intuitively connect me with the shame of others in the room" (Asser, 2022, p. 121). These examples illustrate the importance of professionals being attentive to how they are using and experiencing shame in their work in general. Shame, though, should also be a direct focus of practice.

Shame in NNN

Shame is the focus of the fifth group work session in NNN. This session explores how shame features in stories of violence by considering the relationship between judgement and shame, understandings of shame and its experience, and how we manage intense responses to shame. The Shame Coat activity in this session engages young people in an experiential exercise of mapping what shame is and what it does for us over time. The activity explores the idea that other people can put "shame" on you, some actions or experiences can be experienced as "shameful", and we can also feel "ashamed".

The NNN approach to shame helps young people identify, name, and experience the differences between destructive "image shame" and more constructive "moral shame". For practitioners and young people, these concepts are presented as "shame" and "guilt", being more accessible concepts. We recognise shame and guilt are connected emotions and that increases in guilt can be associated with increases in shame, but consistent with others (e.g., Izard, 1991), we don't see them as interchangeable descriptions of the same experience. While relating their connection, in our work, we tend to focus on shame because of its links to identity and how our experienced and, also, presumed identity can influence outcomes and opportunities in a cyclical and compounding way.

Table 10.1 Program structure and session focus: Shame

Program structure	*Session*	*Focus*
		Beginnings
	1	Emotions
	2	Voice
	3	Empathy
	4	Power and Control
	5	**Shame**
	6	Choice
		Endings

Consistent with understandings of social identity (e.g., Tajfel, 1982), concepts of identity migration explained by the Māori identity migration model (Rata, 2015) and identity migration in recovery from trauma (Duvall & Béres, 2007), we acknowledge that young people who use and experience violence can simultaneously hold multiple identities, with what Rata (2015) describes as push-pull factors motivating "migrations between identity spaces" (pp. 3). We are interested in the role of shame as a potential push-pull factor and how it relates to the use of violence. With a focus on addressing the connections between shame and identity, our work with shame in NNN is necessarily concerned, too, with experiences of stigma. NNN practice recognises the stigma that many young people in the program have experienced on the basis of their social class, the suburbs they live in, the family arrangements they have, their cultural background, and connotations associated with "criminality". In NNN we are also sensitive to the role gender may play in shaping the relationship between shame, stigma, and identity. The NNN practice approach provides an opportunity for the young person to differentiate these stigmatised and unwanted identities from who they are as a person.

Practice approach

Our practice approach to working with shame is shaped by a trauma-informed and culturally safe ethos enacted through relational practice, that is, person-centred and sensitive to privilege, power, and place. The activities we use in working with shame involve experiential learning and rely on practitioners' skills of validation and reciprocal communication. Our practice approach to working with shame aims to reduce the potential threat to identity that shame causes by externalising narratives of shame to explore and reframe shame as related to a behaviour and not identity. Experiential learning activities in this session explore the idea that other people can put "shame" on you, we can see some actions or experiences as "shameful", and we can feel "ashamed". In approaching work related to shame, we were very clear that we wanted to ensure we took a balanced approach in validating and naming experience, sensitive to culture and context and supportive of present and future safety.

In developing the activities used, we consulted widely and were particularly grateful for the contribution of Felicity Cocuzzoli – an Aboriginal equity practitioner and artist who has been a NNN facilitator, cultural reference group member, and practitioner working party peer. Felicity brings to her work a passion and expertise in creative methodologies. Felicity identified the weight of shame and that shame is often put on us by others. In a series of collaborative conversations, we developed the Shame Coat activity (see practice note following) to provide an embodied experience of the socially constructed labels used to shame, their temporal and situational context, and their potential "stickiness" in permeating our sense of identity and self.

The Shame Coat activity involves the use of a heavy coat as a learning tool or prop. A practitioner or, if judged safe and appropriate, a member of the group is recruited to wear the coat during the activity. Ideas about shame are then brainstormed in the group to establish shared understandings of the construct and its experience. Using the prompts described in the practice note for this activity, practitioners then introduce a brainstorming activity to explore, in scaffolded progression, known and familiar narratives about the practice of shaming others. Modelling reciprocal communication, practitioners participate in this activity alongside young people. After the brainstorming activity and adding of words to the coat is complete, practitioners prompt reflection on what would happen if the (sticky) masking tape was to remain stuck to the coat, using this analogy to explain how shame put on us can become part of us if it is experienced often, across multiple aspects of our life, or in meaningful relationships that result in the insult mattering to us. Participants are then invited to start removing the brainstormed words, with practitioners using the analogy that shame that is put on us can also be removed. A final aspect of the activity is to arrange the removed word prompts to explore the "first", "worst" and "last" (most recent) to chart our developmental experiences of shame and also identify indicators of shame that matter most for us. Once removed, the coat is then taken off the volunteer/practitioner and they are asked how it feels to have the coat now off. Common responses of "it was hot", "it was tight", "it felt so heavy, did you put weights in that" are then able to be used as an analogy for the "weight of shame" on us and in our lives.

Delivering this activity requires considerable skill and requires practitioners to carefully assess the viability of each step in the activity for its safety and appropriateness to the cohort and dynamics of past and present experience. Practitioners should have access to an established psychological distress protocol and culturally restricted information protocol to ensure there are sufficient safeguards in place. There should also be considered consultation with local cultural elders to ensure the activity is culturally endorsed and supported as an appropriate method of exploring shame. Multiple strategies of safekeeping are also employed in the design and delivery of the activity. There is an explicit intention on extracting "words" rather than relating or recalling "experience". In practice, consideration has to be given to how to manage what words are shared and how. There has to be a balance struck between invalidating

Table 10.2 Practice note: The Shame Coat activity

Practice note: Shame Coat activity	
Description:	This experiential learning activity explores narratives of shame, how these are experienced by young people, and the developmental sequence and meaning of experiences of shame.
Time:	15 minutes
Purpose:	This activity seeks to externalise narratives of shame and show how shame can be "put on" you, can "come from within you", and can "become a part of you and how you see yourself". It explores the "weight" of shame and how shame can be lifted.
Resources:	Large heavy coat, masking tape, Sharpie pens
Presentation:	Understandings of shame are explored. Shame is described as something that can be "put on" you, can "come from within you", and can "become a part of you and how you see yourself". A volunteer/practitioner wears the coat while the group brainstorms and writes down words representing their experiences of shame and add to the coat. Brainstorm prompts: • What words cause people to feel shame? • What words have you used to shame someone? • What words have caused you to feel shame? • What were the first, worst, and last words that caused you shame? The order in which prompts are explored is important. Work from the outside in – start with words that we hear other people use to shame others. It is important to focus on others first. Remember it is essential that practitioners participate in this process and match the level of vulnerability in young people's input. For example, if young people do disclose words that others have used to shame them facilitators should do so too – to their own level of comfort and safety. Remember to always emphasise that the words being added to the coat are NOT about the wearer. Check in about their safety and comfort.
Rationale:	This activity engages young people in mapping out what shame is and what it does for us over time. It is worthwhile noting here the difference between guilt and shame. Put simply, shame is self-focused, while guilt is behaviour-focused. This activity is focused on shame rather than guilt. Shame is a contextualised experience, and its experience is determined by the meaning of behaviours in social and cultural contexts (Farmer & Andrews, 2009). By naming and narrating known and familiar beliefs and practices associated with shame, we can support the young person to a place of critical reflection on choices and consequences and movement towards what is possible to know and do (Duvall & Béres, 2011).

people's experience by saying they can't share words that have been used to cause them shame and realising the personal significance of some words to others participating. Careful discussion continually reiterates sharing to be personal reflections and not directed towards anyone in the group. Safety is also established by focusing first on an externalised narrative of known and familiar practices that happen "around here" (referencing contextual aspects of place) towards our own practices and experiences. Both aspects of extraction and externalising create psychological distance from experiences that might threaten perceived or experienced safety of those participating. Safety is also supported by attuned relational communication practices, including careful and considered participation of the practitioners in sharing their own experiences, matching intensity and language used by the young people. Seeing practitioners add words they've used to shame others or words that have been used to shame them distances the activity as being one that could be experienced as "shaming" the young people involved. Reciprocal communication in this respect both balances power by showing shared and common experiences and reveals and acknowledges privilege and power divides where young people shared words representative of ongoing colonialist violence, marginalisation, racism, and structural disadvantage. To further ensure safety, this activity is immediately followed by work focused on mindful and experiential practice of strategies for distress tolerance, providing an in-situ experience of migration of states of mind through physiological and psychological distress tolerance learning.

What we've learned

In practice experience of NNN, we have consistently seen young people's experiences of the destructive effects of shame that arises from messages that they themselves are not okay. These messages arise within interpersonal relationships but also from immediate and broader social context. Insights to young people's experiences characterise shame as a complex emotional experience, often interwoven with other emotions and situated in cultural and contextual meanings characteristic of different points in time and place. In our work, there have been few occasions where the activation of guilt/moral shame has been possible and, as such, the potential for restoration and reintegration are largely not existent for this cohort at present. Where this has occurred, we have seen it happen through acts of co-creation and care, situating naturalistic restoration as possible. In the following section, we present what we have learned so far about the role and experience of shame in the lives of young people who use and experience violence.

Shame and stigma

In our work with both young women and young men, it has not been uncommon to hear them recount actions that place them at risk of harm or serious legal consequences to avoid shame or "loss of face". Often this involves stepping up or stepping in to defend others, demonstrate allegiance, and define their identity as "part of" or "like". The repercussions of this for young people we've worked with can be involvement (or escalation of their involvement) with the justice system, which can then be associated with further stigma and shame. In a recent delivery of NNN with young men in detention, we were confronted with examples of justice-related and justice-imposed labels creating stigma and shame. Reflections shared here are drawn from the practitioner's own notes on the experience of working with one young man in the Shame Coat activity (see Figure 10.1).

Figure 10.1 An example of the words young people identify as being used to cause shame

Box 10.1 What we've learned . . .

"Working with Cruz was an interesting study of contrasts. While characterised to us as someone with convictions for serious crimes who could be at risk for leading more, our experience of him in NNN was as a consistently polite, engaged, and articulate young man. It was obvious he had assumed or was afforded leadership status in the group, perhaps owing to some combination of age, size, acts, connections, or reputation. His engagement in group activities in previous weeks had endorsed them as viable prospects for the other young men and his engagement with the practitioners endorsing them as an unthreatening presence.

Cruz willingly volunteered to model the Shame Coat. As standard practice, we continually noted that the words brainstormed and stuck to the coat were not about Cruz and frequently checked in on his felt safety and willingness to continue on with the activity. We noticed that a lot of the young men in sticking their notions of shame to the coat would apply them to Cruz's back – something we had also observed in other settings. There was something in this that was quite unsettling for Cruz. It seemed to replicate having people say negative things behind your back in ways that mean they're unknown to you, but you still sense or still have an experience of them.

Some of the words the young men shared were racial slurs, others sexualised slurs, others related to stigma about drug use and poverty, and, for the first time, some related to justice involvement. We noticed that with additions to the coat, Cruz was visibly shifting in his stance, moving backwards and towards a corner so to avoid the placement of labels on his back. Again, we checked he was okay, and he remained adamant he wanted to continue.

When contributing his own feedback to the activity, Cruz noted that the "worst" word used to put shame on him was "criminal". Once scribed to a piece of masking tape, Cruz couldn't bear for the label reading "criminal" to be attached to the Shame Coat he was wearing. Standing beside him, I offered to hold the label for him during the activity, and it sat in my hand – displaced and suspended till the activity finished. When mapping the words commonly described as the "first", "worst", and "last" to occasion shame for these young men, "criminal" was listed as the worst and last (most recent) by others too. But not with the same reaction as having it attached to them as had been the case for Cruz. He was visibly relieved taking off the coat, convinced the coat was weighted, commenting on how heavy it felt".

Despite perceptions that being a criminal may be worn as a badge of honour among young people, this young person demonstrated the opposite, not being able to bear it attached to him. Crewe et al. (2020) found among long-term prisoners that while the offence of murder can carry a certain status in the prison population, the interviewees in their research felt no pride in that label, feeling instead that they would forever be seen as someone "evil", "monstrous" or "psychotic" (p. 259). The experience with Cruz challenged existing assumptions we had as practitioners about criminalised identity formation for young people and how this might shape future behaviours and meaning and attributions made about them. Cruz had described that a number of his siblings had been involved with the justice system, but this wasn't identified as a point of connection between them. The label of "criminal" was for him associated with judged consequences of his actions but not his sense of self or identity. This observation led us to contemplate whether and with what sensitivity interventions with this cohort actively appraise the role of shame in the formation of identity. We were struck in the context of our work with this cohort that any active exploration of identity or expression of identity was shut down or expressly prohibited through signs warning against it. While this is explained as deterring gang-affiliated antisocial behaviours, it effectively stifled the capacity of interventions to better understand what contributes to identity for these young men, how aspects of that identity that are no longer viable can be explored, and how movement away from problem states can be supported. This reflects our emerging thinking that the embodied experiences related to youth violence mean interventions need to better understand how these experiences shape self-concept.

Shame and gender

Practice experience with NNN has helped us to see important parallels between young men's and young women's relationships with shame as well as some significant differences. For both young men and young women that we have worked with, culture and contexts of marginalisation and disadvantage commonly frame the words used as weapons of shame. While some young men referenced sexualised slurs as known and familiar ways of enacting shame, this was more common for young women. Almost all young women we have worked with report their first experiences of shame as either a sexual slur or a combination of a racial and sexual slur. Young women reported that they experienced these from the time they started school. Connected with crime, but with a heavier gaze towards notions of betrayal or cowardice, young women consistently report that the worst word used to enact shame is "snitch" (see Figure 10.2). Even symbolically the idea of snitching was serious and threatening and associated with significant (anticipated) shame.

Figure 10.2 Words used to describe shame by young women in NNN

We've also witnessed self-directed violence for young women (particularly self-harm) associated with shame. Young women in the group have noticed and been uncomfortable with evidence of self-harm among peer participants. When we explored this discomfort, connotations made links to weakness, a characteristic that was othered and inconsistent with their sense of self as strong, self-reliant, and self-protective. As noted earlier, families were often discussed by young women as a frequent source of frustration, disappointment, and shame. This was rarely raised by young men, though in work with incarcerated young men, one participant shared in a Postcard to Practice that shame "stops me from believing that family will change".

Concerningly for us, we also saw systems and supports use shame to connect notions of criminality with young women's identity. We saw both untrained and highly trained practitioners openly make witnessed comments to young women about their future actions linked to either their past justice involvement or that of their family; for example, "Oh, don't worry, next time you get charged you'll have me again" (intimating a future likelihood that the young woman would get charged again) or "At least you're doing better than your mum. By the time she was your age. . . . What was more troubling was that these examples, which amount to shaming, were enacted by women, in relational ways. In both instances (and there were other examples), the relation between the young woman and the practitioner was inferred and referenced familiarity with the young woman's history and likely future. This (false) relationality conferred mixed messages for the young women, with it being common for them to not see this as problematic and as genuine affection or positive regard. At face value, these findings sit at odds with other reflections that young women we have worked with are hypersensitive to perceived potential for threat from other women. Yet we wonder if perhaps they also reflect the power of perceived connection and how powerful this can be in the context of unmet needs for female support.

Image shame versus guilt/moral shame

How young people thought about shame differed according to their age, length of time involved with the justice system, psychological maturity, and the space and safety they had available to them in which to reflect on things that had happened and their connection to their current circumstance. The vast majority of young people we have worked with identify that shame stops them from doing things, trying new things, joining with others, and communicating their feelings, needs, and desires. In conversations with Ray, a young man involved with NNN, he reflected deeply on shame.

Box 10.2 What we've learned . . .

In discussion about how much of a role shame plays in young people's anger and violence, Ray reflected:

> "At least, 40–45% [is the role of shame], yeh".
>
> "When you're angry at the world, you're angry at yourself. When you're angry at the world, like, everything you think is about you and what you're thinking, I guess, about the world, but when you're screaming it out you're letting everyone know who you are and what you are, yeh".
>
> "Like when you're angry, I don't think you're telling the full truth".
>
> "You sort of lie to yourself and everyone else around it".

He continued . . .

> "People can feel the shame in what they wear, how they act, how other people act, what other people wear, they can feel shame in a lot of things . . . Mainly, like, you feel shame when you're either angry with yourself or arguing with someone. You realise it, but, yeh, no, you have more shame and, like, the anger is pushing that out. It's like the shame you see not anger".

I pondered with Ray whether that's why it's hard to help someone's anger, because it's shame they're showing, and it's hard to sort that out for someone else? He responded:

> "Yeh, pretty much, that's what I feel, yeh. I don't want to burden anyone with my stuff. You've got to do it yourself, like, people need support but . . . " (he trailed off shrugging).

Yet not all young people who use violence experience shame in relation to their actions. Farmer and Andrews (2009) found while justice-involved young males reported higher levels of anger than their non-justice-involved peers, their levels of shame were comparatively low and not associated with anger. The authors suggest shame is a contextualised experience, and its experience is determined by the meaning of behaviours in social and cultural contexts.

Few young people we worked with openly discussed shame related to their use of violence though some did, demonstrating developed self-awareness and a real readiness for identity migration. For many young people, as Ray describes, anger is shame projected. It was common amongst the young people we worked with to see blame for their current circumstances (sometimes quite legitimately) externalised to others. Further, a number of young people commented that adults/practitioners needed to know that "shaming" them for their actions was unhelpful.

Box 10.3 What we've learned . . .

Postcards to Practice sent anonymously by young people in NNN had the following advice for adults and practitioners regarding young people and shame:

> "Leave me alone to reflect on choices".
>
> "Time to myself, to relax, right and wrong".
>
> "Adults shaming kids doesn't work".

We've observed that when shame is lifted from its tie to identity (who I am), there is a greater capacity for empathy driven by recognition of impacts of behaviour (what I did).

In NNN we have witnessed naturalistic restorative outcomes for peer participants. Collaborative acts of co-creation and learning in a peer environment led to experiences of caring and sharing for program participants. These participants had often been co-offenders but less frequently victims and offenders against each other. For these young people, impacts of their own trauma alongside and amongst complex community and cultural obligations, norms, and expectation meant that traditional models of restorative justice would, more than likely, replicate structures of power and control, oppression, and loss. Instead, participatory, creative, and collaborative actions provided these young people with chances to make restoration in ways that also increased empathy and care. This seems to reflect critiques of restorative justice that argue that outcomes are rarely actualised remedially (Acorn, 2004) and that the traditional process forces undue burden on the person who experienced harm to quickly excuse or forgive the person who caused them harm (Curtis-Fawley & Daly, 2005).

Takeaways for practice

1. Shame must be considered as a high possibility for young people who have used violence, especially where this has been in their relationships.
2. Shame is difficult to spot, cloaked in a range of behaviours including separation and isolation, displacing blame, defending honour, and lashing out.
3. Being able to work with shame requires building a reciprocal working relationship, acknowledging past trauma, attending to invalidation, and increasing abilities of emotional recognition and regulation.
4. As practitioners, we must be aware of our power to inflict shame and focus on creating the safety required to connect with moral shame.

Conclusion

This chapter has provided a multi-disciplinary, present, and historical overview of shame, especially as it relates to justice contexts and to young people and violence. It recognises the developmental resources required for shame to be present without being debilitating, the relational contexts in which shame can be provoked and worked differently with, and the potential for social shame and stigma to impact on young people in programs such as NNN. We have detailed how NNN approaches work with shame in the program, identified specific activities involved, and set out findings from the program of research incorporated into NNN.

This directs us towards the following chapter which explores the role of choice.

References

Acorn, A. E. (2004). *Compulsory compassion: A critique of restorative justice*. UBC Press.

Ahmed, E. (2002). Shame management: Regulating bullying. In E. Ahmed, N. Harris, J. Braithwaite, & V. Braithwaite (Eds.), *Shame management through reintegration* (pp. 211–314). Cambridge University Press.

Ahmed, E. (2006). Understanding bullying from a shame management perspective: Findings from a three-year follow-up study. *Educational & Child Psychology*, *23*(2), 25–39.

Asser, J. (2022). Shame/violence intervention. In R. Gerodimos (Ed.), *Interdisciplinary applications of shame/violence theory: Breaking the cycle* (pp. 119–135). Springer International Publishing AG. https://doi.org/10.1007/978-3-031-05570-6_1

Bear, G. G., Uribe-Zarain, X., Manning, M. A., & Shiomi, K. (2009). Shame, guilt, blaming, and anger: Differences between children in Japan and the US. *Motivation and Emotion*, *33*(3), 229–238.

Benade, L. (2015). Shame: Does it have a place in an education for democratic citizenship? *Educational Philosophy and Theory*, *47*(7), 661–674. https://doi.org/10.1080/00131857.2014.880644

Bennett, D. S., Sullivan, M. W., & Lewis, M. (2005). Young children's adjustment as a function of maltreatment, shame, and anger. *Child Maltreatment*, *10*(4), 311–323.

Blagg, H. (1997). A just measure of shame? Aboriginal youth and conferencing in Australia. *The British Journal of Criminology*, *37*(4), 481–501. https://doi.org/10.1093/oxfordjournals.bjc.a014193

Blagg, H. (2017). Doing restorative justice otherwise: Decolonising practices in the global south. In I. Aertsen & B. Pali (Eds.), *Critical restorative justice* (pp. 61–78). Hart Publishing.

Blagg, H., & Anthony, T. (2019). *Decolonising criminology: Imagining justice in a postcolonial world*. Palgrave Macmillan UK. https://doi.org/10.1057/978-1-137-53247-3_6

Braithwaite, J. (1989). *Crime, shame and reintegration*. Cambridge University Press.

Braithwaite, J. (2020). Restorative justice and reintegrative shaming. In C. Chouhy, J. Cochran, & C. L. Jonson (Eds.), *Criminal justice theory, volume 26: Explanations and effects* (pp. 281–308). Routledge.

Braithwaite, J., & Mugford, S. (1994). Conditions of successful reintegration ceremonies – dealing with juvenile offenders. *British Journal of Criminology*, *34*, 139–171.

Brown, B. (2006). Shame resilience theory: A grounded theory study on women and shame. *Families in Society*, *87*(1), 43–52. www.doi.org/10.1606/1044-3894.3483

Cairns, P., & Howells, L. (2019). Angry young men: Interpersonal formulation of anger to effect change. In J. A. Barry, R. Kingerlee, M. Seager, & L. Sullivan (Eds.), *The Palgrave handbook of male psychology and mental health* (pp. 351–368). Springer International Publishing. www.doi.org/10.1007/978-3-030-04384-1_18

Crewe, B., Hulley, S., & Wright, S. (2020). *Life imprisonment from young adulthood: Adaptation, identity and time*. Palgrave Macmillan UK. www.doi.org/10.1057/978-1-137-56601-0

Curtis-Fawley, S., & Daly, K. (2005). Gendered violence and restorative justice: The views of victim advocates. *Violence Against Women*, *11*(5), 603–638.

De Boeck, A., Pleysier, S., & Put, J. (2018). The social origins of gender differences in anticipated feelings of guilt and shame following delinquency. *Criminology & Criminal Justice*, *18*(3), 291–313. www.doi.org/10.1177/1748895817721273

Duvall, J., & Béres, L. (2007). Movement of identities: A map for therapeutic conversations about trauma. In C. Brown & T. Augusta-Scott (Eds.), *Narrative therapy: Making meaning, making lives* (pp. 229–250). SAGE Publications. https://doi.org/10.4135/9781452225869

Duvall, J., & Béres, L. (2011). *Innovations in narrative therapy: Connecting practice, training, and research*. W. W. Norton & Company.

Farmer, E., & Andrews, B. (2009). Shameless yet angry: Shame and its relationship to anger in male young offenders and undergraduate controls. *The Journal of Forensic Psychiatry & Psychology*, *20*(1), 48–65.

Fattore, T., & Mason, J. (2020). Humiliation, resistance and state violence: Using the sociology of emotions to understand institutional violence against women and girls and their acts of resistance. *International Journal for Crime, Justice and Social Democracy*, *9*(4), 104–117.

Foucault, M. (1991). *Discipline and punish: The birth of the prison*. Penguin Books.

Fox, B. H., Perez, N., Cass, E., Baglivio, M. T., & Epps, N. (2015). Trauma changes everything: Examining the relationship between adverse childhood experiences and serious, violent and chronic juvenile offenders. *Child Abuse & Neglect*, *46*, 163–173.

Gibson, M. (2016). Social worker shame: A scoping review. *British Journal of Social Work*, *46*(2), 549–565.

Gibson, M. (2019). *Pride and shame in child and family social work* (1st ed.). Bristol University Press. www.doi.org/10.2307/j.ctvdtpj6t.13

Gilligan, J. (2003). Shame, guilt, and violence. *Social Research*, *70*(4), 1149–1180. www.doi.org/10.1353/sor.2003.0053

Goffman, E. (1963). Embarrassment and social organization. In N. J. Smelser & W. T. Smelser (Eds.), *Personality and social systems* (pp. 541–548). John Wiley & Sons. https://doi.org/10.1037/11302-050

Gosling, P., Denizeau, M., & Oberle, D. (2006). Denial of responsibility: A new mode of dissonance reduction. *Journal of Personality and Social Psychology*, *90*, 722–733. www.doi.org/10.1037/0022–3514.90.5.722

Gross, Y. (2020). Erikson's stages of psychosocial development. In J. S. Mio & R. E. Riggio (Eds.), *The Wiley encyclopedia of personality and individual differences, models and theories* (Vol. 1). John Wiley & Sons.

Hamblet, W. C. (2010). *Punishment and shame: A philosophical study*. Lexington Books.

Harris, N. (2007). Shame, ethical identity, and conformity: Lessons from research on the psychology of social influence. In *Regulatory Institutions Network Occasional Paper 12*. Australian National University.

Herman, J. L. (2011). Posttraumatic stress disorder as a shame disorder. In R. L. Dearing & J. P. Tangney (Eds.), *Shame in the therapy hour* (pp. 261–275). American Psychological Association. https://doi.org/10.1037/12326-011

Izard, C. E. (1991). *The psychology of emotions*. Springer Science & Business Media.

Jenkins, A. (2009). *Becoming ethical: A parallel, political journey with men who have abused*. Russell House Publishing.

Kerig, P. K., Becker, S. P., & Egan, S. J. (2010). From internalizing to externalizing: Theoretical models of the processes linking PTSD to juvenile delinquency. In S. J. Egan (Ed.), *Posttraumatic stress disorder (PTSD): Causes, symptoms and treatment* (pp. 33–78). Nova Science Publishers.

Kitayama, S., Markus, H. R., Matsumoto, H., & Norasakkuankit, V. (1997). Individual and collective processes in the construction of the self: Self-enhancement in the United States and self-criticism in Japan. *Journal of Personality and Social Psychology*, 72, 1245–1267. https://doi.org/10.1037/0022-3514.72.6.1245

Lewis, M. (1998). Shame and stigma. In P. Gilbert & B. Andrews (Eds.), *Shame: Interpersonal behavior, psychopathology, and culture* (pp. 126–140). Oxford University Press.

Lewis, M. (2016). Self-conscious emotions: Embarrassment, pride, shame, guilt, and hubris. In L. Feldman Barrett, M. Lewis, & J. M. Haviland-Jones (Eds.), *Handbook of emotions* (4th ed., pp. 792–814). The Guildford Press.

London, R. (2011). *Crime, punishment, and restorative justice: From the margins to the mainstream*. Lynne Rienner Publishers. https://doi.org/doi:10.1515/9781935049678

Mayer, C.-H. (2019). Crime and shame: Reflections and culture-specific insights. In C.-H. Mayer & E. Vanderheiden (Eds.), *The bright side of shame: Transforming and growing through practical applications in cultural contexts* (pp. 117–130). Springer Nature.

McWilliams, J. A. (2017). The neighborhood school stigma: School choice, stratification, and shame. *Policy Futures in Education*, *15*(2), 221–238. www.doi.org/10.1177/1478210317705740

Morrison, A. P. (2011). The psychodynamics of shame. In R. L. Dearing & J. P. Tangney (Eds.), *Shame in the therapy hour* (pp. 23–43). American Psychological Association. https://doi.org/https://doi.org/10.1037/12326-001

Muris, P., & Meesters, C. (2014). Small or big in the eyes of the other: On the developmental psychopathology of self-conscious emotions as shame, guilt, and pride. *Clinical Child and Family Psychology Review*, *17*(1), 19–40.

Nussbaum, M. C. (2004). *Hiding from humanity: Disgust, shame, and the law*. Princeton University Press.

Nussbaum, M. C. (2008). Hiding from humanity: Replies to Charlton, Haldane, Archard, and Brooks. *Journal of Applied Philosophy*, *25*(4), 335–349.

Owen, T., & Fox, S. (2011). Experiences of shame and empathy in violent and non-violent young offenders. *The Journal of Forensic Psychiatry & Psychology*, *22*(4), 551–563. https://doi.org/10.1080/14789949.2011.602096

Paulo, M., Vagos, P., Ribeiro Da Silva, D., & Rijo, D. (2020). The role of shame and shame coping strategies on internalizing/externalizing symptoms: Differences across gender in adolescents. *European Journal of Developmental Psychology*, *17*(4), 578–597. Retrieved April 21, 2023.

Rata, A. (2015). The Mäori identity migration model. *MAI Review*, *4*(1), 3–14.

Rebellon, C. J., Wiesen-Martin, D., Piquero, N. L., Piquero, A. R., & Tibbetts, S. G. (2015). Gender differences in criminal intent: Examining the mediating influence of anticipated shaming. *Deviant Behavior*, *36*(1), 17–41.

Routt, G., & Anderson, L. (2016). Building respectful family relationships: Partnering restorative practice with cognitive-behavioral skill learning. In A. Holt (Ed.), *Working with adolescent violence and abuse towards parents: Approaches and contexts for intervention* (pp. 15–33). Routledge.

Rutter, N., & Barr, U. (2021). Being a "good woman": Stigma, relationships and desistance. *Probation Journal*, *68*(2), 166–185. https://journals.sagepub.com/doi/abs/10.1177/02645505211010336

Ryan, M. T. (1993). Shame and expressed emotion: A case study. *Sociological Perspectives*, *36*(2), 167–183.

Schalkwijk, F., Stams, G. J., Stegge, H., Dekker, J., & Peen, J. (2016). The conscience as a regulatory function: Empathy, shame, pride, guilt, and moral orientation in delinquent adolescents. *International Journal of Offender Therapy and Comparative Criminology*, *60*(6), 675–693. www.doi.org/10.1177/0306624X14561830

Scheff, T. J., & Retzinger, S. M. (1991). *Emotions and violence: Shame and rage in destructive conflicts*. Lexington Books/D. C. Heath and Company.

Schulz, P. (2020). *Male survivors of wartime sexual violence: Perspectives from northern Uganda*. University of California Press.

Stuewig, J., & McCloskey, L. A. (2005). The relation of child maltreatment to shame and guilt among adolescents: Psychological routes to depression and delinquency. *Child Maltreatment*, *10*(4), 324–336. www.doi.org/10.1177/1077559505279308

Tajfel, H. (1982). *Social identity and intergroup relations*. Cambridge University Press.

Tangney, J. P., & Dearing, R. L. (2002). *Shame and guilt*. Guilford Publications.

Tangney, J. P., Stuewig, J., & Mashek, D. J. (2007). Moral emotions and moral behavior. *Annual Review of Psychology*, *58*, 345–372. www.doi.org/10.1146/annurev.psych.56.091103.070145

Tangney, J. P., Wagner, P. E., Fletcher, C., & Gramzow, R. (1992). Shamed into anger? The relation of shame and guilt to anger and self-reported aggression. *Journal of Personality and Social Psychology*, 62, 669–675. www.doi.org/10.1037/0022-3514.62.4.669

Theisen-Womersley, G. (2021). *Trauma and resilience among displaced populations: A sociocultural exploration*. Springer Nature. https://doi.org/10.1007/978-3-030-67712-1

Tomkins, S. S. (1987). Shame. In D. L. Nathanson (Ed.), *The many faces of shame*. Guilford Press.

Weiner, B. (2006). *Social motivation, justice, and the moral emotions: An attributional approach*. Lawrence Erlbaum Associates, Inc

11 Choice, change, and identity

Tamara Blakemore, Louise Rak, and Graeme Stuart

Choice, change, and identity

This chapter considers the role of choice, change, and identity in youth violence. It provides an overview of theories and evidence regarding the links between choice, change, and youth violence and choice, change, and identity migration. It describes how we've approached choice and change in the Name.Narrate.Navigate (NNN) program and the practice approaches we've found useful to strengthen skills of self-awareness and self-regulation. Concluding the chapter, we share the voices and experiences of young people who have participated in NNN. This de-identified information was collected with appropriate ethics approval through practitioner reflections on group work sessions, referencing narratives shared as part of group work activities. These narratives frame a deeper understanding of young people's engagement with crime, violence, or other concerning behaviour as not occurring through a singular or stable pathway. The narratives show young people's use of violence does not follow from initiation to continuation or increase predictably or uniformly but, rather, is shaped by and, in turn, shapes contexts and circumstances bound by context and culture and changing over time and place.

Choice, change, and desistance

The notion of choice pervades our everyday discussions about youth violence and our policies, legislation, and practice in response. Despite a growing understanding of the multiple, dynamic, and contextualised factors that contribute to youth violence, the underpinning narrative of violence as a conscious and directed choice remains persuasive. While this framing of youth violence has its roots in the general theory of crime (Gottfredson & Hirschi, 1990), known today as classical criminology, it remains persuasive because it supports discrete, rather than diffuse, attributions of blame for what is a deeply troubling phenomenon. There's a

DOI: 10.4324/9781003177883-11

sense of certainty, predictability, and safety in a worldview built around such attributions, one that is reinforced by strategic choices of the media in deciding how to discuss the knowns and unknowns of stories relating to youth violence (Nichols, 2011) and the political imperatives of governments faced with tackling the alternative.

The inevitability of scapegoating and victim blaming associated with such worldviews can raise tricky questions about how we tackle choice in our work with youth violence, especially when we recognise that young people who use violence have often also experienced violence. If we consider our work with youth violence to be motivated by goals of desistance and we assume that involves change, then, ultimately, we are challenged to consider, "How do people change?" and, relatedly, "What is the role of choice in change towards desistance?" Answers to these interconnected questions will depend on what we understand desistance to be and how we understand people come to make and sustain changes it requires.

The notion of desistance is about change that involves cessation, stopping, abstaining, refraining, or *desisting* from particular acts (McNeill & Maruna, 2007). In relation to crime, the notion of desistence refers to a process encompassing implicit but distinguishable phases of cessation and *sustained* cessation from criminal acts (Uggen & Kruttschnitt, 1998). These phases have been referred to by Laub and Sampson (2001) as termination versus desistance and by Maruna and Farrall (2004) as primary versus secondary desistance. McNeill (2016) suggests a third phase of desistance signifies when change and desistance are socially recognised. Weaver (2019) explains that while these phases are not understood to be sequential or linear, the language used to describe them can often mean they are interpreted as such. The author references Nugent and Schinkel's (2016, p. 570) alternate framework that describes phases of desistance as "act-desistance" (ceasing criminal acts), "identity desistance" (where ideas about the self shift alongside changed behaviour), and "relational desistance" (when these changes are recognised by others) (Weaver, 2019).

Theories of desistance differ in their explanations of how people make and sustain change. They alternately describe factors and processes involved as individual and agentic, social, and structural, or interactionist (Barry, 2010; Maruna, 1997). The earliest ideas about desistance emphasised biologically driven change (experienced in the natural process of development, ageing, and maturation) amd explained that people simply grow out of crime (Goring, 1919; Glueck & Glueck, 1937). Referred to as developmental, ontogenic, or maturational reform theories, these understandings of desistance remain influential, bolstered by evidence from large-scale longitudinal studies demonstrating an age-crime curve, explaining involvement in crime peaks around 18 years and steadily decreases thereafter (Hirschi & Gottfredson, 1983; Moffitt, 1993). Neuroscience-informed studies suggest this may be due to psychological and physical manifestations of reward sensitivity peaking during adolescence, while skills for cognitive control are still developing, meaning young people may be more likely to engage in risk-taking behaviours compared to younger or older cohorts (Shulman et al., 2016). While age remains one of the strongest predictors of desistance (McNeill et al., 2012), critiques of ontogenic theories observe they don't provide enough detail about what it is about maturation (e.g., biological changes, social transitions, learning, and life experience) that explains variable experiences of change towards desistance (Maruna, 1997).

The emergence of volition, agency, and choice in our understandings of desistance began to gain prominence in the 1980s. Rational choice theories (Clarke & Cornish, 1985) suggest people make a conscious decision to desist from crime because of reappraising the relative costs and benefits associated with crime (Paternoster, 1989; Shover, 1983). Haigh (2009) observes underscoring this is some sense of emerging doubt about known beliefs and practices, which may have developed in response to an aversive experience (Haggard et al., 2001) or an accumulation of negative experiences (Cusson & Pinsonneault, 1986). This is characterised by Paternoster and Bushway (2009, p. 1121) as a "crystallization of discontent" or dissatisfaction with life. Referencing Alfred Schutz's (1973) analysis of systems of relevance, Haigh (2009) emphasises that without doubt or dissatisfaction, deliberation and decision-making about change will not occur. Haigh (2009) sees the experience of doubt and deliberation as a vulnerable state of transition involving an element of loss as the taken-for-granted world is dismantled. The author notes Schutz (1973) suggests transition occurs over time rather than being an immediate choice between two competing options (Haigh, 2009). Choices towards change and desistance are also influenced by whether we think the outcomes of our behaviour are within our control (Ahlin, 2014). Locus-of-control theories argue that when people believe they have control over their life and their outcomes, they are more likely to see outcomes as directly attributable to their behaviour and, hence, amenable to change (Lefcourt, 1982; Ahlin, 2014).

Choice is thought to play a necessary, but perhaps not entirely sufficient, role in explaining change and desistance (McNeill et al., 2012). Social control theories suggest "turning points" in life (e.g., marriage, employment, parenthood) contribute to desistance by altering our social bonds or ties to institutions of social control (e.g., family, work, school) (Laub & Sampson, 1993). These events bring with them expectations and obligations incompatible with involvement in crime, disrupt accustomed routines, and establish new routines and activities of daily life that reduce opportunities for involvement in crime (Farrall, 2002; Giddens,

1979). Other ideas of desistance informed by social control theories suggest the social bonds offered by adulthood can see young people "drift" away from crime (Matza, 1964), sentiments echoed by social learning–informed observations that once young people disassociate or weaken ties with peers in the context of new or evolving roles and relationships, they are less likely to engage in crime (Warr, 1998). The power and potential of life events to support change depend on the meaning or symbolic weight afforded to them (Giordano et al., 2002; Maruna, 2001). Interactionist theories, while still emphasising the importance of exchanges between the individual and their social and structural contexts, extend our understanding of desistance as involving subjective changes to the person's sense of self and identity that have important effects on people's behaviour (Bottoms et al., 2004; Barry, 2010; Weaver, 2015). These theories acknowledge cognitive and agentic change happens either in response to or preceding social and structural experiences and events and that these changes can evoke and sustain desistance.

Choice, change, and identity

Interventions for youth violence, at their core, hope to stimulate change and assist young people to move towards more adaptive (and socially acceptable) ways of being and doing. Stein and Markus (1996) suggest that successful and sustained change involves a corresponding change in our sense of self and our identity. Similarly, Maruna and Roy (2007) suggest desistance is likely to result from changes in our "self-identity and worldview" (p. 115). The construct of youth identity is complex and thought about in many different ways across disciplines, with debate spanning its meaning, the processes involved, and its goals and objectives (Abrams & Hyun, 2008). Understandings of youth identity tend to conceptualise it as a dynamic process involving conceptions of our current self, what we were like in the past, and our hopes and fears about what we will be like in the future, shaped by feedback from our social interactions and structural power arrangements, including gender, culture, and socioeconomic position (Strahan & Wilson, 2004).

Adolescence is a critical period for the contemplation of *possible future selves* and identity exploration and formation (Erikson, 1968). The notion of possible future selves (hereafter, possible selves) is explained by Markus and Ruvolo (1989) as our ideas of ourselves in the future, reflecting our aspirations, expectations, and concerns. Possible selves are thought to motivate us towards change and growth (Markus & Nurius, 1986) by serving as reference points for evaluating our current selves (Strahan & Wilson, 2004). In a search for self, Phelan et al. (1993) explain that young people find themselves confronted by multiple and sometimes competing representations of the self, according to different reference points (e.g., gender, culture, age, sexuality, and socioeconomic status), as they traverse the "multiple worlds" of everyday life, with each new situation and setting having its own values, norms, beliefs, expectations, and obligations to negotiate (p. 7). How well young people are able to find and form an integrated sense of self as they travel across and between spaces will be determined by the congruence or dissonance of norms and values of different settings and the strategies young people have access to for navigating difference (Phelan et al., 1993).

For some young people, justice involvement brings with it a new context in which to negotiate their identity. Abrams et al. (2008) argue that, for young men, justice involvement and, particularly, incarceration can reinforce norms, beliefs, and practices of hegemonic masculinity (Connell, 1995), privileging power, status, hierarchy, misogyny, and homophobia. Juxtaposed with this, intervention programs both overtly and covertly impose norms of middle class and normative citizenship, constructing a dichotomy between future and current notions of the self as "good" versus "bad" and encouraging incarcerated young men to envision more socially acceptable notions of who they want to be (Abrams et al., 2008). The dissonance between intervention and setting is compounded by expectations implicit in interventions of profound and rapid change, involving self-reflection that young people describe as painful and threatening (Abrams & Hyun, 2008).

The possible selves model of change explains change (as is required in youth violence interventions) requires contemplating possible selves and reassessing our values and goals before settling on which possible self to pursue and shifting away from previous ideas of self that are no longer useful (Wurf & Markus, 1991; Dunkel et al., 2004). This process has been linked to the stages of change model (Prochaska & DiClemente, 1982), which argues change (including desistance) occurs through five nonlinear stages: (1) *precontemplation*: where people are unaware or have little awareness that a problem exists and/or change is needed; (2) *contemplation*: where people have become aware there is a problem and are actively contemplating change; (3) *preparation*: where people have decided to take action and are planning or testing out steps toward change; (4) *action*: where people are putting their plans into action and are actively modifying their behaviour, experiences, and/or environment; and (5) *maintenance*: where people are working to sustain change (Prochaska & DiClemente, 1982; Prochaska et al., 2013).

In mandated or involuntary contexts, it is suggested that people are likely to be pre-contemplative of change (Babcock et al., 2005; Begun et al., 2001), not seeing a need for change and not desiring change or defensive about being pushed to change (Willoughby & Perry, 2002).

It should be noted that when people are in a pre-contemplative stage of change, they may have yet to consider a range of possible selves or may have fewer hoped-for possible selves (Dunkel et al., 2004). Studies have found justice-involved young people report fewer possible selves and are less likely to endorse positive possible selves compared to non-justice-involved peers (Oyserman & Markus, 1990; Oyserman et al., 2002). Reasons for this may relate to whether justice-involved young people perceive they need to change and the centrality of the problem (e.g., youth violence) to the person's concept of self (Dunkel et al., 2004). By implication, if youth violence is central to a young person's self-concept, changing the problem means restructuring of the identity as well, while if, on the other hand, youth violence is not seen as central to the young person's self-concept, then they may change the problem without changing their identity (Dunkel et al., 2004). Whether young people perceive violence as central and/or a problematic aspect of their identity may also reflect the messages they receive through feedback from social interaction. Oyserman and Fryberg (2004) observe that any possible or alternative selves we envisage for ourselves will be shaped by the perceived value of alternative identities and the probability of achieving them according to what we've learned in our social world. In this way, social contexts can either be empowering or undermining of aspirations, growth, and change (Oyserman & Fryberg, 2004). The subjective temporal distance (Ross & Wilson, 2000, 2002) between justice-involved young people's current sense of self and any possible future selves is also important. Strahan and Wilson (2004) suggest that where possible future selves feel too far away or too out of reach, they are less likely to motivate people's actions towards change.

The cognitive transformation theory (Giordano et al., 2002) offers an alternative idea of how change occurs, particularly as it relates to desistence from crime. The authors suggest a necessary precondition for desistence is an openness or motivation towards change (Giordano et al., 2002). Further, that in such conditions, real and tangible scaffolding to support, enable, and sustain change needs to be present. This can include housing, employment, or education and emotional connections and relationships. Giordano et al. (2002) explain that these factors (which they refer to as "hooks") provide a context through which new identities develop and, over time, replace old ones. Giordano et al. (2002) note this process may not be linear and that progress towards desistence relies on interrelated individual, social, and structural factors that shape access to and control over resources and opportunity. This theory articulates that if we consider our behaviours and actions as part of our identity, then contemplating change can involve what White and Epston (1990) described as identifying an aspect of our identities that is no longer viable.

How successful young people will be at navigating and negotiating choices towards positive change will depend on their readiness or openness to change (Giordano et al., 2002). Some authors have suggested that the factors and processes involved in our readiness to change seem to be poorly understood (Ward & Eccleston, 2004), leading to a situation where we know more about *what* works for youth violence than *when* these interventions are best implemented (Burrowes & Needs, 2009). Existing theories of readiness for change for young people who use violence draw upon the notion of treatment readiness originally developed by Serin and colleagues in justice contexts (Serin, 1998; Serin & Kennedy, 1997). They variously point to the influence of internal factors (including cognitive, affective, volitional, and behavioural states) and external factors (such as voluntary/involuntary status, location, supports, and resources) in explaining what helps position people to make choices towards positive change (Ward et al., 2004). Arguably, the first model to explain people's readiness to change was Prochaska and DiClemente's (1982) stages of change model, focusing on the processes used to achieve change (Carroll et al., 2013). This model has been used with justice-involved young people (Hemphill & Howell, 2000), suggesting that their readiness for change is determined by whether they are in the contemplation or action states of change (Burrowes & Needs, 2009). As Drieschner et al. (2004) point out, though, knowing a young person is contemplating change doesn't tell us what they are contemplating and what motivates that contemplation. Burrowes and Needs (2009) suggest that in this way, the stages of change model offers a limited understanding of readiness to change.

In response, they propose a readiness-to-change framework, suggesting contextual factors that support choices for change (described in the context-for-change model) interact with internal barriers that might hinder such choices (described by the barriers-to-change model) to explain a person's readiness to change (Burrowes, 2006; Burrowes & Needs, 2009). Contextual factors that support readiness to change are identified as including factors that characterise the individual and their environment but also, importantly, what the author describes as the *catalyst* for change (Burrowes, 2006), a construct like the idea of turning points discussed earlier. Ten barriers to readiness to change are identified, all related to perceptions the person may have about the importance of change, the need for change, personal responsibility for change, urgency of change, cost benefits of change, costs associated with the means of change, suitability and efficacy of the means for change, abilities required to achieve and maintain change, and the realities of change (Burrowes & Needs, 2009). The significance of self-perception and its roots in broader cognitive processes of beliefs, attitudes, schemas, and strategies has been noted in a number of discussions relating to readiness for change (Carroll et al., 2013; Chambers et al., 2008; Lopez & Emmer, 2002). Carroll et al. (2013) note an important observation across these discussions is that the same cognitive factors and processes likely to influence *readiness for change* are also themselves the *target of change*. The implication of this for youth violence interventions is that choices for change are likely part of a movement towards change that could take time to develop in strength and momentum.

Choice in NNN

Choice is explored in the final group work session of NNN. The session commences with a mindfulness-focused activity: Mindful Jenga. This activity involves choice (which block to pull to prevent the tower from tumbling) and mindful consideration of prompts that focus on self-awareness, self-regulation, and contemplation of possible future selves. Other activities in the session explore ideas of equity and choice in relationships and concrete strategies for choice making.

Our work with choice in NNN is focused on creating opportunities and strengthening skills for the safe exploration of possible future selves. The work is framed by an understanding that when young people contemplate making choices towards desistance, this can implicate required changes in their sense of self and their identity. Our thinking about choice, change, and identity is consistent with the postmodern and social constructionist philosophies of narrative therapy that perceive identities as fluid and pluralistic rather than fixed, static, and singular (White, 1995). Thinking about identities as fluid allows for the possibility for movement from an identity defined by actions and experiences towards one that is reflexive and strengths-focused, including aspects of survival, resistance, and growth (Duvall & Béres, 2007). As practitioners, we believe this stance is critical in warning against pathologising interactions with the young people we work with and crucial to creating

Table 11.1 Program structure and session focus: Choice

Program structure	*Session*	*Focus*
		Beginnings
	1	Emotions
	2	Voice
	3	Empathy
	4	Power and Control
	5	Shame
	6	**Choice**
		Endings

a relational experience where it is possible for them to experience themselves in different ways than they might have had the opportunity to in other service, support, and learning contexts.

Practice approach

Narrative therapy's understanding of identities as socially constructed, contextually (and structurally) influenced, and fluid over time is a particularly fitting frame for our work with young people who use violence. Consistent with this frame, we work from the position that we're not there to uncover the absolute right or wrong choice (or truth) but, rather, to explore the experience and outcomes of multiple interpretations and multiple truths. As noted by Duvall and Béres (2007), "This philosophical position that we take in our work informs our interactions and our way of being in relation to people" (p. 234). Essential to this is creating a safe distance between the young person and acts or experiences which have the potential to define or characterise them in negative ways. We tend to do this by using the narrative therapy technique of externalising (White & Epston, 1990). This involves naming acts and experiences as external constructs, separate from the young person. For example, we might start by discussing "the role of choice in violence", scaffolding towards "choices people (in general) make" before approaching "choices you might make". Externalising choice does not mean excusing actions or nullifying harm associated with that choice. Rather, by considering choice (or, relatedly, shame, violence, etc.) as separate from the young person, any threats to the sense of self are lessened, and there is a greater chance of being able to collaboratively deconstruct problems, evaluate behaviours, and reconsider possible futures.

We also find the idea of a conversational map, based on the notion that "people's lives are multi-storeyed experiences" (Duvall & Béres, 2007, p. 234), a useful, implicit guide to our practice conversations with young people who use violence. Duvall and Béres (2007) suggest conversational maps can capture the significance and meaning in people's stories, allowing them to find similarities and differences and identify themes and context to their experiences. The authors suggest five primary "elements of inquiry", including the *points of stories* (in our work, what the young person thinks is important to convey); the *backstory* (outlining the social and spatial context of experience); *pivotal events* (the things that have happened for the young person that give their experience meaning and contribute to their sense of self); *evaluation of effects* (for us, this relates to how young people have responded to experiences and events and how they perceive the outcomes of this); and *summary* (which relates to our reflections on what young people have shared and our tentative observations towards possible alternative futures).

Narrative therapy techniques can also be used to frame in-the-moment awareness of experience, consistent with the practice of mindfulness (Beaudoin, 2020; Percy & Paré, 2021a, 2021b; Zimmerman, 2018). Mindfulness-based activities are scaffolded throughout the NNN program with the aim and objective of strengthening skills for self-awareness and self-regulation. In our work, we are guided by Jon Kabat-Zinn's (1991) understanding of mindfulness as both the practice and experience of purposefully paying attention in the moment and noticing, without judgement, our unfolding thoughts, feelings, and physical states. It involves openness, curiosity, acceptance, and compassion towards the self, with the aim and objective of improved wellbeing (Bishop et al., 2004; Eberth & Sedlmeier, 2012; Kabat-Zinn, 2003). Mindfulness achieves this through its dual focus on the self-regulation of attention and nonjudgemental awareness, which means, with practice, we can become more aware of our cognitive and emotional response to events or experiences and this awareness can facilitate re-configured, more regulated responses, ultimately resulting in improved outcomes (Bishop et al., 2004).

The relationship between narrative and mindful approaches is well-explained by Percy and Paré (2021a, 2021b), who observe that while narrative work has a discursive focus on the dominant stories that contextualise the meaning we make of our experience, mindfulness draws attention to what captures (and distracts) our attention. Percy (2008) reflects "both narrative (approaches) and mindfulness foreground embodied experience, promote curiosity and an exploratory attitude toward our lives" (p. 362). Percy and Paré (2021b) argue that mindfulness is a valuable tool in narrative work (focused on identity migration) because it enhances skills for self-awareness and self-regulation required to unpack familiar and known practices, beliefs, and meanings. Further, practicing paying attention in a detached way to our experiences simulates an autonomous practice of externalising experience and can de-couple the seemingly automatic meanings we tend to attach to events, emotions, or experience by virtue of our socialisation and acculturation to dominant discourses (Percy & Paré, 2021b). Mindfulness improves our capacities for self-regulation by increasing our self-awareness and our ability to recognise and tolerate distress (Barrett et al., 2001; Witkiewitz et al., 2013). This is thought to occur through the overlapping processes of sensitisation and desensitisation involved in focusing our awareness on our experiences from a nonjudgemental and distanced space which provides time for cognitive reappraisal to occur (Schuman-Olivier et al., 2020).

Mindfulness in NNN

As a practice and experience, mindfulness can be achieved through a variety of techniques (Bishop et al., 2004). While often taught and practiced through meditation (Linehan, 2015; Schuman-Olivier et al., 2020), "not all meditation is mindfulness and not all mindfulness is meditation" (Schuman-Olivier et al., 2020, p. 372). In NNN, we focus on what Linehan (2015) describes as the "what" skills for mindfulness, including the "intentional process of observing, describing, and participating in reality nonjudgementally, in the moment, with effectiveness (i.e., using skilful means)" (p. 154). Referencing Linehan (2015), we describe these skills as involving (1) *observing*: noticing or paying attention to things inside or outside of ourselves using our senses; (2) *describing*: putting our observations into works, sticking to observable facts without judgement; and (3) *participating*: completely engaging in an activity while letting go of judgement.

Activities involving these skills are intentionally scaffolded in each NNN session. These activities seek to strengthen young people's capacities to observe and describe their feelings, thoughts, and behaviours and those of others around them. Greater self-awareness as well as a practice in nonjudgementally noting, but not reacting to, environmental cues achieved over the course of the program may then assist young people to achieve a point of readiness and regulation for more targeted recidivist-focused or therapeutic interventions.

Mindful Jenga

In the choice session, the mindfulness activity is Mindful Jenga. It involves participants and practitioners taking turns to choose and remove pieces from the Jenga tower and respond to a mindful prompt written on each piece (see Figure 11.1). Prompts capture mindful observation (e.g., "What can you hear right now?"), mindful description (e.g., "Name one thing that always makes you laugh") and mindful participation (e.g., "Take three deep breaths"). The prompts also capture conceptions of past selves (e.g., "What is your favourite memory") and possible future selves (e.g., "Describe your ideal day"); the identification of difference (e.g., "Name one thing that is going well right now" versus "Name one thing that's not going well right now") and intentionality for change ("Name three things you want to work on"). While we always advise that people can skip the prompt if they want and we offer to read out prompts if we think it will overcome literacy challenges, we have rarely experienced young people opting out of the activity, and where the tower does fall, there's often calls to repeat the activity. This activity seems to establish a settled, sometimes reflective but usually engaged, presence in the session, which enables deeper exploration of concepts of choice and change.

Figure 11.1 Mindful Jenga

Table 11.2 Practice note: Mindful Jenga

Practice note: Mindful Jenga	
Description:	A participatory mindfulness activity stimulating self-reflection and requiring self-regulation and choice.
Time:	15 minutes
Purpose:	To practice and model observational, descriptive, and participatory mindfulness, using prompts exploring past, present, and future conceptions of self; points of difference; and intentionality for change. The content and process of the activity stimulates self-awareness and self-regulation.
Resources:	A Jenga set – with mindfulness prompts added to each piece.
Presentation:	Young people and practitioners take turns in removing one piece from the tower, reading the mindful prompt, and carrying out the instruction before returning their piece to the top of the tower. You can remove any piece except the one on the top. The activity is over when the tower falls.
Rationale:	Studies show executive functions we rely on for self-regulation (including those responsible for focusing and shifting our attention and inhibiting or activating our behavioural responses in flexible ways) are strengthened by mindfulness practice (Hölzel et al., 2011; Vago & Silbersweig, 2012). Further, a body of research finds positive effects of mindfulness for justice-involved young people's experience of anger (Barnert et al., 2014; Himelstein et al., 2012b, 2015; Milani, 2013), aggression and violence (Singh, 2017), anxiety and stress (Barnert et al., 2014; Himelstein et al., 2012a, 2012b), psychological wellbeing and behavioural function (Himelstein et al., 2012a, 2012b; Shonin et al., 2013), self-awareness and self-regulation (Barnert et al., 2014; Barrett et al., 2016; Himelstein et al., 2012a, 2012b, 2014) attentional focus, and engagement (Himelstein et al., 2012a, 2012b; Leonard et al., 2013).

What we've learned

Over the course of the group work sessions in NNN to date, young people have shared with us rich narratives of their experiences that refute stereotypes of youth violence as a homogeneous or unitary construct. These narratives also generally reject notions of young people's use of violence as typically mindless, unthinking, or unconsidered. Instead, some young people describe violence to find and form connection, for acceptance and protection, to communicate needs, to redress injustice, and to establish identity. These findings are consistent with previous studies (e.g., O'Driscoll, 2011; Mares, 2001) where choice, volition, and agency play a contextualised role in young people's narratives of their use of violence. This is not to advocate for violence or excuse the harm caused, but rather, like others (e.g., Garot, 2007; Jones, 2004), we think it calls for a deeper understanding of the social and structural contexts that give rise to violence becoming a viable option for some young people. We also think some social and structural contexts need to be considered in how we support desistance. Where young people we work with are considering, have considered, or have achieved change towards desistance, the role of choice in this process has been contextualised and sometimes constrained. Where change has been achieved, we see young people making pragmatic choices and often experiencing both gain in the loss of former identities and loss in the gain of new ones.

Choice is contextualised

Mindfulness activities across the program provide an interesting insight into how young people experience and use choice. We see real synergies in the Mindful Jenga activity (described previously) and the notion of choice as it relates to change. As participants and practitioners take turns in choosing which piece to remove, weighing up different choices, sometimes attempting to remove one but then selecting another, attention is usually concentrated and focused on not making the tower fall and less on avoiding prompts that could cause vulnerability or discomfort.

Box 11.1 What we've learned . . .

Tasmin is a 15-year-old Aboriginal woman who participated in NNN. Tasmin's cultural identity was important to her, but it was also something she wanted to be deeper and set apart from the violence she saw daily at home and on the mission. She was not encouraged to seek more knowledge from her parents, particularly her father – so it was a conscious choice to want more for herself and one that was not without risk.

It was through the Jenga prompt "I wish I knew more about" that allowed Tasmin the introduction she needed to share her desire to learn more about her Aboriginal cultural heritage with the NNN group:

> "Yeah, I wish I knew more about being Aboriginal and stuff. It's hard though because he [father] is so angry, like, all of the time . . . you can't ask him . . . so I need to think about ways to do it".

When we explored choice in the context of relationship behaviours, we found young people were less certain and less agreed on what this could look like compared to power and control (see Chapter 9). In a reverse of the activity described to map power and control in relationships, in the session focused on choice, we explore with young people what equity and choice might look like and what gives people equity and choice in their relationships. Again, using a large drop sheet to brainstorm ideas and NNN cards to explore visual examples of the concepts mapped, we explore questions including, "Do we have a choice over the types of relationships we have?", "What choices can we make (in our relationships)?", "What influences our choices?"; and "Is it a choice to use violence?" (see Figure 11.2).

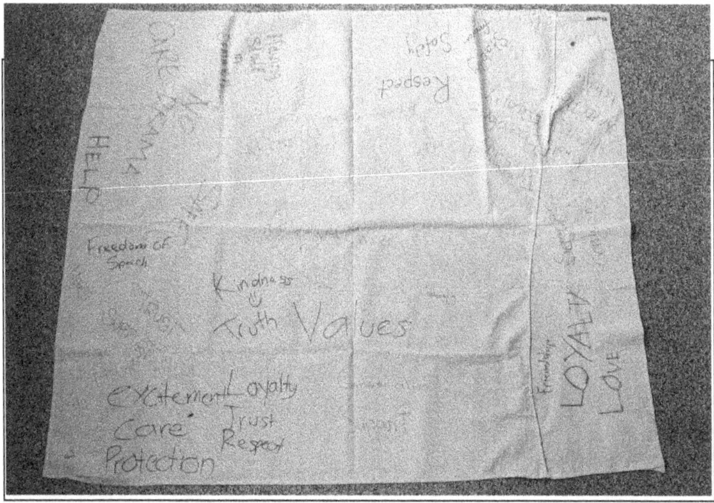

Figure 11.2 Equity and choice map

Box 11.2 What we've learned . . .

Young men in detention identified relationship behaviours associated with equity and choice that they valued most (but felt they had the least) as:

> "Love, loyalty, trust, honesty and respect".

In discussion they all agreed these relationship behaviours involve choice. They noted they tend to rely on what they've experienced before to inform the choices they make in relationships and were deeply reflective about the different types of choices they might need to make to have these much longed for characteristics in their lives.

Reflecting on work with young men in detention, there was uniform agreement with the idea that it is a choice to use violence. This is consistent with what we have been told by young people in community settings, though, there, the contextualised and sometimes constrained nature of choice has been more readily discussed. For some young people, their use of violence and/or their subsequent justice involvement has sat uncomfortably with their sense of self or how they wish to be perceived by others (see discussion of the Shame Coat activity in Chapter 10). As reflected in one young man's Postcard to Practice, many were at pains to tell us, "I'm really a nice guy". These observations of contradictory behaviour and shifting presentations of self align with Goffman's (1959) dramaturgical perspective on how we can enact different "selves" in various situations and Hewitt's (1988) idea of the situated self as shaped by and towards the different situations we find ourselves in. Further support for these ideas was found in the observation that for some young people, their use of violence portrayed a public identity that meant they weren't someone to be messed with or gave them certain kudos or capital in particular settings. These observations fit with Emler and Reicher's (1995) model of delinquency, which emphasises how criminal acts can be "a form of self-presentation through which young people manage their public reputations" (p. 7). This idea was certainly consistent with what we observed for young men we worked with in detention. The deep contemplation we observed for some of these young men at varying points of the group work program gave us pause to wonder whether they felt trapped by the identities their use of violence conveyed and how easy it would be to make choices towards change and desistance, especially where these identities held protective or contextually endorsed value.

Choice can be challenging

The challenges associated with choice have been highlighted for us through an activity we use in NNN to scrutinise the concrete steps involved in choice-making. Inspired by Linehan's (2015) "pros and cons grid", we have explored how young people evaluate the positives and negatives of making (or not making) choices informed by instinct or impulse in scenarios meaningful to them. The aim of this activity is not to convince participants to make a particular choice but, rather, to establish a shared understanding of the considerations that might be involved in choice-making for young people who use violence.

Box 11.3 What we've learned . . .

Considering the positives and negatives of choices that might result in getting involved in crime after his release from detention, Jamal engaged readily in listing what he saw as potential negatives of such choice:

> "Being back in here, missing out on time and special events with family, the food here, not having freedom, missing family".

But considering the positives of these same choices was readily as easy:

> "Money, excitement, family, being part of it, . . . it's just what you do".

When considering positives and negatives of choices to get involved in crime or choices not to get involved in crime, Jamal ultimately explained:

> "I probably will, even though I know . . . even knowing what it's like here and all these things . . . I probably will".

Jamal's mention of excitement as a potential motivator for getting involved in crime (including violence) may be explained by opponent-process theory. Baumeister and Campbell (1999) suggest that while causing harm might be experienced as aversive at first, over time, this aversion diminishes while positive feedback responses grow, hence outweighing natural aversion. There was real resignation in Jamal's narrative, a sense that some choices (and outcomes) were inevitable. We had heard this before from a young man in the community who, having not been in detention, felt he'd "probably end up in jail". This was despite him having limited contact with the justice system to date and having considerable access to personal skills and abilities that could serve as strong protective factors for future justice involvement. In further conversation with Jamal, there was a sense that there would be real loss in any gains associated with desistance. Barry (2006) reported similar findings, suggesting the agency required in desistance means not only choosing not to get involved in criminal activity but also giving up sources of stability, continuity, and sociability.

By contrast, some young women saw any such loss as inconsequential to loss associated with choices that could lead them to (continue) to get involved with crime. Two young women, considering the positives and negatives of a choice to use violence against a residential caseworker with whom there had been considerable conflict, discussed how this choice would breach bail conditions and would almost certainly lead to a custodial sentence. As one young woman explained to the other:

> Yes it's shit being in resi, but you've spent a week inside before right? You do your plan, you go back in. I've had over two years, and it's worse than resi . . . I could have made different choices.

Another young woman, amid considerable conflict with peers and considering using violence, explored positives and negatives of such a choice before coming to the decision that doing nothing was a viable alternative for her though a peer reflected, "*Sometimes doing nothing can be a good choice, sometimes it's not*".

Choice is possible and probable in the right conditions

We observe young people we work with who have made changes towards desistance have often done so in the context of different relationship choices involving distancing or disassociating themselves from peers involved in criminal activity. This is consistent with findings long reported in the literature (e.g., Knight & West, 1975; Barry, 2006) and sometimes associated with developmental understandings of desistance. Stewart et al. (1994) document the influence of peers diminishes rapidly with age, noting while 45% of 17-year-olds in their study report having been influenced by peers, only 18% of 23-year-olds report the same level of influence. Commencing relationships was also associated with changes towards desistance for some young people we worked with. Commenting on what had changed for him, one young man said, "I met a nice girl that believed in me and helped me like do things that I didn't think I could

Figure 11.3 Self made

do". Other young people re-engaged with education or entered employment while also disassociating from contexts or connections where they were previously engaged in criminal activity (see Figure 11.3).

For young people we have worked with who have made choices and changes towards desistance, there has been both loss in the gain and gain in the loss. One young woman who had gone on to find independent accommodation, complete educational qualifications, enter the workforce, and start a family lamented often missing the connections she once had and was noted by her former caseworkers to still "call to check in". While the identity shift to partner, worker, and mother for this young woman seems outwardly complete, there were ties to her former life that seemed to offer reassurance and without which her new identity may have seemed less stable. This observation gave us pause to consider the tension between narratives of connection and independence for young people in transitioning to new identities. The desire to be seen as self-made, self-reliant, and self-determining was common among many of the young people we have worked with, and striking out independently was common in their achieving desistance. Yet, we reflect that the human need for connection is also critical in sustaining change and, echoing Sauma (2008), wonder how practice best supports not only possible future selves but also possible future connection.

There was also considerable gain in the loss of former identities tied to criminal activity and the use of violence. Choices to get involved or desist from crime were described in young people's narratives as contextual, consequential, cumulative, and exhausting.

Box 11.4 What we've learned . . .

One young man explained it as being free from what he recalled as an exhausting experience:

> "You start out sad, sad turns to anger, anger gets you locked up. Getting locked up means you get out and put on parole. You can't do any drugs, so you start drinking. You see your mates going out and doing stuff, and you want to go out doing it with them and then . . . you end up getting over it, and then you wanna just live your life".

Stronger skills for self-awareness, self-regulation, and connection have seen young people we have worked with enter meaningful employment, re-engage with education, and form positive peer associations that bring with them new identities and ways of being and doing in the world. Importantly these new identities seem to be endorsed by others and have involved the narrative re-storying of how young people see themselves considering their previous experiences (McNeill & Maruna, 2007). For those who have made the most significant shifts, we saw an interest and willingness to participate in generative activities (Maruna, 2001).

Box 11.5 What we've learned . . .

For some young people, there is a sense that new identities that emerge out of old ones are sometimes strengthened by experience:

> "Sounds fucked, but I wouldn't change anything. Like, I am who I am now through all of my experiences, I'm doing somewhat good for an 18-year-old, I'm doing better than most 18-year-olds. You know this is just a part of my life that's only

> just starting, and I'm really trying to knuckle down and get shit done, so yeh I wouldn't change much of my choices. Besides, I dunno, like, being an absolute, like, little shit to my old case-workers and stuff, like, being a little more engaging and get a bit more further, but that's about it". (Ray)

And for others that they had something important to give back to young people like them:

> "I want to help those kids as much as I can to change, I've been in those ways before, and I want to see them change. It's how far I've come, and I can see where I was then . . . I enjoy people see how I have changed". (Jazz)

Maruna's (2001) landmark research on "going straight" suggests desistance is sustained when people who have been involved in crime find new identities with a care-oriented, other-centred focus. For people found to desist from crime, this focus on generative activity is often accompanied by a desire for lasting accomplishment and self-concepts that incorporate life histories as redemptive, hopeful, and strengths-based stories of survival (Maruna, 2001; White, 2007). These findings implore practice with youth violence to better consider how we support the development of generativity to achieve and sustain identity migration and desistance.

Takeaways for practice

1. Interventions for youth violence can be enhanced by supporting young people to consider possible future selves and strengthening skills and conditions that support choices towards change.
2. Choice can involve agentic change and/or be shaped by social and structural factors – it is rarely simple, often constrained, and rarely linear.
3. Choices towards change and desistance can involve loss in the gain. The agency required for change towards desistance can, at least in the short term, involve not only choosing to desist from criminal acts (including violence) but also foregoing human and social capital.
4. Choices towards change and desistance can also involve gain in the loss, particularly when new identities are able to incorporate old ones and result in generative good.

Conclusion

This chapter has considered the role of choice in change towards desistance. It has presented a selective overview of the ways in which choice has been understood in relation to change and desistance and in relation to shifts in self-concept and identity. The chapter presented an overview of the practice approach to work with choice in NNN, highlighting how concepts and techniques from narrative therapy have framed mindfulness to strengthen self-awareness and self-regulation in readiness for moving towards new ideas of what's possible to know and do.

References

Abrams, L. S., Anderson-Nathe, B., & Aguilar, J. (2008). Constructing masculinities in juvenile corrections. *Men and Masculinities*, *11*(1), 22–41.

Abrams, L. S., & Hyun, A. (2008). Mapping a process of negotiated identity among incarcerated male juvenile offenders. *Youth & Society*, *41*(1), 26–52. https://doi.org/10.1177/0044118x08327522

Ahlin, E. M. (2014). Locus of control redux. *Journal of Interpersonal Violence*, *29*(14), 2695–2717. https://doi.org/10.1177/0886260513520505

Babcock, J. C., Canady, B. E., Senior, A., & Eckhardt, C. I. (2005). Applying the transtheoretical model to female and male perpetrators of intimate partner violence: Gender differences in stages and processes of change. *Violence and Victims*, *20*(2), 235–250. https://doi.org.10.1891/vivi.2005.20.2.235

Barnert, E. S., Himelstein, S., Herbert, S., Garcia-Romeu, A., & Chamberlain, L. J. (2014). Exploring an intensive meditation intervention for incarcerated youth. *Child & Adolescent Mental Health*, *19*(1), 69–73. https://doi.org/10.1111/camh.12019

Barrett, L. F., Gross, J., Christensen, T. C., & Benvenuto, M. (2001). Knowing what you're feeling and knowing what to do about it: Mapping the relation between emotion differentiation and emotion regulation. *Cognition & Emotion*, *15*(6), 713–724. https://doi.org/10.1080/02699930143000239

Barrett, L. F., Quigley, K. S., & Hamilton, P. (2016). An active inference theory of allostasis and interoception in depression. *Philosophical Transactions of the Royal Society B: Biological Sciences*, *371*(1708), 20160011. https://doi.org/10.1098/rstb.2016.0011

Barry, M. (2006). *Youth offending in transition: The search for social recognition*. Routledge.

Barry, M. (2010). Youth offending and youth transitions: The power of capital in influencing change. *Critical Criminology*, *15*(2), 185–198.

Baumeister, R. F., & Campbell, W. K. (1999). The intrinsic appeal of evil: Sadism, sensational thrills, and threatened egotism. *Personality and Social Psychology Review*, *3*(3), 210–221.

Beaudoin, M. N. (2020). Affective double listening: 16 dimensions to facilitate the exploration of affect, emotions, and embodiment in narrative therapy. *Journal of Systemic Therapies*, *39*(1), 1–18. https://doi.org/10.1521/jsyt.2020.39.1.1

Begun, A. L., Shelley, G., Strodthoff, T., & Short, L. (2001). Adopting a stages of change approach for individuals who are violent with their intimate partners. *Journal of Aggression, Maltreatment & Trauma*, *5*(2), 105–127. https:// doi.org/10.1300/J146v05n02_07

Bishop, S. R., Lau, M., Shapiro, S., Carlson, L., Anderson, N. D., Carmody, J., Segal, Z. V., Abbey, S., Speca, M., Velting, D., & Devins, G. (2004). Mindfulness: A proposed operational definition. *Clinical Psychology: Science and Practice*, *11*(3), 230–241. https://doi.org/10.1093/clipsy.bph077

Bottoms, A., Shapland, J., Costello, A., Holmes, D., & Grant, M. (2004). Towards desistance: Theoretical underpinnings for an empirical study. *The Howard Journal*, *43*(4), 368–389.

Burrowes, N. (2006). *Time to change? Offender readiness to change their offending behaviour* [PhD dissertation submitted to the British Library]. University of Portsmouth.

Burrowes, N., & Needs, A. (2009). Time to contemplate change? A framework for assessing readiness to change with offenders. *Aggression and Violent Behavior*, *14*(1), 39–49. https://doi.org/10.1016/j.avb.2008.08.003

Carroll, A., Ashman, A., Bower, J., & Hemingway, F. (2013). Readiness for change: Case studies of young people with challenging and risky behaviours. *Australian Journal of Guidance and Counselling*, *23*(1), 49–71. https://doi.org/10.1017/jgc.2012.17

Chambers, J. C., Eccleston, L., Day, A., Ward, T., & Howells, K. (2008). Treatment readiness in violent offenders: The influence of cognitive factors on engagement in violence programs. *Aggression and Violent Behavior*, *13*(4), 276–284. https://doi.org/10.1016/j.avb.2008.04.003

Clarke, R. V., & Cornish, D. B. (1985). Modeling offender's decisions: A framework for research and policy. In M. Tonry & N. Morris (Eds.), *Crime and justice: An annual review of research* (Vol. 6, pp. 147–185). University of Chicago Press.

Connell, R. W. (1995). *Masculinities*. University of California.

Cusson, M., & Pinsonneault, P. (1986). The decision to give up crime. In D. B. Cornish & R. V. Clarke (Eds.), *The reasoning criminal: Rational choice perspectives in offending* (pp. 72–82). Springer-Verlag.

Drieschner, K. H., Lammers, S. M., & van der Staak, C. P. (2004). Treatment motivation: An attempt for clarification of an ambiguous concept. *Clinical Psychology Review*, *23*, 1115–1137.

Dunkel, C. S., Kelts, D., & Coon, B. (2004). Possible selves as mechanisms of change in therapy. In C. Dunkel & K. Kerpelman (Eds.), *Possible selves: Theory, research, and applications* (pp. 187–204). Nova Science Publishers.

Duvall, J., & Béres, L. (2007). Movement of identities: A map for therapeutic conversations about trauma. In C. Brown & T. Augusta-Scott (Eds.), *Narrative therapy: Making meaning, making lives* (pp. 229–250). Sage Publications.

Eberth, J., & Sedlmeier, P. (2012). The effects of mindfulness meditation: A meta-analysis. *Mindfulness*, *3*(3), 174–189. https://doi.org/10.1007/s12671-012-0101-x

Emler, N., & Reicher, S. (1995). *Adolescence and delinquency: The collective management of reputation*. Blackwell Publishers.

Erikson, E. (1968). *Identity, youth, and crisis*. W. W. Norton & Company.

Farrall, S. (2002). *Rethinking what works with offenders*. Willan Publishing.

Garot, R. (2007). "Where you from!" Gang identity as performance. *Journal of Contemporary Ethnography*, *36*(1), 50–84.

Giddens, A. (1979). *Central problems in social theory: Action, structure and contradiction in social analysis*. Palgrave Macmillan.

Giordano, P. C., Cernkovich, S. A., & Rudolph, J. L. (2002). Gender, crime, and desistance: Toward a theory of cognitive transformation. *American Journal of Sociology*, *107*, 990–1064.

Glueck, S., & Glueck, E. (1937). *Later criminal careers*. Kraus.

Goffman, E. (1959). *The presentation of self in everyday life*. Penguin Books.

Goring, C. (1919). *The English convict* (Abridged ed.). His Majesty's Stationery Office.

Gottfredson, M. R., & Hirschi, T. (1990). *A general theory of crime*. Stanford University Press.

Haggard, U. A., Gumpert, C. H., & Grann, M. (2001). Against all odds: A qualitative follow-up study of high-risk violent offenders who were not reconvicted. *Journal of Interpersonal Violence*, *16*(10), 1048–1065.

Haigh, Y. (2009). Desistance from crime: Reflections on the transitional experiences of young people with a history of offending. *Journal of Youth Studies*, *12*(3), 307–322. https://doi.org/10.1080/13676260902775077

Hemphill, J., & Howell, A. (2000). Adolescent offenders and stages of change. *Psychological Assessment*, *12*(4), 371–381.

Hewitt, J. (1988). *Self and society*. Allyn and Bacon.

Himelstein, S., Hastings, A., Shapiro, S., & Heery, M. (2012a). Mindfulness training for self-regulation and stress with incarcerated youth: A pilot study. *Probation Journal*, *59*(2), 151–165. https://doi.org/10.1177/0264550512438256

Himelstein, S., Hastings, A., Shapiro, S., & Heery, M. (2012b). A qualitative investigation of the experience of a mindfulness-based intervention with incarcerated adolescents. *Child and Adolescent Mental Health*, *17*(4), 231–237. https://doi.org/10.1111/j.1475-3588.2011.00647.x

Himelstein, S., Saul, S., & Garcia-Romeu, A. (2015). Does mindfulness meditation increase effectiveness of substance abuse treatment with incarcerated youth? A pilot randomized controlled trial. *Mindfulness*, *6*(6), 1472–1480. https://doi.org/10.1007/s12671-015-0431-6

Himelstein, S., Saul, S., Garcia-Romeu, A., & Pinedo, D. (2014). Mindfulness training as an intervention for substance user incarcerated adolescents: A pilot grounded theory study. *Substance Use & Misuse*, *49*(5), 560–570. https://doi.org/10.3109/10826084.2013.852580

Hirschi, T., & Gottfredson, M. R. (1983). Age and the explanation of crime. *American Journal of Sociology*, *89*, 552–584.

Hölzel, B. K., Lazar, S.W., Gard, T., Schuman-Olivier, Z., Vago, D. R., & Ott, U. (2011). How does mindfulness meditation work? Proposing mechanisms of action from a conceptual and neural perspective. *Perspectives on Psychological Science*, *6*(6), 537–559. https://doi.org/10.1177/1745691611419671

Jones, N. (2004). "It's not where you live, it's how you live": How young women negotiate conflict and violence in the inner city. *The Annals of the American Academy of Political and Social Science*, *595*(1), 49–62.

Kabat-Zinn, J. (1991). *Full catastrophe living: Using the wisdom of your body and mind to face stress, pain and illness*. Delta.

Kabat-Zinn, J. (2003). Mindfulness-based interventions in context: Past, present, and future. *Clinical Psychology: Science and Practice*, *10*(2), 144–156. https://doi.org/10.1093/clipsy.bpg016

Knight, B. J., & West, D. J. (1975). Temporary and continuing delinquency. *British Journal of Criminology*, *15*(1), 43–50.

Laub, J. H., & Sampson, R. J. (1993). Turning points in the life course: Why change matters to the study of crime. *Criminology*, *31*(3), 301–325.

Laub, J. H., & Sampson, R. J. (2001). Understanding desistance from crime. In M. H. Tonry & N. Morris (Eds.), *Crime and justice: An annual review of research* (Vol. 26, pp. 1–78). University of Chicago Press.

Lefcourt, H. M. (1982). *Locus of control: Current trends in theory and research* (2nd ed.). Lawrence Erlbaum Associates, Inc.

Leonard, N. R., Jha, A. P., Casarjian, B., Goolsarran, M., Garcia, C., Cleland, C. M., Gwadz, M. V., & Massey, Z. (2013). Mindfulness training improves attentional task performance in incarcerated youth: A group randomized controlled intervention trial. *Frontiers in Psychology*, *4*. https://doi.org/10.3389/fpsyg.2013.00792

Linehan, M. M. (2015). *DBT skills training manual* (2nd ed.). The Guilford Press.

Lopez, V. A., & Emmer, E. T. (2002). Influences of beliefs and values on male adolescents' decision to commit violent offenses. *Psychology of Men & Masculinity*, *3*, 28–40.

Mares, D. (2001). Gangstas or lager louts? Working class street gangs in Manchester. In M. W. Klein, H.-J. Kerner, C. L. Maxson, & E. G. M. Weitekamp (Eds.), *The Eurogang paradox: Street gangs and youth groups in the U.S. and Europe* (pp. 153–164). Kluwer Academic Publishers.

Markus, H., & Nurius, H. (1986). Possible selves. *American Psychologist*, *41*, 954–969.

Markus, H., & Ruvolo, A. (1989). Possible selves: Personalized representations of goals. In L. A. Pervin (Ed.), *Goal concepts in personality and social psychology* (pp. 211–241). Lawrence Erlbaum Associates, Inc.

Maruna, S. (1997). Going straight: Desistance from crime and life narratives of reform. In A. Lieblich & R. Josselson (Eds.), *The narrative study of lives* (Vol. 5, pp. 59–93). SAGE Publications.

Maruna, S. (2001). *Making good: How ex-convicts reform and rebuild their lives*. American Psychological Association.

Maruna, S., & Farrall, S. (2004). Desistance from crime: A theoretical reformulation. *Kolner Zeitschrift fur Soziologie und Sozialpsychologie*, *43*, 171–194.

Maruna, S., & Roy, K. (2007). Amputation or reconstruction? Notes on the concept of "knifing off" and desistance from crime. *Journal of Contemporary Criminal Justice*, *23*(1), 104–124. https://doi.org/10.1177/1043986206298951

Matza, D. (1964). *Delinquency and drift*. John Wiley & Sons.

McNeill, F. (2016). Desistance and criminal justice in Scotland. In H. Croall, G. Mooney, & M. Munro (Eds.), *Crime, justice and society in Scotland* (pp. 200–216). Routledge.

McNeill, F., Farrall, S., Lightowler, C., & Maruna, S. (2012). How and why people stop offending: Discovering desistance. In *Insights evidence summary to support social services in Scotland*. www.iriss.org.uk/sites/default/files/iriss-insight-15.pdf

McNeill, F., & Maruna, S. (2007). Giving up and giving back: Desistance, generativity, and social work with offenders. In P. Raynor & G. McIvor (Eds.), *Developments in social work with offenders* (pp. 224–339). Jessica Kingsley Publishers.

Milani, A., Nikmanesh, Z., & Farnam, A. (2013). Effectiveness of mindfulness-based cognitive therapy (MBCT) in reducing aggression of individuals at the Juvenile correction and rehabilitation center. *International Journal of High Risk Behaviors & Addiction*, *2*(3), 126. https://doi.org/10.5812/ijhrba.14818

Moffitt, T. (1993). "Life-course persistent" and "adolescent-limited" antisocial behaviour: A developmental taxonomy. *Psychological Review*, *100*, 674–701.

Nichols, S. L. (2011). Media representations of youth violence. In C. Barter & D. Berridge (Eds.), *Children behaving badly? Peer violence between children and young people* (pp. 167–179). https://doi.org/10.1002/9780470976586.ch12

Nugent, B., & Schinkel, M. (2016). The pains of desistance. *Criminology and Criminal Justice*, *16*(5), 568–584.

O'Driscoll, A. (2011). *Creating shared meaning: Narratives of youth violence, mindfulness, and counselling psychology* [Unpublished Doctoral thesis]. City University London. https://openaccess.city.ac.uk/id/eprint/11663/

Oyserman, D., Coon, H. M., & Kemmelmeier, M. (2002). Rethinking individualism and collectivism: Evaluation of theoretical assumptions and meta-analyses. *Psychological Bulletin*, *128*(1), 3–72. https://doi.org/10.1037/0033-2909.128.1.3

Oyserman, D., & Fryberg, S. (2004). The possible selves of diverse adolescents: Content and function across gender, race and national origin. In C. Dunkel & K. Kerpelman (Eds.), *Possible selves: Theory, research, and applications* (pp. 17–39). Nova Science Publishers.

Oyserman, D., & Markus, H. R. (1990). Possible selves and delinquency. *Journal of Personality and Social Psychology*, *59*(1), 112–125. https://doi.org/10.1037/0022-3514.59.1.112

Paternoster, R. (1989). Decisions to participate in and desist from four types of common delinquency: Deterrence and the rational choice perspective. *Law and Society Review*, *23*(1), 7–40.

Paternoster, R., & Bushway, S. (2009). Desistance and the feared self: Toward an identity theory of criminal desistance. *Journal of Law and Criminology*, *99*(4), 1103–1156.

Percy, I. (2008). Awareness and authoring: The idea of self in mindfulness and narrative therapy. *European Journal of Psychotherapy and Counselling*, *10*(4), 355–367.

Percy, I., & Paré, D. (2021a). Narrative therapy and mindfulness: Intention, attention, ethics, part 1. *Journal of Systemic Therapies*, *40*(3), 1–14. https://doi.org/10.1521/jsyt.2021.40.3.1

Percy, I., & Paré, D. (2021b). Narrative therapy and mindfulness: Intention, attention, ethics, part 2. *Journal of Systemic Therapies*, *40*(4), 1–11. https://doi.org/10.1521/jsyt.2021.40.4.1

Phelan, P., Davison, A. L., & Yu, H. C. (1993). Students' multiple worlds: Navigating the borders of family, peer, and school cultures. In P. Phelan & A. L. Davison (Eds.), *Renegotiating cultural diversity in American schools* (pp. 52–88). Teachers College Press.

Prochaska, J. O., & DiClemente, C. C. (1982). Transtheoretical therapy: Toward a more integrative model of change. *Psychotherapy: Theory, Research & Practice*, *19*(3), 276.

Prochaska, J. O., Norcross, J. C., & DiClemente, C. C. (2013). Applying the stages of change. *Psychotherapy in Australia*, *19*(2), 10–15.

Ross, M., & Wilson, A. E. (2000). Constructing and appraising past selves. In D. L. Schacter & E. Scarry (Eds.), *Memory, brain and belief* (pp. 231–258). Harvard University Press.

Ross, M., & Wilson, A. E. (2002). It feels like yesterday: Self-esteem, valence of personal past experiences, and judgments of subjective distance. *Journal of Personality and Social Psychology*, *82*, 792–803.

Sauma, J. (2008). Street encounters: Betrayal and belonging in youth gangs. *Public Policy Research*, *15*(1), 32–35.

Schuman-Olivier, Z., Trombka, M., Lovas, D. A., Brewer, J. A., Vago, D. R., Gawande, R., Dunne, J. P., Lazar, S. W., Loucks, E. B., & Fulwiler, C. (2020). Mindfulness and behavior change. *Harvard Review of Psychiatry*, *28*(6), 371–394. https://doi.org/10.1097/hrp.0000000000000277

Schutz, A. (1973). *Collected papers 1: The problem of social reality*. Martinus Nijhoff.

Serin, R. (1998). Treatment responsivity, intervention and reintegration: A conceptual model. *Forum on Corrections Research*, *10*, 29–32.

Serin, R., & Kennedy, S. (1997). *Treatment readiness and responsivity: Contributing to effective correctional programming*. Correctional Services.

Shonin, E., Van Gordon, W., Slade, K., & Griffiths, M. D. (2013). Mindfulness and other Buddhist-derived interventions in correctional settings: A systematic review. *Aggression and Violent Behavior*, *18*(3), 365–372. https://doi.org/10.1016/j.avb.2013.01.002

Shover, N. (1983). The later stages of ordinary property offender careers. *Social Problems*, *31*(2), 208–218.

Shulman, E. P., Smith, A. R., Silva, K., Icenogle, G., Duell, N., Chein, J., & Steinberg, L. (2016). The dual systems model: Review, reappraisal, and reaffirmation. *Developmental Cognitive Neuroscience*, *17*, 103–117.

Singh, S. (2017). Understanding aggression among youth in the context of mindfulness. *Indian Journal of Health and Wellbeing*, *8*(11), 1377–1379.

Stein, K. F., & Markus, H. R. (1996). The role of the self in behavioral change. *Journal of Psychotherapy Integration*, *6*(4), 349–384.

Stewart, J., Smith, D., & Stewart, G. (1994). *Understanding offending behaviour*. Longman.

Strahan, E. J., & Wilson, A. E. (2004). Temporal comparisons, identity, and motivation: The relation between past, present and possible future selves. In C. Dunkel & K. Kerpelman (Eds.), *Possible selves: Theory, research, and applications* (pp. 1–16). Nova Science Publishers.

Uggen, C., & Kruttschnitt, C. (1998). Crime in the breaking: Gender differences in desistance. *Law and Society Review*, *32*(2), 339–366.

Vago, D., & Silbersweig, D. (2012). Self-awareness, self-regulation, and self-transcendence (s-art): A Framework for understanding the neurobiological mechanisms of mindfulness. *Frontiers in Human Neuroscience*, *6*. https://doi.org/10.3389/fnhum.2012.00296

Ward, T., Day, A., Howells, K., & Birgden, A. (2004). The multifactor offender readiness model. *Aggression and Violent Behaviour*, *9*(6), 345–673.

Ward, T., & Eccleston, L. (2004). Risk, responsivity, and the treatment of offenders: Introduction to the special issue. *Psychology, Crime, & Law*, *1*(3), 223–227.

Warr, M. (1998). Life-course transitions and desistance from crime. *Criminology*, *36*(2), 183–216.

Weaver, B. (2015). *Offending and desistance: The importance of social relations*. Routledge.

Weaver, B. (2019). Understanding desistance: A critical review of theories of desistance. *Psychology, Crime & Law*, *25*(6), 641–658. https://doi.org/10.1080/1068316x.2018.1560444

White, M. (1995). *Re-authoring lives*. Dulwich Centre.

White, M. (2007). *Maps of narrative practice*. W. W. Norton & Company.

White, M., & Epston, D. (1990). *Narrative means to therapeutic ends*. W. W. Norton & Company.

Willoughby, T., & Perry, G. P. (2002). Working with violent youth: Application of the transtheoretical model of change. *Canadian Journal of Counselling and Psychotherapy*, *36*(4).

Witkiewitz, K., Bowen, S., Douglas, H., & Hsu, S. H. (2013). Mindfulness-based relapse prevention for substance craving. *Addictive Behaviors*, *38*(2), 1563–1571. https://doi.org/10.1016/j.addbeh.2012.04.001

Wurf, E., & Markus, H. (1991). Possible selves and the psychology of personal growth. In D. J. Ozer, J. M. Healy, & A. J. Stewart (Eds.), *Perspectives on personality* (Vol. 3, pp. 39–62). Jessica Kingsley.

Zimmerman, J. (2018). *Neuro-narrative therapy: New possibilities for emotion-filled conversations*. W. W. Norton & Company.

12 NNN, a (new) way of working

Tamara Blakemore and Chris Krogh

What we've learned (so far)...

We imagine this book may have taken you, the reader, on quite a journey, contemplating what youth violence means, how we respond to it, what the Name.Narrate.Navigate (NNN) program has looked like, and what it has found and foretold about practice in this context. For us, this book presents a moment-in-time snapshot of taking stock in a long and continuing journey of learning in, through and from our practice. In this final chapter, we draw together our learnings (so far) and offer an overview of the place we have come to in thinking about work with youth violence. We recognise this is vastly different from the place we started and that it will not be the place we remain over time. We see synergies here with the final group work session of the NNN program where, after reflecting on their progress, we invite participants to complete a final Postcard to Practice sharing words of advice for us as workers but also for their future selves. In this chapter, we share some of these Postcards as reflective prompts for practitioners, noting that what young people want us to know and think about can provide great clarity and perspective to our work.

Contrasts and contradictions

Our work with youth violence has taught us that the young people we work with exist in space that is neither protected by notions of childhood nor aided by the independence of adulthood. This betwixt and between space is characterised by innumerable contrasts and contradictions. The first of which is the plain observation that young people who use violence often experience violence; they are positioned as both harmed and harmful.

Harmed and harmful

In some contexts, young people who use and experience violence simultaneously hold the labels of both victim and offender. As noted, robust

DOI: 10.4324/9781003177883-12

evidence for and from practice substantiates high rates of trauma among justice-involved youth. Reported rates of adverse childhood experiences (ACEs) for these young people are up to 8 times greater than those reported in the community (Abram et al., 2004). Additionally, many belong to what has been referred to as a "crossover" cohort (e.g., Baidawi, 2020), involved with both child protection and youth justice systems. Aboriginal young people are over-represented in this cohort, a finding similarly observed across other countries carrying historic legacies of settler-colonialism such as Canada and Aotearoa/New Zealand.

It is important to emphasise that the majority of young people impacted by trauma do not become involved in crime (Malvaso et al., 2021). In short, risk does not equal destiny. Rather, both the occurrence and outcomes of trauma are multi-determined, situated, enacted, experienced, and sometimes reproduced through shifting sociopolitical and historical landscapes, moderated and mediated by individual and collective strengths. This reality creates a high need for supportive responses from communities and services systems. Yet many young people who use and experience violence have been kept out of much needed systems of support because addressing their use of violence seems to outweigh remediation of the violence used by others against them (see Figure 12.1).

Exploring the realities of justice-involved young people, Levenson and Willis (2019, p. 481) remark, "People convicted of crimes rouse little sympathy". They reason, in societies where crime and justice policy

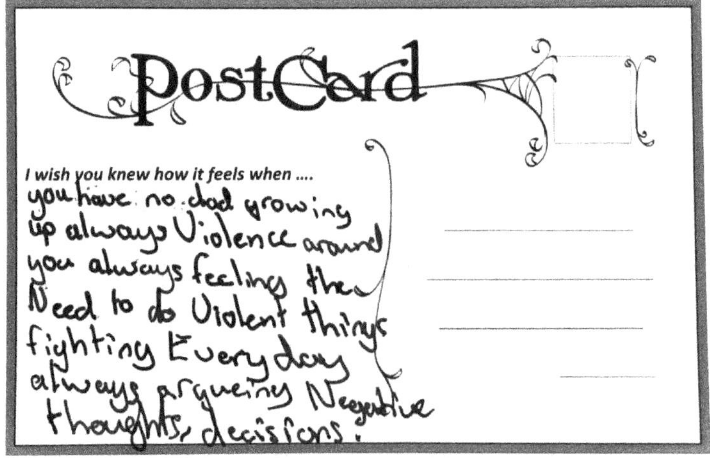

Figure 12.1 Postcard to practice: I wish you knew how it feels when . . .

emphasizes notions of culpability and punishment, it is unsurprising that practice with justice-involved youth has, to date, rarely addressed the role of trauma in crime (Levenson & Willis, 2019). It is our experience that for young people who use violence, the violence, abuse, and trauma in their lives is normalised, or taken for granted, by both practitioners and young people themselves. This seems effectively to disregard the significance of trauma and its impact in conceptions of youth violence. As Levenson and Willis (2019) point out, a trauma lens can enrich our understanding of life course trajectories of crime and better inform prevention and intervention efforts.

Known and unknown

Another contrast and contradiction we observe is that young people who use violence are at once known and unknown, continuously seen but largely unheard. We also reflect on how awareness of youth violence is shaped by media discourse as a highly visual and visceral social problem, which the public feel both familiar with but also at a loss with how to respond. We see this reflected in practice where a sense of familiarity with youth violence does not seem to equate to nuanced understandings of its meaning and motivation. As we noted in the Preface, our work was precipitated by practitioner concern that youth violence was increasing and that needs for available, accessible, and appropriate responses went unmet. While recognising the validity of these concerns, we have worried whether perceived increases in youth violence might reflect an increase in scrutiny and criminalisation of the impacts of trauma, particularly for young women.

It appears to us that something which is both common and troubling intensifies responses to nullify its problematic place in our awareness and its calls on our accountability. This has been most apparent to us in considering young women's use of violence, which seems to raise challenging questions for policy and practice, is often relational, and sometimes is situated in a reciprocated process, oscillating between using violence and experiencing violence, abuse, and trauma (Azad et al., 2018; Odgers et al., 2005). When trauma-related behaviours result in criminal charges, we see a "double penalty" issued – young people are criminalised for their behaviours but also, inherently, for their own victimisation (Blakemore et al., 2021; Segrave & Carlton, 2010; Stubbs, 2011). Notions of the criminalisation of trauma are also highly relevant to understanding the experiences of Aboriginal young people, who live in the aftershocks of violent colonisation, state-sanctioned systematic removal from families and culture (Atkinson et al., 2014), and complex intersections of systemic and structural racism and discrimination and social marginalisation (Barnes & Motz, 2018; Cunneen & Tauri, 2019).

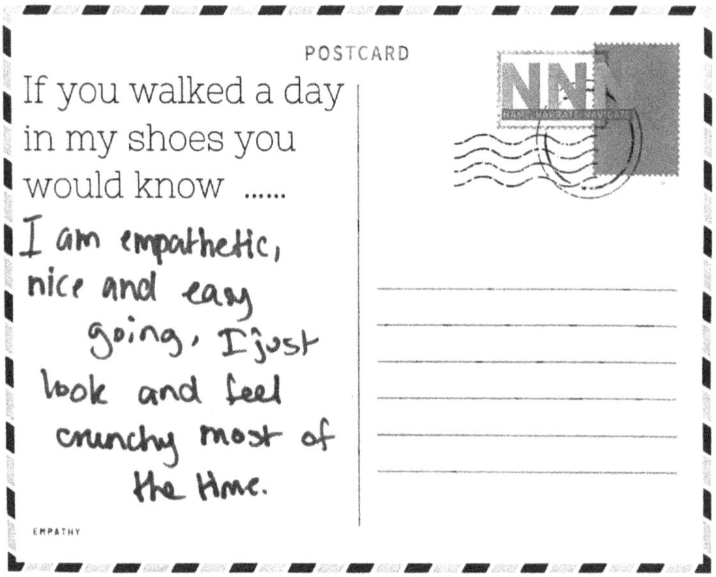

POSTCARD

If you walked a day in my shoes you would know ......

I am empathetic, nice and easy going. I just look and feel crunchy most of the time.

EMPATHY

Figure 12.2 Postcard to practice: If you walked a day in my shoes you would know . . .

Research and practice knowledge about young people who use violence is extensive. What strikes us, though, is how little we know from the perspectives of these young people themselves and how our systems of service and support so often silence their voices. This seems quite different to how policy and practice has engaged with consumer-led responses to mental health and addiction, and we wonder whether this relates to a growing awareness that youth violence is too complex to categorise as an illness or disorder. What is clear to us is that justice-involved young people often feel invalidated in their interactions with practitioners, systems, and structures where apriorist agendas regarding crime and prevention preclude them from being seen for who they are, what they know, and what they need (Fasulo et al., 2015).

This discord is mirrored by youth violence interventions that seek to build young people's capacities for empathy, with limited reference to empathy-led, connection-based design. In our practice we observe connection as an often fraught experience for justice-involved youth, frequently marred by interpersonal and intergenerational trauma as well as structural and systemic disadvantage and disengagement (Blakemore et al., 2018, 2019). We see empathy as a bridge between how young people see and think about themselves and how they see and think about others in relation to themselves. Yet, we don't often see this reciprocated in practice approaches seeking to bolster empathy. Our hunch is empathy in the lives of young people who use violence deserves a much richer narrative that captures the intersubjective experience of both knowing and being known. This reminds us of Carl Rogers' (1964) notions of empathy *as a way of knowing* and the value we see for practice in his description of this as involving subjective, interpersonal, and objective strategies to make sense of the experiences of others.

Agentic and vulnerable

Another contrast and contradiction we observe is that young people who use violence can be at once agents of power and control and vulnerable citizens who may be marginalised and oppressed. Young people who use violence enact different forms of power and control in their interactions with people and systems. They express acts of agency and choice, reaction, and resistance, including but not limited to the use of violence or acts of harm towards themselves, others, and/or their property. Young people who use violence also commonly experience being disempowered and controlled in their interactions with social and structural contexts. How these differing aspects of engagement with power and control

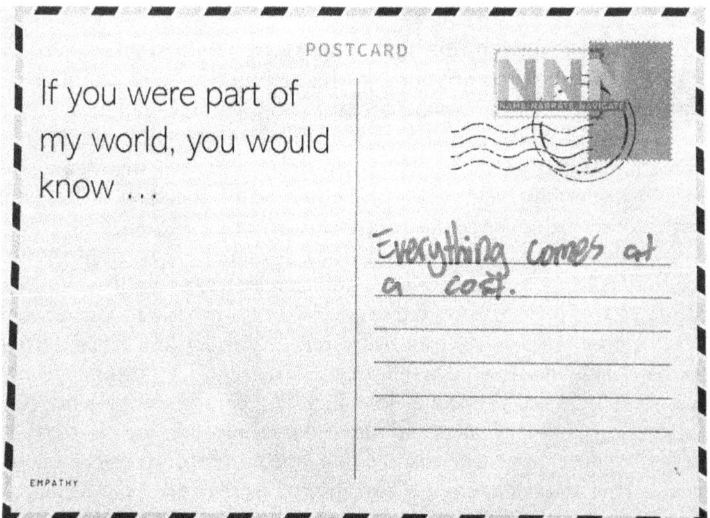

Figure 12.3 Postcard to practice: If you were part of my world you would know . . .

influence each other in temporal order and intensity of effect varies according to context and accumulation. What we tend to see in practice, however, is that these different aspects of power and control are thought about quite separately. Like the distinction between having used and experienced violence, negative acts of power and control are seen and responded to far more than being disempowered and controlled. Even when these contextual factors of young people's violence are described, they are rarely incorporated into programs and interventions.

It is perhaps unsurprising then that young people who use and experience violence seem to have expectations of service systems and practitioners that are bound up in and informed by prior experiences of invalidation, oppression, and control. In thinking about our practice, we have given pause to consider Jenkins' (2009, p. 5) observation that when working with young people in the context of violence/abuse, especially towards adults, "hierarchies are contradictory and inconsistent". Recognising that practitioners typically have a genuine desire to support young people towards safer, healthier, and happier lives and more socially acceptable behaviours, we realise that systemic and structural constraints on practice can mean that it is easy to fall into the trap of applying the power we have to stop young people from using the power they have. This seems to perpetuate dynamics of power and control and potentiate its own influence on youth violence.

Parallel process in practice

The work presented in this book finds practice with youth violence is complex. We think contributing to this complexity is the fact that the challenges faced by practitioners seem to exist almost symbiotically with experiences of young people who use and experience violence. That is, practitioners may experience their own voices silenced in many contexts, their own options limited, and their own actions controlled. Relevant to this observation is the idea of parallel process (Searles, 1955), referring to the ways in which unconscious dynamics experienced by two separate cohorts can be reflected in their interactions with each other. Miller (2004, p. 383) notes the value of parallel process to our practice lies in our willingness and capacity to reflect critically and act reflexively so that "here and now" dynamics between us and the other can be the source of rich and rewarding learning. The parallels we see between experiences of practitioners and the young people they work with relate to individual experiences and the common, if not universal, need for establishing and maintaining a homeostatic sense of power and control.

In reflecting on what we've learned from young people who use violence, we noted that their prior experiences of violence, abuse, and

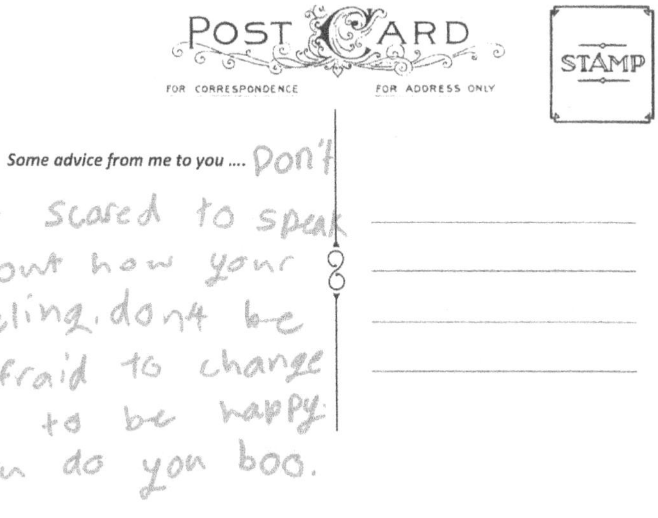

Figure 12.4 Postcard to practice: Some advice from me to you . . .

trauma are often normalised and taken for granted. Said another way, in the vast majority of cases, violence entered the lives of these young people long before they ever used violence against others, and the legacy of traumas they live with are never far from the surface. We think that this may well be the case for us as practitioners, too, when we have had our own life experiences with violence, trauma, and vulnerability. Among the helping professions, it has been well-established that practitioners often come to their work with pre-existing experiences of adversity and trauma, with this likelihood compounded for women (Lee et al., 2017; Steen et al., 2020). Indeed, the desire to help others may be linked to past experiences of needing/receiving help or an allied ethos of religion, spirituality, culture, or personal values and beliefs. Research on career motivation suggests a choice to enter the helping professions can be associated with: (birth) order in family; previous history of or exposure to substance abuse; exposure to other psychosocial trauma including addictive/abusive behaviours, mental or physical ill-health, and other traumatic life events including marriage, separation, and death; and exposure to the profession (i.e., receiving help) (Biggerstaff, 2000; DiCaccavo, 2002; Usher et al., 2013).

Despite being well-intentioned and invested, skilled and experienced, practitioners show signs that this work takes its toll. This is sometimes articulated in their narratives as cynicism, detachment, and despondency about the experiences and likely outcomes for young people. At other times, it is expressed as disconnection from the worlds inhabited by them. We wonder in these contexts whether practitioners experience secondary or vicarious trauma in their work or whether what we are observing is an almost parallel process for practitioners and their clients, with both wanting to be heard yet lacking an authentic and safe common language. Relatedly, the other parallel we see is how practitioners and the young people they work with can vie for power and control. As discussed, power and control represent a pervasive context of our work with youth violence, and often interventions presume a need to enforce control over or reinforce capacities for increasing self-control. Yet, as noted, very little has been written about whether or how interventions with young people who use violence attend to practitioner power in this work. This would address what Jenkins (2009, p. 14) calls the "politics of intervention", recognising that work with violence occurs within dominant social power structures and that practitioners largely represent these social dynamics, including working within powerful institutions and carrying significant social privileges. Jenkins (2009, p. 10) argued, "We have a responsibility to be vigilant for and to critique violent practices whether they are enacted by our clients, statutory and community institutions or (especially) by ourselves".

A (new) way of working

The NNN program for young people was developed with and for the community to address an unmet need for trauma-informed and culturally safe ways of working with youth violence. Our pilot research (Blakemore et al., 2018, 2019) involved conversations with practitioners across sectors of health, justice, policing, education, out-of-home care, mental health, youth work, Aboriginal-led services, and housing. It identified that our colleagues in practice were aware of this gap in accessible and appropriate service delivery as well as a corresponding gap in training to work with young people who experience and use violence. This was the catalyst for NNN, a program that requires practitioners to embrace a distinct way of working. We found that a shift in practice approach and perspective is important, recognising the limited effectiveness of existing programs and the need for a new ethics in practice.

The NNN way of working intentionally merges the neuroscience of trauma with reflexive and relational practice, grounded in an ethic of care, shared power, and reciprocity, consistent with Aboriginal ways of knowing and doing. Key to this is the indivisible nature of trauma-informed and culturally safe practice, especially when working with Aboriginal young people. A culturally safe lens includes an understanding of sociopolitical histories and the complex interplay between overlapping experiences of marginalisation and inherent strengths, all of which shape lives and narratives at collective and individual levels. We often share the observation that "trauma impacts how we tell our story and how we perceive our interactions with others and the world around us". The NNN way of working understands "trauma is directly relevant to understanding the driving factors" underlying young people's involvement in crime and the "driving factors that are likely to contribute to desistence or recidivism" (Kerig, 2013, p. 2). It also appreciates the healing power of cultural identity where collective ties to family, kin, and community are imbued with spiritual connections to Country and honours Aboriginal ways of being, knowing, doing, and belonging (Krakouer et al., 2018).

In our experience, there is both a need for and good engagement with the prospect of working in this way. Practitioners, services, and interventions are working hard to integrate understanding of trauma and culturally competent practice as well as to have culturally informed adaptations of programs available. We see that there is an appetite for extending, improving, and deepening practice in these areas to more fully realise the power of these approaches. We hope the NNN makes a contribution in this domain. Integral to the development and continuous improvement of NNN is that Aboriginal knowledge and ways of doing are respected and foregrounded in the program, for *all* young people, not just those of Aboriginal heritage. We respect the intrinsic fit between what the neuroscience of trauma tells us about impacts of trauma and what we need to heal and Aboriginal wisdom and practices that are inherently strengths-based and healing-informed, emphasising connection as intrinsic to wellbeing (Garvey et al., 2021; Hine et al., 2023; Parter & Wilson, 2021). This approach is consistent with Atkinson's (2013) recommendations that the synergies between Indigenous healing and the neuroscience-informed approaches be realised and Perry's (2009) observations of the relevance of Aboriginal healing practices to the neurosequential model of therapeutics (NMT).

The NNN way of working is guided by practice principles of mindful engagement, the validation of trauma, relationality and reciprocal communication, a power-with approach, and experiential learning. These elements are fundamental to the program's theory of change and have been explored and unpacked in Chapters 6 through 11 in this book. Implementing these principles relies on practice focused on creating significant connections with young people and placing them at the centre of the work. Starting from a trauma-informed and culturally safe ethos, the work is person-centred and sensitive to privilege, power, and place. Further, it is strengths-based and narratively shaped (Levine & Kline, 2006; Scott et al., 2021), recognising young people bring knowledge, skills, stories, and experience that can act as important road maps for practice. Implementing the NNN practice principles involves using reciprocal communication (Linehan, 2015) and creative and experiential methodologies including photo elicitation (Harper, 2002) and Photovoice (Wang & Burris, 1997) to better understand youth violence by positioning young people as experts in a relational and collaborative process of knowing and growing. This process is led by young people's perspectives, reconsidering and restorying social constructions of identity, culture, and Othering. The NNN way of working avoids assumptions about class and cultural and racialised identities that often inform dominant ideas about risk and (criminogenic) needs related to violence. Instead, NNN focuses on the young person's whole story, considering the wider determinants of experience at the intersections of trauma, class, culture, and gender.

Implications for practice and practitioners

We recognise that for some practice settings and some practitioners, the NNN way of working will feel familiar and comfortable. For others, it will involve unpacking previous thinking and ways of relating to and working with young people and, importantly, considering how they conceive of and position themselves in this work. Often this begins with a conversation about the power that practitioners hold in their roles and the ways in which they think about the role of power and control in youth violence and its remediation.

Position and power

The body of work reported in this book reflects what we have found in NNN, that young people's use of violence is not what we commonly think it is. We find that when we are working with young people who have acted violently, we are working as much with vulnerability as with violence, as much with fragility as with danger. This challenges commonly held beliefs that youth violence is about a lack of control and is best remedied by sanctions and practices that reinforce powerful (or dominant) societal norms and expectations. Instead, a central tenet of the NNN way of working is that as practitioners, we need to be critically aware of our own positionality and power, recognising that in our roles, we are often charged with responsibilities that invite us to exercise "power-over" the people we work with. This may be in the form of enacting sanctions or consequences but can also include implications of our actions or inactions in advocating for those with whom we work. There is also the subtle (or not so subtle) invitation in our work to exercise power via our "expert" status in determining what the people we work with need and problem-solving to meet these needs or resolve crises. Resisting the urge to problem-solve and, by association, give advice is one of the most relatable ways that we've found to talk with practitioners about being self-reflective of power in our practice. We are clear that the NNN way of working requires practitioners to sit outside of the need to advise, instruct, coach, or "manage" and instead step into a reciprocal and relational way of working where power is understood to flow between practitioners and young people in ways that are interdependent and can be negotiated (Duck, 2007; Poggi, 2005).

In this way of working, practitioners assume that young people know their life, their situation, and their context better than the worker does. NNN is premised on the idea that time, space, and positive relational conversations, along with effective and engaging activities to explore their realities and needs, provide the foundations for change. Using these resources, young people in the program will come to try out the new knowledge and skills the program offers when they feel ready and safe to do so. From this starting point, practitioners can take a position of learning from and learning with the young person and avoid giving unrealistic advice or trying to direct the young person to change. This approach aims to avoid the pitfalls of challenging or confronting the young person as a pathway to change, which can impact significantly on engagement and reinforce negative experiences of professionals and systems (Linehan, 1997). We find this process requires practitioners to find, collect, and value the momentary and minute signs of respect and change that young people demonstrate rather than expecting or accepting compliance as a measure of meaningful migration in identity and behaviour. We reflect that when we see the harm that is happening to some young people and the harm that they are inflicting on others, a sense of need for radical and urgent change can take hold. We can find ourselves trying to force change which, we have found, rarely ends well.

We are commonly asked how we *manage* or *control* behaviour. Our response relates to how we understand young people's behaviour, how we conceive our role, and how we see both as intertwined with notions of power and agency. Our conception of power in our practice is consistent with Gallagher's (2008) interpretation of Foucault that power "is a form of action, that transforms and influences other actions" (p. 144). We recognise challenging behaviour can be an invitation to vie for power and control over the use of time, what is done, and how it is done. From a trauma-informed perspective, we understand these invitations to be informed by expectation and experience, anxiety and fear, and a self-protective need to establish safety and separation from any source of potential threat, coercion, or control. From a culturally safe lens, we appreciate how dominant social and structural contexts shape experience in ways that can perpetuate marginalisation. As practitioners, we must be conscious of the power that we hold and use it in service of the young people with whom we are working rather than in the service of the systems within which we are embedded. We need to be able to recognise the power that we hold and use it in ways that don't reproduce violence in the service of our responding to the violence abuse these young people have dealt to others.

Vulnerability and self-awareness

As well as recognising our positionality and power, as the preceding chapters have shown, the young people we work with require us to have considered, be self-aware about, and have developed atunement to our own vulnerabilities in our working relationships with them. We must be able to be relationally present with the young people we work with and not overwhelmed by our own emotional states as their vulnerabilities remind us of our own vulnerabilities, their shame reminds us of our own shame, and their trauma reminds us of our own trauma. None of us is immune to trauma and, as noted, many of us come to practice with our own experiences of it. The impacts of existing trauma on professionals can be exacerbated by experiences of burnout, compassion fatigue, and vicarious or secondary trauma. These commonly characterise the impacts of the organisations in which, or with which, we work. (Jacob & Lambert, 2021). In our work as NNN practitioners, we are influenced by Laura van Dernoot Lipsky's (2009) notion of *trauma stewardship*, recognising we hold, simultaneously, an incredible honour and a tremendous responsibility in working with trauma. Trauma stewardship requires us as practitioners to develop a deep sense of self-awareness and recognition of the need to support our own wellbeing while supporting others.

This calls on us as practitioners to undertake what might be thought of as a "parallel journey" (Jenkins, 2009) with our clients, such that everything we require of young people we work with, we must also require of ourselves as workers. In essence, this requires us as practitioners to be vulnerable and to skilfully balance that vulnerability with self-awareness and self-regulation in realising relational and reciprocal practice. Self-awareness is generally considered core to practice effectiveness in the social and human services (Blakemore et al., 2019). It involves an awareness of our own values, beliefs, and ideals; our assumptions; our own prior experience; and our positionality. The fact that our work in these sectors is so often trauma-facing means that skills of self-awareness, critical consciousness, the conscious use of self, emotional intelligence, and reflexivity are critical to the effectiveness of our work and our own wellbeing. Self-awareness is inherent to building helping relationships. It underpins the effective use of interpersonal communication skills like verbal and nonverbal communication and listening (Geroski, 2016) that are core to relational and reciprocal ways of working.

Relationality is "central to Indigenous understandings of kinship" (Dudgeon & Bray, 2019, p. 3) and understood as the "the process of connecting" and ties between people and place (Rose et al., 2003, p. 61). Learning from Aboriginal ways of knowing and doing, we recognise that connecting and building a relationship with the young people we work with is "more than just establishing rapport it is about understanding and honoring history, setting context, and whole-heartedly *hearing* the story" (Bessarab & Ng'andu, 2010, p. 42). Bennett et al. (2011) stress the importance of time, stillness, and silence in being able to effectively hear peoples' stories. Brearley (2014) describes this as *deep listening*, a way of learning and togetherness, involving listening, being present, and developing relationships where listening happens respectfully, responsibly, and with reciprocity. Relational practice requires and inspires regulation. A relational approach understands that practitioners and the young people we work with are often intertwined in generating and experiencing the challenging emotions involved in and instigated by work with youth violence. Effective work in this context involves reflexive processes of negotiation (Campos et al., 2011) that require us to consider how and why our goals may differ, and then relinquishing, modifying, or persevering (Campos et al., 2011) towards consistent, trust-based, and respectful relationships. Working in a relational way that prioritises connection informed by deep listening has supported us to acknowledge the unrecognised, normalised, or delegitimised experiences of trauma for young people we work with.

Creativity and engagement

NNN values creative methods of expression and connection. These methods give voice and visibility to young people's experiences in the context of their cultures and communities. The use of creative practices with justice-involved cohorts has a lengthy history (Ursprung, 1997; Teasdale, 1999). These practices can be easily categorised as art therapy programs or diversional practices with both having been shown to have positive benefits for participants across therapeutic, educational, quality of life, and prosocial engagement outcomes (Johnson, 2008). Yet, creativity in the NNN way of working is not "art therapy". Instead, it involves creative means to story and elicit narratives via processes of observation, recognition, and representation. Our commitment to the methods of photo elicitation (Harper, 2002) and Photovoice (Wang & Burris, 1997) is informed by the fact that they are not only a trauma-informed and culturally safe way to learn about youth violence from young people intimately involved in its experience and use but also that they can be transformative for participants, largely through their capacity to validate previously unrecognised strengths (Budig et al., 2018).

These methods also support the practice of mindful observation, description, and participation. The NNN way of working embraces mindfulness as a means of building skills for self-regulation in the context of the often-chaotic life circumstances of young people who use and experience violence. Consistent with the work of Linehan (2015) and Kabat-Zinn (2015), there is a focus across these activities on noticing and building awareness without falling into "black-and-white" thinking and making judgements. Creative and visual methods are significant in this regard as they can "blur the line between subjectivity, semiosis, visual observation and the performative reflection-in-action required" in practitioners (Chand & Blakemore, in press). The participatory nature of creative methods can also help to flatten power imbalances amongst and between young people and practitioners and open up opportunities for reflective sharing and storytelling. Story is universally central to Aboriginal knowledge systems (Kovach, 2021) and in Western practice recognised in work influenced by Paulo Freire (1970) and his notion that action (and change) occur through reflection inspired by self-awareness, the awareness of others, and the capacity for perspective-taking. Story can also provide a form of safety. As noted in forthcoming work (Chand & Blakemore, in press), "Structure to the affordances of freedom of expression offered by creative methods both contrasts with and complements the unpredictability" of the lives of young people who use and experience violence. These methods provide a safe opportunity for young people to consider alternative perspectives and ways of being and doing in readiness for identity migration.

Next directions

This book has presented our learnings to date from practice with young people who use and experience violence. Sitting alongside this is a broader body of work that has focused on how we strengthen self-awareness, self-regulation, and skills for connection in practice to increase capacity for work that is relational, reciprocal, and balanced in power. Our work with practitioners in this regard has taken the form of intensive, immersive, short- and longer-term training scaffolding trauma awareness; the NNN way of working with youth violence; and latterly, managing the impacts of working with and alongside violence, abuse, and trauma. There is more work to do in this space.

Next directions for the NNN team include exploring how these lessons from young people and practitioners can more deeply shape our teaching in the tertiary sector as we prepare students in social work, human services, and law for a sustainable life of practice. We also look forward to expanding delivery of the NNN program to meet the needs of young people who demonstrate sexually harmful behaviour; those

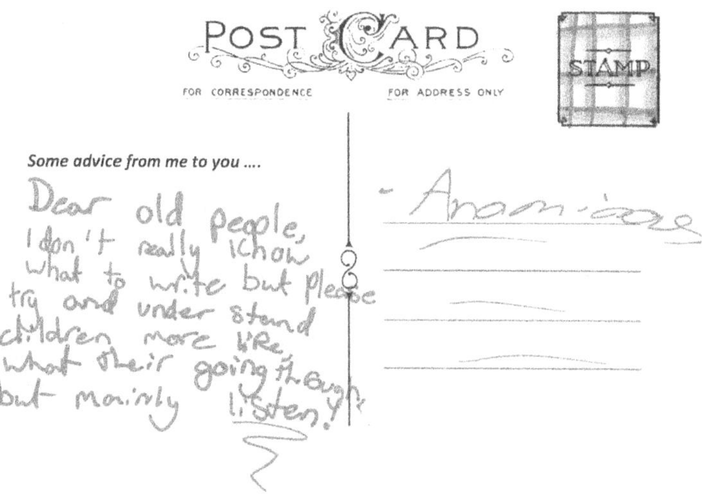

Figure 12.5 Postcard to practice: Some advice from me to you . . .

with diverse gender identities; and to parents, carers, and kin impacted by experiences of violence, abuse, and trauma.

We hope that in reading our learnings to date, whether you have dipped in and out of one chapter or two or read every page from beginning to end, you have found something to take with you as you work in this area, whatever form that work takes. We also hope this is the beginning of a conversation and a new story about what practice with young people who use and experience violence could and should look like into the future.

References

Abram, K. M., Teplin, L. A., Charles, D. R., Longworth, S. L., McClelland, G. M., & Dulcan, M. K. (2004). Posttraumatic stress disorder and trauma in youth in juvenile detention. *Archives of General Psychiatry*, *61*(4), 403. https://doi.org/10.1001/archpsyc.61.4.403

Atkinson, J. (2013). *Trauma-informed services and trauma-specific care for Indigenous Australian children* (Resource sheet no. 21). Produced for the Closing the Gap Clearinghouse. Canberra: Australian Institute of Health and Welfare & Melbourne: Australian Institute of Family Studies.

Atkinson, J., Nelson, J., & Atkinson, C. (2014). Trauma, transgenerational transfer and effects on community wellbeing. In P. Dudgeon., H. Milroy., & R. Walker (Eds.), *Working together: Aboriginal and Torres Strait Islander mental health and wellbeing principles and practice* (pp. 135–144). Kulunga Research Network.

Azad, A., Hau, H. G., & Karlsson, M. (2018). Adolescent female offenders' subjective experiences of how peers influence norm-breaking behavior. *Child and Adolescent Social Work Journal*, *35*(3), 257–270. https://doi.org/10.1007/s10560-017-0526-0

Baidawi, S. (2020). Crossover children: Examining initial criminal justice system contact among child protection-involved youth. *Australian Social Work*, *73*(3), 280–295.

Barnes, J. C., & Motz, R. T. (2018). Reducing racial inequalities in adulthood arrest by reducing inequalities in school discipline: Evidence from the school-to-prison pipeline. *Developmental Psychology*, *54*(12), 2328–2340. https://doi.org/10.1037/dev0000613

Bennett, B., Zubrzycki, J., & Bacon, V. (2011). What do we know? The experiences of social workers working alongside Aboriginal people. *Australian Social Work*, *64*(1), 20–37. https://doi.org/10.1080/0312407x.2010.511677

Bessarab, D., & Ng'andu, B. (2010). Yarning about Yarning as a legitimate method in Indigenous research. *International Journal of Critical Indigenous Studies*, *3*(1), 37–50.

Biggerstaff, M. (2000). Development and validation of the social work career influence questionnaire. *Research on Social Work Practice*, *10*(1), 34–54. https://doi-org.ezproxy.newcastle.edu.au/10.1177/15527581-00010001-06

Blakemore, T., Agllias, K., Howard, A., & McCarthy, S. (2019). The service system challenges of work with juvenile justice involved young people in the Hunter Region, Australia. *Australian Journal of Social Issues*, *54*(3), 341–356.

Blakemore, T., Rak, L., Agllias, K., Mallett, X., & McCarthy, S. (2018). Crime and context: Understandings of youth perpetrated interpersonal violence among service providers in regional Australia. *Journal of Applied Youth Studies*, *2*(5), 53–69.

Blakemore, T., Randall, E., Rak, L., & Cocuzzoli, F. (2021). Deep listening and relationality: Cross-cultural reflections on practice with young women who use violence. *Australian Social Work*, *75*(3), 304–316. https://doi.org/10.1080/0312407x.2021.1914697

Brearley, L. (2014). Deep listening and leadership: An indigenous model of leadership and community development in Australia. In C. Voyageur, L. Brearley, & B. Calliou (Eds.), *Restoring Indigenous leadership: Wise practices in community development* (pp. 91–128). Banff Centre Press.

Budig, K., Diez, J., Conde, P., Sastre, M., Hernán, M., & Franco, M. (2018). Photovoice and empowerment: Evaluating the transformative potential of a participatory action research project. *BMC Public Health*, *18*(1), 1–9.

Campos, J. J., Walle, E. A., Dahl, A., & Main, A. (2011). Reconceptualizing emotion regulation. *Emotion Review*, *3*(1), 26–35. https://doi.org/10.1177/1754073910380975

Chand, A., & Blakemore, T. (in press). Not just art therapy: A case study embedding a design practitioner in youth violence intervention program "Name.Narrate.Navigate" (NNN). In *Design in action: Reflections on social and inclusive practices*. Intellect Books.

Cunneen, C., & Tauri, J. M. (2019). Indigenous peoples, criminology, and criminal justice. *Annual Review of Criminology*, *2*(1), 359–381. https://doi.org/10.1146/annurev-criminol-011518-024630

DiCaccavo, A. (2002). Investigating individuals' motivations to become counselling psychologists: The influence of early caretaking roles within the family. *Psychology and Psychotherapy: Theory, Research and Practice*, *75*(4), 463–472. https://doi.org/10.1348/147608302321151943

Duck, S. (2007). *Human relationships* (4th ed.). SAGE Publications.

Dudgeon, P., & Bray, A. (2019). Indigenous relationality: Women, kinship and the law. *Genealogy*, *3*(2), 23. https://doi.org/10.3390/genealogy3020023

Fasulo, S. J., Ball, J. M., Jurkovic, G. J., & Miller, A. L. (2015). Towards the development of an effective working alliance: The application of DBT validation and stylistic strategies in the adaptation of a manualized complex trauma group treatment program for adolescents in long-term detention. *American Journal of Psychotherapy*, *69*(2), 219–239. https://doi.org/10.1176/appi.psychotherapy.2015.69.2.219

Freire, P. (1970). *Pedagogy of the oppressed*. Herder & Herder.

Gallagher, M. (2008). "Power is not an evil": Rethinking power in participatory methods. *Children's Geographies*, *6*(2), 137–150. https://doi.org/10.1080/14733280801963045

Garvey, G., Anderson, K., Gall, A., Butler, T. L., Whop, L. J., Arley, B., Cunningham, J., Dickson, M., Cass, A., Ratcliffe, J., Tong, A., & Howard, K. (2021). The fabric of Aboriginal and Torres Strait Islander Wellbeing: A conceptual model. *International Journal of Environmental Research and Public Health*, *18*(15), 7745. https://doi.org/10.3390/ijerph18157745

Geroski, A. M. (2016). *Skills for helping professionals*. SAGE Publications.

Harper, D. (2002). Talking about pictures: A case for photo elicitation. *Visual Studies*, *17*(1), 13–26. https://doi.org/10.1080/14725860220137345

Hine, R., Krakouer, J., Elston, J., Fredericks, B., Hunter, S.-A., Taylor, K., Stephens, T., Couzens, V., Manahan, E., DeSouza, R., Boyle, J., Callander, E., Cunningham, H., Miller, R., Willey, S., Wilton, K., & Skouteris, H. (2023). Identifying and dismantling racism in Australian perinatal settings: Reframing the narrative from a risk lens to intentionally prioritise connectedness and strengths in providing care to First Nations families. *Women and Birth*, *36*(1), 136–140. https://doi.org/10.1016/j.wombi.2022.04.007

Jacob, K. M., & Lambert, N. (2021). Trauma exposure response: How secondary trauma affects personal and professional life. *MedEdPORTAL*, 17. https://doi.org/10.15766/mep_2374-8265.11192

Jenkins, A. (2009). *Becoming ethical: A parallel, political journey with men who have abused*. Russell House Publishing.

Johnson, L. M. (2008). A place for art in prison: Art as a tool for rehabilitation and management. *Southwest Journal of Criminal Justice*, *5*(2).

Kabat-Zinn, J. (2015). Mindfulness. *Mindfulness*, 6, 1481–1483. https://christinilleborg.dk/wp-content/uploads/Et-kursus-i-Mindfulness_links.pdf

Kerig, P. K. (2013). *Trauma-informed assessment and intervention*. National Center for Child Traumatic Stress.

Kovach, M. (2021). *Indigenous methodologies: Characteristics, conversations, and contexts*. University of Toronto press.

Krakouer, J., Wise, S., & Connolly, M. (2018). "We live and breathe through culture": Conceptualising cultural connection for Indigenous Australian children in out-of-home care. *Australian Social Work*, *71*(3), 265–276.

Lee, K., Pang, Y. C., Lee, J. A. L., & Melby, J. N. (2017). A study of adverse childhood experiences, coping strategies, work stress, and self-care in the child welfare profession. *Human Service Organizations: Management, Leadership & Governance*, *41*(4), 389–402. https://doi.org/10.1080/23303131.2017.1302898

Levenson, J. S., & Willis, G. M. (2019). Implementing trauma-informed care in correctional treatment and supervision. *Journal of Aggression, Maltreatment & Trauma*, *28*(4), 481–501.

Levine, P. A., & Kline, M. (2006). *Trauma through a child's eyes: Awakening the ordinary miracle of healing*. North Atlantic Books.

Linehan, M. M. (1997). *Validation and psychotherapy*. American Psychological Association.

Linehan, M. M. (2015). *DBT skills training manual* (2nd ed.). The Guilford Press.

Malvaso, C. G., Cale, J., Whitten, T., Day, A., Singh, S., Hackett, L., Delfabbro, P. H., & Ross, S. (2021). Associations between adverse childhood experiences and trauma among young people who offend: A systematic literature review. *Trauma, Violence, & Abuse*, *23*(5), 1677–1694. https://doi.org/10.1177/15248380211013132

Miller, S. (2004). What's going on? Parallel process and reflective practice in teaching. *Reflective Practice*, *5*(3), 383–393. https://doi.org/10.1080/1462394042000270682

Odgers, C. L., Moretti, M. M., & Dickon, N. R. (2005). Examining the science and practice of violence risk assessment with female adolescents. *Law and Human Behavior*, *29*, 7–27.

Parter, C., & Wilson, S. (2021). My research is my story: A methodological framework of inquiry told through storytelling by a doctor of philosophy student. *Qualitative Inquiry*, *27*(8–9), 1084–1094. https://doi.org/10.1177/1077800420978759

Perry, B. D. (2009). Examining child maltreatment through a neurodevelopmental lens: Clinical applications of the neurosequential model of therapeutics. *Journal of Loss and Trauma*, *14*(4), 240–255. https://doi.org/10.1080/15325020903004350

Poggi, G. (2005). Classical social theory, III: Max Weber and Georg Simmel. In A. Harrington (Ed.), *Modern social theory: An introduction* (pp. 63–86). Oxford University Press.

Rogers, C. R. (1964). Toward a science of the person. In T. W. Wann (Ed.), *Behaviorism and phenomenology: Contrasting bases for modern psychology* (pp. 109–140). University of Chicago Press.

Rose, D. B., James, D., & Watson, C. (2003). *Indigenous kinship with the natural world in New South Wales*. NSW National Parks and Wildlife Service.

Scott, J., Jaber, L. S., & Rinaldi, C. M. (2021). Trauma-informed school strategies for SEL and ACE concerns during COVID-19. *Education Sciences*, *11*(12), 796. MDPI AG. http://dx.doi.org/10.3390/educsci11120796

Searles, H. F. (1955). The informational value of the supervisor's emotional experience. *Psychiatry*, *18*, 135–146.

Segrave, M., & Carlton, B. (2010). Women, trauma, criminalisation, and imprisonment. *Current Issues in Criminal Justice*, *22*(2), 287–305. https://doi.org/10.1080/10345329.2010.12035887

Steen, J. T., Senreich, E., & Straussner, S. L. A. (2020). Adverse childhood experiences among licensed social workers. *Families in Society*, *102*(2), 182–193. https://doi.org/10.1177/1044389420929618

Stubbs, J. (2011). Indigenous women in Australian criminal justice: Over-represented but rarely acknowledged. *Australian Indigenous Law Journal*, *15*(1), 47–61.

Teasdale, C. (1999). Report: Developing principles and policies for arts therapists working in United Kingdom prisons. *The Arts in Psychotherapy*, *26*(4), 265–270.

Ursprung, W. A. (1997). Insider art: The creative ingenuity of the incarcerated artist. In D. Gussak & E. Virshup (Eds.), *Drawing time: Art therapy in prisons and other correctional settings* (pp. 13–24). Magnolia Street Publishers.

Usher, K., West, C., MacManus, M., Waqa, S., Stewart, L., Henry, R., Lindsay, D., Conaglen, J., Hall, J., McAuliffe, M., & Redman-MacLaren, M. (2013). Motivations to nurse: An exploration of what motivates students in Pacific Island countries to enter nursing. *International Journal of Nursing Practice*, *19*(5), 447–454. https://doi.org/10.1111/ijn.12095

Van Dernoot Lipsky, L. (2009). *Trauma stewardship: An everyday guide to caring for self while caring for others*. Berrett-Koehler Publishers.

Wang, C. C., & Burris, M. A. (1997). Photovoice: Concept, methodology and use for participatory needs assessment. *Health Education and Behavior*, *24*(3), 369–387.

Index

Note: Page numbers in *italics* indicate a figure or photo and page numbers in **bold** indicate a table on the corresponding page.

For Product Safety Concerns and Information please contact our EU representative GPSR@taylorandfrancis.com
Taylor & Francis Verlag GmbH, Kaufingerstraße 24, 80331 München, Germany

www.ingramcontent.com/pod-product-compliance
Lightning Source LLC
Chambersburg PA
CBHW050333270326
41926CB00016B/3438

* 9 7 8 1 0 3 2 0 1 2 4 9 0 *